The Nature Study Movement

The Nature Study Movement

The Forgotten Popularizer of America's Conservation Ethic

Kevin C. Armitage

University Press of Kansas

Published by the University Press of Kansas (Lawrence, Kansas 66045), which was organized by the Kansas Board of Regents and is operated and funded by Emporia State University, Fort Hays State University, Kansas State University, Pittsburg State University, the University of Kansas, and Wichita State University

Chapter 3 was previously published as Kevin C. Armitage, "The Child Is Born a Naturalist: Nature Study, Woodcraft Indians, and the Theory of Recapitulation," *Journal of the Gilded Age and Progressive Era* 6, no. 1 (January 2007). Copyright 2007 by the Society for Historians of the Gilded Age and Progressive Era (SHGAPE).

Chapter 4 was previously published as Kevin C. Armitage, "Bird Day for Kids: Progressive Conservation in Theory and Practice," *Environmental History* 12, no. 3 (July 2007). Copyright 2007 by *Environmental History* and the American Sociey for Environmental History and the Forest History Society.

Library of Congress Cataloging-in-Publication Data
Armitage, Kevin C.
The nature study movement : the forgotten popularizer of America's conservation ethic / Kevin C. Armitage.
p. cm.
Includes bibliographical references and index.
ISBN 978-0-7006-1673-2 (cloth : alk. paper)
1. Nature study—United States. 2. Nature conservation—United States. 3. Environmentalism—United States. I. Title.
QH51.A73   2009
508.071—dc22

2009026494

British Library Cataloguing-in-Publication Data is available.

Printed in the United States of America
10 9 8 7 6 5 4 3 2 1

The paper used in this publication is recycled and contains 30 percent postconsumer waste. It is acid free and meets the minimum requirements of the American National Standard for Permanence of Paper for Printed Library Materials Z39.48-1992.

Contents

An illustration section follows page 136

Acknowledgments

I am happily indebted to many colleagues, friends, and family, all of whom helped me see this project to its conclusion. Its strengths are due to them, its weaknesses are due to me alone.

If I did one thing right at the University of Kansas, it was to surround myself with the best scholars in the field. Most important, I was fortunate to have the ear of Donald Worster in the Department of History. In addition to being the greatest practitioner in his field, he is a dedicated, welcoming mentor and keen editor. Don has an amazing ability to zero in on the core of an argument and understand its implications. Any scholar of American history would be lucky to work with him. I was equally fortunate to work with Robert Antonio in the Department of Sociology. Like Don, Bob is a master of his field and a dedicated teacher. A true historian, he has the great ability to translate abstractions of social theory into concrete, historical situations. No one who shares my interests in environmental history and social theory could hope for better mentors than Don and Bob. Other colleagues I would like to acknowledge are Jim Woelfel, who is a great example of what a professor should be, and Jon Earle, who is a fountain of energy and ideas. I would also like to thank David Katzman, Peter Mancall, Jeffrey Moran, Barry Shank, Karl Brooks, Gregory Cushman, and Ray Hiner. They all have my gratitude and my admiration.

Nature study is gaining the attention of a number of scholars, many of whom have shared the podium with me at conferences. In particular, I would like to thank Cynthia Watkins Richardson, Amy Green, and Dawn Chávez, all of whom helped me think critically about the field. Cynthia, in particular, has shared her work and interests with me at a number of conferences and through many an e-mail. Curt Meine shared his expertise on Aldo Leopold. I thank my writing group for their hard work and for indulging my interests. Lisa Brady and Dale Nimz are fine scholars and good friends, and they are responsible for helping me weed through many early drafts. Maril Hazlett deserves special recognition for her keen insights, editorial efforts, and unflappable good cheer. Many other colleagues helped as well. Mark Hersey shared both my interest in rural life and, most generously, his research. I would also like to thank Jay Antle, Rob Campbell, Kip Curtis, Brian Drake, Mark Frederick, Mark Horowitz, Todd Ormsbee, and Paul Sutter, all of whom are friends and intellectual brothers. The Linda Hall Library of Science granted me research monies and access to its wonderful archives at a key moment. Beth Berninger provided essential child-care help during my last year in Minnesota, enabling me to focus on my research and writing. Finally, my fellow union members in the Graduate Teaching Assistants Coalition at the University of Kansas fought the good fight to win decent working conditions that let me do the work that led me to writing this book. Their volunteer efforts have my respect and gratitude.

The last four years in southwestern Ohio, where I researched and revised this book amid new class preparations, have been full of learning and great fun. I have found a genial home and many new friends at Miami University. Special thanks are due to Drew Cayton for reading this manuscript. Mary Kupiec Cayton, Mary Jean Corbett, Nik Money, Carla Pestana, and Allan Winkler are all good friends and exemplary mentors.

Colleagues around the country have shaped this work; they are too numerous to name, but they have my profound gratitude. Anonymous reviewers of my articles and this manuscript provided thoughtful and helpful commentary. They are fine examples of academic professionalism; now that I, too, am reviewing manuscripts, I keep them in mind as models to emulate. The staff at the University Press of Kansas deserves all good things that can come to them. Kalyani Fernando and Jennifer Dropkin in particular have my thanks for much hard work. They made the difficulties of manuscript preparation not only manageable but even enjoyable.

This book is dedicated to my family. My brother Keith and sister Karole have supported me in countless ways over the years; they also exemplify the rewards of serious engagement, whether with medicine or art. My parents, Kenneth Barclay Armitage and Katie Hart Armitage, passed on to me the love of learning and provided summers in the mountain wilderness near Gothic, Colorado. My father introduced me to many a marmot friend. Without knowing it, I lived a nature study childhood. Helen Sheumaker is my love, my life partner, and my companion in adventures of all kinds. We have had thirteen great years; I can only imagine what the future holds. Our daughter, Rita Karole Armitage, has my love and, thankfully, shares my passion for books and nature. Hey Rita, let's go find some horn corals or, better yet, let's catch some salamanders.

The Nature Study Movement

Introduction

Nature, Science, and Sympathy

in the Progressive Era

"Nature," declared Cornell University horticulturalist Liberty Hyde Bailey, "may be studied with either of two objects: to discover new truth for the purpose of increasing the sum of human knowledge; or to put the pupil in a sympathetic attitude toward nature for the purpose of increasing the joy of living."[1] Nature study proponents believed—passionately—in both these propositions. In an era of revolutionary advances in science and technology, nature study advocates embraced the investigation of nature as a scientific endeavor, the key to unlocking nature's secrets. Students needed training in basic science because it was essential to intellectual development and social progress. Progressive nature study advocates understood that science underpinned the modern world, so educated citizens needed to understand and use it. They also wholeheartedly believed in the ability of nature study to increase the joy of living. For nature study advocates, the green world was a source of delight, instruction, and nourishment for the soul. Nature study advocates recognized the ineffable and magic nature of the nonhuman world and insisted that humans could know its enchantments if only they opened themselves to the experiences that intimate commerce with nature offered.

Yet these two purposes were often in conflict. Quantifiable research seeks to eliminate human emotion insofar as it might impinge on the scientific understanding of nature. The objective, rational, and quantitative values of modern science precluded the idea that people could find in nature the personal, spiritual, and qualitative values that bring joy to life. Then, as now, many scientists, especially biologists, were deeply attached to the natural world they studied, but their research methodology aimed to channel such emotions. The empirical, mathematical formalism of the scientific method reduced nature to its component parts, sacrificing holistic understanding of the green world. "Nowadays science teaches the places of the stars by lines and angles . . . but the heavens are more vitally peopled," averred one widely read nature study supporter. "We cannot all be positive scientists, and heaven help the world if we could be! The spirit of things would be dried away by letter, and the affections ranged in systems about material suns."[2]

The problem was not science itself. By "science," nature study advocates meant more than professional methods for investigating natural phenomena. They construed the term broadly to mean the objective, quantitative, and systematic values that characterized industrial society writ large as well as scientific method. The efficient, maximizing production of industrial capitalism bequeathed to society the values of selfish individualism and an ethos of functional rationality whose values forcefully impacted thought and feeling—the very culture of American life. Could industrial regimentation possibly enhance the spiritual exploration, aesthetic pleasure, and intellectual adventure that fulfilled individuals? Nature study advocates wondered how industrial culture could bring a person "to love, appreciate, and utilize wisely the environment placed around him by a benevolent creator."[3] Nature study attempted to embrace scientific modernity while simultaneously recoiling from the narrow, instrumental, and ugly society engendered by industrial civilization. Even essays touting "A Practical Angle in the Aesthetic Side of Nature Study" bewailed modern life, which "seems . . . to be depleted more and more of idealism, and is daily being lowered to a mere battle for existence, a battle with hostile forces over which often we have no control, and which tends to take the joy out of life."[4]

This debate was especially intense in the late nineteenth and early twentieth centuries because of the dramatic changes wrought by the second industrial revolution. The scientific worldview entered the daily lives of people as never before through the union of science and technological rationality in the workplace. People used complex machinery in their work (and, increasingly, in their private) lives, and their supervisors embraced "scientific management" to ensure that machinery operated with maximum productivity. Scientific management, most prominently associated with Frederick Winslow Taylor, employed the methods and assumptions of scientific rationality to increase labor efficiency. Wielding stopwatches and clipboards, managers timed each action of the worker, subsequently prescribing in numbing detail his or her every movement. Though these time and motion studies increased efficiency, workers suffered a profound loss of autonomy. Many Americans experienced science, then, not through the wonder of discovery but through the loss of autonomy and the flattening of experience that accompanied industrial regimentation.

As Progressive Era Americans embraced scientific modernity, they were uneasy about the impersonal and dispassionate nature of social and economic life.

The systematic organization of public and personal life promised a society of maximum productivity and efficiency, but it debilitated the intuitive and subjective side of life. As Robert Wiebe observed in his classic study of industrializing America, at the turn of the twentieth century, citizens "groped for some personal connection with the broader environment, some way of mediating between their everyday life and its impersonal setting."[5] Against this streamlined warping of the human fabric, nature appeared to be a place of liberation, a place that allowed for greater self-realization than that offered by social institutions. Nature could, in the words of photographer and social reformer Jacob Riis, "prevent our children [from] becoming senseless automatons in the industrial grind."[6] Nature study advocates were typical of an important thread in American culture that embraced scientific investigation while being repulsed by the quantification and bureaucratic systemization that modern society imposed on life. Many Americans experienced industrial systemization as a loss of autonomy and turned to nature to regain the unmediated experiences that, unlike so much of bureaucratic culture, enhanced the joy of living.

Such reasoning helped many Progressive Era educators conclude that the betterment of America lay in the direct interaction with nonhuman nature. Armed with guidebooks, cameras, collecting jars, and unrestrained curiosity, Americans flocked from their homes and classrooms to nearby forests, prairies, rivers, and mountains to gain greater insight into the wondrous workings of nature. "Nature study," as its enthusiasts dubbed the movement, used instruction in basic natural history, such as plant identification, animal life histories, and school gardens, to promote the skills needed to succeed in industrial life and to cultivate the spiritual growth that modern life occluded. Nature study classes bred animals, raised chickens, learned to identify local birds, watched tadpoles develop into frogs, or eradicated mosquitoes. They planted, grew, and tended gardens whose products they sometimes sold. Nature study pedagogy focused on the nature that students encountered in their day-to-day lives. Knowledge of the green world close to home opened the door to science; it "leads to a knowledge of the sciences of botany, zoology and geology as illustrated in the door-yard, the corn field, or the woods back of the house."[7] At its best, nature study intended to make children into active citizens who were skilled in reasoning and were committed workers on behalf of their environments. Underlying the nature study movement's attention to the natural world was the assumption that knowledge and sentiment would evoke concern for the well-being of nature itself.

The nature study movement included teachers and their students, as well as many popular nature writers, professors, and amateur naturalists around the country. Children studying the green world in school brought nature study into their homes. Families walking in the woods or looking for birds' nests or planting gardens in vacant lots described their activities as nature study. Most important of all was to interact with nature itself, rather than with representations of it. Because unmediated contact with nature was essential to both the beginnings of a scientific mind-set and the enhancement of spiritual satisfaction, teachers should take their charges out of the classroom and into the fields and forests to foster the children's healthy, natural development.

Millions of schoolchildren ventured outside to experience nature firsthand. The nature study movement gained great momentum in the 1890s and soon became an integral part of school curricula nationwide. By 1907 nature study proved so popular that it was being taught in schools throughout the country; the movement also enjoyed the support of many prominent intellectuals and boasted an established professional society and a scholarly journal. One study conducted in 1915 found that fourteen states required elementary schools to teach nature study, and twenty-three states issued outlines for nature study instruction. A 1921 survey found that "1905 to 1915 saw the incorporation of nature study outlined in the Course of Study of almost every state in the union."[8] A leading part of the new education, nature study swept the country as both a curricular ideal and a popular pastime.

As this new way of knowing nature entered American homes, so did its contradictions. Nature study attempted to reconcile objective scientific investigation with spiritual experience. This was no easy task. The modern worldview represented by scientific inquiry thrust entirely new and exclusive ways of knowing nature on a changing world. The meanings that humans granted to nature were in flux. This epistemological rupture forced Americans to come to terms with new ways of understanding the world and to invent methods of retaining what was good and useful about the old ways. Nature study advocates sought to embrace the modern world of science while retaining the older methods of fellowship with nature that yielded the unique experiences and ethical insights that science could not. The phrase "nature study" came about because it implied both the rational virtues of the scientific endeavor and an openness to ethical and personalized experiences derived from immediate interaction with nature. Proponents of nature study cherished both the intellectual clarity of scientific investigation and the experiential possibilities of immersing oneself in nature.

This struggle over ways of understanding nature reveals a great deal about one of the central goals of the nature study movement—the conservation of wildlife and natural resources. Nature study advocates reasoned that perceptions of nature affected responses to it. Lamenting that children were taught to despise "a great many creatures," one typical nature study proponent recoiled at "the ruthless and utterly purposeless slaughter of the harmless members of the so-called brute creation." The slaughter occurred because of "utter ignorance of the function of these creatures" and "groundless fears."[9] Only nature study that combated ignorance (with science) and fear (with sympathy) could staunch such behavior. Nature study embodied and promoted a radical change in Americans' attitudes toward the natural world they inhabited.

With its commitment to fostering healthy relationships between nature and people, it is not surprising that nature study was at base a pedagogical movement whose chief object was the reform of children. Nature study advocates—and progressive educators more broadly—conflated the flourishing of nature with the flourishing of children. Education and conservation were both considered in the language of natural processes and organic development. Thus the *Nature-Study Review* regularly published articles that instructed teachers to grow "A Better Crop of Boys and Girls."[10] The green world and the human nature of children both required social care: each demanded tending, development, and the preservation of those unique qualities found in nature and childhood. To thrive, children and nature needed each other.

Leading conservationists considered children—and their education—vital to the conservation movement. President Theodore Roosevelt believed that "the preservation of the useful and beautiful animal and bird life of the country depends largely upon creating in the young an interest in the life of the woods and fields."[11] Roosevelt's right-hand man, forester Gifford Pinchot, elaborated on these themes in his classic text *The Fight for Conservation*. Emphasizing that conservation was a "moral" issue, Pinchot argued:

> Conservation goes back in its direct application to one body in this country, and that is to the children. There is in this country no other movement except possibly the education movement—and that after all is in a sense only another aspect of the conservation question, the seeking to make the most of what we have—so directly aimed to help the children, so conditioned upon the needs of the children, so belonging to the children, as the conservation movement.[12]

Children needed nature, and genuine, lasting reform depended on inculcating into children the new, progressive values of conservation.

The conflation of childhood and conservation is not surprising, given the centrality of childhood to reformers of the late nineteenth and early twentieth centuries. Historian David Macleod described this era as the "age of the child." Child-centeredness grew from many of the same countermodern impulses that helped nourish the conservation movement. By the late nineteenth century, many children served the psychological rather than the economic needs of their parents. As systematization imposed itself more and more on American life, those nervous about such changes found in childhood the very premodern qualities they wished to retain in adult life. As historian Daniel T. Rodgers asserted, adults found in childhood an "oasis of the imagination where drama and spontaneity could rule unhindered by systematization run to excess." Childhood seemed an idyll of wholeness, serenity, stability, play, and unfettered expression, in contrast to the fragmented and alienated adult world. Progressive adults, suffering from "covert restlessness and half disguised anxiety," made childhood over into an expression of nature—the very antithesis of the machine.[13] Like conservation, the movement for child welfare grew from modern science as well as from romantic longings. Experts in the behavioral and applied sciences as diverse as sociology, psychology, and education advocated for the expression of child instinct through play in and exploration of the natural world. Both countermodern and objectively scientific sources argued that interaction with nature was vital to the development of healthy children.

How would nature be introduced to children? A child's healthy maturation and commitment to conservation would arise if the child developed "sympathy" with nature. "If one is to be happy, he must be in sympathy with common things," wrote Bailey. "He must live in harmony with his environment."[14] By "sympathy," nature study advocates meant an affinity between people and the green world that created a harmonious relationship between nature and human beings. This meaning of sympathy originated with Scottish commonsense moral philosophers who believed that ethics were grounded in the possibility of imagining the feelings of others. John Ruskin, a Victorian pioneer of the arts and crafts movement, explained that sympathy is "the imaginative understanding of the natures of others, and the power of putting ourselves in their place, [it] is the faculty on which virtue depends."[15] Nature study advocates insisted that to enact healthy values toward the nonhuman world, people must imagine, as far as possible, the point of view of nonhuman nature. Sympathy could increase happiness and move people to broaden their moral concern to include nonhuman nature. This was a radical sentiment in a culture fundamentally at odds with the natural world. Though nature study advocates continually proclaimed that humans benefited most from such ethics, the most vociferous, heated condemnations of nature study denounced the idea that society should grant moral standing to nonhuman nature.

Nature study advocates insisted that sympathy helped the social and spiritual development of people and promoted the need to conserve the natural world.

In this way nature study advocates theorized their pedagogy as fundamental to the conservation movement. First nature study advocates decried the destruction of the natural order. Charles B. Scott's widely read *Nature Study and the Child,* for example, lamented that "we have adapted ourselves to our physical environment by stripping our land of its forests, our air of its birds, our waters of their fish, by using up in the most reckless manner our natural resources. Nature has been our slave, from whom we could take anything, to whom we owed nothing." However, Scott averred, "we are learning that such adaptation is in the end unprofitable, unwise, utterly wrong. . . . We are discovering as a nation that we must protect our forests, and are just beginning to plant where we formerly used our energies in destroying our trees."[16]

Nature study combated such destruction by educating the child that he "owes something to the world about him. He protects what he once destroyed. He takes care of the flowers which before he trod upon. The birds are his friends. He is learning to love them. . . . He is adapting himself to his physical environment; not merely appropriating, but giving in return." The key to living with nature rather than destroying it was the development of sympathy. "Without sympathy," argued Scott, "nature study may be . . . disastrous in its effects on the child's environment." Calamitous results occurred because ethics did not constrain the investigations of science. Without ethical sentiment to guide scientific inquiry, "Our wild-flowers will be pulled up, our birds destroyed, our shade-trees mutilated ('sacrificed to the cause of science')." Such science students did not become conservationists; they became "cold blooded anatomists and collectors." But if teachers developed sentiment and scientific objectivity, students would "care for or work for nature."[17]

Nature study adopted the two-pronged political strategy of Progressive Era conservationists. Reform consisted of legislation that protected the natural world and the cultivation of an ethos that valued nonhuman nature and thus protected it as a matter of course. As nature study proponent Mabel Osgood Wright put it, conservationists needed to "educate the moral nature so that it will not desire to do the wrong act." Simultaneously, conservationists must work for "the establishment and enforcement of laws that shall punish those who do the wrong."[18] Writing about efforts to legislate the protection of birds, Wright noted, "The bird protective societies are tireless, but the ground must be prepared for the message they send forth."[19] Education would prepare citizens for laws that advanced the conservationist agenda, and it would shift the moral thinking about nature. The education that nature study advocates called for was not disinterested but laced with moral deliberation.

That moral rectitude of nature study advocates reveals a great deal about the kind of education they offered. Nature study demonstrates that the social critique proffered by romantic critics such as Thoreau found a wide audience in the late nineteenth century. Guided interaction with nature offered people beauty and solace while at the same time providing a fascinating subject of investigation. Nature study was a way to bring holistic perspectives into atomized lives. As Anna Botsford Comstock wrote in her best-selling field guide, nature study should consist "of simple, truthful observations that, like beads on a string, may finally be threaded upon the understanding and thus held together as a logical and harmonious whole." It should help people discern truth and give "practical and helpful knowledge," all the while cultivating "the child's imagination" and the "love of the beautiful."[20]

Truth, imagination, and beauty are the language of people's desires—how they hope to feel about nature. Americans used nature to enhance their lives and critique their society. Nature became one of the most powerful ways of adjusting to the vicissitudes of modern life; through nature one could gain the necessary, unique qualities that industrial civilization relentlessly processed into bulk form. Becoming a naturalist was a way to meet modern life on its own terms while maintaining one's humanity. Nature study conservationists were not simple or naïve scientific modernizers but thoughtful citizens examining what science could offer society and what it could not. Nature study was "science brought home," wrote Comstock.[21] As such, it was both more narrowly focused and much larger than science could ever aim to be.

Conservation, then, was not just one component of a modernizing state but a resolution of deep tensions roiling American culture. It tied science to social purposes rather than letting it sprawl, unfettered, beyond social usefulness. The protection of nature was necessary because contact with the green world allowed for moral conviction and aesthetic growth. Nature study conservationists sought to create the physical and cultural space that allowed values other than regimentation to bloom. Nature study conservationists bound together moral and institutional reform. Nature study demonstrated in the language of its time what has become the central social message of contemporary ecology: what we do to nature, we do to ourselves. In other words, conservationists sought to conserve human as well as natural resources. They had to, because the development of the American people was inextricably bound to the flourishing of nature.

Despite these overtly political aims, nature study perspectives have not been included in the historiography of the conservation movement. The nature study debate over science and the meaning of nature is one reason for this omission. The classic exposition of the conservation impulse, Samuel P. Hays's *Conservation and the Gospel of Efficiency,* viewed conservation as "above all . . . a scientific movement" whose essence was "rational planning" and "efficient development."[22] According to this view, the progressive conservation movement was an acute departure from the search for individual expression and the romantic love of nature espoused by nineteenth-century figures such as Emerson, Thoreau, Whitman, and Melville; rather, it favored scientific management and its corollary interests in technology and efficiency. Even those historians who have defended the democratic nature of conservation by linking social equity to the efficiency of applied science delineate a tradition that, with the exception of John Muir, largely turned its back on its nineteenth-century forebears.[23]

The interpretation of conservation as essentially bureaucratic and efficiency minded depicts the typical conservationist as a scientific expert who yoked individual expertise to federal power, giving conservation the utilitarian and dispassionate cast of objective, quantifiable science. Yet there are no figures in the conservation movement who comfortably fit such a narrow profile.[24] Given this perspective, it is not surprising that Hays found the "moral crusade" behind the conservation impulse to be only a small part of the movement, one that stood in the way of rational development policy. This viewpoint derived from Hays's concentration on bureaucratic structures and his focus on the role of conservation in transforming the United States from a "loosely organized society" to a "highly organized, technical, and centrally planned and directed social organization."[25]

Other historians have paid more attention to the ethical and aesthetic side of conservation, only to label it "preservation" and oppose it to conservation. The iconic moment of this historiography concerns the battle over California's Hetch Hetchy valley, which pitted the ostensibly exclusive motives of the aesthetic preservationist John Muir against the utilitarian conservationist Gifford Pinchot.[26] Yet Muir himself was an excellent and enthusiastic amateur scientist, and Pinchot was not a scientist but a politician and a moralist who reveled in spiritual communion with the natural world.[27] Like most figures in the conservation movement, neither Muir nor Pinchot was an aesthete or a technocrat; they both reflected sometimes harmonious, sometimes contradictory scientific and sentimental impulses. Pinchot's biographer Char Miller suggested that these tensions fueled conservation to such an extent that without them, "conservation would not have emerged as one of the most important Progressive Era credos."[28] It was not technocracy and bureaucracy but the nature study movement's attempt to reconcile bureaucratic science with individual and social flourishing that typified progressive conservationists.

Moreover, the historians who write about conservation as a movement for scientific efficiency have generally failed to examine grassroots impacts of federal resource policy. A number of superb recent books have substantially rectified this oversight by focusing on the local effects of conservation policy. Other studies have challenged the idea that conservation impacted mostly rural people by demonstrating the achievements of urban conservation. Many of these newer studies examine the ambiguous social legacy of conservation and its contradictions concerning natural resources as well.[29] All these examinations have enriched our understanding of conservation, proving its ongoing fascination as a complex and compelling historical phenomenon with many lessons for today.

Despite these tremendous insights, there has been no substantial revision of the idea that conservation was fundamentally motivated by efficiency and the bureaucratic application of scientific knowledge to resource policy. One recent study argued that conservationists presented themselves as "dispassionate technicians concerned only with solving neatly confined scientific problems."[30] Given this viewpoint, the history of conservation remains a story about the use of state power alone. But as popular, grassroots movements such as nature study reveal, the culture of conservation valued a deep skepticism about the impact of scientific modernity on people and their relationship with the natural world. To see this, we need only take conservationists at their word. Writing in 1910, anthropologist and geologist W. J. McGee, dubbed the "scientific brains of the conservation movement" by Pinchot, noted, "On its face the Conservation Movement is material—ultra material. Yet in truth," he continued, "there has never been in all human history a popular movement more firmly grounded in ethics, in the eternal equities, in the divinity of human rights! Whether we rise into the spiritual empyrean or cling more closely to the essence of humanity, we find our loftiest ideals made real in the Cult of Conservation."[31]

Such fervent and powerful rhetoric was typical of conservationists. Yet I do not propose to substitute a single interpretation emphasizing countermodern impulses for the received characterization of conservation as guided by objective bureaucrats; I only want to recognize the multitudinous cultural complexities of the conservation movement. If we continue to ignore its intricate ethos, our understanding of conservation will continue to be skewed. Minimizing the conservationist debate over science creates a conservation movement bereft of its nuanced moral sensibilities and philosophical distinction. In my view, aesthetic and ethical preservation and scientific conservation were not separate ideologies but inexorably intertwined components of conservation itself. To shortchange this multifaceted set of motivations and ideologies that inspired conservationists is to misunderstand both conservation itself and its relationship with the present-day environmental movement. Conservation was a call for both environmental *and* cultural sustainability. The ecological distrust of modern life has always been coupled with a cultural revulsion at systematization run amok. Rationalization smothers nature and culture. In this sense, ecological sustainability and cultural preservation are inescapably entangled.

By viewing conservation as an uncritical embrace of scientific modernity, scholars have missed the profound countermodern anxieties that nourished progressive conservation and continue to nurture contemporary environmentalism. Both movements are multifarious stews of modernizing and countermodernizing impulses. Indeed, in this way, conservation, and nature study in particular, exemplifies a central dilemma of modern life: although the modern ethos of secular rationality creates shared knowledge, individuals must produce for themselves the values that give meaning to life. Premodern, magical worldviews provided ready-made answers to the problem of meaning, but in a world of scientific and economic rationality, no such answers are available. Science cannot replace the old values because its findings are always quantified and contingent on a constant stream of new evidence and interpretation. Its continually changing view of nature forces its adherents to incessantly reinvent their understanding of the world. Put another way, within the scientific method there is no ultimate authority that sanctions some behaviors and condemns others. Individuals are left to bring their own ethical systems into being. Modern science provided conservationists with many tools, but it did not tell them why to use them. Conservationists needed to create the moral discourse that demanded the protection of the natural world.

Thinkers of the time were aware of these contradictions inherent in modern society. In 1914 journalist Walter Lippmann—hardly a countermodern aesthete—explained that his generation, heir to the socioeconomic and intellectual revolutions of the late nineteenth century, did not know "how to behave when personal contact and eternal authority have disappeared. There are no precedents to guide us, no wisdom that wasn't made for a simpler age." Significantly, Lippmann especially pitied urban children because they learn to be "quick about artificial complications," as opposed to rural children, who live close to nature and are thus "competent amidst enduring things." Even language itself degraded under the artificiality of the city: the "uprooted" person's idiom "has gone stale and abstract in a miserly telegraphic speech," unlike "country people [whose] words still taste of actual things. Contact with sun and rain and earth and harvest," concluded Lippmann, "turns the simple prose of the day's work into poetry for the starved imaginations of city-bred people."[32] Like Lippmann, proponents of nature study responded to the modern dilemma with the idea that nature could help guide moral identity. Nature study was thus modern and countermodern, not simply a response to modernity but part of the very dialectic between science and sentiment that is an inescapable part of modern life.

Nature study was also embedded in the modern political movement of social, cultural, and economic reform called progressivism. Progressivism sought to democratize the power of industrial capitalism by enacting legislation geared toward the social good and to house worthwhile values in new institutions. In a world where many traditional values were suspect or no longer spoke to pressing social needs, progressives attempted to reformulate individual values and the institutions in which they could be expressed so they would remain relevant to the industrial world. For many progressive reformers the goals of social and individual reform often intertwined. One reason to break up corporate trusts, for example, was to restore traditional American values of independence and self-reliance. Progressives thus worked fervently for institutional reform and for the reform of individual character.

Given the progressive interest in both social and individual improvement, it follows that such reformers would focus on education. Indeed, progressives had an inordinate faith in the power of education to rectify social ills. The transformation of education promised greater social efficiency and the opportunity for the development of moral character. Progressives recognized that it is easier to shape young individuals than to reform older ones. "A far-sighted policy such as the training of the young," asserted prominent University of Wisconsin sociologist E. A. Ross, "is preferable to the summary regulation of the adult."[33] Nature study advocates wished to impart to their young charges the skeptical and highly rational worldview of modern science while simultaneously using the object of scientific investigation—nature—to nurture their spiritual and ethical development. Part of education was recognizing the limits of the scientific endeavor. At the heart of the nature study worldview, then, was a faith in the redemptive possibilities of nature itself. While working to train students in the fundamentals of scientific investigation, nature study advocates also wanted to keep the unexpected, the subjective, the ethical, and, finally, the exultant feeling of wonder that can be found when a free and open individual explores the nonhuman world.

The story of nature study, then, is inescapably a story of education, but like their counterparts in conservation history, historians of education have ignored nature study despite its popular appeal and centrality to the development of progressive education. For their part, historians of progressivism and American culture of the late nineteenth and early twentieth centuries have also missed this popular movement and its attempts to resolve some of the central dilemmas of its time—and ours. Historians who have looked at turn-of-the-twentieth-century love of nature often derided it as mere sentimentalism, a mawkish nostalgia best forgotten. Leo Marx, in his celebrated study *The Machine in the Garden,* dismissed enthusiasm for nature as flight from reality into "naïve and anarchic primitivism."[34] For Marx, nature study advocates were moral idiots. They were not. Similarly, Peter J. Schmitt viewed nature study as part of the attempted reconciliation between civilization and wilderness that Americans found in pastoral or "Arcadian" life.[35] He treated nature study as shallow sentimentalism attached to nature, missing entirely the cultural depths of such feeling as well as the belief in science that characterized nature study.

This historical neglect of nature study is surprising, given that its effects are still around us everywhere. Our society still struggles with its relationship to science, even as science continues in many ways to dominate our lives. Like nature study advocates, millions of Americans continue to find spiritual and aesthetic meaning through contact with nature. Nature study is clearly the foundation of environmental education and was a forerunner of environmentalist ideologies such as deep ecology. Moreover, many of the central figures in the environmental movement, such as Aldo Leopold and Rachel Carson, were grounded in nature study as children, and their mature thought clearly and explicitly embraced the nature study of their upbringing.

The romantic orientation of Leopold and Carson reminds us of Emerson's dictum that "there is properly no history; only biography."[36] Accordingly, this book provides short biographical sketches of some of the major, if often overlooked, nature study conservationists: Anna Botsford Comstock, Ernest Thompson Seton, Mabel Osgood Wright, Gene Stratton Porter, and Liberty Hyde Bailey. These individuals made significant contributions to the conservation movement. Other names, such as John Dewey and Booker T. Washington, will be familiar to readers, although their contributions to conservationist thought will likely be new. These educators—and all were devoted, by one means or another, to education—helped popularize the nature study ideal. As both a pedagogic and a popular idea, nature study has had a lasting effect on American culture and society. The time has come, then, for a reevaluation of nature study and what it tells us about the American relationship with the nonhuman world.

This book seeks to place nature study in its historical context. The ways that nature study advocates tried to reconcile science with spirit were surprising, incomplete, and contradictory. Given the diverse nature of nature study, what follows is not a straightforward narrative that attempts to impose a linear structure on multifaceted phenomena but rather a collection of interconnected yet separate examinations of the complex ways American culture struggled with science and its application to the natural world. I have tried to elucidate the development of nature study and also the ways that development reflected larger social dynamics inherent to modern industrial society. This is a story worth knowing. Nature study was rooted in a specific era, but it also heralded one of the most powerful relationships Americans have had with the nonhuman world. In the specific example of nature study, one finds much that is universal to modern America.

CHAPTER ONE

"Nature Study Is an American Habit"

Nature Study, Science, and Spirit

Do not all charms fly
At the mere touch of cold philosophy?
—Keats, *Lamia*

Scholastic nature study began on 6 July 1873 on Penikese Island, a small and rocky member of the Elizabeth group in Buzzards Bay, fourteen miles off the southern Massachusetts shore. On this day Louis Agassiz, the renowned Harvard professor of zoology and geology, welcomed almost four dozen students, about a third of whom were women and the majority of whom were public school teachers, to his latest venture, the Anderson School of Natural History. The occasion marked the beginning of the first professional biological field station in American history. Among the guests who attended the event were the governor of Massachusetts and members of the state legislature and school board. Agassiz, always one to memorialize an event with a stirring speech, began by calling on the assembled students to "join silently in asking God's blessing upon their work together."[1] He then outlined the summer's agenda by expounding on his philosophy of education: "Our object is to study nature, but I hope I may lead you in this enterprise so that you may learn to read for yourselves." By the study of nature, Agassiz meant the direct observation of natural phenomena rather than learning about the outdoors from textbooks. The less you learn from books, he explained, "the more you will be left to nature's resources. . . . Our appliances for study are none but what nature affords."[2] Even by Agassiz's high standards, the opening address was a noteworthy speech. Indeed, it proved memorable enough that John Greenleaf Whittier chose to commemorate it in a poem, "The Prayer of Agassiz."

Agassiz's central goal for the field station was not to advance professional scientific investigation but to train teachers in the best methods of natural history instruction. This goal derived from Agassiz's larger ambition to use education to invigorate the popular study of nature; he wished to make an interest in natural history both familiar and popular. To that end, Agassiz trained a generation of leading professional zoologists (and in Nathaniel Shaler, at least one geologist) and lectured extensively to the lay public. In particular, Agassiz set out to train teachers of science. He opened his lectures at Harvard's Museum of Comparative Zoology to public school teachers and insisted that women as well as men be permitted to attend them. Agassiz also worked directly with public school teachers through his support for educational reformers such as Horace Mann. He participated in the Massachusetts State Teachers' Association and helped advance science instruction by lecturing in summertime teachers' institutes in Massachusetts. He also incorporated his own school for girls, which for nine years instructed such students as the daughters of Ralph Waldo Emerson, Ellen and Edith. When asked to identify his profession, he described himself not as a man of science but simply as Louis Agassiz, teacher.[3] His stature was so great among education professionals that the professional journal *Education* enticed new subscribers by offering as a premium a portrait of either Horace Mann or Louis Agassiz.

Agassiz spent so much of his time and energy spreading his pedagogical gospel because he deplored the existing methods of science instruction. Stanford University president David Starr Jordan, a former student of Agassiz's, recalled his professor protesting that "throughout the country the great body of teachers of science went on in the old mechanical way. . . . The boys and girls still kept up the humdrum recitations from worthless text-books. They got their lessons from the book, recited them from memory, and no more came into contact with Nature than they would if no animals or plants or rocks existed on this side of the planet Jupiter."[4] Agassiz continually sought new methods to impart the essentials of natural history. Most fundamentally, he insisted that students study nature by experiencing it firsthand instead of only encountering it through the written word. For decades Agassiz propounded the idea that serious students of natural history "should make nature [their] text book." While discussing pedagogy, he often repeated his aphorism that "if you study Nature in books, when you go out of doors you can not find her." Indeed, Jordan recalled an impassioned Agassiz urging the students at the Anderson School of Natural History to resist textbook sellers: "There are great business concerns engaged in the manufacture and sale of these worthless books who are our greatest enemies. They are really circulating educational poison, and I beg of you don't shrink from rebuking them at every opportunity. I have aroused very serious opposition to my work by stating these things openly, but I shall continue to do it as long as my strength lasts."[5]

Science teachers around the country echoed Agassiz's concerns. *Popular Science Monthly* editorialized that "book teaching of science" not only is "void" and lacking positive pedagogical effect but also "has an actively injurious effect on the mind, which it deadens with meaningless jargon and befogs with ill-comprehended notions."[6] Other writers noted that textbooks failed to promote a comprehensive and integrated view of scientific knowledge, reducing the findings of science to disparate, unconnected facts and concepts. One writer in *Educational Review* charged that such desiccated abstractions "as presented in textbooks" have been "carefully winnowed" of "poetry" and "personality" and thus inhibit an interest in science with the "high and dry" method of teaching.[7] Other critics charged that the "high and dry" method of teaching destroyed the natural affinity for investigation that children possessed. "Until school-life begins, a child is a good observer," claimed J. S. Kingsley in *Popular Science Monthly*, "but the whole training after that period is one adapted, if not intended, to repress the forms of observation."[8] Science pedagogy clearly needed fresh instructional methods that could revitalize the teaching of a discipline whose pedagogy was widely understood to be dull, repetitive, and detached from the lives of students.

To help remedy this dismal state of pedagogical affairs, Agassiz proposed a scientific "camp meeting" where teachers could learn to see nature for themselves and then learn how to teach others to see. He had long pondered creating a scientific field station where science teachers could receive training in the best methods of natural history instruction. Indeed, he hoped the Anderson School might become the "educational branch of the Museum of Comparative Zoology."[9] The idea for a summer school in natural history took definite shape in December 1872, when Agassiz's former student and current Harvard colleague Nathaniel Shaler, a champion of outdoor education, suggested that Agassiz establish one for teachers of natural history. Both Shaler and Agassiz wished to locate the institute at a seaside locale where students could learn natural history through their own explorations.[10]

Seizing on the idea, Agassiz issued a leaflet on December 14, a year to the day before his death, announcing a free "Program of a Course of Instruction in Natural History, to be delivered by the Seaside, in Nantucket, during the Summer Months, chiefly designed for teachers who propose to introduce the Study into their Schools and for Students preparing to become Teachers." The broadside included this declaration by Agassiz: "I do not propose to give much instruction in matters which may be learned from books. I want, on the contrary, to prepare those who shall attend to *observe for themselves.* I would therefore advise all those who wish only to be taught natural history in the way in which it is generally taught, by recitations, to give up their intention of joining the school."[11]

Even before the school had a location, Agassiz assembled a faculty of his former students, all widely recognized as top scientists in their own right; they included Shaler, Burt G. Wilder, Alpheus Packard, Frederick Ward Putnam, Theodore Lyman, and Agassiz's son Alexander. In March 1873, when members of the Massachusetts legislature made their annual visit to Agassiz's museum, he cornered them with an impassioned solicitation for public funds to support his latest venture. One of the legislators remarked, "I don't know much about Agassiz's Museum, but I am not willing to stand by and see so brave a man struggle without aid."[12] Yet before the legislators could formally consider the matter, a wealthy tobacco merchant and landlord named John Anderson, having read in the *New York Times* of Agassiz's plans, offered Penikese Island to the project. The island included a furnished house and a barn; Anderson also provided $50,000 for laboratory equipment and the building of a dormitory.

No doubt due to Agassiz's tremendous reputation and personal magnetism, the gifts kept coming. C. W. Galloupe of Boston donated a yacht, the *Sprite,* to Agassiz's venture. Students used the yacht to dredge for deep-water specimens. The yacht also ferried students to Casco Bay, where they could obtain brachiopods and echinoderms unavailable at Penikese. Reference books came from the Smithsonian Institution, Thomas G. Appleton, and Scribner & Co. Coupled with Agassiz's flair for publicity, these gifts helped the summer institute attract laudatory press coverage. The *New York Tribune* described the school as a "Striking Educational Experiment."[13] Not surprisingly, students from as far away as Colorado flocked to the Anderson School. Agassiz received more than two hundred applications, from which he chose the forty-four students who attended the initial session. A plaque positioned for all students to read as they entered the Penikese laboratory featured one of Agassiz's exhortations that would become a rallying cry of the nature study movement: "Study nature, not books."

Agassiz had long practiced the direct study of nature, a technique he preached at Penikese. Shaler recalled his professor's unique methods of developing the power of observation in his students:

> Agassiz brought me a small fish, placing it before me with the rather stern requirement that I should study it, but should on no account talk to any one concerning it, nor read anything relating to fishes, until I had his permission to do so. To my inquiry, "what shall I do?" he said in effect: "Find out what

you can without damaging the specimen; when I think that you have done the work I will question you." In the course of an hour I thought I had compassed that fish; it was rather an unsavory object, giving forth the stench of old alcohol. . . . Many of the scales were loosened so that they fell off. It appeared to me to be a case for a summary report, which I was anxious to make and get on with the next stage of business. But Agassiz, though always within call, concerned himself no further with me that day, nor the next, nor for a week. At first, this neglect was distressing; but I saw that . . . he was covertly watching me. So I set my wits to work upon the thing, and in the course of a hundred hours or so thought I had done much—a hundred times as much as seemed possible at the start. I got interested in finding how the scales went in series, their shape, the form and placement of the teeth, etc. . . . In another week of ten hours a day I had results which astonished myself and satisfied him.[14]

Shaler was not the only pupil to suffer what students sometimes referred to as Agassiz's "fish method" pedagogy. Samuel H. Scudder, who went on to become a widely respected professor of entomology at Cornell, remembered feeling an initial "disappointment" in Agassiz's methods, "for gazing at a fish did not commend itself to an ardent entomologist." It also smelled. "My friends at home, too, were annoyed, when they discovered that no amount of eau-de-Cologne would drown the perfume which haunted me like a shadow." Moreover, Agassiz forbade the use of scientific instruments, even those meant to improve observation; Scudder recalled using only "my two hands, my two eyes, and the fish: it was a limited field." Days passed with the "wretched fish," yet even as the knowledge gained by observation increased, Professor Agassiz implored his student to "look, look, look." After four days Agassiz added another fish to the examining table, gradually increasing the number until representative members of the entire genus *Haemulon* lay before his anxious student. But by this time, Agassiz had won over his diffident entomologist. "At the end of eight months," recalled Scudder, "it was almost with reluctance that I left these friends and turned to insects; but what I had gained by this outside experience has been of greater value than years of later investigation in my favorite groups."[15]

Agassiz's fish method of science instruction was widely used following the summer on Penikese Island. Another student at Penikese, Helen B. C. Beedy, recalled that it was Agassiz "who gave the impetus to the study of natural history in America—not from books but from nature herself."[16] Agassiz's pedagogical methods seemed to inspire everyone who came into contact with them. The preeminent pragmatist philosopher and educator William James, who accompanied

Agassiz on a sixteen-week voyage up the Amazon, remained unimpressed with Agassiz as a scientist but nevertheless declared that "Agassiz's influence on methods of teaching was prompt and decisive." Indeed, the methodology of direct interaction with the things of nature had an "electric" effect on pedagogy. "The good old way of committing abstractions to memory," observed James, "seems never to have received such a shock as it did at his hands." Moreover, James noted that the fish method was not just appropriate to the classroom but was a way of being in the world. The pedagogy that produced Agassiz's astonishing command of natural history also created a life lived in "the light of the world's concrete fullness."[17]

Agassiz translated these laboratory methods to his field institute. He mingled freely with his Penikese Island charges, and his enthusiasm for study galvanized the students, who spent a good deal of their time examining the fish they captured along the shore. At times students worked well into the evening, dissecting their fish specimens by candlelight. The students also formed a Natural History Club to discuss methods of natural science teaching.[18] A seriousness of purpose characterized the participants; one sullen student griped that the women were very "schoolma'amy" and "the gentlemen are not a whit behind."[19] All agreed with the pedagogical necessity of teaching with actual specimens; Agassiz volunteered that "there should be a little museum in every school room."[20] The students at Penikese fell into an agreeable routine. Mornings often involved lectures or working closely with the faculty, afternoons were devoted to collecting, and evenings brought more lectures or laboratory work. One student recalled the summer as "wonderful . . . what a rich experience it was, what a high spot in our lives!"[21]

Some professional scientists, however, were not pleased with Agassiz's methods. The emphasis on teaching rather than research elicited derogatory commentary from Europe, where research laboratories flourished. The well-regarded British morphologist E. Ray Lankester described the Anderson School as an attempt "to make bricks without straw." Indeed, Lankester derided the "class of students . . . on Penikese" who undertook "a sort of holiday picnic of some weeks."[22] The Anderson School of Natural History offered little for those yoked to an advanced research agenda that dismissed any serious consideration of pedagogy.

Such criticism did not deter the Anderson School from boasting a larger student body and another distinguished faculty for its second annual session in 1874. But without the spirited and guiding presence of Louis Agassiz, who had died the previous December, the location's drawbacks became more apparent. The island's isolation made travel difficult and expensive.[23] Moreover, the island

and its surrounding waters were not especially blessed with study specimens. The Anderson School of Natural History thus folded after only two years. Penikese Island itself was put to unusual uses in the years following the school's demise. After it was purchased by the state of Massachusetts, the island served as a leper colony from 1905 to 1921. It was declared a bird sanctuary in 1942, and in 1973 Penikese gained its current status as the site of a school for troubled youth.

The short life of the Anderson School of Natural History should not be confused with the esoteric history of its location. The Anderson School served as a model for the development of field stations dedicated to biological research. Many of Penikese's alumni went on to found other maritime laboratories, including the renowned station at nearby Woods Hole, Massachusetts.[24] Most significantly, the pedagogical principles touted at Penikese helped transform American education. Jordan argued that the brief weeks on Penikese Island achieved nothing less than a transformation of American education: "The school of all schools in America which has had the greatest influence on American scientific teaching was held in an old barn on an uninhabited island some eighteen miles from the shore. It lasted barely three months, and in effect it had but one teacher. The school at Penikese existed in the personal presence of Agassiz; and when he died it vanished."[25]

Although the Anderson School had vanished, its former students immediately began pondering ways to incorporate their newfound knowledge and Agassiz's pedagogical methods into the teaching of schoolchildren. This pondering brought about many questions. Members of the Natural History Club wondered at what age students should be introduced to a thoroughgoing study of the natural world. One, James Johonnot, had queried Agassiz on the matter. How old do children need to be before "we commence to teach natural history?" he asked. Agassiz, striking the keynote of his teaching philosophy, replied, "at once, using the material at hand."[26] The response was not meant to be flippant; it merely emphasized the necessity of introducing the study of natural history to children. The problem was one of method: At what age could students benefit from scientific instruction? And how might teachers modify difficult and systematic science to make it palatable to children?

The answers took form in the nature study movement. Nature study advocates followed Agassiz's lead by contending that students required direct contact with the green world to learn about nature's workings. They believed that such contact imparted a love of learning and the spiritual and moral resources needed to buffer the intensely materialistic values of American society. In an era of greatly expanding access to education, they wished to ground the entire

American people in the basics of natural history—a difficult proposition in an increasingly industrial and urbanized nation. In such a society, the reliance on books might dominate scientific study, as Agassiz feared. "We have so many books even about the out-of-doors," lamented nature study's most prominent intellectual, Liberty Hyde Bailey, "that we do not need to go out-of-doors to learn about it."[27] Despite the prevalence of books, nature study advocates maintained that direct contact with nature provided the best way to become a naturalist. And although the general term "naturalist" seemed somewhat outmoded in the modern era of highly specialized, quantifiable, and reproducible laboratory science, nature study advocates felt that a thorough grounding in the principles of natural history was necessitated rather than obviated by industrial society.

Louis Agassiz was not the only member of his family concerned with educating children in basic natural history. His second wife, Elizabeth Cabot Agassiz, writing under the pseudonym Actaea, published a book for children in 1859 titled *First Lesson in Natural History.* Elizabeth Agassiz attempted to bring complex subject matter to the attention of children by writing in a warm and accessible style. The book took the form of a letter to Elizabeth Agassiz's nieces, Lisa and Connie, and presented itself as "true stories . . . about animals."[28] Yet the reader was also informed that the book, written "under the direction of Professor Louis Agassiz," imparted accurate and detailed scientific information. In training children to understand their surroundings, Elizabeth Agassiz followed her husband's injunction to "select such subjects that your pupils can not walk without seeing them. Train your pupils to be observers, and have them provided with the specimens about which you speak."[29] Twenty years later the book reappeared as part of the Guides for Science Teaching series sponsored by the Boston Society of Natural History. By introducing children to accurate portrayals of nature through accessible narratives, Elizabeth Cabot Agassiz prepared the way for popular nature study writers for children, such as Mabel Osgood Wright and Ernest Thompson Seton.

Meanwhile, a pedagogical method imported from Europe was transforming American education. Called "object teaching," this new form of pedagogy, derived from the teachings of Swiss educator Johann Pestalozzi, used tangible objects instead of textbooks to impart lessons. The inductive assertion that children learned more readily from direct sensory experience rather than memorization and recitation—the essential idea of object teaching—became a cornerstone of the nature study movement and progressive education more broadly. The state normal school at Oswego, New York, became the American institution most closely associated with object teaching, but the new method quickly spread to schools across the country.[30] Object teaching became the leading subject for discussion in teachers' institutes, and by 1870, object lessons began to develop into a method of natural science instruction for elementary children.

Object teaching at Oswego evolved toward nature study under the tutelage of H. H. Straight, a graduate of Oberlin College who had studied with Louis Agassiz at Penikese Island. Straight expanded the idea of object teaching into nature study by taking children on extended field trips to nearby swamps, forests, and lakes. On such trips students learned basic natural history by interacting with nature rather than relying on textbook representations of it. Straight's expanded method took account of the limits of object study; objects, if used only to invoke memorization, could become as stultifying as other forms of recitation. As John Dewey noted, object lessons cannot "afford even the shadow of a substitute for acquaintance with the plants and animals of the farm and garden acquired through actual living among them and caring for them."[31]

Straight's career at Oswego and other institutions illustrates early innovations in pedagogy that led to the introduction of nature study in public schools. Born in Chautauqua County, New York, Henry Harrison Straight graduated from his local common school despite being orphaned as a young boy.[32] By age sixteen he was teaching at his common school before enrolling at Oberlin. He moved from Oberlin to Galena, Ohio, where he became principal of the public school system. Straight intended to save his salary so that he could study in Germany, which at the time had the most advanced system of university science education. While in Galena he taught natural science by having his students investigate tangible natural objects. Upon graduation from Oberlin, Straight's plans changed, and rather than pursuing his studies abroad, he took the job of president of Peru State Normal School in Peru, Nebraska. While at Peru, Straight advanced the then radical idea that schools needed to promote what he called the "complete life" of human beings.[33]

Straight left Peru for Cook County Normal School to work with a recognized leader in school reform, Francis Parker. Instructing students in the complete life began with a thorough scientific investigation of "man's proper relationship to the universe"; on that basis one could improve physical health, mental acuity, and moral bearing. Straight argued that education must investigate the physical world of nature and consider humans "as an organism subject to the same laws of growth as other living organisms." Such study helped humans understand God's intentions as revealed "in Scripture, in Nature, and in human history."[34] The holistic emphasis of nature study allowed for an integrated understanding of the interrelation of nature and human society. In his natural history pedagogy, Straight concurred with Dewey, who warned that if nature is isolated from the child's world, "the original open and free attitude of the mind to nature is destroyed; nature has been reduced to a mass of meaningless details."[35] Straight's dedication to holistic and integrated nature study was cut short when he succumbed to tuberculosis in 1886.

Progressive educators such as Straight and Dewey intended to inculcate children with the instrumental, problem-solving side of scientific investigation as well as with a love of nonhuman nature and natural piety. The tensions between these goals defined nature study and much of what would become known as progressive education, a dynamic I explore in detail in the following chapter. Yet the linkage of the spiritual and the scientific deserves comment. In a century marked by frequent and intense religious revivals among Protestant denominations, proponents of nature study often justified new curricula with an emphasis on rudimental science in spiritual terms.[36] For example, consider an 1892 book published by the supervisor of teachers in Boston, Louisa Parsons Hopkins, titled *The Spirit of the New Education.* Like Agassiz and other advocates of educational reform, she attacked the "medievalism" of the schools and their reliance on "an exclusively book education." But after she visited a kindergarten where time was devoted to play and song as well as to study, she proclaimed the "baptism of the spirit" that new educational methods could provide.[37] For reformers such as Hopkins, the scholarly investigation of nature would promote the new scholastic emphasis on spirit. The development of spirit sought by Hopkins implied important lessons for teachers of nature study: "Not too much analysis at first, and no drudgery, should accompany the observation of nature in the school-room," proclaimed Hopkins. "Because a sense of sympathy with nature is the highest end of such study; the growth of the soul is the final object of all study, and the soul grows by exercise of its powers of love and aspiration."[38]

The linkage of science and piety by progressive nature study reformers also developed from traditions that emphasized the personal benefits derived from the study of natural history. Indeed, the popularity of natural history study drew in part from its perceived moral as well as practical benefits. Many nineteenth-century Americans believed that "a good naturalist cannot be a bad man."[39] This feeling was clearly rooted in earlier forms of natural theology that viewed nature as the product of a beneficent God and thus extolled the study of natural history as moral inquiry. As the nineteenth century progressed, the secular rhetoric surrounding natural history increased. Yet even as natural history became a professional concern ensconced in universities—a gradual and messy process that saw natural history evolve from a primarily subjective and often amateur pursuit to a specialized academic research subject—the rhetoric of moral uplift remained an important part of the study of nature. Nature study advocates, like their fellow students of natural history and like their fellow conservationists, remained moral reformers as well as popularizers of science, including their championing of the concept of Darwinian evolution.

Nature study's emphasis on experience and learning from tangible objects, embodied by Agassiz's mantra "study nature, not books," might be misread as antiliterature if not simply anti-intellectual. After all, the vibrant print-based democracy of the nineteenth century led to a culture of argument that flowed from the circulation of printed material. Literate citizens were inculcated into the virtues of coherent argument well supported by evidence. Cogent readers must be intellectually armed, able to ferret out misdirection and superficial thought. They must weigh ideas and make sound judgments. Nature study advocates did not wish to escape this culture but rather to expand it to include the interpretation of nature. The book of nature must be read with the same diligence as the printed word. The same qualities that make for good readers— serious engagement, the ability to wield common sense and to evaluate information—also make for good observers of the wonderful, complex, buzzing natural world. Sustained, observant, and thoughtful inquiry need not stop at doorways; it is useful whether one is inside or out.

The literary quality of nature study naturalists drew on another tradition long associated with natural theology: using the metaphor of the "book of nature." John Muir typified this tradition when he noted in his journals that his travels in Yosemite took him through "forty miles of canyon-wall rocks [that] are stone books gloriously illustrated, and in pursuing my studies I must return to them again and again, as to a library where many a secret in mountain-building may be explained."[40] Naturalists pursued their study of nature with the same reverence, duty, energy, and precision with which biblical scholars pored over scripture. Both sought the word of God, whether that word took the form of language or landscape.

Nature study was not only a movement within schools; it was always a popular pastime as well as a set of curricular practices. The method of direct contact with the natural world united the scholastic and popular expressions of nature study. Thus Pestalozzian theory influenced pedagogy as well as popular interest in natural history. A good example of the popular influence of Pestalozzian methods is found in the work of Almira Phelps.[41] Phelps wrote a popular textbook, *Familiar Lectures on Botany,* to better the education of women in the sciences; the book sold more than 275,000 copies over the next forty years. The pedagogical methods Phelps advocated—such as placing a flower in the hands of students as they studied its parts—derived from object teaching and complemented the wide topical range of the text. Phelps's book introduced students to botanical classification and included a thorough introduction to plant anatomy, botanical geography, and the history of botany; practical advice on naturalizing plants; and a chapter on the "language of flowers." In short, Phelps encouraged her readers to become studious amateur botanists. For Phelps and the many nature study advocates who followed her, the direct contemplation of nature was not for students alone but was a pleasurable pastime for interested laypersons as well. Millions of Americans took up Phelps's call over the years, as natural history study became a broadly popular pastime.

The early history of nature study followed the pattern created by Agassiz and Phelps and other promoters of the study of natural history. The initial story was one of the popularity and importance of science as reflected in its inclusion in school curricula, as well as the widespread embrace of natural history study as a pleasurable and stimulating activity for enthusiastic amateurs. Thus, a great many Americans (especially those of the middle and upper classes) knew nature as an object of scientific curiosity. For such nature enthusiasts, the outdoor world was a fascinating subject for investigation, and one whose study yielded practical, moral, and even spiritual benefits.

Yet the history of the nature study movement is not just a story about the professionalization and popularization of scientific study. Nature continued to have powerful meanings beyond being an object of study, even to many scientists. Nature came to be seen as a spiritual and aesthetic antidote to modern life, and contact with nature became not just a pedagogical method but also a way to ameliorate the stresses and anxieties of the modern world. This response to nature joined the popularization of science to form the two dominant streams of the nature study movement. By the late nineteenth century the stupendous advances in industrialization and technology, the growing dominance of the urban core over the peripheral countryside, new forms of routinized labor, and the transformation of a disorganized, entrepreneurial economy into a consolidated, corporate, capitalist world power produced significant new meanings attached to nature. The scholarly study of nature was central to this transformation, for advances in science and technology were fundamental to the changes wrought by industrial America. Simultaneously, the study of nature pointed Americans to new methods of spiritual expression, new ways to find aesthetic pleasure, and a place from which to criticize modern life.

The anxieties embodied within the nature study movement largely reflected—but were not exclusive to—the social and cultural concerns of white, middle-class Protestants. In an age in which many children no longer grew up on farms, white Anglo-Saxon Protestants' contact with nonhuman nature provided a way to preserve and perpetuate the values that guided their culture. (Although the nature study movement included people from a wide variety of social locations, its most important figures were middle-class Protestants of northern European lineage.) The flexibility of liberal Protestantism accounts for its pervasive cultural power and its deep influence on progressivism.[42] As nature study demonstrates, it helped legitimize the scientific worldview by insisting that critical inquiry could not be at odds with God's purposes. Many people came to believe that contact with nature provided the physical and spiritual intensity of experience that had supposedly characterized premodern life. Middle-class Protestants embraced the ostensibly frontier values of self-reliance, independence, and thrift and the analytic, problem-solving habits of mind that ostensibly arose from contact with an untamed continent. Moreover, they believed that contact with American wildlands created a unique and stable American character in a way that the cultural products of a diverse and urban immigrant society could not emulate. In a secular and pluralistic world, nature became the place where identities were confirmed and the established values of the Protestant middle classes were enacted.

The nature study movement thus reflected the scientific aspirations as well as the spiritual longings of the professional middle class. Just as nature came to invoke scientific modernity, it also connoted the cultural opposite of modernity: a place of primitive and authentic spiritual and aesthetic refuge, a place both physically and psychically disassociated from industrial life. Drawing on the rhetoric of moral uplift associated with the natural history tradition, nature study advocates viewed the green world as a necessary refuge from modern society, even as they continued to promote the scientific worldview central to cultural modernity. Contact with nature became important not just for popular and professional scientific understanding but also for moral clarity and a sense of coherent selfhood against the dislocations of industrial society. The specter of the new industrial world that separated Americans from nature haunted the denizens of urban areas, who were most exposed to modern life, as well as those in the countryside, who also felt the displacing effects of industrial civilization.

The new industrial world depended on scientific investigation as a cultural form. Many critics felt that the mania for science and industry was constricting the possibilities of human experience. Was a narrow scientific expediency crowding out other ways of being in the world? Sociologist Thorstein Veblen—best remembered for his caustic criticism of the "leisure class," which established social prestige by flaunting its affluence through displays of "conspicuous consumption"—also worried about the effects of science on culture.[43] Veblen worried about what kind of culture arose from a mechanical as opposed to an organic worldview. "Modern civilization is peculiarly matter-of-fact," observed Veblen; its denizens "are in peculiar degree capable of an impersonal, dispassionate insight into . . . material facts." Such dispassionate consciousness arises when a "machine process" dominates culture. This phenomenon produces "the spiritual and intellectual life of this cultural era [which must] maintain the character . . . the machine process gives it."[44] A critique of machine processes led to the devastating criticisms of Muir, who charged that modern "people are on the world, not in it; have no conscious sympathy or relationship to anything about them, undiffused, separate, and rigidly alone like marbles of polished stone, touching but separate."[45] Similar concerns led nature study advocates such as Bailey to declare that nature study was "a revolt from the teaching of mere science" because it endeavored to help "every person . . . live a richer life."[46] Nature study advocates wished to embrace the advancements of science, but not at the expense of reducing human experience to machine-like efficiency.

Nature study, then, was both a science and a reaction to modern life that historian T. J. Jackson Lears has termed "antimodernism." This deep ambivalence toward modern life mostly affected those of the middle and upper classes. The bureaucratic and compartmentalized experiences of modernity led to the worry that modern people were becoming the empty drones that Max Weber, borrowing from romantic critics, described as "specialists without spirit, sensualists without heart." Even such highly successful champions of modernity as Theodore Roosevelt complained of "overcivilization" and advocated "The Strenuous Life" as training for manhood that could combat the ostensible physical inertia and lack of authenticity of modern existence. Crucially, this dissonant attitude did not involve the rejection of civilization but rather an accommodation to modern life that was simultaneously nostalgic and progressive, spiritually vital yet broadly secular.[47]

For those Americans imbued with an antimodern malaise, contact with nature could combat the sense of loss they associated with urban, industrial life, easing their transition to modernity. Antimodern malaise thus affected the very people most embedded in the culture of modernity, such as scientists and promoters of science. Devotees of rugged nature such as Theodore Roosevelt (himself the product of a nature study boyhood) advised the wilderness traveler not to abandon civilization altogether but rather to "take books with him as he journeys; for the keenest enjoyment of the wilderness is reserved for him who enjoys also the garnered wisdom of the present and the past."[48] Although antimodern anxiety grew from the feeling that civilization sacrificed organic unity, physical vitality, and emotional ease to industrial progress, it did not demand a repudiation of modern conditions of living. Antimodern dissenters found ways to accommodate their longings within industrial civilization, rather than rejecting modern life wholesale.

The quest for organic experience personifies a powerful and abiding criticism of industrial modernity. In this sense, antimodern Americans followed the great European social theorists of the late nineteenth century, who understood well the depth of capitalist culture's moral and spiritual destructiveness. Though they did not find refuge in nature, the most insightful social theorists of the late nineteenth century recognized the quest for authenticity as a fundamental aspect of modern society. For example, even such champions of industrial production as Karl Marx decried the unreality of modern life with his famous *Communist Manifesto* injunction that, in capitalist social relations, "all that is solid melts into air, all that is holy is profaned." For Marx, capitalist social relations alienated humans from their authentic selves, dissolving human interaction into the "icy water of egotistical calculation."[49]

Marx's contemporary Friedrich Nietzsche warned of a "weightless" culture severed from moral foundations. He viewed the degradations of modernity as arising not from capitalist social arrangements but from the increasing impotence of modern culture. Secular modern society engendered simple accommodations to bland systems of belief characterized by easy but ultimately vacuous meanings that emptied human experience of vitality, authenticity, and purpose. In the first years of the twentieth century, Weber developed these ideas in his critique of modern society as producing only one type of human consciousness, a culture correlated to the massive structures of bureaucratic authority that capitalist society produced in abundance. At its worst, modern society devolved human consciousness into a flat, one-dimensional "instrumental rationality" that reduced thought and expressiveness to the imperatives of bureaucratic structures. Weber worried that the "iron cage" of bureaucratic rationality was greatly constricting the possibilities of human fulfillment, leading human life toward a state of "mechanized petrification." Instrumental rationality threatened to bring about a "polar night of icy darkness." The insidious side of the modern dilemma is well represented by an aphorism of Emerson: "Every spirit makes its own house," wrote this favorite author of nature study advocates, "but afterwards the house confines the spirit."[50]

Visual artists as well as philosophers offered similar criticisms of modern society. The Barbizon school of landscape painters embodied what would become known as the nature study perspective. Barbizon painters—named for the bucolic village where they made their homes—insisted on direct interaction with nature, painting outside—*en plein air*—to help in their quest for the precise reproduction of landscape. Importantly, the landscape for these painters was not mere background, a stage for melodrama, or allegorical device: they depicted nature as they found it. This nature included the rural, working-class people who made a living in those same landscapes. These painters were very popular in romantic circles in America, influencing transcendentalist philosophy and poets such as Walt Whitman, who once claimed that his seminal book of poetry, *Leaves of Grass,* was the work of Barbizon painter Jean-François Millet in another form. For Barbizon painters, nature was real, and through contact with it, one could find a more satisfactory way to live.

Lears argued that the cultural crisis engaged by these philosophers and painters was a powerful factor in twentieth-century American history:

> This sense of unreality has become part of the hidden agenda of modernization. Throughout the twentieth century, a recoil from the artificial, over-civilized qualities of modern existence has sparked a wide variety of quests for more intense experience, ranging from the fascist fascination with violence and death, to the cults of emotional spontaneity of avant-garde artists to popular therapies stressing instinctual liberation. Antimodern impulses, too, were rooted in longings to recapture an elusive "real life" in a culture evaporating into unreality.[51]

The longing for real life and vital experience characterized much of the American relationship with nature in the twentieth century. It distinguished the romantic critique of industrial civilization, and antimodern sentiment was largely expressed through the use of nature as a place to criticize modern America.

The power of antimodern insight was that it understood and condemned the materialistic, self-striving, and ultimately empty (if bloated) rhetoric of those who proffered the dominant ideology of industrial progress. Antimodern dissenters knew that modern bureaucratic structures and culture made authentic individual experience problematic. Nor should the recognition that the authentic is itself a socially constructed category of being prevent us from realizing the historic (and contemporary) power of the desire for real existence. Similar ideas animated American romantic thought. For the purposes of this book, I have conflated antimodernism with the powerful romantic critique of industrial society and science leveled by American transcendentalist philosophers.

The nature study movement did not need to seek out highbrow European critiques of modern society; it could—and often did—turn to indigenous traditions of American romanticism that lodged similarly scathing criticisms toward industrial modernity. This point highlights another weakness in the interpretation of conservation as a movement motivated by efficiency and expressed primarily through bureaucracy. If this were true, then Progressive Era conservation was a radical departure from the romantic tradition. According to this interpretation, just as Emerson and especially Thoreau were being canonized and widely appreciated, the conservation movement rejected them in favor of the kind of narrowly materialist science that romantics fiercely rejected. Indeed, conservation as efficiency implies that the romantic critique flourished through the middle of the nineteenth century and then disappeared during the early twentieth century, only to be reborn with the rise of environmentalism in the 1960s. Instead of such a convoluted lineage, the nature study movement demonstrates that progressive conservation was rife with such undeniably romantic themes as the search for holistic understandings of the self and nature, criticisms of positivist science, and an appreciation of sentiment as a way of knowing the natural world.

Romantic themes are prominent in the major works of transcendentalist philosophers and nature study advocates. For example, Emerson's insistence on holism—"Nothing is quite beautiful alone: nothing but is beautiful in the whole"—led him to argue that art and science are united in both method and result: "Truth, and goodness, and beauty, are but different faces of the same All." Emerson rejected faraway searches for wild nature in favor of immersion in the nature near his home. "I embrace the common," wrote the naturalist; "I explore and sit at the feet of the familiar, the low." Following this immersion of self and world, Emerson favored holistic natural history against the emerging modern, materialist science that was atomized, fragmented, and narrowly empirical. Thus naturalists should investigate the green world through "untaught sallies of the spirit" rather than mere "addition and subtraction." "I cannot greatly honor minuteness in details," explained Emerson, "so long as there is no hint to explain the relation between things and thoughts; no ray upon the metaphysics of conchology, of botany, of the arts, to show the relation of the forms of flowers, shells, animals, architecture, to the mind, and build science upon ideas."[52]

The spiritual side of nature study grew from this deep emotional distrust of modern life. Nature study advanced the powerful romantic critique of modern dualism. Separated from the vital currents of the natural world, human life withered like drought-ridden crops. Body and soul degenerated—which is why nature study essayist (and Episcopal minister) Dallas Lore Sharp found that if nature study "is not communion with nature, I know that it is at least a real pleasure, and rest, peace, contentment, red blood, sound sleep, and, at times, it seems to me, something close akin to religion."[53] If immersion into nature provided soundness of mind, it follows that nature itself was a kind of hymnal, prayer book, and church. Modern life created the conditions that inhibited satisfaction; nature could repair the damage.

Henry David Thoreau articulated the universally true life of nature more forcefully than his mentor Emerson. Thoreau bequeathed unreserved passion to the study of nature. Part of the passion derived from his childhood; Thoreau benefited from a nature study upbringing. Both his parents enjoyed nature and spent much time exploring the countryside near Concord. Soon young Henry enjoyed similar outings. He recalled his childhood as being immersed in the natural environment: "Formerly methought nature developed as I developed and grew up with me. My life was ecstasy. In youth, before I lost any of my senses, I can remember that I was all alive and inhabited my body with inexpressible satisfaction."[54] Thoreau thus linked personal with natural vitality. People and nature needed each other to thrive.

For Thoreau, the interaction with nature was intellectual but also bodily; he wanted to taste the green world—sometimes literally. In one famous passage Thoreau articulated his visceral enthusiasm for wild nature: "I caught a glimpse of a woodchuck stealing across my path, and felt a strange thrill of savage delight, and was strongly tempted to seize and devour him raw."[55] This hunger to consume nature's vitality was rarely stated with such force by nature study advocates, who had the practical limitation of trying to convince parents and teachers to adopt the new pedagogy. The dominant tone of nature study was one of earnest reformism, not ecstatic, physical communion with nature. But they too believed passionately in the power of nature's vital currents to nourish bodily energies.

How quantifiable science fit such ardor vexed romantic naturalists. Like nature study theorists, Thoreau went so far as to worry about the effects of materialist science on his own consciousness: "I fear that the character of my knowledge is from year to year becoming more distinct and scientific," wrote Thoreau in 1851. "In exchange for views as wide as heaven's cope [sky] I am being narrowed down to the field of the microscope—I see details not wholes nor the shadow of the whole. I count some parts & say 'I know.'"[56] Science could inhibit the full range of human responses to the wild. "If you would make acquaintance with the ferns you must forget your botany," wrote Thoreau. "You must get rid of what is commonly called knowledge of them."[57] Thoreau continued to explore this theme in his journals, though he maintained his commitment to knowledge. "I fear that the dream of the toads will not sound so musical now that I know whence it proceeds," confessed Thoreau, "But I will not fear to *know*."[58] One method Thoreau deployed against utilitarian expedience was humor. Brooding over the "poor dry compilation" that was the *Annual of Scientific Discovery,* Thoreau pilloried the idea of the Society for the Diffusion of Useful Knowledge—which intended to spread scientific facts to the broad reading public—with his own proposal for a "society for the diffusion of useful Ignorance."[59] Like Emerson, Thoreau wished for knowledge that opened up the world, rather than the spread of instrumental reason that foreclosed new discovery.

Importantly, this romantic critique did not eschew knowledge or science. As much as Thoreau criticized science, he also loved it. But Thoreau did critique knowledge stripped of its integrity and subsumed into systematic classification. As he wrote in his journal:

> In the true natural order the order or system is not insisted on. Each is first and each is last. That which presents itself to us this moment occupies the whole of the present and rests on the very topmost point of the sphere, under the zenith. The species and individuals of all the natural kingdoms ask our attention and admiration in a round robin. We make straight lines, putting a captain at their head and a lieutenant at their tails. . . . It is indispensable for us to square her circles, and we offer our rewards to him who will do it.[60]

The argument is one of relational knowing, of holism; systems impose order and hence distortion on that which is classified. Moreover, such classification stops subjective interaction with the natural world, inhibiting the expression of compassionate values: "Nature must be viewed humanely to be viewed at all; that is, her scenes must be associated with humane affections, such as are associated with one's native place, for instance. She is most significant to a lover. A lover of nature is preëminently a lover of man. If I have no friend, what is Nature to me? She ceases to be morally significant."[61]

To recognize the value of nature, one needs to acknowledge both its otherness—the absolute difference of people from the rest of the natural world—and the fact that we are intertwined, members of the same community. Without sympathy, how can one cultivate values that acknowledge nature's worth? Thoreau contended that the "unsympathizing man . . . regards the wildness of some animals . . . as a sin; as if all their virtues consisted in their tamableness."[62] "Thus the true man of science," wrote Thoreau, "will know nature better by his finer organization; he will smell, taste, see, hear, feel, better than other men. His will be a deeper and finer experience. We do not learn by inference and deduction and the application of mathematics to philosophy, but by direct intercourse and sympathy. It is with science as with ethics—we cannot know truth by contrivance and method."[63] Just as positivist science could constrict broad experience with nature, so could this utilitarian vision of science constrict the types of knowledge that could be gained through interaction with the green world.

Thoreau and his fellow romantic critics bequeathed a theory of how people should relate to the natural world to nature study activists. Nature was a fascinating object for scientific inquiry and a standpoint for social critique, including criticism of the very science that took nature as its object. The conservation embraced by nature study advocates embodied all these diverse understandings and uses of the natural world: we needed to preserve nature to use it wisely as an object of scientific investigation and as a place from which we could see and rectify social inadequacies.

One social failure that needed remedy was the flatness of experience stemming from the new forms of systematization inherent to industrial life. Assembly-line labor, social regimentation, and mass consumerism all molded experience into standardized forms. Quantification reduced and flattened experience, heightening the sense that the mind and body were divorced. This criticism was found in American romanticism as well as in pragmatist thought, and it is one of the crucial ways these two strains of American thinking (which contain great disagreements) came together to influence the nature study movement. Nature study advocates wanted people to interact with nature because it was effective pedagogy and because it allowed unmediated experience to flourish.

As with progressive education more broadly, John Dewey theorized experience. For Dewey, the human experience with nature was an irreducible interaction with nonhuman others, not merely an encounter with nature as it exists inside the human mind. "Experience" wrote Dewey, "is of as well as in nature. It is not experience which is experienced, but nature—stones, plants, animals, diseases, health, temperature, electricity, and so on. Things interacting in certain ways are experience; they are what is experienced. Linked in certain other ways with another natural object—the human organism—they are how things are experienced as well. Experience thus reaches down into nature; it has depth."[64]

This notion of experience had particular resonance for those nature study advocates who found in nature an antidote to stultifying industrialism. This notion of using nature to enrich experience pervaded nature study rhetoric. But industrialism only expanded the mind in certain ways. "This is an age of fact, and we are glad of it," wrote Bailey. "But it may be also an age of the imagination. There need be no divorce of fact and fancy; there are only the poles of experience."[65] Romantic theorists and pragmatic philosophers agreed that it was contact with nature that allowed both these poles of experience to thrive. This pluralistic rendering of experience derived from contact with actual nature—not books.

These romantic concerns were embedded in American nature study in two primary ways. Professional scientists worried that the increasing specialization of disciplinary inquiry inhibited broad knowledge and deep appreciation of scientific achievement. In 1884 *Science* magazine editorialized that the division of scientific labor was "an evil" because it worked against diverse learning and thus created "a thousand little hermit cells" each tenanted by an "intellectual recluse" who, blinded to the "true purpose of learning," dismissed the larger world "to look after itself."[66] In other words, the overspecialized scientist suffers the same narrowing of interest and flattening of experience as the bureaucrat. Like Emerson, *Science* could not greatly honor minuteness in details. Nature study aimed to combat the intellectual narrowing of specialization by creating in students a love for continuous, broad-based learning by grounding them not in specialized scientific investigations but in the broad and immediate concerns of natural history.

Moreover, nature study proponents held that contact with nature reinvigorated the sense of intellectual possibility that industrial life stamped into bureaucratic form. As Dorothea Lange, supervisor of nature study in the city schools of St. Paul, Minnesota, put it, nature study worked "against the narrowing, blinding, specializing of modern life." "What better remedy [for intellectual narrowness] is there," asked Lange, "than an introduction into the great and universally true life of nature?"[67] The critique also extended to the authors of nature study books. C. A. and Lida B. McMurray's 1896 text *Special Method in Natural Science* argued for a holistic worldview against the ordered abstractions of scientific categorization: "the subject before us is not natural science (classified knowledge) but nature study. We are seeking to know nature in her real form as she shows herself in the field, forest and shop, not the classified orders and systems of scientific books."[68]

Nature study was thus an attempt to spread learning in natural history and a rebellion against the modern ethic of instrumental rationality that desanctified the green world of nature and, with it, the inner realm of the self. Nature study advocates asserted that contact with nature served the pedagogical purpose of introducing children to science and the moral purpose of combating the iron cage of rationality by rooting individuals in the real world of physical nature. In his text *Nature Study and Life*, Clifton Hodge described direct contact with nature as the "anchor of elementary education," a necessary mooring because "modern life tends to drift away from nature into artificialities of every sort."[69] Those artificialities included the cheap remedies so many people used to combat modern nervousness. Anna Botsford Comstock, in an editorial in *Nature-Study Review*, contrasted nature, "with her effective balm, her soothing ministrations, her rejuvenating influences," against the patent medicines, tobacco, and alcohol that so many Americans imbibed "to soothe overwrought nerves." Indeed, "we have only to open our windows to let in the healing air, that nervousness, batlike, is banished by good sun light."[70] Comstock's colleague Bailey concurred, explaining that "this return to nature is by no mean a cure for all the ills of civilization, but it is one means of restoring the proper balance and proportion in our lives."[71]

A great deal of antimodern anxiety fixated on the city. The contemporary reader should pause to remember the radical changes to the sensory experiences of the industrial city's first generation of denizens. Urban residents were no longer greeted at dawn by the overwhelming sound of birdsong or able to see the "real" landscapes of the farm or forest. Moreover, the separation from nature and the striking dependence on others emphasized what many Americans felt as a loss of autonomy. Historian Frederick Jackson Turner famously articulated this anxiety over the loss of autonomy when he worried that the closing of the frontier would end the struggles with nature that gave Americans their independence and self-reliance that sustained the republic. Nor was Turner alone in his worries. "The man of to-day is less independent than the Greek," argued art historian Charles Eliot Norton. "He cannot get along alone, he is more helpless by himself with every advance of our complicate civilization."[72]

Nature study writer Mary Dickerson concurred with Turner's assessment of modern life, worrying over the loss of rural life that created American independence and noting that "very little of the old environment is left." Dickerson then argued that the urban landscape that replaced the old environment created "greater dangers than ever came from forest or prairie," dangers that may "eventually threaten the life of the nation." The peril stemmed from the lack of independence and the supposed ease of corruption inherent to modern life; thus the "city children of today" might become "the very opposite of their forefathers in regard to the qualities of earnestness, determination, self-reliance and high-mindedness."[73] Likewise, country-life champion Bailey proclaimed the need to maintain the rural values of "steadiness" and "freedom from speculativeness and from great temptation to evil doing," because "the machine" has "come between us and the essentials" of life.[74]

The historical peak of the nature study movement from the 1890s through the 1910s occurred at a time when advances in science and technology created profound tensions in American thought and patterns of culture. Miles Orvell contended in *The Real Thing* that for most of the nineteenth century, science and technology were generally received as agents of democratization.[75] Science promised to bring high culture to a mass audience in a variety of forms: quality reproduction promised the availability of literature, visual arts, and other genres of genteel culture to the greater part of the literate populace. But by the twentieth century, many Americans viewed technologies such as mechanical reproduction as akin to an automated confidence man, perpetuating the false and the dubious. What part of life remained personally authentic in an age of assembly-line production that depersonalized labor and mechanical reproduction that depersonalized consumption?

Responding to this phenomenon, many Americans attempted to create unique, authentic experience. The quest for authenticity took many forms, from avant-garde art that exalted irrationality over bourgeois respectability to philosophical vitalism, fascination with the medieval world, and the literary and popular romanticism that exalted the rustic simple life as more real and vital than modern urban existence. Americans of the middle and upper classes were propelled by a notion of attaining experience that could not be duplicated. Although mass production helped create unprecedented material wealth, it also engendered the feeling that individuality was sacrificed to the institutions of modern society. This dialectical tension between imitation and authenticity remains one of the defining categories of American life.

The problem of attaining authentic experience in a mass society is especially important when considering the cultural meanings attached to nature. Nature is the very definition of that which is authentic and real, the stuff from which imitation arises, yet at the same time, nature is a concept open to endless abstraction, the essential character of any specific thing. Even in the conventional sense of nature as that which humans have not made, distinctions between imitation and authenticity break down. For example, landscapes clearly altered by human intervention will likely be thought of as natural if the human interference took place far enough in the past. Despite such etymological conundrums, Americans at the beginning of the twentieth century turned to the nature of the nonhuman world and to nature as depicted in art and literature in response to the "weightlessness" or unreality that defined their lives. Modern life was inauthentic, so people sought to get in touch with the real—with nature itself. Many Americans sought the authentic in nature, attempting to locate and solidify what Emerson called "an original relation with the universe."[76]

Antimodern anxiety thus plagued thinkers such as Comstock and Bailey in the scholastic side of the nature study movement. It also appeared in popular nature study literature as well. Naturalist John Burroughs—the most widely read nature writer of the early twentieth century—clearly concurred with the nature study teachers who worried that the overspecialization of scientific inquiry inhibited holistic thought and feeling. Speaking of scientific inquiry, Burroughs charged, "We approach nature in an exact, calculating, tabulating, mercantile spirit. We seek to make an inventory of her storehouse." Such an approach blinded the modern investigator to the spiritual side of contact with nature. "He is so intent upon the bare fact that he does not see the spirit or the meaning of the whole," argued Burroughs. "He does not see the bird, he sees an ornithological specimen; he does not see the wild flower, he sees a new acquisition to his herbarium."[77] For Burroughs, "Science is impersonal and cold and is not for the heart but for the head."[78] The separation of intellect and emotion desanctified the self, reducing it to a commodity like any other—the mercantile spirit that Burroughs wanted to reject in his relationship with nature. Nature lovers such as Burroughs maintained that contact with nature could rejuvenate one's sense of wholeness and wonder, but only if one jettisoned the detached, objective attitude at the heart of modern society.

Other writers and thinkers less directly concerned with natural history repeated and elaborated on romantic uses of nature. For example, consider the writings of poet and essayist Bliss Carman. Carman counseled his readers that one "use of the out-of-doors" is that it alleviates "the demands which civilization imposes upon us." We "turn to nature for relief from the petty exactions and disordering complexities of life with which we have become encumbered." By combating such industrial imperatives, immersion in nature "restores us to ourselves. Its profound essential satisfactions build themselves into the character and become part of the personality."[79] The full development of human consciousness demanded intimate contact with nature; Carman thus considered contact with nature a necessity, not a luxury. "There is in reality a power in Nature to rest and console us." Those who partake in nature's power become more fully realized as individuals and better, more caring human beings. Indeed, people who "have been reared not far from the wild school of the forest make the best citizens and friends." For Carman, the human "friendship with nature" gives us "first of all" our "sanity" as well as our "health."[80] In a modern society that manufactures flat and bureaucratic personalities, contact with the green world could restore the instinctual vitality and moral ballast of human personality lost to industrial imperatives. "We may put up with factory-made commodities and all the impositions of commerce, if we will, but there is no substitute for open air," argued Carman. "It is not only a choice between outdoors and indoors, it is a choice between out-of-doors and death."[81]

Millions of Americans followed, in one way or another, the injunctions of popular nature study authors. "For rest, stimulus, solitude, [and] recreation, men and women are turning more and more to the fields and woods every year," observed the *Outlook* in 1903. This movement was vital because it "has contributed immensely to the health, vigor, and joy in life of the American people." Moreover, the movement was a democratic one because the aids to nature study were available to all. "No sign of the times is more significant of the change in American habit," editorialized the *Outlook*, "than the number of volumes on flowers, trees, shrubs, [and] birds, which are constantly coming from the press."[82] Sharp characterized "the present great nature movement" as an attempt to "discover . . . trees, birds, flowers, [nature's] myriad forms." This quest for discovery traced "directly to Agassiz, and the host of teachers he inspired."[83]

The nature study movement thrived by attempting to reconcile quantifiable and romantic methods of knowing nature. In a humorous example of the antimodern anxieties associated with finding authentic nature in a business civilization, the nature study movement could also claim at least one confidence trickster. The "News Notes" section of the September 1907 issue of *Nature-Study Review* warned readers about a successful con: "An imposter has for several months been working among nature-study teachers in New York and New Jersey. His specialty is paid-in-advance subscriptions to a magazine 'Birds and Nature,' including sixty colored plates." The charlatan claimed to represent a business incorporated as the Nature Study Company and apparently enjoyed considerable success swindling nature study advocates; the offices of *Nature-Study Review* were swamped with "many letters of complaint." The description of this confidence man appeared to leap from the imagination of Herman Melville. "The agent signs his name F. W. Cooley," reported the *Review*. He "is a Quaker, about 70 years old, gray hair, blue eyes, slender form, not well dressed (probably he can afford better clothing now), and minus two fingers on his right hand." The notice concluded with a note of tired optimism: "Even an amateur Sherlock Holmes should be able to identify him at sight after reading this description."[84]

Although the *Nature-Study Review* never again mentioned this trickster, this superficially benign anecdote highlighted the profound antimodern anxieties within the nature study movement. The questions vexing the movement concerned authenticity: How should one know nature? What is the proper way to study it? How should individuals and society use the knowledge gained from interaction with nature? Does the scientific method provide the best means of knowing nature? The nature study movement never formulated systematic and thorough responses to these questions. Yet this failure did not result from a lack of intellect on the part of nature study advocates. Rather, it reflected an entire culture in a deep state of epistemological crisis in which once stable categories of knowledge and experience melted with the profound changes that capitalist industrialization visited upon the world. If confidence men could fake the intellectual tools that provided a privileged and knowing relationship to nature, what touchstones of reality were left for those seeking unmediated experience?

The confidence trickster's art—the possibility of perpetuating a fraud—arises most forcibly when its cultural opposite—the authentic—is in a state of flux. Authenticity as a category of cultural experience is especially precious in modern capitalist society: mass production, advertising, and the constant revolutionizing of technology and modes of production all work to continually undermine tangible experience and stable notions of the real. Although few proponents of nature study engaged in such philosophically complex cultural commentary, many elaborated on the important antimodern criticisms leveled by their contemporaries.

Quandaries over authenticity affected the intertwined pedagogical and romantic sides of the nature study movement. Dallas Lore Sharp, a popular writer and a favorite of Rachel Carson (she wrote that his essays have "about them the tang and freshness of a sea breeze, the limpid beauty of a mountain pool"), depicted the problems of science and authenticity in his essay "The Nature Student."[85] Sharp began by describing an encounter he had as a student with his science professor. Viewing Sharp's precise dissection of a dog's nerves, the professor observed, "Doesn't a revelation like that take all the moonshine about the 'beauties of nature' clean out of you?" Of course, for Sharp and other nature study enthusiasts, it did not. Despite his appreciation for the dog's nervous system, he "persisted in a very unscientific love for live dog." But laboratory work did not encourage a love of nature either. "Sentiment," concluded Sharp, "is not science." Yet sentiment is as real as a dog's nerves. Echoing the criticisms of science forwarded by Burroughs, Sharp noted that without sentiment, the scientist "sees no such difference between live and dead nature, nature in the fields and in the laboratory." The scientist's dissected nature is just as unreal as nature viewed through maudlin sentiment. Knowledge itself is not the problem; Sharp insisted that "the nature-lover may turn nature-student and have no fear of losing nature."[86]

And yet the segregated, classified, and, to some, desiccated knowledge that can cause scientists to miss the forest for the trees—or the dog for its nerves—remained deeply problematic to the proponents of nature study. In direct contact with nature, Sharp found the same solution to the problem of reconciling science with sentiment as the rest of the nature study movement did. "We know that a real, ordinary, yet marvelous world does exist, and right at hand," argued Sharp. "The present great nature movement is an outgoing to discover it—its trees, birds, flowers, its myriad forms. This is the meaning of the countless manuals, the 'how-to-know' books, and the nature study of the public schools."[87]

The nature study movement, then, exposed one of the contradictions at the very heart of modern industrial society. Along with its profound achievements, modern science helped produce a culture based on bureaucracy, methodical thinking, adherence to system, and quantification; in short, modern science helped create the instrumental rationality that worried Max Weber as well as American nature lovers. Yet millions of Americans longed to find in nature the very values that objective, quantifiable science suppressed—subjectivity, spirituality, and communion with the nonhuman world. Thus nature study arose when modern science and industry became a dominant force in social and cultural life. Millions of Americans ascribed new and vitally important meanings to nature at exactly the time that bureaucratic rationality and science were eliminating through quantification the subjective interaction between people and nature. American nature study advocates wished not to discard the impressive achievements and precise rationality of laboratory science but to retain the holistic habits of mind necessary for spiritual contact with nature. In the final analysis, then, nature study was an attempt to reconcile science with sentiment. The popular appreciation for natural history proffered by Louis Agassiz combined, in the years following his death, with the romantic sentiments of many Americans who felt disaffected with modern life. In that and many other ways, nature study embodied the American relationship with nonhuman nature. It is in this sense that Sharp was correct to claim that "nature study is an American habit."[88]

CHAPTER TWO

"A Living Sympathy with Everything That Is"

Nature Study and the Roots of Progressive Education

> For at least two decades the leaders in nature-study were also the leaders in the progressive thought concerning elementary schools.
> —Dora Otis Mitchell, "A History of Nature-Study"

In a 1907 essay titled "The Great Mother as an Educator; or, the Child in Nature's Workshop," Benjamin O. Flower, the muckraking editor of *Arena* magazine, bemoaned the "feverish, abnormal, artificial, and demoralizing influences of modern urban life" on the "future life of the child." But if children turned to nature, the "true teacher [of] the normal mind," they could develop in a "wholesome and normal way." To mitigate the deleterious effects of industrial life, children must develop an "intimate *rapport* with nature." Thus, "parents and all who have the priceless treasure of childhood entrusted to their care should make it a glorious labor of love to drive out the false, the artificial and the morally enervating influences that invade the child-mind, by flooding its imagination with the light, the beauty and the wonder of nature." Flower, following his progressive instincts, hinted that nature study served social purposes by creating healthier, fully formed citizens. Indeed, contact with nature would turn the "listless" and "unobserving" child into a "man or woman who is at once a philosopher, an idealist and a lover."[1]

Flower's rhetoric concerning the "demoralizing" and "artificial" conditions of urban life echoed mainstream progressive critiques of established pedagogy. With real justification, Flower and other progressives produced a chorus of criticism that chastened the dominant mode of repressive and pedantic pedagogical practice—the overuse of corporal punishment, stultifying lectures, and the quiet memorization and recitation that dominated classrooms. Reformers questioned what relationship the stale repetition of basic information bore to problem solving in the real world. How, they asked, did current methods of instruction encourage originality or prepare students to tackle the challenges inherent to an industrial democracy? Did the dominant modes of pedagogy fit the way children actually learned? Like many others, Flower advocated a "new education" that would respond to social needs, an education propagated by skilled teachers whose students would be "fascinated into goodness and lured into greatness."[2]

Students of the myriad educational reform impulses that coalesced first as the "new education" and later under the banner of "progressive education" will recognize Flower's heated tone as typical of the progressive rhetoric. Reformers in the field of education combined evangelical zeal with the confidence of professionals wielding the latest discoveries from psychology and pedagogy. Progressives noted that many if not all of the institutions that had traditionally socialized children—particularly the family, the church, and the apprentice system of industrial labor—had been drastically transformed by the second industrial revolution. These changes were summarized by the rapid urbanization of the country. "The father who as a boy knew every plant in the field, every animal in the forest, and every rock on the hillside, is raising his son in machine-made town," wrote one proponent of nature education.[3]

The urban and industrial revolutions transplanted children away from nature while simultaneously flattening their experiences at home. When children matured in rural environments, their own investigations and encounters with the world taught them how to solve problems; imagination and the ability to resolve dilemmas developed as a matter of course. But since mechanization removed work from the home and, most importantly, distanced native problem solving from work, children no longer had the opportunity to develop their native intelligence. The goal of the new education, then, was to create pedagogical situations that exercised children's native capacities by solving problems. This was achieved by having children solve problems that arose from their native interests, not by having them memorize abstract data.

Child-centered progressive education was only one part of the varied humanitarian movements responding to industrialization. These reformers, many of them professional, middle-class denizens of northern cities, combined their faith in the possibilities of science and progress with an unmediated horror at the social and natural dislocations stemming from industrial, capitalist civilization.[4] As historian of education William J. Reese argued, "In its American phase, child centered progressivism was part of a larger humanitarian movement led by particular men and women of the northern middle classes in the antebellum and postbellum periods. This was made possible by changes in family size, in new gender roles within bourgeois culture, and in the softening of religious orthodoxy within Protestantism."[5]

Scholastic nature study clearly embodied the main tenets of progressive education. Although the various movements, ideologies, and pedagogical ideas that formed progressive education were pluralistic and at times contradictory, one can still apply education historian Lawrence Cremin's distillation of the defining principles of progressive education to see that nature study exemplified progressive pedagogical practice.[6] First, proponents of nature study viewed their pedagogical principles as a means to improve human health both individually and communally, physically and morally. Moreover, nature study advocates sought to do this through the practical application of the latest principles derived from psychology and the social sciences; nature study was, in other words, "child centered." Finally, the advocates of nature study sought a broad application of their discipline to all kinds of students, regardless of their geographic or social location. This principle reflected their belief in the power of the study of nature to uplift human culture. In short, nature study was fundamental to the larger response of progressive educators to industrial civilization.

Most nature study advocates considered the relationship between children and nature an intensely moral one. They asserted that contact with nature helped children achieve the habits of mind they needed to understand their world. That habit of mind included an embrace of science: "Our daily bread depends as never before on a comprehension of physical and biological phenomena. The average man, not the expert alone, must be scientific."[7] But rather than being coolly instrumental, that science needed to be cloaked in concern for nonhuman nature. By developing respect for nonhuman life, nature study expanded students' realm of moral concern. Yet nature study did not displace the progressive concern with social life. Theorists of progressive education, such as nature study advocate Wilbur Jackman and philosopher John Dewey, built on the intellectual legacy of romanticism by elaborating on the intertwined fates of nature and culture, highlighting the holistic character of human experience.

Nature study advocates' attempts to achieve sound pedagogical practice by combining their progressive zeal for rigorous scientific research with their romantic view of children and nature exposed many of the incongruities that shaped progressive education. Faith in the beneficence of scientific inquiry existed in constant tension with the romantic view of nature held by many nature study advocates. "All youths love nature," wrote one widely read proponent of nature study, "none of them, primarily, loves science. . . . A rigidly graded and systematic body of facts kills nature-study; examinations bury it."[8] The relentless categorization of knowledge and the narrowly positivist view of experience employed by some scientists and their followers in the public schools contradicted the romantic ideal of a holistic and child-centered curriculum.

Nature study thus elucidates progressive education because it engendered a sophisticated debate over the meaning and place of specialized knowledge in modern society. Inherent to that debate over nature study was the universal quandary of education, the problem of knowing. How were students to know nature during an era that juxtaposed a marked increase in specialized knowledge against an acute awareness of the inevitably social impact of its diffusion? How can empirical science and moral sentiment inform the human relationship with nonhuman nature? To understand these conflicting meanings of nature study, one must examine the romantic ideology that grew into progressive education. Yet the history of nature study is not a contest of ideas alone. As we shall see, many of the prominent experimental curricula that gave rise to progressive education featured nature study at their center. Moreover, the debates over the proper methods to teach nature study illuminate the tensions surrounding science and modernity that informed progressive education.

Like the progressivism it helped spawn, romanticism cannot be reduced to a single, readily definable set of historic events, philosophical viewpoints, or aesthetic values. Indeed, many different romanticisms can be inferred from the rich variety of intellectual trends, aesthetic movements, and social revolutions that took place from the late eighteenth century through the middle of the nineteenth. Part of the difficulty in defining romanticism is that it represented an impulse or set of feelings as much as a well-defined set of ideas. Still, some general themes connect romanticism's philosophical outlook and aesthetic spirit, especially with regard to the great European theorists of education whose ideas did so much to instigate American progressive education.

Most broadly, romanticism is best understood as growing out of eighteenth-century thought in reaction to the Enlightenment's excessive rationality and narrow empiricism. In contrast to the matter-of-factly mechanistic worldview proffered by Enlightenment rationalism, romantics asserted a philosophy that critic Morse Peckham aptly termed "dynamic organicism."[9] This worldview valued holistic over mechanistic thinking and individuality and creativity over uniformity and rationalization. Romantics tended to view the problems of individuals as stemming from their relationship to a corrupt society rather than arising from attributes inherent to their human nature. Crucially, romantics valued nature both for its own intrinsic value and as a place of spiritual and aesthetic refuge. In his magisterial study of ecological thought, Donald Worster reminded us that "at the very core of this Romantic view of nature was what later generations would come to call an ecological perspective: that is, a search for holistic or integrated perception, an emphasis on interdependence and relatedness in nature, and an intense desire to restore man to a place of intimate intercourse with the vast organism that constitutes the earth."[10] Where Enlightenment rationalists detected in nature that which was uniform, mechanistic, and bound by law, romantics found a dynamic world of intrinsic worth that offered access to unmediated feelings and unspoiled communion between self and world.

Romantic attitudes pervaded the thinking of the theorists of pedagogy whose insights would eventually form the basis of progressive education. The earliest of these theorists was a seventeenth-century Moravian monk named John Amos Comenius. Exiled during the political and sectarian upheavals associated with the Thirty Years' War, Comenius resolved to invent methods of education that might help restore his homeland to religion and piety should he once again be free to work there. "Reform in education," asserted Comenius, "would bring about a reform of works" that would result in "less ignorance, confusion, and dissent" while bringing about "more light, order, peace and silence."[11] In the meantime, Comenius found refuge in Poland, where he gained employment as a teacher at the Moravian Gymnasium in the town of Lesna. This appointment gave fresh impetus to his pedagogical work. Importantly, Comenius sought to build a general theory of learning rather than focusing solely on the teaching of Latin. His pedagogical philosophy was published in 1657 as *The Great Didactic*.[12]

Comenius is generally credited with being the first philosopher to theorize a system of education that began with early childhood and ended with the university. His proposed school system was to be universally available to children up to eleven years of age, and he felt that the schools should concentrate on developing socially useful skills as well as imparting scientific knowledge of the natural world. Comenius thought that such knowledge must come from contact with actual things rather than representations of things. For Comenius, the material world was not a mere representation of a greater eternal truth but a tangible reality that gave rise to the metaphysical world of ideas. Following the implications of this insight, Comenius argued that "since the beginning of knowledge must be with the senses, the beginning of teaching should be made by dealing with actual things. The object must be a real, useful thing, capable of making an impression upon the senses."[13] Comenius thus theorized the educational methods that in their American incarnation became known as "object teaching."

Like the nineteenth-century pioneers of nature study he would inspire, Comenius extrapolated from the idea of teaching with objects to the idea of teaching through contact with the natural world. "Do we not dwell in the garden of Nature as well as the ancients?" asked Comenius. His view of the garden of nature anticipated that of romantic thinkers, who almost two centuries later found so much pedagogical value in contact with the green world. "And why should we need to know the works of Nature?" wrote Comenius in his *Physics*. "Why, say I, should we not, instead of these dead books, lay open the living book of Nature, in which there is much more to contemplate than any one person can ever relate and the contemplation of which brings much more of pleasure, as well as of profit?"[14]

Humans and nature were even more closely linked in the philosophy of the great romantic theorists of education. For example, radical social philosopher Jean-Jacques Rousseau began his treatise on education, the 1762 novel *Emile,* by linking aberrant socialization to the domination of nature. "Everything is good as it leaves the hands of the Author of things," claimed Rousseau, yet "everything degenerates in the hands of man. He forces one soil to nourish the products of another, one tree to bear the fruit of another." Indeed, the human "disfigures everything," for "he wants nothing as nature made it, not even man; for him man must be trained like a school horse; man must be fashioned in keeping with his fancy like a tree in his garden." Explicit in the opening lines of Rousseau's volume, then, is a powerful exhortation to recognize the intertwined fates of the external nature of the living earth and the internal nature of human beings.[15]

Yet as Rousseau's analogy indicates, humankind has not learned to respect life. Rousseau's writings emphasized metaphors that bound people with organic nature. In doing so, he stressed the complicated necessity of replacing the predominant methods of socialization that distort human nature with new pedagogical methods appropriate to the healthful maturation of the individual. A human being entering into civil society without suitable development was like "a shrub that chance had caused to be born in the middle of a path and that the passers-by soon cause to perish by bumping into it from all sides and bending it in every direction." Organic metaphors further illustrate Rousseau's theory of human nature. Humans, like the living things of nature, have a core being that is either facilitated or thwarted during its course of development. Rousseau scholar Grace Roosevelt correctly contended that Rousseau viewed each person "like an individual tree." Every child "has his own individual form or constitution, his own dispositions and inclinations, which are prior to the influences of external shaping."[16] Rousseau viewed human development as analogous to that of nature, and he also believed that contact with nature was essential to learning. Leaving aside the fictional Emile to "seek in myself an example" that is "evident" to the reader, Rousseau expounded on the benefits of contact with nature. "I would always stay as close as possible to nature, in order to indulge the senses I received from nature—quite certain that the more nature contributed to my enjoyments, the more reality I would find in them."[17]

Rousseau advocated teaching according to nature, but by the impractical pedagogical method of shielding children from society until young adulthood. Yet his organic metaphors and insistence on theorizing the relationship between nonhuman and human nature set the stage for the theories of the two thinkers who exerted the greatest influence on American progressive education: Swiss educator Johann Pestalozzi and German educator Friedrich Froebel.

Rousseau influenced Pestalozzi to such an extent that Pestalozzi tried to raise his own child as the tutor raised Emile. Finding Rousseau's methods impractical, however, Pestalozzi studied children to ascertain how they learned, and he eventually opened a series of schools that implemented his findings. He believed that children learned best through direct experience with real objects of the world. Yet such contact needed to occur in a nurturing environment; Pestalozzi became well known for his insistence that children's learning required a caring and positive atmosphere. A member of the political Left, he also championed the idea that educational opportunities be made available to women and the poor.

Like Rousseau, Pestalozzi presented his educational philosophy in the form of the novel; *Leonard and Gertrude* appeared in 1781, followed by *How Gertrude Teaches Her Children* in 1801. In the later work Pestalozzi expanded on his philosophy of education according to nature, by which he meant that humans must understand the greater environment as well as their place in it. For Pestalozzi and other romantic thinkers, human nature was part of physical nature. "The mechanism of [human] nature," wrote Pestalozzi, "is essentially subject to the same laws as those by which physical nature generally unfolds her powers." It follows that "all instruction of man is then only the Art of helping Nature to develop in her own way."[18] Pestalozzi delivered adamant injunctions regarding the human relationship with nature:

> Man! Imitate it. Imitate this action of high Nature, who out of the seed of the largest tree first produces a scarcely perceptible shoot, then, just as imperceptibly, daily and hourly, by gradual stages, unfolds first the beginnings of the stem, then the bough, then the branch, then the extreme twig on which hangs the perishable leaf. Consider carefully this action of great Nature: how she tends and perfects every single part as it is formed, and joins on every new part to the permanent growth of the old.[19]

Pestalozzi, like other romantics, viewed the analogy between natural growth and human maturation as a demonstration of the interdependence between humans and physical nature.

For Comenius, Rousseau, and Pestalozzi, the human relationship with nature was an intensely moral one; contact with nature was believed to spur piety toward nature's creator. Friedrich Froebel, a former student of Pestalozzi's who is best known as the innovator of the kindergarten, continued to promote this connection between moral fervor and physical nature. Froebel believed that contact with nature raised children's moral stature, as they learned to find examples of moral behavior in nature. For example, Froebel cited the loving care displayed by mother birds as proof of familial obligation. "Every contact with nature," asserted Froebel, "elevates, strengthens, purifies." Froebel urged the following practice to parents: "Take your little children by the hand; go with them into Nature as into the house of God. Allow the wee one to stroke the good cow's forehead, and to run about among the fowl, and play at the edge of the wood. Make companions for your boys and girls of the trees and the banks and the pasture land."[20] Froebel took the idea of using nature as a companion for children seriously. During their jaunts to farm or forest, children should be taught not to alter or possess nature; they should be taught to have reverence for life. It is little wonder that he thought optimal early learning occurred in a child's garden.

Though well known for his insistence on the importance of play to childhood learning, Froebel, like other romantic theorists of education, also placed a great deal of emphasis on practical work as a pedagogical method. "Particularly helpful at this period of life is the cultivation of gardens owned by the boys and cultivated for the sake of the produce. He would see his work bearing fruit in an organic way, determined by logical necessity and law—fruit which, although subject to the inner laws of natural development, depends in so many ways upon his work and upon the character of his work."[21]

Children were to nurture not only plant life in their gardens but also animals such as insects and birds. Froebel felt that this experience with nature would induce in children humility and reverence, practical skills, and the desire to learn. Interaction with nature was the source of experience that would foster children's development. Froebel repeated the romantic insistence on the analogy between human and nonhuman nature to describe the work of the kindergarten: "As in a garden, under God's favor, and by the care of a skilled, intelligent gardener, growing plants are cultivated in accordance with Nature's laws."[22]

As with the criticisms of industrial modernity, however, American nature study practitioners could look to indigenous romantic traditions for critical and innovative pedagogy. Almost all the widely published transcendentalists—Ralph Waldo Emerson, Henry David Thoreau, Margaret Fuller, and Bronson Alcott—worked as teachers. Emerson and Thoreau in particular wrote as much about education as they did about nature; indeed, nature study advocates merely repeated the transcendentalist intertwining of these themes, which included key nature study ideas such as the insistence on individualism and self-reliance and the belief that intercourse with nature provided spiritual guidance.

Emerson and Thoreau investigated nature education in their writings. Emerson asserted that the "world exists for the education of each man."[23] Because he believed that physical facts were doorways to higher, transcendent truths, the role of the educator was to dismiss the collection of mere facts in favor of developing intellectual curiosity, which could bring deeper truths to the forefront of student consciousness. Learning was thus a process of making truths, not one of discovering them lying about, as if truth existed in commodity form. To do this would require a radical reconfiguration of the relationship between education and the larger culture—a reconfiguration that Emerson called for in his famous essay "The American Scholar." The purpose of education was not merely to transmit knowledge but to allow students to hone experience and modify their own interpretations of the world.

That interpretation of the world did not end with scholastic endeavors. Emerson noted, "Our institutions, of which the town is the unit, are all educational, for responsibility educates fast. The town meeting is, after the high-school, a higher school."[24] Democracy itself was an educative process, a position most forcibly articulated by John Dewey. "Full education comes only when there is a responsible share on the part of each person, in proportion to capacity, in shaping the aims and policies of the social groups to which he belongs," argued Dewey.[25] Both Emerson and Dewey emphasized that education must be sufficient to help people function as intelligent citizens, the very goal of progressive education.

Thoreau wrote about education—especially about lifelong education—and also spent much of his life as an educator, beginning when he was an undergraduate at Harvard and continuing with his own school, the Concord Academy. The unthinking routine, cautious pedagogy, and acceptance of authority that characterized conventional education horrified Thoreau. "What does education often do?" exclaimed Thoreau. "It makes a straight cut ditch of a free, meandering brook."[26] Anticipating progressive thinkers such as Dewey, Thoreau, like Emerson, viewed education as central to creative democracy, to the community building that was essential to the democratic life. For Thoreau and the progressive educators who followed him, there was continuity between the process of learning and the rest of experience. That experience could be richly invigorating due to the individual's ability to grow from it, or it could be narrowly expedient, an instrumentalism that confined human potential. Moreover, education needed to be ecological; as Thoreau once quipped, Harvard taught all the branches of knowledge, but none of the roots.

Thoreau's Concord Academy adopted curricular nature study *avant la lettre.* Although other parts of the curriculum were conventional, the Thoreau brothers (Henry hired his brother John, a teacher from Roxbury, to help with the school) also engaged in a great deal of study that took students outside the classroom. The brothers frequently took their charges on field trips to local businesses and outside to study nature, led by the master naturalist himself. In the spring, each student plowed a small plot of land. This "nature work" was coordinated with other skills; the students learned to use surveying equipment, for example. The school was a success, closing only due to John's struggle with tuberculosis, the disease that would eventually fell Henry as well.

Among the projects that Henry was working on at the time of his death was a textbook undertaken at the urging of Bronson Alcott, who became Concord's school superintendent in 1859. Alcott envisioned that Thoreau would write a guide to the local geography and natural history of Concord. Alcott valued Thoreau's experience, writing, "Happily we have a sort of resident Surveyor-General of the town's farms, farmers, animals, and everything else it contains."[27] Moreover, students would not just read this book; Thoreau himself would guide students through the local landscape on field trips. The basis of this pedagogy—immersion in the local, use of the senses, the interweaving of natural history with other subjects—became the basis of nature study pedagogy.

Given the power and prominence of the romantic intellectual legacy, one can easily see how a movement devoted to the study of nature would grow from these pedagogical roots. Proponents of nature study themselves acknowledged the debt. In his book *The Nature-Study Idea,* Cornell University horticulturist Liberty Hyde Bailey, one of the nation's most prominent champions of nature study, asserted that the beginnings of nature study "are certainly as old as the time of Socrates and Aristotle." Yet the contemporary movement is "a fruit of the great educational reformers—Comenius, Pestalozzi, Emile [*sic*] Rousseau, Froebel. . . . It represents a reaction from the dry-as-dust science teaching."[28]

The dual concern for moral instruction and nonhuman nature that typified romantic thought flourished in America at a time of immense social upheaval that, among other changes, redefined gender roles. Indeed, the romantic legacy prospered in America partly due to the social changes that brought many women into elementary schools as teachers during the nineteenth century.

Given the lack of a national church or other institutionalized forum of moral instruction, many Americans looked to the family to instill moral rectitude in the nation's youth. Because children were at home with their mothers, motherhood itself became charged with the transmission of moral culture. The separation of gender roles in the nineteenth century thus intensified the domestic duties of women, including the social obligations attached to motherhood. The public role of women as social reformers also helped cement the connection between femininity and social morality. The pressure on women to impart moral values only increased as the nineteenth century's amoral capitalism guided the industrial economy's radical reconfiguration of the structure of society. As public education spread, schools also became the locus of moral instruction. Women seized public education as a means to redefine their capacity as moral guardians through an expanded social role as schoolteachers. By the late nineteenth century, women so dominated the teaching profession that a backlash of commentary decrying the "women peril" in teaching appeared in professional journals of education.[29]

The power of women as educators made sense to Americans steeped in romantic theories of education. Rousseau, Pestalozzi, and Froebel all portrayed nature as female, the giver of life and the nurturer of spirit. Gender roles and ideologies of nature were intimately connected. Women, defined through their bodies, were thought to be closer to nature and therefore able to more thoroughly impart its wholesome wisdom. Moreover, the sentimentality attached to communion with nature fit widespread gender stereotypes that emphasized the supposed tender emotionality of women. Yet always lurking within these complex ideologies of nature and gender was the romantic devotion to discovery and experimentation. Romantic notions of pedagogy flowered into progressive education when nature study advocates began to view growth in nature as a model of personal development and as a teacher of humanity.

Nature study constituted one way to turn the romantic ideals and fanciful pieties of progressive reformers into practical curricula imparted through sound pedagogy. In this regard, nature study evinced less of the naïveté that sometimes characterized the application of the romantic ideas associated with the new education. Indeed, one finds nature study at the core of the brilliant experimental curricula that led to many of the best innovations in what became known as progressive education.

Perhaps Colonel Francis Wayland Parker (1837–1902) carried out the most influential of the early experiments in curriculum and pedagogy when he became superintendent of schools in Quincy, Massachusetts, in 1875. Parker had decided on a career in education early in life. After service in the Union army,

Parker resumed that career but became increasingly dissatisfied with the dominant pedagogy of his day. Like Horace Mann before him, Parker traveled overseas to learn about the latest innovations in pedagogy. In Europe he was able to study the ideas of Pestalozzi and Froebel firsthand. Upon his return he landed the job as superintendent of schools in Quincy and promptly implemented his version of romantic, cutting-edge teaching methods.

Parker jettisoned the standard curriculum and its dull reader, speller, grammar, and copybook. In its place he instituted lessons based on the experiences and interests of children and the innovative ideas of teachers. The new curriculum emphasized children's ability to observe, describe, and understand through direct experience with real objects. Children read from current magazines and newspapers, played with objects to learn arithmetic inductively, and generally avoided lessons based on recitation, repetition, and memorization. More importantly, the unconventional curriculum was built around three unifying subjects: geography, history, and nature study. Other subjects were correlated with these.[30] Parker's students made frequent trips to the countryside, where teachers used contact with the natural world to help children apply their burgeoning observational and deductive abilities to learn everything from basic mathematics to drawing.

Although the program could claim immediate and measurable success, and although it attracted a great deal of national attention, it was also intensely controversial. Conservative critics lambasted the move away from fundamentals and charged that the surveys demonstrating marked improvements in reading and spelling ability were biased. Parker left Quincy in 1880, and after a brief stint as a school supervisor in Boston, he became principal of one of the great laboratory schools, Chicago's Cook County Normal School, in 1883. It was at Cook County that Parker, while educating both students and student teachers, fully developed his pedagogical theories. Most broadly, Parker sought to place the interests, needs, and abilities of students at the center of the educative process and to coordinate and relate the subject matter of the curriculum in such a way that it held immediate meaning for children. That curriculum included nature study.[31] Shortly after Parker arrived, Cook County became the local public school for its neighborhood.

Parker had long sought a specially trained science teacher who could bring holistic and progressive theories of education to bear on the teaching of science. He found that man in Wilbur Jackman. Jackman grew up on a farm near California, Pennsylvania. At a young age he developed a great love for plants and animals (a common trait among nature study advocates) and spent the rest of his life attempting to translate that love into practical and effective pedagogy.

After graduating from Harvard (where he studied with prominent geologist and conservationist Nathaniel Shaler) he accepted a job as a science teacher in Pittsburgh. Parker discovered Jackman on a visit to Pittsburgh and immediately brought him to Cook County.[32] "Never shall I forget the elation with which Col. Parker introduced Mr. Jackman," recalled Jackman's colleague Orville Bright. "For years he had been in search of a teacher of natural sciences who could bring these subjects into rational touch with young lives."[33]

Jackman's theories of childhood education easily coalesced with the child-centered curriculum developed by Parker. He believed that children expressed broad rather than particular interests and that they needed physical contact with actual nature to develop their skills in observation and reason. Jackman developed these ideas in two books: *Nature Study for the Common Schools* (1891), dedicated to "the common school teacher," and *Nature Study for Grammar Grades* (1899). *Nature Study for the Common Schools* remains a small classic of progressive educational thought. Jackman carefully studied the manner in which children learn and then translated that knowledge into science lessons for children. His primary pedagogical concern was to prevent the introduction of disciplinary thinking at too early an age: "It is a radical error to attempt to make specialists of the pupils from the beginning." Children naturally acquire knowledge that is "all breadth and no depth"; early specialization destroys the interest of children and blinds them to inquiry that they would otherwise enjoy.[34] Given proper methods of introduction, however, science in the form of nature study could become a vital part of the elementary school curriculum. Jackman advocated that nature study lessons correlate with the changing seasons, a strategy that emphasized the mutability of nature and brought the subject matter to bear on children's immediate experience and broad but superficial interests.

Like his fellow progressive educators, Jackman was a staunch critic of the dominant modes of pedagogy. Writing in the *Journal of the Proceedings of the National Education Association,* Jackman argued that "the introduction of nature-study into the common schools has made it obvious to the most obtuse that complete reorganization of the course of study is imperative." Indeed, Jackman claimed that "nature-study found the grammar school utterly poverty-stricken from the standpoint of thought material"; thus nature study "was like sunlight breaking through gloomy clouds. . . . It actually seemed as though the three R's were about to loose their grip."[35] The introduction to *Nature Study for the Common Schools* contained Jackman's justification for jettisoning the three Rs and instituting nature study in their place. Beyond the "reasoning power" his methods would enhance, he noted a "pressing need" for "pupils to be taught the truth about the laws of nature." In an age of patent medicines, popular "mind cures," belief in occult powers, and other examples of quackery that thrived on scientific illiteracy, Jackman lamented that "there are enough people about us, so grossly ignorant of natural laws, that they are the willing victims of a base fraud."[36]

The Cook County Normal School quickly developed a wide reputation for educational excellence and attracted many distinguished visitors. Among these were psychologist G. Stanley Hall, who stopped at Cook County annually "to set my educational watch," and Hall's former student John Dewey, who, upon taking a new position as head of the departments of Philosophy, Psychology, and Pedagogy at the University of Chicago, promptly enrolled his children in Cook County Normal School.[37] In January 1896, however, Dewey opened his own school, the Laboratory School at the University of Chicago, popularly known as the Dewey School. Dewey intended the school to be wholly experimental, an institution founded to test and reform his educational theories and to use experimentation as a pedagogical tool. Francis Parker was an enthusiastic observer of Dewey and his experiments in education. Indeed, Parker contended that he and Dewey shared the same ideas but that Dewey articulated them in philosophical terms.[38] By October 1896 the Dewey School had thirty-two students and two full-time teachers: one in nature study, the other in history and literature.

By 1898 Dewey had organized the school faculty on a departmental basis that featured teacher specialists in literature, history, woodworking, science, physical education, textiles, cooking, and music. Ida B. DePencier's *The History of the Laboratory Schools* described the curriculum this way: "All the groups learned history, which Mr. Dewey viewed as a way of giving children 'insight into social life.' What was called science was largely nature study—observation of the world about them."[39] The curriculum included frequent field trips, often for the purpose of nature study. Dewey's pedagogy reflected his general agreement with much of the progressive critique that existing methods of education failed to connect to the interests and abilities of children.

Less understood is Dewey's insistence that teachers connect the curriculum to students' interests and abilities.[40] Indeed, Dewey's pedagogy called on teachers to "reinstate into experience" the various subject matters of the curriculum.[41] Dewey concurred with nature study advocates that learning was inseparable from experience. According to Dewey, positing ideas as hypotheses to be tested by experiment undermined the harmful Cartesian split between mind and body (manifested as the divorce between theory and practice) and provided all students with the skills needed to build a democratic society in a technologically complex world. Again, such problem solving begins most successfully with the existing interests and abilities of students but ends with the mastering of organized subjects. In short, Dewey intended his pedagogy to equip students with the ability to analyze and act on "social realities—including the evils—of industrial and political civilization."[42]

The role of the teacher, then, was a most demanding one. Teachers needed to be expert enough to take the native interests of children and translate them into practical, hands-on activities. It was not enough for students to merely have experiences; students had to use their own language to reflect on and analyze their lessons. This required both disciplinary competence and imaginative and excellent pedagogical practice. Few teachers could create such wide-ranging, learned, and imaginative pedagogy. Among the many factors inhibiting the creation of such classrooms was that very few teachers were trained in science. One of the great challenges of the nature study movement—and a problem that still plagues American education today—was finding scientifically qualified teachers. One success of the nature study movement was its education of teachers, as well as students, in the basics of natural history at a time when scientific education was in its infancy. But the fact that the nature study movement had to spend so much time educating teachers demonstrated the profound lack of scientifically capable instructors.

As if such pressures were not profound enough, the public rarely missed an opportunity to impart its own wisdom to teachers. Due to its experimental and private nature, Dewey's school remained relatively free from public intrusions, though it was constantly on the edge of bankruptcy. But because Parker's school was public, its progressive curriculum and pedagogy were subject to a great deal of conservative criticism and meddling by the local school board. Upon receiving a generous endowment from Mrs. Emmons Blaine, daughter of industrialist Cyrus McCormick (inventor of the reaper), Parker privatized his institution. The new school was also located at the University of Chicago, which briefly boasted two experimental elementary schools. When Parker died in March 1902, the two schools merged under a leadership that included Dewey as director of the School of Education, Jackman as dean, and Dewey's wife, Alice, as principal of the elementary school.[43]

One year later Dewey resigned his position to take a job at Columbia University. At that time Jackman became principal of the elementary school and, at Dewey's urging, also assumed editorship of the *Elementary School Teacher*. As editor, Jackman continued his support of nature study, writing in the June 1905 issue, "it is simply ridiculous to keep children confined in a schoolroom learning *about* a world while they must live *in* it." Jackman's profound contributions to nature study were cut short when he died from pneumonia at age fifty-two on Monday, 28 January 1907; he had spent that previous Saturday at a

School of Education social gathering. Yet his intellectual legacy lived on through his contact with John Dewey and Deweyan ideas. Jackman's published advocacy of nature study had adopted a decidedly Deweyan tone, and Dewey himself became a strong advocate of nature study.[44]

Dewey's interest in nature study was a long-standing one. In 1897 he gave an address to the parents and teachers of the Laboratory School that presented a detailed account of how the school's practices related to his theoretical principles. In it he described nature study this way:

> Both nature study (that is the study through observations of obvious natural phenomena) and experimental work are introduced from the beginning. The science is very much more difficult to arrange and systematize. There is so little to follow, so little that has already been done. It is impossible to exaggerate this statement. The slight amount of work in science that has been developed in any systematic way for the use of children, which purposes to cultivate their powers of noting the habits of plants and animals is almost negligible. The earth is, perhaps, the focus for the science study as practically all of the work relates to it sooner or later, and in one way or another.[45]

Both Jackman and Dewey wished to blend into the school a holistic and integrated curriculum that reflected their romantic understanding of knowledge itself. Dewey argued that nature study must embody a holistic approach:

> To make the child study earth, air or water, bird, beast, or flower apart from environment and out of relation to their use by other factors in the environment, their function in the total life process, cuts the ties that relates and binds natural facts and forces to people and their activities. The child's interest fades for he misses the way. His imagination finds no avenue of connection that makes object, fact or process concrete to him. He loses his original open, free attitude toward natural facts. Nature herself is reduced to a mass of meaningless details. In contrast, however, when a natural object is clothed with human significance and human association, a road lies open from the child's mind to the object through the connection of the latter with life itself. The unity of life, as it presents itself to the child, thus binds together and carries along the different occupations of living. The diversity of plants, animals, and geographical conditions . . . are ways to carry certain features . . . to a completed mental and emotional satisfaction."[46]

Dewey emphasized that he viewed nature study as holistic science—and much more. In an essay titled "Imagination and Expression," he argued that nature study developed aesthetic sensibilities:

Drawing in connection with nature study affords excellent means for development in technical definiteness and accuracy. It is necessary to image parts in definite, not in haphazardness relations, in order that the idea of the whole may be realized. But even here, especially with younger children, it is necessary to bear in mind that the primary interest is not in the external appearance of the object as an object, but in function, use, aesthetic quality and relation to life.[47]

Dewey maintained his belief in the efficacy of nature study long after he left the Laboratory School. Moreover, his philosophical work continued to build on his insistence on the active role of nature in human life. In his seminal 1915 text *Democracy and Education,* Dewey theorized nature as an active historical agent. "This setting of nature" wrote Dewey, "does not bear to social activities the relation that the scenery of a theatrical performance bears to a dramatic representation; it enters into the very make-up of the social happenings that form history."[48] History and nature influenced each other and thus should be taught as complementary, not antagonistic, subjects.

Dewey's philosophical and pedagogical goal of replacing Cartesian dualisms with holistic thinking led him to advocate a method of studying the past that combined narrative and natural history, a position also held by Jackman. It remains a good example of progressive educators searching for romantic pedagogy that integrated rather than categorized human knowledge. Dewey argued that if history failed to consider its basis in the natural environment, it lost its vitality as a discipline. "When this interdependence of the study of history, representing the human emphasis, with the study of geography, representing the natural, is ignored," wrote Dewey, "history sinks to a listing of dates with an appended inventory of events." Dewey ridiculed the teaching of history that overlooked the influence of nature as a "literary fantasy." Indeed, history that ignored the agency of nature became a literary fantasy because "in purely literary history the natural environment *is* but stage scenery."[49]

A holistic view of nature also helped spur sympathy for nonhuman life. "When nature is treated as a whole" argued Dewey, "its phenomena fall into their natural relations of sympathy and association with human life." Indeed, one of the primary goals of nature study was "to cultivate a sympathetic understanding of the place of plants and animals in life and to develop emotional and aesthetic interest." The tending of classroom animals was important because it taught "humaneness to animals and a general sympathy for animal life."[50] Meanwhile, nature study advocates adopted Deweyan language to describe their pedagogy. "The nature-study method," wrote Maurice A. Bigelow, "consists largely in *learning by doing.*"[51]

The repeated insistence that humans must develop sympathy for nonhuman nature remained one of the outstanding features of the nature study movement. Commentators at the time noticed this trend. Margaret W. Morley, writing in *Outlook,* praised nature study for its multidisciplinary approach because the sciences are "all interrelated, all threads in one design." Because that single design included the human world, "there is a duty owed by us to the trees, and through them to our fellow-men." This attitude also supported utilitarian approaches to conservation: "A knowledge of tree life, a love for trees, and a knowledge of the reasons for preserving them, if instilled in early years, will make an intelligent interest in trees part of mature life, and there will be no difficulty gaining advocates for forest laws when the question is raised."[52]

But such values were not universally held. Much of the controversy surrounding scientific specialization and nature study focused on the moral value attached to nonhuman life. A stunning support for the nature study point of view appeared in *Science* magazine in an article written by L. H. Baekeland, a professor of chemical engineering at Columbia University and the inventor of Bakelite plastic. Deploring the overspecialization that "reduces us to mere automatic machines," Baekeland focused on the corollary concern that specialization engendered a "narrow-mindedness" that may, in turn, "lead to a short-sighted pettiness." For Baekeland, the consequences of overspecialization affected every part of public life. "Busily burrowing along like moles, in the pursuit of our own little specialties, we are dizzily preoccupied with our specialized routine work." Thus, "in science as well as in politics . . . we are willing to join the herd of docile and unthinking sheep who are following a leader." This attitude had especially deleterious effects on the study of nature because "we lose the desire of coming once in a while upon the surface of the earth to take a stimulating look at the grand view of nature and its inspiring entity." In words that were surely appreciated by those nature study advocates worried about the moral effects of highly specialized academic study, Baekeland argued:

> Our lack of broad-mindedness is shown in many other ways. We admit the principle of evolution, but when it comes to concede rights and friendliness toward animals—fellow beings—we fall short of our theories: we eagerly forget that other living creatures enjoy life and suffer, feel and think as we ourselves, if not exactly in the same way. Some of us claim to be civilized and yet find high pleasure and recreation in hunting, killing, maiming and

torturing defenseless animals, although we go on criticizing the Spaniards who enjoy the gore of a bull-fight.[53]

Yet Baekeland's view was certainly in the minority among scientists who, by professional necessity, embraced specialization to the detriment of "broad-mindedness" and surely at the cost of ethical attachments to nature. John M. Coulter, head of the Department of Botany at the University of Chicago, expressed the dominant viewpoint in his essay "Nature Study and Intellectual Culture," a work that clearly anticipated C. P. Snow's famous critique of academic life as divided into "two cultures."[54] For Coulter, the split between the humanities and the sciences depended on the role of the self during intellectual pursuit. "If the proper intellectual result of the humanities is *appreciation,* whose processes demand *self-injection,*" wrote Coulter, "the proper and distinctive intellectual result of the sciences is *law,* to obtain which there must be rigid *self-elimination.*" Thus Coulter rejected "the study of nature" conducted "so as to cultivate merely a sentimental appreciation of natural objects," for it belonged to the humanities, not science.[55] Disciplinary science rejected the very foundation—sympathy—on which many nature study advocates built their pedagogy and justified the rationale for conservation.

Other critics of sympathetic attachments to nature were more forthright in their rejection of the moral basis of nature study. Many thinkers simply could not abide the granting of moral standing to nonhuman nature. One particularly vehement example of such criticism came from renowned psychologist Edward Thorndike, a proponent of a reductive stimulus-response theory of learning. Writing in the *Educational Review,* Thorndike charged that "the work which is now being done is often so useless that the stoutest supporters of nature-study ought to be always exercising their critical sense in reforming it." The expression of sympathy for animals and plants was "unreasonable and therefore mischievous idolatry." Nor did such love lead to a future interest in science: "St. Francis is no patron saint for science or science teachers. . . . Science and scientific observation are not the results of an emotional or ethical, but of a purely intellectual, interest in things."[56] Thorndike did not appreciate the distinction nature study advocates made between the practice of science and the motivation for it, nor their argument about childhood development and disciplinary thinking.

Even more alarming for Thorndike was the ostensible moral confusion of elevating nonhuman life into the realm of ethics; this idea provoked his most bitter outrage. Nature study encouraged a "vicious lack of discrimination" because "birds, insects, snails and plants . . . are all credited with life in the sense of human life." Thus a "loving interest" in nature is an "atrocity. . . . Nature is . . . an unchanging machine, a master against whom our revolt is beginning to succeed . . . [nature remains] a mere collection of things to be turned to the service of our conscious ends."[57] By embracing an ethical justification for conservation, proponents of nature study encouraged the very moral dialogue that ensured at least some condemnation of their pedagogy. The moral dialogue sought by nature study advocates thus contributed to the debate and confusion about nature study's relationship to the scientific endeavor and the intellectual foundations for conservation.

These controversies presented severe challenges to advocates of progressive education. How would the abstract and specialized epistemology of scientific inquiry suit the core romantic ideology of unmediated intercourse with a beneficent nature? What was the relationship between scientific method and the educational capabilities of children? Progressive science education emanated from the contradictions inherent to the rationalizing imperatives of the scientific method and the moral commitment to pedagogy built on the holistic and natural development of the child.

The nature study movement grew out of these contradictions that constituted the very heart of progressive education. Progressive educators embraced science by pushing for a "science of education" and for the introduction of the latest findings and methodologies of experimental disciplines into the school system. Many others sought to expand the experimental methodologies of laboratory science into a pedagogy appropriate for elementary school children.[58] More broadly, the progressive commitment to science and modernity fueled much of the broad social agenda that backed the new education.

Yet the very scientific method embraced by progressive reformers often proved anathema to progressive pedagogy. The empirical, formal, and disciplinary spirit of scientific investigation too easily lent itself to the traditional pedagogy of catechism and memorization that so repelled reformers committed to new and innovative methods of instruction. For example, W. M. Davis, writing in *Science,* lamented, "Much that has been taught under the name of nature study is not properly a study of nature, but a *memoriter* drill or an empirical abstract of what some one else has learned by a study of nature."[59] Cornell University professor of nature study Anna Botsford Comstock concurred: "If nature study is made a drill, its pedagogic value is lost." Indeed, when nature study "is properly taught, the child is unconscious of mental effort or that he is suffering the act of teaching."[60]

Nature study advocates followed this history by once again seeking an effective means of bringing into the classroom the insights into nature brought about by modern science. Writing in *Educational Review,* Massachusetts Institute of

Technology professor William Sedgwick argued that "physical and natural science should be taught in the schools for many reasons, but chiefly because they are better adapted than any other subjects to illustrate and enforce scientific method." Despite his adherence to scientific method, Sedgwick expanded on the pedagogical value of unmediated intercourse with nature. Indeed, observation and experiment as an educational method "cannot be over-estimated, for it is actual personal intercourse with nature."[61] Was education in science an unfortunate return to passive memorization and recitation, or a liberating embrace of the technological and modern? Would nature help lead students, or would it remain the quiescent subject of empirical investigation?

Advocates of nature study attempted to reconcile scientific investigation with the innovations of the new education by emphasizing pedagogical methodology rather than discrete subject matter and disciplinary cohesion. Bailey described the "value" of nature study this way: "It cannot be reduced to a system, is not cut and dried [and] cannot become part of rigid school methods. Its very essence is spirit. It is as free as its subject matter."[62] Nature study thus attempted to attach subject matter to children's interests, yet it always kept an eye toward a future of systematic, scientific thought: "When the interest passes from the heart to the head, nature-love has given way to science," wrote Bailey. "Fortunately it can always remain an affair of the heart with a more perfect engraftment of the head."[63]

Other writers more forthrightly viewed nature study as a precursor to advanced study in disciplinary science. "Nature study," wrote high school science teacher E. R. Whitney, "aiding so directly, as it does, in observation and deduction, is thus a decided help in the higher work of science by becoming a link between the abstract and the concrete, and showing the bearing of abstract principles upon human life."[64] Yet others were not so sure. Responding to Whitney's paper, biology professor Otis Caldwell castigated what he viewed as the sentimental, rather than rational, basis of nature study. Indeed, Caldwell thought nature study embraced feeling at the expense of science: "If so-called elementary science for grade work were more truly elementary science, and less legendary, mythical, imaginary, and impersonating, it would do something toward establishing some elementary notions of the scientific method of thinking; it would remove elementary science from its present position of well-earned disrepute; and would give it the support of science men."[65]

The attempt to attract the support of men of science drove the founding of the American Nature Study Society. Its first meeting took place in Chicago on 2 January 1908; the meeting's time and place were chosen to follow the convention of the American Association for the Advancement of Science. The society thus positioned itself as a scientific rather than a primarily educational organization, likely to the satisfaction of its membership, which largely comprised high school and college science teachers.[66] Commenting on the first meeting, the editor of *Nature-Study Review*, M. A. Bigelow of Columbia Teacher's College, promoted the connection between nature study and science. Despite the fact that "many of these men [of science] have long been inclined to regard nature-study as merely a fad," Bigelow boasted that "it was evident that interest in nature-study was in the ascendancy so far as men of science are concerned." Yet Bigelow ended his remarks with a note of caution: "All this does not mean that the scientific men are now heartily approving nature-study in general. . . . On the contrary expressions of approval were commonly coupled with qualifying remarks concerning the kind of nature-study."[67] Few scientists openly opposed nature study, but many remained wary of its pedagogical value unless it conformed to standards of experimental investigation.

Stated in the form of "nature study versus science," the question of the relationship between progressive pedagogy and disciplinary cohesion hounded the nature study movement. Despite a great deal of thinking and writing and several symposia devoted to the subject, nature study advocates were ultimately unable to resolve this dilemma.[68] In one sense, the question lingered because nature study attempted to ascertain truths and promote experiences and moral influences that remained outside the realm of scientific endeavor. Nature writer John Burroughs expressed the nature study point of view (even though he was ostensibly rejecting the "study" of nature) when he wrote:

> I . . . never study nature . . . I have loved nature . . . but a student of nature in any strict sense I have never been. What knowledge I possess of her creatures and ways has come to me through contemplation and enjoyment, rather than through deliberate study of her. I have been occupied more with the spirit than the letter of her works. In our time, it seems to me, too much stress is laid upon the letter. . . . Of that sympathetic and emotional intercourse with nature which soothes and enriches the soul, [the clerk of the fields] experiences little or none. . . . He is so intent upon the bare fact that he does not see the spirit or the meaning of the whole.[69]

Nature study advocates wanted students to learn natural history but also to find spiritual and aesthetic meanings that were just as real as the facts of natural history.

Nature study advocates insisted that nature's "real form" consisted of a great deal more than arid abstractions of its classifications. "Mere facts are dead," wrote Bailey, "but the meaning of the facts is life." In short, nature study advocates attempted to teach science while simultaneously engaging students' emotions by grappling with questions of meaning. Understanding that individuals try to make sense of the world through symbols, many teachers added lessons in poetry and fiction to their nature study syllabi. "The artist and poet know this world [of nature]," asserted Bailey, "yet they do not know it by mere knowledge or analysis." Science alone cannot account for the multifaceted human relationship with nature; indeed, "we have a right to a poetic interpretation of nature."[70] Although a "poetic interpretation of nature" appeared to conflict with the nature study movement's fundamental injunction that children experience nature directly, it also realized many of the romantic goals of progressive education.

The debate between science and nature study did not represent a split between scientists and common school educators. Indeed, many prominent scientists supported the romantic goals of nature study. "The child comes to know nature through its imagination and feeling and sympathy," claimed Bailey, a prominent horticulturalist.[71] As the child matures, such feelings of sympathy develop into a more systematic appreciation of the natural world. By high school, the pupil is ready for specialized training in science. Dr. Harold W. Fairbanks of the University of California at Berkeley concurred with Bailey's point of view:

> Nature-study should lead the child back to this natural intimacy with nature and to delight in her company. This cannot be done by feeding him upon courses of study made up of scientifically arranged facts, but by fitting him in a broad way through the exercise of his observational and reasoning powers so that he not only takes pleasure in the world around him but is able to use it more fully to his material advantage.[72]

The ideology of making children sympathetic to nature also satisfied the deeply felt emphasis on moral character. Nature study advocates felt that the amoral outlook of experimental science failed to connect actions to the moral realm of choices and consequences. Furthermore, the insistence on including moral deliberation in the study of nature came about as preeminent scholars challenged the ethical implications of modern science. For example, Nathaniel Shaler wrote of the need to reconcile religious faith and natural law, observing that "some sense of spiritual reconciliation with nature is the necessary support for all the higher work of the mind, whatever the nature of that work may be." Shaler rejected resolutely mechanistic understandings of nature in favor of freer understandings so that "in such a realm the spirit may contentedly dwell feeling that it is in its own fit house."[73] Harvard president Charles W. Eliot concurred, insisting on the harmonious development of both scientific and sentimental attachments to nature. "The idea of culture has always included a quick and wide sympathy with men," asserted Eliot; "it should hereafter include sympathy with nature, and particularly with its living forms, a sympathy based on some accurate observation of nature." Without dismissing specialized science, Eliot propagated the faith of nature study: "A brook, a hedgerow, or a garden is an inexhaustible teacher of wonder, reverence, and love."[74]

Like Eliot, proponents of nature study attempted to reconcile their embrace of experimental science and moral instruction with their rejection of formalized pedagogy. They did this by retaining many of the romantic meanings of nature while accepting the lessons in critical observation, thought, and deduction provided by the scientific method. Development according to nature meant intimate contact with the natural world, and such contact facilitated the broad skills in reasoning and moral sensibility on which a sound education is based. Thus the attack on old methods of education by nature study advocates was an intensely moral affair. Stanford University president David Starr Jordan stressed the connection between responsibility and pedagogy in his essay "Nature Study and Moral Culture":

> When a child is taken from nature to the schools he is usually brought into an atmosphere of conventionality. Here he is not to do, but to imitate; not to see nor to handle, nor create, but to remember. He is, moreover, to remember not his own realities, but the written or spoken ideas of others. He is dragged through a wilderness of grammar with thickets of diacritical marks into the desert of metaphysics. He is taught to do right, not because right action is in the nature of things, the nature of himself and the things about him, but because he will be punished somehow if he does not.[75]

However, the responsibility fostered by direct interaction with the world made nature study a moral and political affair: "Democracy," argued Jordan, "is a nature study on a grand scale."[76] Pedagogy that embraced individual creativity and responsibility within an unalterably holistic worldview coalesced with the progressive commitment to democratic politics.

Despite such heavyweight theorizing by the supporters of nature study, critics chastised their philosophy as a mere celebration of nostalgic sentimentalism. The very power of the charge that an intellectual position is nostalgic reveals how deeply the norms of progress and objective science were (and are) ingrained in American culture. Only in a culture deeply committed to progress could the charge of "nostalgia" alone do so much to discredit an argument or, as in the case of nature study, an entire pedagogy. And yet the charges stuck.

Nature study, quick to bring a moral and ethical dialogue to the study of nature, appeared to many critics to be incompatible with disciplined scientific inquiry.

Disciplinary challenges aside, the nature study emphasis on moral and aesthetic development meant that many—but certainly not all—of its prominent practitioners were on the margins of scientific careers. This is true in the case of one of the greatest champions of nature study, Anna Botsford Comstock.[77] Comstock engineered a career that used her talents as a biologist, writer, and educator; in doing so, she provided a model for women who wanted careers that expanded beyond traditional prospects. Born in a log cabin in Cattaraugus County, New York, Anna Botsford was the daughter of prosperous farmers. Her mother, a Hicksite Quaker, often took young Anna on rambles through the countryside, where she imparted to her daughter an abiding love of nature and a keen interest in natural history. A group of wealthy female neighbors, recognizing Anna's intellectual talents, persuaded her to pursue a university education. Anna's life took a decisive turn when, as a Cornell undergraduate studying languages and literature (she was part of the third class of women enrolled at the school), she took a zoology course offered by John Henry Comstock. Soon the young professor was accompanying his student on long walks in the countryside, and the two were married shortly after Comstock received tenure and was promoted to assistant professor of entomology. Anna Botsford Comstock quickly found herself immersed in several different and demanding roles: faculty housewife, science student, and research assistant to her husband.

Although Anna Comstock relished entomological fieldwork, her duties for her husband soon focused on her artistic abilities. She began her career as a wood engraver in January 1877, working with tools provided by John Henry; soon she was producing insect illustrations for him. In 1885, 1887, and 1890 Comstock traveled to New York City to study with John P. Davis, a master engraver at the Cooper Union Institute. Her talents as an artist were quickly recognized. The American Society of Wood Engravers elected her into its ranks, only the third woman to garner this professional distinction. Upon receiving this honor, Comstock articulated the nature study philosophy, arguing that her work had been recognized because of her unique method of copying from a live insect. Comstock exhibited her work worldwide. Her engravings of moths and butterflies appeared in Berlin and San Francisco as well as at the 1893 Chicago World's Fair and the 1900 Paris Exposition. She also won prizes at the New Orleans Exposition of 1885 and the Pan-American Exposition of 1901.

Meanwhile, Comstock's artistic talents paved the way for her to publish scholarly work and gain a professional reputation among scientists. She had already helped her husband write professional papers, including a scientific report on the cotton worm for the U.S. Department of Agriculture. It was Comstock's engravings, however, that opened the door to scientific publication. When John Henry Comstock published his *Introduction to Entomology* in 1888, the title page credited the "many original illustrations drawn and engraved by Anna Botsford Comstock." The book sold well, and the following month Anna Comstock became one of the first four women inducted into Sigma Xi, the national honor society of the sciences.

Anna Comstock attained true professional equality with her husband when they produced their second book, a monumental text titled *A Manual for the Study of Insects.* The text listed Anna as coauthor—John Henry Comstock was one of the few male scientists of the time who credited the contributions of his wife—and featured hundreds of her original drawings as well as her written depictions of the life histories of a variety of insects. The lively prose and beautiful drawings distinguished the Comstocks' volume from others in the field. The book instantly found its audience; within a month, thirty schools had adopted it as a classroom text. Meanwhile, Anna Comstock returned to her undergraduate studies at Cornell—interrupted when she married—and earned her degree by completing a thesis titled "The Fine Anatomy of the Interior of the Larva of *Corydalus cornutus,*" better known as the dobsonfly.

Anna Comstock's professional activity increased as she became actively involved in the nature study movement. She wrote dozens of books and articles and lectured widely to rural schoolteachers during her summer travels. Every summer also found her lecturing about nature at Chautauqua. She continued to coauthor books with her husband. In collaborating on *The Spider Book,* both Anna and John Henry spent a great deal of time in the field collecting specimens; Anna produced illustrations for the book, while John Henry provided photographs. Anna's professional productivity appeared to pay off when in 1898 she was appointed assistant professor of nature study in the Cornell University Division. The prejudice against women entering the world of academic science quickly stopped her advancement, however; the Board of Trustees balked at giving a woman professional status and reduced Comstock's position (but not her salary or responsibilities) to that of lecturer. Yet she remained an active member of the Cornell faculty, helping her husband build one of the world's premier entomology departments and, with Liberty Hyde Bailey, making Cornell the intellectual center of the nature study movement. In 1919 Cornell eventually promoted Anna Comstock to professor; she was sixty-five years old and would retire two years later.

Anna Comstock's artistic creativity and scientific achievement exemplified the nature study movement's attempt to combine aesthetic and ethical appreciation for the natural world with the stringent and objective method of professional scientific inquiry. The tensions inherent in this merger showed up in Comstock's written work. As Marcia Maria Bonta explained, the nature study articles Comstock collected in her book *Ways of the Six Footed* revealed her profound countermodern sympathies.[78] In her chapter on the maple-leaf cutter, Comstock wrote of the power of contact with nature to relieve the pressures of the workaday world. "Tired of a world that lectured and talked and argued and did many other noisy things that wore on one's nerves," she preferred the quiet company of nature. The forest provided her respite from the "world of work and care." Comstock's social vision also appeared in her evaluations of insect life. She titled her chapter about bees, ants, wasps, and termites "The Perfect Socialism" and compared the ostensible altruism of these insects to the blind acquisitiveness and competitiveness of human beings. Comstock insisted that, in contrast to the failures of socialist theorists, "insects had already solved the problem of practical socialism." Human morality paled in comparison: "The generosity of these insect citizens toward each other is an ideal which still lies beyond the horizon of accomplishment in the human world."[79]

Like other nature study proponents, Comstock sought to realize human ideals in her relationship with nature. The relationship between humans and nature gave people physicality, a sense of possibility and exploration, as well as the creative and authentic experience typical of the relationship between an artist and her medium. Comstock's relationship with art was similar to the one she had with nature. She spent a great deal of time with her engravings, relishing the feel of wood and the tangible expression of her artistic vision. She thus used her abilities as a wood engraver to escape the displacement from nature and Taylorized regimentation that characterized modern labor. In this way, Comstock, like other school arts and nature study advocates, used aesthetic experience in the manner prescribed by William Morris and his followers in the arts and crafts movement.

As historian Amy Green makes clear, Comstock most clearly articulated her artistic motivations in a novel she penned about academic life, *Confessions to a Heathen Idol*.[80] The novel appeared under the pseudonym "Marian Lee" because Comstock felt it "would be scandalous for a scientific woman to write a novel." However, readers quickly guessed the identity of the author due to Comstock's thinly veiled references to herself and to Cornell campus politics. The second edition of the novel was published under her married name. The novel was a celebration of creative labor. Comstock, through the character of Marian Lee, described her greatest happiness and fulfillment while wood carving. Marian

Lee eventually informed her readers that "productive labor is the best of all our activities to make the day happy and the night satisfied."[81]

Although Comstock clearly reveled in her woodcraft, it was her writing and communion with nature, maintained throughout her adult life, that produced her deepest satisfactions. In 1909 Comstock seized on a new idea: she decided to write a general handbook for nature study teachers. No publisher was interested, but two years later *Handbook of Nature Study* was published by her husband's company, Comstock Publishing Associates. The massive work of nearly nine hundred pages proved an immediate success and kept the small Comstock press—a venture started to publish scientific books—alive for decades. The work reached twenty-four printings, was translated into eight languages, and remains in print today.

The textbook justified nature study because it cultivated "the child's imagination" and "a love of the beautiful." Most important, "nature-study gives the child a sense of companionship with life out-of-doors and an abiding love of nature." Echoing Bailey and other fellow romantic naturalists, Comstock stressed that the love of beauty and companionship with nature were vital because "this is an age of nerve tension, and the relaxation which comes from the comforting companionship found in woods and fields, is, without doubt, the best remedy for this condition." Like other nature study and school arts advocates, Comstock held that aesthetic experience and direct contact with nature could abate antimodern anxieties. Nature could heal frayed nerves because of its beauty and intrinsic qualities and also because it allowed people to be authentic, free, and creative. Thus Comstock maintained that "the correlation of nature-study and drawing is so natural and inevitable that it need never be revealed to the pupil."[82]

Despite Comstock's criticism of modern life and her struggle to establish a professional identity as a female scientist, she devoted little attention to women's issues such as the battle for suffrage. Although she supported women's right to vote, she did not actively fight for the cause. Comstock once explained this apparent discrepancy in her activism by noting that her political energies were consumed by the struggle for progressive education. "I had been using all of my strength to fight narrowness, prejudice, and injustice, in the curriculum of the common schools" she wrote; "I was weary with fighting."[83] Nonetheless, her example of creating a rich professional and personal life within the constraints of her day inspired many people. The Phi Kappa Phi honor society initiated her as a member in 1923. Comstock learned of another honor that same year when she opened the *New York Times* and found that the League of Women

Voters had chosen her—along with luminaries Jane Addams, Carrie Chapman Catt, and Edith Wharton—as one of the twelve greatest women in America.[84] In 1988 the National Wildlife Federation inducted her into its Conservation Hall of Fame. Clearly, Comstock's example of professional success in a male-dominated field won her the appreciation of many of her peers.

Comstock's career exemplified the many tensions within the nature study movement. Linking aesthetic interests with nature study suggested to several critics that nature study was sentimental rather than academic, imprecise rather than scientific. The powerful gender norms that equated women with an emotional and artistic relationship to nature rather than an intellectual or scientific one caused many educators to dismiss nature study as undisciplined sentimentalism. Interest among educators in the beauty of nature connoted instruction in naïve sentimentalism rather than practical academic pedagogy. The feminine connotations of aesthetic nature study emphasized to its detractors that, like school arts, nature study could be safely classified as a pleasant supplement to the curriculum but was not a central part of it. Science was central to industrial modernity. Those plagued by romantic spiritual yearnings might find a balm for their nerves in an aesthetic appreciation of the outdoor world, but they were unlikely to find through education a cure for their disease.

CHAPTER THREE

"The Child Is Born a Naturalist"

Nature Study, Woodcraft Indians, and the Theory of Recapitulation

> I had a vision for my people, a figure of perfect manhood,
> a being physically robust, an athlete, an outdoors man,
> accustomed to brunt of flood, wind and sun—rough road
> and open spaces—a man wise in the ways of the woods,
> sagacious in council, dignified, courteous, respectful to all,
> and kindly as a good natured giant; a man whose life was
> clean, picturesque, heroic, and unsordid; a man of courage
> equipped for emergencies, possessing his soul at all times,
> and filled with a religion that consists, not of mere occasional
> observances, not of vague merits hoarded in the skies, but of
> a strong kind spirit that makes him desired and helpful here
> to-day.
> —Ernest Thompson Seton, "The Woodcraft League or
>   College of Indian Wisdom"

Speaking to the 1889 meeting of the National Education Association from a podium surrounded by schoolchildren, Francis Parker—the crusading school reformer dubbed the "father of the progressive education movement" by John Dewey—announced, "I am a firm believer in children living out their lives in the mythical stage: in the period when they ask and answer themselves questions about nature."[1] For Parker, that mythical stage corresponded to life as Native Americans ostensibly lived it: "a little child is a little 'Injun'. . . . He begins with the same natural love and instinct . . . the wrong comes later." Like Indians, children had an innate interest in the natural world: "*the child*," asserted Parker, "*is born a naturalist*." Turning to the children around him, Parker asked, "Don't you want to be an Indian little boy, and put feathers in your hair? Wouldn't you like to dig a hole and live in the ground, and wouldn't you like to roam at will in the big woods? Certainly you would."[2]

The idea that children, like Indians, were born naturalists and were instinctively interested in the natural world gained wide support among education professionals at the turn of the twentieth century. Intellectual justification for this belief came from the theory of recapitulation—the idea that the individual child's maturation repeated, or recapitulated, the evolutionary history of the human race.[3] Developmentally, then, children were thought to be like Indians; they were in a savage state and needed to satisfy that part of their evolutionary history to mature into responsible adults. Furthermore, because growing children repeated the evolutionary history of the human race, teachers needed to use educational materials that coincided with the child's stage of development. The savage child needed to interact with the natural world. As Katherine Dolbear, a high school teacher from Holyoke, Massachusetts, told the National Education Association, do not "forget to consider man's animal ancestry, and to allow for it in supplying suitable foods for his mind during its various stages of development." Interaction with the green world had to be among the educational materials used to fortify a student's mind because "the child naturally turns to the same things which were of utmost importance and interest to his ancestors; that is, to the study of living things."[4]

Other nature study writers put the matter even more starkly. "A boy is no more a miniature man than a larva is a moth," contended Cyril A. Stebbins of the University of California. "He is the caterpillar stage of a man, the growing stage. Interference with nature in producing a moth results in a weak moth. Interference with nature in building a man results in a weak man." This "caterpillar stage" of development "is spread over some twelve years," during which time educators must devote themselves to the "fundamental" needs of human development. Those needs included "civic and moral history," because the child has a "racial mind" as well as a "racial body."[5] In the theory of recapitulation, nature study advocates found scientific justification for their bedrock belief that children needed unmediated interaction with the natural world to develop both mind and body.[6] Just as Indians knew nature's secrets and led deeply spiritual lives, so too must the children of industrial society develop those skills to become productive and happy adults.

At first glance, the idea that children were akin to primitive humans appeared to resolve many tensions within the nature study movement. Proper education demanded contact with nature because the long evolutionary history of the human race determined that children required contact with the outdoor world.

Conversely, a lack of intercourse with nature explained aberrant behavior because, as one prominent researcher suggested, modern urban life, "with its temptations, prematurities, sedentary occupations, and passive stimuli ... suppressed, perverted or delayed" children's healthful primal instincts.[7] Contact with nature, then, induced intellectual and psychological well-being. Healthy and educated children would protect scarce resources because, like Indians, they understood and valued the natural world.

Yet many telling incongruities remained at the core of this new evolutionary understanding of human development. The theory was progressive, in that it perceived science as advancing the work of civilization, yet its proponents worried that civilization harmed children's healthful maturation. How could this version of cultural evolution account for the wonders—and the problems—of industrial civilization as well as the ostensible closeness to nature and lack of reason displayed by aboriginal peoples? Furthermore, how could it explain the social effects of science, which simultaneously unlocked nature's secrets and created the modern society that seemed to remove people from nature as never before? Despite these difficulties, progressive educators used recapitulation to bridge the modernist and antimodernist tendencies within the movement. So too might nature study inculcate both utilitarian and spiritual foundations for conservation. Students needed direct contact with nature to develop the instincts that would allow them to adjust to the modern world, an adjustment that would also help bring the modern world into harmony with nonhuman nature. In the nature study movement's use of recapitulation, we see an attempt to bring industrial society into harmony with the natural world by discovering within the child an Indian who is spiritually fulfilled through harmonious contact with nature.

The idea that the physical and psychic development of children mimicked the ascendancy of humankind from savagery to civilization had been circulating for several decades in American intellectual circles. Nature study patriarch Louis Agassiz popularized the idea during his extremely successful second series of Lowell Lectures delivered in Boston during the winter of 1848–1849. The idea fit well with Agassiz's taxonomic contention that all species could be grouped and classified according to their degree of physiological complexity. For Agassiz, this vision of a tightly structured universe evinced the intelligent design of a divine Creator. Indeed, the discovery of order in nature prompted Agassiz to proclaim that humans can "think God's thoughts after him. . . . Natural History must, in good time, become the analysis of the thoughts of the Creator of the Universe."[8]

The theory of recapitulation also supported Agassiz's contention that the human species could be divided and ranked into various components according to a system of racial classification.[9] Although few nature study teachers drew the same overtly racist conclusions that Agassiz did, many thought the theory provided scientific support for the idea that children learned through contact with nature because, developmentally, they were in a savage state. For nature study advocates, learning from nature was simply another way of describing the thorough grounding in basic natural history they aimed to impart to ready students. The theory of recapitulation "proved" that children had natural affinities for basic scientific exploration.

The use of the theory of recapitulation to justify innovative pedagogy gained its greatest support from one of the intellectual pioneers of American psychology, G. Stanley Hall.[10] Hall based his version of the theory of recapitulation on his readings in the classic texts in romantic education and on the burgeoning science of evolutionary biology. Although romantic theorists of education such as Jean-Jacques Rousseau pointed toward pedagogy based on the latest science regarding the biological nature of humans, recapitulation did not gain more widespread intellectual credibility until the swirl of theorizing brought about by the interpretations of and reactions to Charles Darwin's *Origin of Species*. First, German embryologist Fritz Müller, in his defense of Darwin, *Für Darwin* (translated into English as *Facts and Arguments for Darwin*), used his research into the development of crustaceans to suggest the possibility of recapitulation. More importantly, biologist Ernst Haeckel used recapitulation to formulate what he considered the fundamental biogenic law: ontogeny recapitulates phylogeny. This "law"—the strict version of which is rejected by present-day biologists—states that the development of the embryo of a given species (ontogeny) repeats the evolutionary development (phylogeny) of that species.[11]

Hall used the theory that the intellectual development of the child repeats the development of the human species as the foundation for his genetic psychology. Echoing Haeckel's decisive scientific language, Hall identified recapitulation as the general psychonomic law. He used this insight to help differentiate the various stages of development from infancy to adulthood. Because Hall, along with many contemporary anthropologists, believed that cultures passed through a fixed series of stages, he concluded that the virtues of adulthood grew out of the lesser qualities of savage civilizations.[12] For Hall, the years prior to adolescence were an extension of embryonic development, and educators needed to treat students in a manner befitting such a developmental stage. Hall believed that each stage of development began with a burst of new instincts; ages six and seven were years of crisis that led into the comparatively uncomplicated preteen years. Most significantly, Hall distinguished between childhood and a new period of maturation that he termed adolescence. Adolescence itself was a "new birth" in which unique "qualities of body and soul" emerged in the maturing organism; it marked the phyletic transition from an animal-like state to conscious humanity.[13] Followers of Hall and recapitulation theory often modified his stages of development, preferring the vague notion that healthy childhood demanded the expression of pent-up instinct over precise calculations of instinctual age.[14]

For Hall, proper pedagogy derived from understanding the deep history of the human race reflected by the individual's development: "The principle that the child and the early history of the human race are each keys to unlock the nature of the other applies to almost everything in feeling, will and intellect," contended Hall. "To understand either the child or the race we must constantly refer to the other."[15] Crucially, because the history of the race took place in a state of nature, educators believed that children must also find themselves in an untrammeled world. "Every department of knowledge must be taught by inculcating in every possible way the love of nature," asserted Hall. "For what is nature? The great Mother of us all."[16] Educators thus needed to "perpetually incite" children to explore "field, forest, hill, shore, the water, flowers, animals, the true homes of childhood in this wild, undomesticated state from which modern conditions have kidnapped and transported him."[17]

Hall's concern with citizenship echoed an important theme in the history of progressive theories of childhood and natural resource conservation: the conservation of character and vitality. Right conduct and proper hygiene played an important role in conservation because they combated the wastefulness of disease. Even such utilitarian documents as the report of President Theodore Roosevelt's National Conservation Commission included a section on the conservation of "national vitality" through what it hoped would become "a great movement to conserve human life and health."[18] The report argued for a number of public health (and eugenic) measures that could improve national vitality, including playgrounds, which provided the "physical training that accords with child instincts." The report stressed, "The suppression by civilized and urban life of the instinct for play and amusement is responsible for much of what we call 'crime' and 'depravity.'"[19] Outdoor activity put children in touch with a beneficent nature and promoted moral development through the healthful expression of primal instinct.

Although nature study advocates drew from the ostensibly orderly and scientific basis of recapitulation to promote their pedagogy, they used recapitulation in an imprecise and fluid manner to justify a variety of pedagogies. Some teachers, for example, used the theory of recapitulation to support the superiority of freewheeling "nature play" over compartmentalized "nature study."

Writing in *Popular Science Monthly,* Charles Lincoln Edwards, the director of nature study for the city schools of Los Angeles, argued that "the spirit of play" must animate nature study because "a deep living sympathy, bred through the ancestral ages of growth near to the heart of nature, shall lead the child into the joy of living and the happiness of love and knowledge. Nature-play, rather than nature-study, is the key to this wonder fairyland of which the child is a part."[20] Like Charles Scott, Edwards believed that education devoid of ethical sentiment harmed the psychic development of the student.

The assumptions of recapitulation also led Edwards to a sharply bigoted perception of the cultures of people who were assumed to be primitive in their relationship with nature. Edwards argued that field trips should be buttressed with "the stories and songs of negroes and Indians" because "these more primitive people are but grown children, living in closer touch with nature," unlike modern "dwellers in brick apartments."[21] In the theory of recapitulation, Edwards found scientific support for widespread prejudice expressed in the idea of a simple, and hence noble, savage. This use of recapitulation to support early-twentieth-century racist attitudes was typical of many theorists who saw recapitulation as an ostensibly scientific validation for race and gender hierarchies.[22]

Although nature study advocates rarely theorized about race and gender hierarchies, many cited recapitulation as justification for the use of myth and fairy tale in nature studies. Because children were considered to be in the same evolutionary stage as "primitive" peoples, teachers expected children's interests in nature to be "savage" rather than "scientific." Intellectuals such as Dr. Harold Fairbanks could thereby proclaim in the pages of *Nature-Study Review* that "the child in his mental growth goes through in epitome the history of the race. He is first interested in folk-tales and nature myths and in getting answers to the meaning of things about him." After passing through a myth and folktale stage, children eventually matured, acquiring the mental capacities necessary for scientific thought. Therefore, teachers should not make the mistake of using methods of instruction beyond the developmental stage of the child. "We may look at the child as a possible future scientist," proclaimed Fairbanks, "but that should not affect our present method of treating him."[23]

Other theorists of education extended the justification for myth and fairy tale in nature study to a critique of imaginative literature. According to N. Cropsey of Indianapolis, the "deeper significance" of the connection between the child and nature was found "in his love of harmony and beauty, and in his vague knowledge or intuition of the correspondence between his own life and life of nature." Yet perverted understandings of nature could demoralize the higher spiritual significance of nature study. Fortunately, modern science provided the true account of nature's mysteries, and that explanation could be applied to other kinds of creative thought. "Perhaps the intuitions of the poet prepare the way for the more definite investigations of science," suggested Cropsey, "and in turn science must influence the view of the poet." Poets no longer found divinities in nature: "As science began to discover one law in all the contradictions of the external world, poets began to write of nature as harmony in itself, which again finds response in the harmony of the soul."[24] Poets might reach into the deep history of the human connection with nonhuman nature, but only if they eschewed fanciful representation for the precision of scientific observation.

Advocates of nature study also used the theory of recapitulation to proclaim a role for myth in establishing a future love of science. Speaking to the National Education Association, W. A. Hoyt of Brookfield, Massachusetts, argued that the love of science grew from the myths that characterized "savage life." "If [the child's] individual development does run parallel with that of the race," asserted Hoyt, "it must needs be that Science, instead of exterminating superstition, as she strives to do in the adult, should rather foster it in the child. . . . Crude and fond myths, lying so warm and so long about the heart, fertilize the roots of love of science in childhood."[25] The love of myth itself was merely nature's way of preparing the human mind for the greater but more mature and taxing work of scientific investigation. In this way, the justification of myth by the theory of recapitulation helped reconcile science with sentiment.

By 1907 the recapitulation justification for nature study was so widespread that a small controversy erupted when Maurice Bigelow questioned its efficacy.[26] Writing in Nature-Study Review, Bigelow asserted that the evidence so often cited by nature study professionals as demonstrating children's innate appreciation for nature was instead "reflections or imitations of the interests of their elders." Indeed, Bigelow cautioned, "It must strike the fair-minded observer that the characteristic ethical and esthetic attitude of a naturalist is in most cases a later development of an interpretation of nature which, like poetry and philosophy, is the product of mature minds."[27] Those who held functionalist views of human nature were quick to chime in. Willard N. Clute, editor of American Botanist, concluded that children were not motivated by innate sympathy to nature because "the child is very much like an electric motor. It keeps going and interested as long as you turn on the current."[28]

The controversy over recapitulation in nature study once again restated the hoary "nature versus nurture" debate. Responding to Bigelow's defense of the cultural environment in shaping the interests of children, Clayton F. Parker of the Los Angeles State Normal School recalled his boyhood of "warfare" against "the harmless and defenseless 'critters' of the earth, air, and water." Parker believed most of his actions stemmed from learned behavior, thus demonstrating the need for nature study to counter such conduct with a thorough grounding in the principles of conservation, the child's "true relation to his environment."[29] Whatever the cause of aberrant behavior, all nature study advocates agreed on its usefulness in combating the destruction of nature.

Scholastic nature study advocates were not the only ones who viewed children as savages who required interaction with the green world. The idea that contact with nature could revitalize the victims of "overcivilization" also received support from a variety of nonacademic sources. Episcopal bishop Samuel Fallows supported Hall's idea that physical battles in childhood prepared young men for the moral battles of later life. (Many churchmen found in Hall's theories support for the idea that modern youth were in dire need of religious belief.)[30] Joseph Lee, longtime president of the Playground Association of America, was a vociferous proponent of the "Big Injun age" of childhood development.[31] Most notably, Theodore Roosevelt penned an enthusiastic letter to Hall that asserted the need to foster "the *barbarian virtues*" to keep civilized boys from becoming effeminate "milksops." "Over-sentimentality, over softness, in fact washiness and mushiness are the great dangers of this age and of this people," claimed Roosevelt. "Unless we keep the *barbarian virtues*, gaining the civilized ones will be of little avail."[32] Modern society perverted healthful instinct, harming both individuals and society. For Roosevelt, as well as Hall, contact with nature would allow the healthful instincts to thrive before the civilized world channeled them into productive purposes.

The most prominent educator to adopt Indians as a model for children was artist, conservationist, and popular nature writer Ernest Thompson Seton. Seton looked to American Indians as a model for youthful independence and the benefits of nature study. Seton's interest in Indians grew from his abiding belief that, as his biographer H. Allen Anderson explained, "if men were created in God's image, they should rely on their instincts and the basic wisdom of past generations, rather than on the artificially imposed moral codes of contemporary society."[33] Moreover, Seton viewed Indians as living in harmony with their environment, making them models for how the proper expression of instincts could foster conservation. Seton, like many other romantics, believed that civilized society perverted human instincts; therefore, only those in a natural state were able to pursue the authentic life according to nature.

Born in England with the name Ernest Thompson, Seton moved with his family to Canada in 1866. The young Thompson chafed under his father's overbearing manner and strict adherence to conservative Calvinist doctrine; he often sought solace in the wildlands near Toronto, where he found a harmony that was unavailable in his unhappy home. As a teenager Thompson began to produce paintings of the natural world, and his family encouraged his burgeoning artistic abilities. He also began adding "Seton" to his name, following a family legend that claimed direct lineage from seventeenth-century Scottish earl George Seton. After a brief stint at London's Royal Academy of Art, in 1882 Thompson joined his brother Arthur at his homestead on the Upper Assiniboine River in western Manitoba. The wilderness near his new home inspired Seton's creativity and furthered his interests in natural history. By 1885 he had left the homestead and began publishing what he claimed were scrupulously accurate nature stories.[34] His wildlife illustrations also appeared in a number of popular magazines. He accepted commissions for wildlife drawings from such organizations as the American Ornithologists Union and the U.S. Biological Survey.

Seton's intellectual gifts, then, developed in art and science, vocations whose worldviews many considered irreconcilable. In the theory of recapitulation, Seton found a scientific idea that seemed to unite his skills while buttressing his moral conviction that communion with the natural world would teach people honor, physical courage, self-reliance, and spiritual harmony. Seton's cosmology exalted natural drives; he first found intellectual support for his beliefs in the writings of William James, which gave him a powerful defense of the idea that instincts were rooted in human history. After reading the work of both G. Stanley Hall and Hall's popularizer William Forbush, Seton translated his reading of James into an embrace of the theory of recapitulation.[35] As historian Robert H. MacDonald pointed out, Seton combined the ideas of James and Hall into his own theory of human nature: boys had the caveman instinct, the hunter instinct, the initiation instinct, and the hero-worship instinct.[36] To give proper expression to this unfolding life history, Seton wished to educate young men in nature study in a manner that gave free rein to the instincts that contemporary civilization ruthlessly suppressed.

Seton's worldview thus evinced a deep antimodern distrust of the industrial world. Indeed, Seton charged that urban and industrial life squandered the virtues that shaped America's greatest achievements: "money grubbing, machine politics, degrading sports, cigarettes, town life of the worst kind, false ideals, moral laxity, and lessening church power, in a word 'city rot' has worked evil in this nation." For Seton, modern life had devolved into a state of "*Degeneracy*."[37]

Seton was not the only thinker who used recapitulation to critique the ostensible corruption and artificiality of modern life. Francis Parker levied a similar charge at the industrial world: "I believe that the cause of materialism, the lack of faith in God, and the absence of a pure, practical religion to-day, is owing to this terrible evil of cutting off in the child its love of the mythical, and destroying this delightful fancy. Give to the child the full measure of pure, sweet fancy, and then in after life he will see heaven and God and the angels."[38]

For Parker and Seton, American Indians embodied the authentic life that modern industrial life eclipsed. Indeed, Seton used an ideal of the premodern Indian to levy his most strident criticisms against industrial life. "The Civilization of the Whiteman is a failure," charged Seton. "It is visibly crumbling around us. It has failed at every crucial test."[39] Seton attributed such malaise mainly to a society overflowing with "money madness"; he bewailed the subjection of individual autonomy to decisions made in distant cities and social processes that effectively insulated people from the natural, primary forces of existence. Seton sensed that the industrial domination of the green world reduced both nature and the self to disenchanted objects, vulnerable to manipulation by rational technique. He therefore criticized industrial capitalism for its class conflict and also for engendering spiritual malaise. Seton's educational goal, then, focused on counteracting "the system that has turned such a large proportion of our robust, manly, self-reliant boyhood into a lot of flat-chested cigarette smokers, with shaky nerves and doubtful vitality."[40]

Seton emphasized civilization's deleterious effects on body, mind, and morals; unalterable damage occurred with the industrial socialization of children. "The most important thing in America today," argued Seton, "is the character of our young people." His particular focus concerned the development of boys: "manhood, not scholarship, is the highest aim of education." Seton agreed with progressive reformers that schools must minister to the whole child and that the memorization and repetition of traditional education blunted, rather than developed, children's best instincts. Just as the natural maturation of instincts produced solid citizens, perverting these instincts led to social ills such as juvenile crime. Rather than warehousing the results of poor upbringing in prisons, Seton argued that society should "go to the source, which is, nearly always, superabundant animal energy and love of play," which must be "properly guided in childhood, the character forming epoch."[41] If society properly guided this primal energy, social ills such as crime would largely disappear.

Seton also maintained that a foundation of proper character would allow people in the modern world to maintain a skilled and creative individuality against the depersonalizing drill of industrial civilization. To illustrate the incapacity of modernity to produce whole people, Seton contrasted differences in the martial virtues of soldiers from different nations. "The drilled soldier is a piece of admirable mechanism—mechanically brave, mechanically obedient—an able fighting machine," argued Seton. But the "trained man is one of all-round development; a man who can ride, shoot, plan, go ahead, and take care of himself in the woods."[42] Seton used this distinctive (and utterly unhistorical) idea to explain the astonishing victory of the Continental army over the British soldiers in the Revolutionary War. Unlike the mechanistic and drilled British, the virtuous soldier-farmer of the Continental army was proficient in the skills of hand and brain, an independent and self-reliant soldier abetted by frontier experience and "careful moral training."[43] For Seton, the modern world exacerbated the worst qualities of mechanical men. To combat this trend, he dreamed of youthful activity dedicated to instilling in America's children the mental and moral independence that modern life occluded. To that end, Seton turned to a form of nature study that, in acknowledgment of the frontier virtues he hoped to recover, he termed "woodcraft."

Seton endeavored to popularize his ideas by promoting a historical embodiment of woodcraft virtues, for "it is a matter of history that no philosophy, however beautiful, has been established without a current example."[44] Yet the frontiersman of the colonial era did not personify the kind of individual Seton desired his woodcraft charges to emulate. Although Seton claimed he would have preferred a white ideal, he could find none. Like many romantic critics of modernity, Seton looked to the medieval world for an exemplar of pure and vital life.[45] He discarded Robin Hood and Rollo the Sea King as potential models because they were not sufficiently well known; King Arthur lacked the requisite outdoor skills. Perhaps in Seton's mind, even medieval whites were too closely associated with the values of industrial civilization to illustrate frontier virtue. Whatever the reason, Seton was unable to find an exemplar of virtue from white civilization; he thus turned to American Indians as his preferred model for urban youth. Seton extolled the fictional "Indian of Fenimore Cooper and Longfellow," as well as the historical example of Tecumseh, as models for contemporary youth.[46] Seton lauded Tecumseh as "the great Redman, the personal embodiment of all that was good in the Red race, a man without fear, without reproach." Indeed, he was "the noblest figure, undoubtedly, that glorifies the pages of American history."[47] In native Indian societies Seton conjured a model of life devoted to the highest development of natural drives, yet one that was fictionalized enough to avoid the inevitable disappointments associated with real people.

Seton's choice of premodern American Indians as exemplars for urban youth found powerful sustenance from Hall's theory of recapitulation. In his most famous book, *Adolescence,* Hall asserted:

The child revels in savagery, and if its tribal, predatory, hunting, fishing, fighting, roving, idle playing proclivities could be indulged in the country and under conditions that now, alas! seem hopelessly ideal, they could conceivably be so organized as to be far more truly humanistic and liberal than all that the best modern school can provide. Rudimentary organs of the soul now suppressed, perverted, or delayed, to crop out in menacing forms later, would be developed in their season so that we should be immune to them in maturer years.[48]

For Seton, children socialized through the organized instruction of the outdoor skills he termed "woodcraft" could achieve Hall's humanistic ideal. Seton presupposed that the tribal instincts of white urban and suburban children were equivalent to instincts in Indian society. "I know something of savages—of boys I mean," wrote Seton; they are "precisely the same thing." Like Parker, Seton felt certain that America's children held innate proclivities for Indian life. "Most boys love to play Indian," asserted Seton:

They want to know about all the interesting things the Indians did that are possible for them to do. It adds great pleasure to the lives of such boys when they know that they can go right out in the holidays and camp in the woods just as the Indians did and make all their own weapons in Indian style as well as rule themselves after the manner of a band of Redmen.[49]

The linkage of Indians and children was not new. Both Seton and Parker were deeply versed in romantic literature that associated children with Indians, dubbing Indians the "children of nature." Seton believed that Indians knew nature in a more authentic manner than did modern Americans, and they translated that knowledge into more humane, humble, and democratic social values. Like Hall, Seton was deeply ambivalent about civilization. Civilized life was progress, but it sacrificed spiritual and physical virility for the advancements of science.

But as historian Philip Deloria demonstrated in his excellent examination of Seton's appropriation of Indian identity, Seton's belief in recapitulation and his use of American Indians to critique industrial civilization were fraught with complexities and contradictory messages.[50] First, if earlier stages of human development were superior to contemporary civilization, how could the theory of recapitulation account for the supposed evils of industrial capitalism as well as the savage nature of children? Second, to many urban Americans, Indians' character as the "children of nature" was intertwined with their degraded condition as dependent wards, impotent and childlike in their relationships with government and white society. Other turn-of-the-century racist stereotypes continued the older view of Indians as savages because they supposedly embodied, paradoxically, the worst facets of human nature under industrial capitalism: ruthlessness, cutthroat competitiveness, and a lack of social consciousness.

Yet Seton's imagined Indians were, like nature itself, uncorrupted by evil; indeed, they were the very antithesis of malevolence. The dominant social construction of the Indian other, then, revealed much about how white, middle-class professionals felt about modernity. For those invested in defending the superiority of urban industrial life, Indians often represented a return to infantile and callous savage values. Yet the antimodern image of the American Indian also assuaged the longings of educated and affluent members of society such as Seton, who anguished over the physically and spiritually enervating effects of industrial capitalism. Such Americans imagined in Indians the physical virility and spiritual piety that had been lost in contemporary life. Rationalized production created an atomized society and a desanctified nature, prompting disgruntled romantics such as Seton to proffer the "Message of the Redman.... We advocate his culture as an improvement on our own."[51]

Antimodern anxiety generated powerful notions about gender as well as affecting whites' understanding of the Indian other. As Andreas Huyssen argued, much of the deeply felt misgiving about modernity stemmed from masculine anxieties over the feminizing effects of consumer culture.[52] Many modernist critics associated women with consumerism and the ostensible artificiality of mass culture, while presuming that the genuine premodern virtues of the frontier remained the prerogative of men. Only men could connect to an authentic past in which they expressed honest virtues without the corrupting touch of mass culture. Accordingly, Seton's critiques of modernity and youth organizations focused on the maturation of young men.

Seton thus echoed the widespread belief that civilization weakened and feminized young men. Mass culture was not the only culprit. Late-nineteenth-century notions of restrained manhood produced the idea that civilization sacrificed physical power and strength of character—the sources of masculine identity—in its demands for respectable social behavior. Seton did not wish to abandon civilized decorum. Rather, he sought a way to allow the expression of instinct that was not simply a release of primordial feeling but a natural maturation of the individual that would benefit modern life by adjusting individuals to civilized existence. Indeed, Seton believed, along with Hall, that the expression of primitive instinct would inoculate boys against the repressive norms of modern life that flattened and depersonalized distinctive ways of being. A more hearty and progressive civilization would result from the natural, unfettered expression of instinct. The vaccination against repressive civilization arrived in the form of direct contact with nature, for communion with nature allowed instinct to reign. For Seton and Hall, modern men needed to emulate premodern Indians' communion with nature to recover what Hall described as the "hot life of feeling."[53]

It would be easy to dismiss the search for the hot life of feeling as the gender foibles of ungracefully aging middle-class men. As T. J. Jackson Lears argued in *No Place of Grace*, however, antimodern anxieties should not be reduced to the fear of losing masculine characteristics alone, because they also indicated the complex struggle to maintain a coherent understanding of the self against the radical dislocations of modern life. An ideal of authenticity—implicit in theories of recapitulation—could form a powerful base from which to examine modern existence. Moreover, using an ideal of authenticity to criticize modernity carried especially forceful connotations for those concerned with nonhuman nature. This was a powerful strand of criticism extending from Emerson's search for an original relation to the universe. Unlike commercial civilization, nature offered unmediated contact with the world, contact that, for people like Seton, held profound spiritual significance as well as the means to create a practical ideal.

Seton popularized his ideas for woodcraft education and the development of modern men in his widely read, quasi-autobiographical children's novel *Two Little Savages*.[54] The story involves two central narratives in which woodcraft skills and philosophy effect a reconciliation of individuals, community, and nature: the story of the two young "savages" Yan (Seton's stand-in) and Sam, and a stereotypical frontier feud between two formerly friendly trappers. Seton's version of recapitulation appears throughout the text. At one point the two little savages dance to the rhythms of an Indian war chant until "their savage instincts seemed to revive."[55] More broadly, through lessons in woodcraft, the two boys rediscover their "savage instincts" and unite with nature and their frontier community. Indeed, due to his woodcraft skills, Yan eventually gains the exalted position of head war chief. Similarly, the appearance of a common enemy reinforces frontier commonalties. A bitter feud between the trapper Rafton and Caleb Clark, the elderly trapper who imparts a lifetime of woodcraft knowledge to the young boys, ends when the pair must join forces to save Yan and Sam from a brutish three-fingered tramp. Like the outcome, the moral of the story is never in doubt; Seton, preferring the hard sell, propagandizes with a heavy hand.

Rather than being a strictly narrative adventure story, *Two Little Savages* includes many long and detailed digressions that describe woodcraft skills. The young boys receive point-by-point lessons in everything from creating an Indian drum to reading signs and blazing trails. The lessons often combine woodcraft ability with practical conservation. Thus Caleb imparts to the young men that hunting is fine unless it is conducted in a "cruel" fashion or in a manner that "wipe[s] out the hull bunch." To that end, Caleb lets the young savages know that "repeatin' guns is a curse. . . . Ef it's sport ye want, get a single-shot rifle; ef it's destruction, get a Gatling-gun. Sport's good, but I'm agin this yer wholesale killin' an' cruelty."[56] Like the distinction between trained and mechanical soldiers, hunters can act either with an independent and thoughtful morality or with mindless repetition. These differences are emphasized throughout the novel. Even before Caleb preaches the conservation gospel, Yan realizes that his newfound relationship with nature can "show men how to live without cutting down all the trees, spoiling all the streams, and killing every living thing."[57] The same woodcraft morality that binds together a frontier community also serves the goals of progressive conservation.

Moreover, woodcraft's conservation morality eased a grating friction in Seton's thought. If millions of boys needed to recover frontier virtues through woodcraft actions such as hunting, the effect on wildlands and wildlife could be devastating. The more people hunted in wild territory, the more they trammeled the land and depleted the game on which the values of the next generation of American manhood depended. The frontier masculinity that Seton, Teddy Roosevelt, and many others wished to recover derived from the destruction of the natural world. Preserving wildlife and wildlands was the way to reconcile this contradiction. Conservation was a moral obligation between people and the natural world on which they depended; it was a way to conciliate individual development with the need to experience wildness over time. The hunt could continue, but only under a regime of conservation. As historian Richard Slotkin argued, Roosevelt "presented himself as a more advanced type [of hunter], capable of an intellectual appreciation of the beast and the hunt, able to exercise a selectivity in killing that was almost aesthetic."[58] Conservation was not just sentimentalism but was, in fact, its very opposite: a way to preserve masculine frontier virtue.

Beyond his literary output, Seton used nature study to model a more harmonious human relationship with nature. According to Seton, the genesis of his nature study boys' club, the Woodcraft Indians, occurred when he intervened with a group of young vandals who consistently desecrated the fences of his rural Connecticut estate with graffiti. Seton devised an experiment built on his theories of childhood instincts. Rather than punish the misbehaving ruffians, Seton invited them to camp. Forty-two young boys arrived early one Friday afternoon, and after regaling them with Indian tales and outdoor adventure stories, Seton had on his hands "a mob of naked, howling savages, tearing through the woods, jumping into the lake." He channeled the exuberant energy of the boys into lessons on woodcraft; the children learned to camp "in real Indian fashion." Seton organized the boys into an Indian "tribe," dubbed the Sinaways, who adopted "the best things of the best Indians" as their motto. Boys in the tribe assumed Indian names. Seton picked for himself the moniker "Black Wolf." Seton used a variety of games and activities to impart lessons in nature study; the children learned plant and animal identification as well as a variety of outdoor skills. The experiment proved wholly successful. The vandalism stopped, and Seton held gatherings for his Sinaway tribe throughout the summer.[59]

Seton quickly endeavored to present his program to a national audience. Through a series of articles in *Ladies' Home Journal,* Seton launched the Woodcraft League in 1902. That youth organization, based on his experience with the Sinaway tribe, taught children spiritual discipline and woodcraft skills through direct contact with the outdoors. Many YMCAs organized tribes, and some sources claimed that Seton's "Indians" numbered as many as 200,000.[60] Yet the lack of a central coordinating institution belied the popularity of Seton's ideas and hampered the organization's expansion, as did some parts of its ideology: few Americans lauded Indians to the extent Seton did, and the organization's criticism of technological values inspired skepticism.[61] For Seton, such criticism was a central purpose of the organization.

Despite these difficulties, Seton's "Indians" attracted widespread attention. Popular nature writer John Burroughs wrote to Theodore Roosevelt that Seton had "a big thing in his boys Indian camp . . . well worthy of your attention and encouragement."[62] The organization also attracted the attention of Robert Baden-Powell, founder of the Boy Scouts, whom Seton met during a 1906 lecture tour of England. When the Boy Scouts of America incorporated in 1910, Seton was the author of the organization's first handbook and its first chief scout.

The cooperation between Seton and Baden-Powell did not last, however; the leadership of the scouting movement split into two ideologically distinct positions. Baden-Powell's militarism and relative lack of interest in woodcraft drove away those who preferred the decentralized structure and nature study emphasis of Seton's Woodcraft Indians. For Seton, the militarism of the Boy Scouts recapitulated the mindless hunting that destroyed wildlife and threatened to turn his charges into the mechanical men he had founded his organization to overcome. John Muir concurred with Seton and the nature study outlook. When invited to join the Sons of Daniel Boone, a precursor to the Boy Scouts that emphasized hierarchy and discipline, Muir declined and replied that society should encourage young men to grow out of "natural hunting blood-loving savagery into natural sympathy with all our fellow mortals—plants and animals as well as men."[63] Seton eventually resigned from the Boy Scouts in 1915. His status as a British citizen and his fierce criticisms of American life certainly hastened his departure from the organization. Others in the Boy Scouts leadership accused Seton of pacifism—an ideologically potent charge, given that war was raging in Europe. The veracity of such charges is difficult to evaluate, for they likely represented a constellation of fundamental ideological differences. Despite his clearly pacifist leanings, at the outbreak of World War I, the fifty-four-year-old Seton volunteered his services to the Canadian, British, and American governments.

Yet the charge of pacifism stuck, and it came from a variety of sources, including Theodore Roosevelt. One of Seton's rivals in the Boy Scouts bureaucracy was James E. West, an attorney and confidant of Roosevelt's. Despite (or because of) Roosevelt's familiarity with Seton, he informed West of his concern that the Boy Scouts contained within its ranks "certain leaders . . . [who] have used the Boy Scouts organization as a medium for the dissemination of pacifist literature and . . . as propaganda for interfering with the training of our boys to a standard of military efficiency."[64] Seton responded by telling the *New York Times* that West was "a man of great executive ability but without knowledge of the activities of boys, and who, I might almost say, has never seen the blue sky in his life."[65] Seton's response clearly defined the divergent philosophies of the woodcraft ideal and the militaristic Boy Scouts: how could someone unfamiliar with the outdoors teach nature study? Moreover, the hierarchical structure of the Boy Scouts repressed the innate tribal instincts that nature study allowed to develop into authentic manliness.

Despite Seton's emphasis on young men, he also encouraged the founding of the Camp Fire Girls, the female equivalent to the mostly male Woodcraft Indians. Although the latter group occasionally included girls in its activities, it never endeavored to become a coeducational organization. Hoping to extend woodcraft's benefits to young girls, Seton's close friends Luther and Charlotte Gulick founded the Camp Fire Girls, drawing substantially from Seton's ideas. In the summer of 1909 the Gulicks held a successful camp for their daughter and some of her friends. For the next camp they decided to follow Seton's suggestion and christen their camp with the Indian-sounding name "Wo-He-Lo"— derived from the first two letters of the camp's motto: "Work, Health, and Love." Copying Seton's methods, Mrs. Gulick immersed the campers in Indian lore, natural history, and outdoor skills.[66]

Nature study advocates suggested that the benefits of contact with nature would repair the deleterious effects of "overcivilization" on young girls. William

Gould Vinal lamented in 1919 the passing of his grandmother's generation of "live" girls. Such women could "climb a tree" and "pick huckleberries" as well as "romp the fields" and "tramp the roads." Sadly, "times have changed." In contrast to such healthy people, modern life produced girls "contented to sit in a stuffy schoolroom, flat-chested and sallow skinned." Rather than exercise, the modern woman "become[s] sluggish, her nerves shriek"; she is known by her "pallid cheeks, pale eyes," and need for "after dinner pills to assist digestion." Outdoor camps combated these diseases that arose from the "nerve racking pace of today." Immersion in outdoor activities helped the modern girl know nature "as the Injun did." Instead of the neurasthenic maladies of overcivilization, outdoor girlhood produced young women with "red blood, sound nerves, a quick ear, keen sight," and "a quick step." In short, effeminate girls became "tom-boyish . . . in the best sense of the word."[67] By rejecting the debilitating accoutrements of civilization, the young women who participated in the girls' camp recovered the same frontier vitality that was also missing from their male counterparts.

Like Seton and other nature study advocates, the Gulicks drew intellectual sustenance from their friend G. Stanley Hall. They believed that adolescence was a transformative period that required able shaping to produce healthy adults. Yet the shaping of the Camp Fire Girls differed greatly from that of the Woodcraft Indians. Whereas Seton's organization attempted to recover masculine frontier virtue, the Camp Fire Girls endeavored to reinforce contemporary professional, middle-class notions of gender. Indeed, enforcing gender distinctions drove the activities of the organization. Dr. Gulick summarized the Camp Fire Girls' philosophy by asserting, "We wish to develop girls to be womanly as much as we desire men to be manly . . . the bearing and rearing of children has always been the first duty of most women, and that must always continue to be."[68] To that end, Camp Fire Girls were immersed in service activities, including following the lead of the Boy Scouts by granting their support to the First World War. The Camp Fire Girls embraced a variety of measures to help with the war effort, adopting the motto "work through the homes" to orient their activities. Camp Fire Girls salvaged waste, conserved food and planted gardens, volunteered with the American Red Cross, and even walked a hundred miles a month to demonstrate their commitment to wartime sacrifice and to become as "hard" as soldiers.

Seton sharply disapproved of the extreme militarism of the Boy Scouts and Camp Fire Girls and their preoccupation with instilling the social norms of industrial civilization rather than pursuing nature study. Indeed, Seton explained his decision to leave the Boy Scouts as a battle over the place of nature study in the organization. "The study of trees, flowers, and nature," explained Seton, "is giving way to wigwagging, drills, and other activities of a military nature, thus destroying the symbolism of the organization."[69] The symbolism extended back to the kind of model outdoorsman the organization promoted. Seton's opponents in the Boy Scouts valued military organization and the example of the frontiersmen who tamed the continent, bringing nature under the control of human culture. Seton revered Indians for exactly the opposite reason, as exemplars of a society that respected nature's limits and understood its spiritual lessons. Accordingly, the Woodcraft Indians stressed conservationist ethics, prohibiting, among other things, the building of fires, the harming (or even frightening) of songbirds, and the breaking of game laws. The early Boy Scouts did not emphasize nature as a teacher or the need to preserve the inhabitants of wildlands. In short, Indians and nature lore competed with army officers and frontiersmen.

Just as important as the study of nature, however, was the type of person the study of nature helped produce. In his introduction to *Library of Natural History*, Seton lauded the multifaceted pedagogical strengths of nature study. Not only did nature study "develop powers of correct observation and clear reasoning from cause to effect," but it also retained the "final advantage of being an active, health-giving, outdoor pursuit." Moreover, nature study remained available to all social classes. Observing that the "well-to-do" spent "enormous sums" on "pictures, music, the drama, and kindred pleasures," Seton argued that nature study, a pleasure "at least worthy to rank with them," remained, unlike the arts, "within the reach of all." Even more important than the pedagogical strength and availability of nature study, however, was the fact that it emphasized the interconnection between humans and the rest of creation. "Man . . . seeking to know himself, must fail utterly," asserted Seton, "unless he remember that he is only a part of the great machine of the universe. He must therefore study . . . the life-forms about him, which are parts of his environment and offspring of the same creative power as himself."[70]

Unless pedagogy accounted for the natural world of which humans were a part, it would produce only the incomplete mechanical men encouraged by modern civilization. Reflecting on his work, Seton averred that "my chief motive, my most earnest underlying wish, has been to stop the extermination of harmless wild animals, not for their sakes, but for ours. . . . I have tried to stop the stupid and brutal work of destruction by an appeal—not to reason—that has failed hitherto—but to sympathy, and especially to the sympathies of the coming generation."[71] Seton held that scientific investigation must be tempered with ethical sentiment to advance the cause of conservation.

Seton's romanticism clearly resonated with a wide audience; his works sold very well and elicited laudatory commentary from popular publications. For example, journalist McCready Sykes, writing in *Everybody's Magazine,* endorsed the Woodcraft Indians through an evocation of masculine frontier virtue: "Put one of the Seton Indians down at random in any part of the world, and it would be hard for him to be bored," surmised Sykes. "They early become learned in the art of self-government, and are a radiating force for the diffusion of the qualities that make for manliness. They are safe and sane."[72] If boyhood instincts were allowed proper expression, civilization would cease to curb the masculine virtues it so needed. Other critics concurred that Seton had "indeed won the right to be called a leader in the campaign against ignorance, prejudice and self-ishness." The *Humane Review* continued by contrasting Seton's "luminous eloquence" regarding the "kinship between animals and men" with the "feverish haste to turn . . . knowledge to material account" that sadly characterized "these days of eager haste."[73] For Seton and his critical admirers, the turn to nature restored virtues lost in a culture that seemed dedicated solely to technology and the commercial exchange of industrial commodities.

Whatever the intellectual merits of such criticism, it proved to be a huge burden for the ideology of nature. Antimodern champions of nature study asserted that contact with nature fostered no less than a love for myth and science, frontier virtue, psychological health, and the desire for conservation. Only nature could overcome the deleterious effects of industrial society. Yet these critics rejected the wholesale reversion to the primitive; they used nature to help adjust the individual to modern life. Although the Woodcraft Indians emphasized the holistic experience thought to characterize premodern life, they always did so with an eye toward establishing coherent selfhood in the industrial world. Children and their adult caretakers ventured to the outdoors to help them cope with the pressures of modern existence. The dislocations of modern life disappeared in the premodern natural environment. Thus refreshed, citizens could tackle the complexities of industrial existence, particularly the need to conserve natural resources. In this way, much of the critique of the nature study movement became part of industrial culture.

Recapitulation fell out of favor with theorists of education because new research in both the biological and anthropological sciences undermined its applicability. An individual organism might recapitulate some of the phylogenic history of the species to which it belonged, but in such a recapitulation there were many discontinuities and omissions, casting doubt on analogies that posited a direct correspondence between the individual and the species. Most important, Mendelian genetics undermined recapitulation theory by disproving the mechanism of recapitulation—terminal addition. Genetics demonstrated the importance of genes that were present in the animal at the moment of conception, rather than new traits that arose from the development of ancestral ontogeny.[74]

The growing sophistication and openness to the virtues of other cultures by anthropology scholars such as Franz Boas also undermined the claims of recapitulation. Appreciation for the achievements and complex societies of ostensibly "primitive" cultures abraded comparisons between aboriginal people and the various stages of childhood. Without scientific justification, the ideological baggage attached to recapitulation no longer fit the needs of progressive thinkers. Educators and psychologists soon turned to other explanations for childhood behavior. Recapitulation, then, passed from the public scene with a final irony: the theory of recapitulation gained prominence as a scientific justification for pedagogical methods meant to unify unbound human nature with modern civilization, but it was undone by the epitome of controlled civilized objectivity—scientific inquiry.

Yet the potent desire to escape to nature remained a conspicuous component of American culture. Champions of modernity could use contact with nature to inculcate science and physical vitality in urban and suburban youth; romantics could revel in wild, premodern authenticity. Both ideologies used nature to prepare children for adult life. As Seton put it, only after an appropriate education established independent judgment in the child could "the nation . . . make of him a soldier or a shoemaker or a teacher, according to the gift of the individual and the need of the time."[75] The use of recapitulation thus furthered the duality between nature and civilization. Nature study advocates located nature as inevitably outside the normal course of American life. Children and Indians were once again linked; both nature and Indian peoples were relegated to an imaginary premodern frontier, forever beyond the contours of industrial civilization.

Yet for many, the very separation of nature and its peoples from modern life enhanced the desirable traits found in the natural order. Contact with nature, like contact with the primitive other, repaired the sense of loss inherent to industrial life. As Burroughs said, referring to the need for contact with the outdoors, nature study "adds to the resources of life, and arms a man against the ennui and vacuity that doth so easily beset us."[76] The theory of recapitulation thus supported those who believed in the feral nature of childhood while aiding the individual's adjustment to the industrial world. Industrial society would not find in recapitulation a way to harmonize its commitment to scientific discovery with a respect for nonhuman nature and a belief in fostering ethical sentiment.

CHAPTER FOUR

Bird Day for Kids

Progressive Conservation
in Theory and Practice

> There are perhaps few ways in which more practical good
> can be accomplished than by establishing in our schools
> a day devoted to the birds.
> ′ —"Bird Day," *Forest and Stream*

In his 1913 conservation jeremiad *Our Vanishing Wildlife*, William Temple Hornaday, director of the New York Zoological Park, proposed a massive campaign of public education to combat the extermination of American fauna. With the righteousness of the true believing convert, Hornaday thundered that

all our school children should be taught, in the imperative mood:

That it is wrong to disturb breeding birds, or rob birds' nests;

That it is wrong to destroy any harmless living creature not properly classed as game, except it be to preserve it in a museum;

That it is no longer right for civilized man to look upon wild game as *necessary* food; because there is plenty of other food, and the remnant of game can not withstand slaughter on that basis;

That the time has come when it is the duty of every good citizen to take an active, aggressive part in *preventing* the destruction of wild life, and in *promoting* its preservation;

That every boy and girl over twelve years of age can do *something* in this cause, and finally,

That protection and encouragement will bring back the almost vanished birds.

"Teachers," concluded Hornaday, "do not say to your pupils—'It is right and nice to protect birds,' but say:—'It is your *Duty* to protect all harmless wild things, and *you must do it!*'"[1]

Hornaday endorsed one "splendid" example of existing pedagogy that emphasized moral duty toward wildlife: Bird Day. Originated in 1894 by Professor Charles C. Babcock, superintendent of schools in Oil City, Pennsylvania, and modeled after Arbor Day, Bird Day immersed children in bird study and protection.[2] Students researched and wrote about birds, performed plays and recited poems that underscored the aesthetic quality of avian life, and engaged in practical conservation by building bird boxes and planting trees. The moral outlook sought by Hornaday was a significant component of Bird Day programs. Children recited a litany of literary works that demanded kindness toward birds, and speakers beseeched them not to shoot birds, collect eggs, or wear birds on their hats and to control their cats. In short, Bird Day was a teach-in for the conservation of birds. It was the precursor to Earth Day and other contemporary celebrations intended to broaden environmental awareness, such as International Migratory Bird Day.

Bird Day proponents believed in combining the moral injunction to save birds with knowledge of their lives and habits. Such a combination fulfilled the educational purpose at the heart of Bird Day: it fostered the beginnings of scientific inquiry. The information gained from the students' investigations into the natural world would make possible a commitment to conservation. "What is most needed [to help preserve birds] is knowledge of the birds themselves," wrote Babcock in his widely read volume *Bird Day: How to Prepare for It.* Such knowledge led to conservation because "to know a bird is to love him."[3] Babcock's book promoted Bird Day and doubled as a field guide to common birds. Bird Day tactics worked well. The celebration met with considerable success and was adopted by schools and communities nationwide. At least twenty-five state legislatures established Bird Day as an official day of commemoration, frequently in conjunction with Arbor Day. Governors often issued special proclamations for the day, and many states produced guides for teachers to help promote and organize Bird Day activities.

But was it true that to know a bird was to love him? Many conservationists questioned whether knowledge alone produced a sentiment for conservation. Even Hornaday admitted that it was "impossible" for educators "to place [conservationist] ideas mechanically within empty minds," and shockingly, those specialists who knew the most about wildlife seemed to care little for it. Hornaday noted that professional scientists were "hopelessly sodden and apathetic" about wildlife preservation.[4] Infuriated, Hornaday condemned the "strange spectacle" of his highly educated colleagues in the zoological sciences who, "as a mass, [are] so intent upon the academic study of our continental fauna that they seem not to have cared a continental about the destruction of that fauna."[5]

The rational detachment of scientific inquiry—"academic study," in Hornaday's parlance—eliminated subjective feeling and with it the moral conviction that spurred citizens to act in favor of wildlife. Rather than work for conservation, "fully 90 percent of the zoologists of America stick closely to their deskwork, soaring after the infinite and diving after the unfathomable." Heads lodged in the clouds, most professional scientists ignored the crisis of wildlife extermination, "never spending a dollar or lifting an active finger on the firing line in defense of wild life."[6]

For Hornaday and many conservationists, the practical question of how to instill the conservation gospel foundered on the epistemology of dispassionate, quantifiable, and reproducible science. What was the relationship between the knowledge generated by the precise and objective laboratory techniques of modern science and the moral responsibility for conservation? If submersion in academic study failed to generate a conservation ethic among professional zoologists, what hope was there that science education could do so for the lay public? In short, conservationists pondered the relationship between the scientific method and the moral duty toward wildlife—and often found science wanting as a method to instill conservationist ideals. Bird Day was an example of this central tension of progressive conservation. Bird Day advocates attempted to imbue students with the moral sentiment to save vanishing birds and at the same time provide them with scientifically grounded information about birds' lives and habits.

A central component of nature study demanded that children leave their books behind to interact with nature directly. Birds were a common source of nature study materials, and instructors of nature study often headed Bird Day celebrations.[7] Bird Day supporters believed their celebration would "add zest to the regular [nature] studies, encourage the pupils to observe carefully, and give them something to look forward to and work for."[8] Teachers of nature study welcomed Bird Day. Soon the phrase "bird study" became virtually synonymous with "nature study." Babcock considered Bird Day to be an adjunct of the nature study movement. He posited nature study as the "missing link between the child's life and his school work." The wanton destruction of birds surrounded children's lives; Bird Day could combat this ugly phenomenon because "birds are beautiful and interesting objects of study, and make appeals to children that are responded to with delight."[9]

Bird Day gained prominence at the same time the Audubon movement was being reborn. Both incarnations of the Audubon Society made popular education central to its conservation efforts. George Bird Grinnell enrolled thousands of children in his short-lived Audubon Society. When the Audubon Society was revitalized under the leadership of William Dutcher, an amateur ornithologist and insurance agent from New York who was utterly devoted to the cause of bird protection, it once again emphasized popular education as the means to lasting bird protection.[10] Indeed, Dutcher viewed schoolteachers as "Audubon Auxiliaries." Through the popular Junior Audubon Clubs, millions of schoolchildren became involved in bird protection. By 1915 Junior Audubon Clubs had enrolled 152,164 children in 7,728 classes; the effort was so impressive that Audubon Society historian Frank Graham credited the Audubon education program with transforming the society from a loosely organized set of local institutions into a cohesive national force.[11] Despite these successes, educational efforts remained fraught with tensions between the instrumental values of experimental science and the unfettered moral sentiments that defined conservation.

Whether conservationists questioned science and its relationship to moral instruction depended on the particular issue at hand. Conservationists rarely considered nature as a unitary thing; rather, they used the term in all its myriad complexities. The quandaries of the specific issue under consideration determined how much they relied on science as a guide for action. For example, when considering the reclamation of arid lands or sustained-yield forestry—that is, industry or government action in need of regulation—conservationists generally believed in policies derived from efficient, applied science. Applied science demonstrated how to turn the desire for prudent and rational policy into concrete action. When the issue was the conservation of wildlife, especially an issue connected to widespread behaviors such as sport hunting or wearing birds on hats, science was less useful. With regard to children who hunted birds or collected eggs—a very popular pastime, especially among young boys—conservationists' aim was to inculcate new standards of behavior, not to advance efficiency. Moral injunction, not rational processes, changed hearts, minds, and conduct. Popular attitudes toward wildlife highlighted the limits of science to conscribe the activities of people.[12]

Hornaday elaborated on the promise of moral instruction—not scientific inquiry—for the conservation movement in a series of lectures he delivered in 1914 before the Yale University School of Forestry, later published as *Wild Life Conservation in Theory and Practice.* In these talks Hornaday asserted that public education was the greatest potential resource of the conservation movement. The conservation crusade should thus turn "to the open-eyed, open-minded general educators and general students and lay before them the appeal of the wild." Such an appeal could work wonders: "Think what it would mean if 30 per cent of the annual graduates of all American institutions should go forth well informed on the details of this work and fully resolved to spread the doctrine of conservation, far and near!"[13] A broad campaign of public education would instill the doctrines of conservation, which would give rise to a revolution in ethics that would reform conduct toward nonhuman nature.

Yet Hornaday remained skeptical that many scientists would heed his call. "Twenty-five or fifty years hence, if we have a birdless and gameless continent," warned Hornaday, "let it not be said that the zoologists of America helped to bring it about by wicked apathy." But the wicked apathy remained. Hornaday lambasted professional zoologists as "zoological Neros" who fiddled while "our best song birds are being exterminated."[14] Professional interest in wildlife appeared to have little effect on the moral necessity to campaign for wildlife preservation.

Though contemporary readers should remain skeptical about the specifics Hornaday cited to support his heated rhetoric, professional scientists who read his work agreed that the relationship between modern, objective science and an ethical commitment to conservation was worth pondering. One such reader, Charles Adams of the New York State College of Forestry, brought the issue of experimental science and conservation consciousness to the readers of *Science* magazine. Adams, a founder of the Ecological Society of America, concurred with Hornaday that "professional zoologists and teachers of zoology have been practicably negligible" to the conservation effort. To explain this behavior, Adams examined the relationship between scientific epistemology and conservation: "Can a factor in the problem be that we have become so engrossed in important laboratory activity and in domestic animals that there is little concern about wild life?" Adams, like Hornaday a champion of using museums to popularize natural history, noted that the entire structure of modern scientific investigation separated zoologists from the actual conditions of wild nature. Quoting W. K. Brooks, Adams asked, "Is not the biological laboratory which leaves out the ocean and the mountains and meadows a monstrous absurdity?" Perhaps if zoologists interacted with nature rather than with laboratory equipment, "some of their lethargy will be thrown off."[15]

Other prominent conservationists joined Hornaday and Adams in questioning the relationship between science and conservation. Even hardheaded thinkers such as Herbert Smith, Gifford Pinchot's close confidant and editor in chief of the *Journal of Forestry,* worried that the greatly specialized knowledge gained through the modern scientific endeavor would hinder the moral impulse for wildlife conservation. The issue was of particular importance to Smith, who worked to introduce the study of forest conservation into the public schools. "We cannot divide the mind into separate compartments and train this particular one and not train that one without paying a penalty," wrote Smith. "We must educate the emotions and sympathies, the idealizing side, the moral, spiritual, and religious side as well as the hand and the brain."[16] But how might laboratory science educate the moral side of the mind?

Bird Day attempted to educate the moral side of the mind by nurturing a sentimental attachment between people—especially children—and nature. In 1894 Charles Babcock forwarded his idea for Bird Day to Secretary of Agriculture J. Sterling Morton, the founder of Arbor Day. Morton responded to the proposal with genuine enthusiasm, writing, "such a movement can hardly fail to promote the development of a healthy public sentiment toward our native birds, favoring their preservation and increase." For Morton, the early inculcation of sentimental attachment to birds would "become a hundredfold more potent [force for conservation] than any law enacted by the State or Congress." Moreover, bird protection appeals "to the best of our natures," as it instructs in "generosity, unselfish devotion . . . industry, patience and ingenuity."[17] The moral uplift needed for conservation also fashioned honorable citizenship.

A number of prominent writers gave their blessing to Babcock's Bird Day idea. John Burroughs, the most widely read nature essayist in America, wished for a "movement that may extend to all the schools in the country." Popular ornithologist Olive Thorne Miller proclaimed herself "delighted" by the idea of Bird Day, arguing that once children get acquainted with "their little brothers in feathers," they would "never again want to throw a stone at one, and no girl ever to have a dead bird on her hat." Nature essayist and Thoreau promoter Bradford Torrey proclaimed that Bird Day would become "a new saints' day in my calendar." The study of the outdoors—and especially birds—continued Torrey, "is one of the surest ways of laying up happiness," thus guaranteeing a life of contentment for children who immersed themselves with "things out of doors."[18] Like Morton, Torrey believed that Bird Day would advance the "Yankee" values that fostered citizenship as well as the preservation of birds.

On 4 May 1894 schoolchildren in Oil City celebrated the first Bird Day with compositions and presentations about birds, trips to view birds in nearby habitats, and discussions of birds in literature. The occasion was a success, and Babcock immediately turned Bird Day into an annual event. After the third Bird Day in 1896 Babcock wrote, "The results of bird study and of Bird Day are interesting. Our children generally know most of our bird residents, they also love them, and feel like protecting them. There has been a complete change in the relations existing between the small boy and the birds."[19] The *Journal of Education* covered Bird Day, reporting to its readers, "The amount of information about birds that was collected by the children was simply amazing. Original compositions were read, informal discussions were held, talks by teachers were given and the birds in literature were not forgotten or overlooked. . . . [Bird Day] simply needs to be known to meet with a warm welcome."[20]

The success of Bird Day in Oil City prompted other localities around the nation to adopt Bird Day celebrations. Mainstream commentators jumped on the Bird Day bandwagon. The *New York Times* strongly supported Bird Day, calling it "a matter of education and preservation."[21] The *Omaha Sunday World-Herald* argued for a Bird Day in Nebraska by declaring, "Laws for the protection of birds can be beneficial and an evidence of a healthy moral sentiment." Bird Day was thus of "inestimable worth." "Save the birds!" concluded the editorial. "Their value is inestimable and the rising generation should be taught the importance of this sentiment by an observance of 'Bird Day' in Nebraska."[22]

Along with support for Bird Day in the popular press, several states explicitly endorsed a variety of Bird Day conservation activities. As one contributor to North Dakota's *Special Day Programs* declared, "This is a day of doing more than saying."[23] Students planted trees, built and distributed bird boxes, tended gardens, and otherwise beautified school grounds. They also recited poems, produced plays, and wrote their own literature of bird appreciation. Bird Day combined sentiment and action. A typical instruction came from C. G. Lawrence, the superintendent of public instruction for South Dakota: "Let [Bird Day be] a day for doing things as well as a day for inspiring love for the trees and birds of our beloved state."[24] Many governors greeted the celebration with bona fide enthusiasm: "The trees and the birds!" exclaimed Illinois governor Frank Lowden. "Let us teach our children in the schools to plant the one and protect the other and to love them both."[25]

Most state manuals endorsed sentiment as the means to conservation. Many suggested the recitation of poems such as Daniel Clement Colesworthy's "Don't Kill the Birds": "Don't Kill the birds, the happy birds / That bless the fields and grove / So innocent to look upon / They claim our warmest love." Kentucky governor Augustus E. Willson's "Arbor Day Proclamation" instructed schoolchildren to plant trees "for ourselves and for all whom we love." Willson, who would become a Supreme Court justice, continued by emphasizing the multiple purposes of conservation: "Let us plant trees for profit, for gladness, for beauty, for conservation, for the storage of rainwater . . . for our own sake, for our children's sake, for our grandchildren's sake and for humanity's sake."[26] Some Kentucky schoolchildren followed their governor's lead by reciting a popular "Nature Lover's Creed" that proclaimed, "I believe in protecting the birds and the animals that live amidst the trees, and the ferns and mosses and blossoming plants. I believe in all the beautiful things of nature, and would preserve, protect and cherish them."[27] Such sentiments were assumed to be widespread, if not universal. As Eva Shelley Voris of Paducah wrote, "Who loves birds? Everybody—surely."[28]

Though the written word could not replace a working interaction with the natural world, it played a tremendously important role in Bird Day celebrations. Teachers published a variety of recommendations for successful Bird Day programs.[29] Many writers produced plays for schoolchildren to perform during Bird Day celebrations. Frederick Leroy Sargent wrote the widely distributed "Wings at Rest: A Bird Day Tragedy in One Act."[30] Grace B. Faxon published her suggestions for Bird Day with her play "Mother Earth's Party."[31] Others used Bird Day to champion broader causes such as humane education.[32] The amount of literature that was either written for Bird Day or suggested for recitation upon the occasion was so vast that collections of such materials were published.[33] The state manuals offered even more possibilities. Teachers were surely thankful—and likely bewildered—by the amount of imaginative literature and outdoor activities that various experts proclaimed would benefit Bird Day celebrations.

Despite their emphasis on using sentiment to encourage conservation, Bird Day celebrations rarely occurred without extended defenses of the economic necessity of birds. As the title of one article put it, "Without Birds Agriculture Would Be Impossible." This was a consistent theme of Bird Day celebrations.[34] Insects inflicted a tremendous amount of damage on commercial crops, resulting in stunning monetary losses. In Ohio's *Bird Day Manual* of 1914, professor of agriculture B. M. Davis of Miami University testified to the accuracy of the "much quoted" amount of $700 million "as the annual loss in the United States occasioned by insects."[35] Other conservationists lauded specific species such as the bobwhite quail (*Colinus virginianus*) because it consumed the seeds of various weeds by the ton. The *West Virginia Arbor and Bird Day Manual* noted that in addition to weed seeds, bobwhites ingested such pests as the Mexican cotton boll weevil, potato beetles, cotton worms, chinch bugs, and Rocky Mountain locusts. Without such help, "the farmer and the fruit grower will have a more difficult battle each year with insect life, and finally their inroad will be so great that it will be almost impossible to overcome it."[36] Thus, according to Edward Hyatt, superintendent of public instruction for California, Bird Day promoted "a spirit of protection towards [nature] and . . . the economic value of natural resources and the desirability of their conservation."[37]

Similarly, Bird Day advocates were certain that their pedagogy developed qualities of personhood and character that benefited society as well as wildlife. Most found it "a fact" that "the man or woman who loves nature . . . possesses a character quality that extends far beyond the objects that originally stimulated it."[38] Some writers reversed the formula by appealing to the requirements of patriotism to preserve birds. Published in the state of Washington's *Arbor and Bird Day Bulletin,* the "Birds' Declaration of Dependence" located the fate of avian life firmly within the ideology of American ideals: "We, the birds of the United States, in order to provide for our protection, promote our general welfare and secure the blessings of safety for ourselves and our posterity, do make to the people of this state a declaration of dependence for life, liberty and happiness."[39] By placing the fate of birds within the language of American constitutionalism, the author elevated animal life into the concerns of human morality and civic duty.

An ideology of civic duty also played a large role in Alabama's Bird Day programming. Arguing that "Our Patriots Were Nimrods" ("nimrod" was once a common synonym for hunter), the 1915 Alabama *Bird Day Book* suggested that the tradition of the American hunter-outdoorsman made victory possible in the Revolutionary War and the War of 1812 and even contributed to the "effective work of Alabama soldiers" during the War Between the States.[40] Yet the wildlife crisis required the implementation of new civic duties. Alabama touted its "progress . . . relating to game and bird preservation" due to newly enacted regulations that protected wildlife and an "efficient game warden service" to enforce them. These new laws also recognized the "reciprocal obligation" of the "Southern States" and "those who reside in the North" to protect "migratory birds" for mutual benefit.[41]

Hunting needed more than laws to control it; it required new ethics to inform its practices. As Hornaday, writing exclusively for Alabama's *Bird Day Book,* argued, forests can be protected by "national forest reserves" that "arrest the hands of the timber destroyer." But "there are no such corresponding reserved areas for wild life" because "parks and game preserves are lost in utter insignificance." This reality demanded ethical education to protect wildlife from the "Goths and Vandals of the army of destruction who are strangers to the higher sentiments."[42] Alabama Bird Day celebrations followed Hornaday's lead by insisting on new moral standards. As Harry Gunnels, Alabama's superintendent of education, asserted, "If we would get the most of what God has given us, we must instill in the minds and hearts of our children, from the kindergarten, a love of nature and nature's things."[43] Rather than murderous killers, hunters could become, in the words of "poet of the people" Sam Walter Foss, "The Bloodless Sportsman."[44] Indeed, one contributor to Alabama's *Bird Day Book* argued that "to kill [a bird] uselessly and wantonly is a near approach to murder."[45]

One of the most successful local incarnations of Bird Day occurred in Carrick, Pennsylvania (now part of Pittsburgh). It was this particular Bird Day that

Hornaday publicized in *Our Vanishing Wildlife*. Bird Day was so successful in Carrick (and elsewhere in Pennsylvania) in no small part due to the efforts of State Game Commissioner John M. Phillips. A towering figure in the history of Pennsylvania conservation, Phillips was a wealthy Pittsburgh businessman who helped found the State Game Commission. An ardent believer in public lands, Phillips sought to use the game commission to create many "little Yellowstone Parks" so that wildlife might thrive throughout Pennsylvania.[46]

Like so many progressive conservationists, Phillips believed in moral education as the best means to instill the ideals of conservation in the population at large. Bird Day suited his purpose well. His insight was not just to preach to children but also to provide them with specific tasks so they could further conservation through their own actions. If adults provided the tools and direction, children would provide the labor and enthusiastic commitment. Phillips put his ideas into action beginning in 1909 by giving away bird boxes and cherry and Russian mulberry (*Morus alba*) trees to students who promised to post the boxes and plant and care for the trees. By 1912 Phillips had given out approximately a thousand bird boxes and fifteen hundred trees.[47]

The 1912 Carrick Bird Day attracted two thousand flag-waving public and parochial school children. The governor of Pennsylvania, a reformer and champion of progressive education named John Kinley Tener, attended the event. According to the *Pittsburgh Gazette Times,* his presence lent "the state's approval to the movement to teach little boys and girls to be kind and considerate toward all living things."[48] Erasmus Wilson, a reporter for the *Gazette Times,* commented, "Children will care for and defend things that are their very own, fight for them and stand guard over them." Sentiment would create eager and devoted conservationists. "The intense interest manifested by the children, and the earnest enthusiasm manifested," reported Wilson, "leaves no doubt about their carrying out their part of the contract."[49]

Students were inculcated in bird conservation in a variety of ways beyond the activities of Bird Day itself. In some states such as Ohio, teachers were required to read to their students materials that encouraged them "to aid in the protection of the song and insectivorous birds."[50] Some states held competitions that rewarded students for their commitment to conservation. Arizona, for example, held a Wildlife Conservation Contest that awarded students prizes in essay writing, freehand drawing, and photography.[51] Forming clubs dedicated to bird preservation was a popular means of advancing conservation. Local branches of the Federation of Women's Clubs often promoted their own Club Bird Days and organized nature study associations that engaged in a variety of conservation activities.

Many schools formed clubs that carried the Bird Day message throughout the year. Seven hundred Milwaukee schoolchildren formed a Children's League for the Protection of Harmless Birds, and its members pledged "to do all we can to prevent the killing or maiming of birds, and to discourage, as far as we can, the wearing of stuffed birds as ornaments of hats, etc."[52] A children's conservation club in Worcester, Massachusetts, was named the Ten to One Club because its goal was "to have ten of our valuable native birds where we have but one now." According to *Colorado Arbor Day Notes,* the Massachusetts organization "aroused so much enthusiasm among children and parents, and proved so successful" that a similar scheme "may be adopted by practical use in the Colorado schools."[53] The most successful Bird Day practitioners provided an organizational basis to continue conservation activities throughout the year.

Bird club membership was especially fruitful to conservation efforts because, through club activities, children gained a material interest in preservation. Children belonging to the Bird Lovers' Club of Peru, Nebraska, for example, built wren houses, which induced "each boy and girl to feel a paternal interest in all the feathered residents in the community."[54] The pedagogical lessons were not lost on schoolteachers interested in nature study and conservation. "Of all the methods of bird study the one which yields the quickest and most lasting results," reported *Nature-Study Review,* "is one which puts children to work doing something." Actions transformed attitudes: "The boy who makes a bird house will have more respect for birds and less desire to destroy them."[55] Active conservation was just one reason to oppose the practice of teaching "people [about] birds by the use solely of pictures and books."[56]

Bird Day grew from a well-established tradition of expressing moral concern for nonhuman wildlife in imaginative writing geared toward children. For example, the magazine *St. Nicholas,* a handsome and multifaceted publication meant to "supplement, to some extent, the work of the schools," regularly featured stories and articles with conservation themes.[57] *St. Nicholas* promoted bird preservation from its beginning. Historian Robert Welker noted that the second issue featured a plea by C. C. Haskin on behalf of "a large family of our friends who are wantonly destroyed and abused by impulsive persons without good reason. . . . They are the birds—all of them—from the eagle and the vulture to the tiniest hummingbird." Haskin proposed the formation of an organization called "Bird Defenders" that would "advocate the rights of birds at all proper times, encourage confidence in them, and recognize in them creations of the great father, for the joy and good of mankind."[58] The June 1875 issue featured fiction by Helen B. Phillips titled "A Story for the Bird Defenders" in which a grieving robin describes the killing of its mate by a thoughtless boy.

Although the Bird Defenders never materialized as an organization, *St. Nicholas* continued its concern with nature study and conservation. A department devoted to natural history called "Nature and Science for Young Folks," edited by prominent nature study advocate Edward F. Bigelow, became a regular feature of the magazine. *St. Nicholas* also organized a Nature and Science Club that boasted more than half a million members. Most of the conservation message propagated by the magazine consisted of promoting an ethics of care when studying nature. Thus children should delight in wildflowers but remember that "next to those who ruthlessly collect large quantities for sale, among the worst enemies of our delicate and beautiful flowers are young folks ... who pick in unreasonably large quantities or thoughtlessly pull up the entire plant." The magazine therefore concurred "in most hearty sympathy" with the Society for the Protection of Native Plants, which advised that "children of the public schools may not only learn to know [wild plants] by name and enjoy them, but leave them to continue their growth."[59]

"Nature and Science for Young Folks" embraced a similar conservation ethic regarding Christmas trees, citing Gifford Pinchot to buttress its contention that cutting trees, "if done in a scientific way ... is not only commendable but is one of the best methods of promoting forestry."[60] *St. Nicholas* also warned its readers of the false rumor that the Smithsonian Institution offered a cash reward for passenger pigeon specimens. Decrying the actions that such a rumor might promote, the magazine editorialized that "if there were to be any reward in this manner, it should be a reward offered by each State for the capture and punishment of any person who kills one of these beautiful and rare birds."[61] *St. Nicholas* provided an early model of teaching natural history coupled with moral instruction as a way to promote conservation to children.

Several prominent conservationists popularized the Bird Day effort by writing for broad audiences that included schoolchildren and their parents. The most widely read Bird Day author was Mabel Osgood Wright, founder and first president of the Connecticut Audubon Society. Wright collaborated with ornithologist Elliot Coues and artist Louis Agassiz Fuertes to create the colorful book *Citizen Bird*, dedicated to "All Boys and Girls Who Love Birds and Wish to Protect Them." Like most Bird Day texts, *Citizen Bird* emphasized the helpful deportment of avian life, thus advocating for its moral standing. Consider its depiction of the bluebird:

As a Citizen the Bluebird is in every way a model. He works with the Ground Gleaners in searching the grass and low bushes for grasshoppers and crickets; he searches the trees for caterpillars in company with the Tree Trappers; and in eating blueberries, cranberries, wild grapes, and other fruits he works with the Seed Sowers also. So who would not welcome this bird, who pays his rent and taxes in so cheerful a manner, and thanks you with a song into the bargain?[62]

Wright did not just rely on her books; she also mounted an aggressive push for Bird Day education in Connecticut schools. She prepared lectures and slide shows, distributed Bird Day programs to 1,350 schools, and donated volumes on general natural history to needy schools and libraries.[63]

In many ways, Bird Day, with its call for moral restraint on individual conduct, typified the development of conservation. This was especially true of the early Audubon movement. In 1899 Babcock championed his idea for Bird Day celebrations in *Bird Lore,* the predecessor to the journal *Audubon,* which had recently begun publication.[64] That same year, an article on bird study by Frank M. Chapman, ornithologist at the American Museum of Natural History and the publisher of *Bird Lore,* appeared in *Educational Review.* Both essays emphasized education as a means to bird protection. This broad focus on education among conservationists was not surprising because, in addition to believing that sympathy with nature would lead to conservation, most ornithologists at the turn of the century were still self-educated amateurs.[65]

Chapman's article, titled "The Educational Value of Bird-Study," declared that nature study formed a precious "permanent bond between us and nature." Bird study in particular would transform the "natural" desires of young boys to hunt birds and the "tender hearted" desires of young women to wear stuffed birds on their hats into a concern for bird preservation. "Bird-study, therefore, not only has its aesthetic side," argued Chapman, "but it involves humane and moral questions of the deepest import."[66] Chapman's *Bird Lore,* a periodical whose masthead boasted that it was "Devoted to the Study and Protection of Birds," helped unify an Audubon movement that was revitalizing on the state level. Education remained a central focus of the devoted amateur conservationists who made up the individual Audubon Societies.

In 1901 state Audubon Societies coalesced into a national organization under the leadership of William Dutcher. Though Dutcher and his successor, T. Gilbert Pearson, differed greatly in management style, they both viewed education as the ultimate means of promoting Audubon goals. The Audubon Society distributed thousands of copies of model and actualized conservation laws, posters listing game regulations, society circulars, and a series of educational leaflets written by Dutcher and Pearson and published by the National Committee of

Audubon Societies. The leaflets were miniature Bird Day lessons. Each one focused on a particular bird, describing its use to humans and the threats to its existence. The leaflets proved to be wildly popular, and dozens more were written; Pearson eventually edited more than a hundred leaflets and authored forty himself.[67] Dutcher remained an evangelical proponent of the power of education to bring about a revolution in values that would result in widespread conservation consciousness. In his 1909 presidential address to the National Association of Audubon Societies, Dutcher argued that education was "the most powerful factor we are using, and is the surest road to success." To that end, he proposed "a great school or university devoted solely to the work of fitting teachers to be instructors about birds in their relations to man."[68]

Although no such university ever came into being, thousands of educators took up Dutcher's cause. Given that women dominated both the Audubon movement and the underpaid field of public education, it was not surprising that a disproportionate number of female nature writers heeded the Audubon Societies' call to champion education. *Bird Lore* featured a regular section edited by Mabel Osgood Wright entitled "For Teachers and Students," where writers such as Olive Thorne Miller promoted the need for personal interaction with the great outdoors not for economic or scientific purposes but for "the delight of a close acquaintance with nature."[69]

Like Bird Day celebrations, *Bird Lore* writers and the Audubon movement took pains to stress the economic benefits that accrued from bird protection. They also staunchly refused to define bird protection in solely utilitarian terms. Wright, for example, reported with satisfaction on the success of economic arguments that stressed the "status of the bird as a citizen and a laborer" who is "worthy of . . . hire" and therefore "has a right to protection and a living." Yet in an "age of marvelous material progress," should not the "ethical qualities of song and beauty" also be reasons to protect birds? "For is not beauty," queried Wright, "the visible form of the spiritual?" Wright bewailed that "our standards . . . are becoming pitifully [and] intensely material. Let us, therefore, dwell first upon the undeniable beauty and cheer of the birds of the air, and less upon their economic value."[70] Education remained fundamental to the Audubon movement, but it was education in spiritual and ethical values, rather than instruction in how to reduce human interaction with nature to an instrumental calculus.

Given the emphasis on instilling sentiment as the key to spreading conservation, it was not surprising that many wildlife advocates used fiction and other forms of literature to spread the conservation gospel. Creative writing can bring nonhuman characters into narrative fiction, and such individuals become part of readers' moral concern. That is the magic of storytelling. Metaphor and plot convey and construct values that, by means of the narrative, enlarge the ethical concerns of the story's audience. Sentiment in particular can induce emotional responses in readers—that is, it can make them care about the fate of human or nonhuman characters. In short, the components of storytelling do what science cannot: they create avenues of consideration and meaning that explicitly advocate for broader moral concern. Unlike science, literature can be an effective conduit for the moral instruction that conservationists such as Hornaday felt was essential to advance their cause.[71]

Among the best of the nature study fiction is Wright's *Tommy-Anne and the Three Hearts*, a tale that boldly preaches respect for nonhuman life. The title character (Wright was known as "Tommy" in her own home) receives a gift of eyeglasses that reveal nature's secrets and translate the languages of animals. As Welker noted in his discussion of *Tommy-Anne*, instead of following the well-established tradition in children's literature of portraying the use of magical powers to control nature, Wright employs her character's gift to interact with animals from the animals' point of view. This technique places humans and animals on a more equal moral plane, strengthening the emotional impact when Tommy-Anne learns about human cruelty toward other creatures directly from the victims. Despite such literary imagination, Wright clearly intended her work to remain faithful to the known facts of animal behavior. "The lives and habits of plants and animals, however fancifully treated in this book," explained Wright, "are in strict accordance with the known facts of their existence."[72]

Other writers used the literary device of granting human voice to animals to encourage policy makers to adopt laws that enacted an ethical concern for nonhuman nature. The senior U.S. senator from Massachusetts, George F. Hoar, for example, authored and circulated the "Birds' Petition," an appeal for bird protection written from the birds' point of view. Though Hoar is best remembered as a staunch proponent of clean government and for his anti-imperialist views, his sentimental "Birds' Petition" created enough of a stir to appear in a variety of publications, including the *Educational Gazette* and *Current Literature*, as well as several state-issued Bird Day pamphlets.[73]

The "Birds' Petition"—addressed "To the Great and General Court of the Commonwealth of Massachusetts"—begins with the birds explaining to the reader, "We know how good you are." Birds know about human goodness because "we have hopped about the roofs and looked in at the windows of the houses you have built for poor and sick and hungry people." The birds then deftly translate progressive pride in the amelioration of human suffering into horror at their own plight:

Thoughtless or bad people kill us because our feathers are beautiful. Cruel boys destroy our nests and steal our eggs and our young ones. People with guns lie in wait for us as if the place for a bird is not in the sky, alive. If this goes on, all the song birds will be gone. Now, we humbly pray that you will stop all this and save us from our sad fate.

The petition ends by elucidating the ample reward humans will receive through efforts at preservation: the beauty of birds in flight and song, as well as their indispensable help in destroying "wicked insects and worms." Thirty-seven common birds "signed" the petition.[74]

The "Birds' Petition" worked as political propaganda. Copies found their way into the reading room of the Massachusetts senate, where it garnered attention due to its literary quality and the political prominence of Senator Hoar. Indeed, *Current Literature* described the petition as unique because its author was known for "political rather than playful or tender utterances," yet it provided a "most graceful example of the union of dexterous persuasion with sentimental argument and literary charm."[75] Using the potency of the sentiments aroused by the petition, Massachusetts senator Alfred S. Roe introduced a bill that strengthened the state's efforts at bird protection by making it an offense "to sell, wear or have possession of the feathers of song birds for the purpose of ornament." The bill was unopposed in the senate, sailed through the house, and the governor signed it into law on 11 June 1897. The episode remains one of the few instances in which a work of imaginative literature decisively affected the outcome of pending legislation. It also provided powerful sustenance to those who insisted that the intertwined fate of humans and nature remained in the hands of people who were moved to widen their moral concern to include the rights of nonhuman nature.

Bird Day advocates and their colleagues in the nature study movement concurred that conservation could advance only when scientific understandings of nature were coupled with the moral sentiments that moved people to protect it. "Who that has watched the growth and strength of the bird protection propaganda," asked Anna Botsford Comstock, "would for a moment say that it had its inception or gained its strength because of its economic importance?" Instead of utilitarian arguments, conservation was furthered by "pure sentiment—a love of birds in the hearts of thousands of people all over the land."[76] Yet, to be effective, pure sentiment must thrive within a context of scientific information: "It stands to reason," asserted Comstock, "that to respect the rights of any plant or animal, we must know it when we see it, and know something of its habits. No other force will be so potent in preserving the wild life in our great reservations as Nature-Study, taught thoroughly and sanely in the Public Schools."[77]

Education was crucial, but the quandary of how to include moral concern for nonhuman life in popular science education remained. Even such strident moralists as Hornaday advocated a pedagogical philosophy that allowed little room for moral deliberation. In a critique of nature study, Hornaday insisted that students "should be required to memorize facts and definitions" aimed at teaching "classification," which is the "bed rock foundation" of nature study. Yet Hornaday's continued criticism of both zoologists and zoological education was closer to the nature study outlook than he acknowledged. According to Hornaday, most students required "a good *general* knowledge of the most interesting animal forms of his own country." What students did not need was "*to be trained as laboratory investigators, at the expense of practical knowledge in zoology.*" The specialization of laboratory investigation created teachers of science who were "specifically unfit for teaching what the youth of America desire and need to know about animal life." Moreover, Hornaday's conception of general information included the moral conclusion that "birds are useful to man and deserving protection." Indeed, educators should highlight "the birds that men and women are ruthlessly exterminating in ways that constitute crimes against nature."[78] Try as they might, most conservationists could not separate knowledge from moral responsibility.

Such a coupling was so difficult because many conservationists intuited that, left to its own devices, rationalized science would, through an ardent dismissal of subjectivity, depersonalize the relationship between humans and nature. Engrossed in laboratory activity, even professional zoologists had little concern for wildlife. This was the essential difference between experimental science and nature study conservation. Bird Day and nature study sought to integrate knowledge of nature with ethical convictions, rather than insisting on the separation of moral values and scientific facts. Furthermore, the values of interconnection and sympathy stressed by so many nature study conservationists contrasted with the economic and empirical values that guided and funded the bulk of the scientific endeavor. A call for moral duty to nonhuman life did not fit with the relentless quantification demanded by the dominant understandings of scientific precision. Sentiment produced doggerel, not knowledge. Consequently, the sympathy sought by nature study advocates appeared to be irrelevant to the contemporary world, an easy nostalgia or mawkish sentimentalism that was out of step with the tough-minded individuals who embraced contemporary life.

The difficulties of furthering a conservation ethic through a widespread campaign of education took the form of two interrelated questions: What types of knowledge engendered a moral commitment toward conservation? And, more important, did the detached and highly rationalized scientific method as practiced by laboratory researchers deaden their emotional investment in and moral sympathy for nonhuman life? The romantic view of nature held by Bird Day and nature study advocates conflicted with the socially sanctioned faith in the rightness and beneficence of highly technical scientific inquiry. The very modernizing social tendencies embraced by progressives worked to separate ethical and secular modes of understanding human affairs. The "wicked apathy" of zoologists, in other words, was encouraged by the objective nature of scientific inquiry. As society more frequently turned to the scientific establishment for the final verdict on intellectual matters, broad-based amateur knowledge gave way to the results produced by highly educated specialists. These professionals shaped the production and distribution of knowledge and thus much of the political context of intellectual life.[79]

The new forms of science affected Bird Day conservationists in two key ways. The ethic of instrumental rationality helped prompt firebrands such as Hornaday to inject their subjective and ethical beliefs into political discourse with a special vehemence. The combination of detached scientific inquiry and the crisis in wildlife populations seemed to demand the righteous clarity of ethical sentiment in favor of nonhuman nature. As Herbert Smith insisted, wildlife lovers sought to educate the emotions, sympathies, and idealizing side of the mind. Conservationists used events such as Bird Day as vehicles to inundate the public sphere with their moral convictions.

Yet the moral certainty displayed by conservationist rhetoric belied the quandaries faced by progressive moralists. The dynamic set up a vicious circle for conservationists. The more they (usually implicitly) criticized science for its lack of moral content, the more their positions drifted from the social endorsement bequeathed to the production of scientific knowledge.[80] Shorn from a scientific foundation, injunctions to preserve wildlife lost power; yet scientific information bereft of moral content failed to enact the passion for wildlife that spurred its conservation. Bird Day activities were typical of the rhetoric of progressive conservation, in that they continually sought ways to couple the separate worlds of moral and scientific certainty.

For those invested in the moral rhetoric of wildlife protection, the consequences were profound, for it revealed the anxious relationship between wildlife conservation and modernity itself. As Hornaday wrote, "I greatly fear that by the time [proper zoological education] arrives 'in our midst' the most interesting of the world's wild life will have been ground to dust under the iron-shod heel of Modern Civilization."[81] In the last analysis, moral suasion was so important to wildlife conservation because conservationists understood that without it, the progressive embrace of modern society would destroy the very nature they sought to protect. In future decades these tensions were only partially resolved by the widespread embrace of ecology as the science of conservation. Indeed, the difficulties of embracing scientific inquiry while demanding moral consideration for nature dogged the conservation movement throughout the twentieth century.

CHAPTER FIVE

Sticking a Finger into Nature's Pie

The Garden in Nature Study and Conservation

The nature desire may be perpetual and constant, but
the garden desire returns with every new springtime.
—Liberty Hyde Bailey, "A Reverie of Gardens"

How do activists transform a nature-hating culture into one that fosters an "abiding interest in the out-of-doors, a calm appreciation of the landscape?" Many Progressive Era conservationists found the answer not through spiritual exultation in communion with sublime wilderness or in rugged excursions to frontier landscapes but in prosaic experiences with nature found much closer to home. Conservationists theorized that interacting with nature in urban and suburban neighborhoods taught children the "realization of nature's inexorable laws. Slowly, perhaps almost unconsciously, the truth is born in upon them that they must work with nature not against her."[1] The source of this lesson was the humble garden. Accessible to all, managed by people yet also wild, the garden was wild nature rooted in domestic, day-to-day life, and it figured more prominently to Progressive Era conservation, and hence the beginnings of environmentalism, than has commonly been acknowledged. As a vital tool for conservationists, gardens revealed the myriad human relationships with the landscape that conservationists sought to reform. Gardens were especially important to conservationists because they embodied the notion that people and nature need each other. Interest in gardens illustrated the variety of landscapes valued by conservationists and, crucially, the variety of people who valued them.

Consider three prominent exponents of gardening: the teachers and students of the nature study movement, Audubon activist Mabel Osgood Wright, and educator Booker T. Washington. These educator-activists were united in their belief that gardening could inculcate citizens with a love of nature that would improve their lives and promote conservation. School gardens, created with the express intent of fostering a love of nature in children, swept the nation during the first decades of the twentieth century. Wright, like many middle-class, suburban women, championed gardens as a means of personal development and environmental reform. In her novel *The Garden of a Commuter's Wife* (suffused with gardening tips and digressions into natural history), Wright advised:

> Gardening is the most cheerful and satisfactory pursuit for women who love the outdoors. Field and forest often hold one at bay. We may admire, worship, love, but neither advise nor argue with them nor add one cubit to their stature. In a garden one's personality can come forth, stick a finger into nature's pie, and lend a hand in the making of it, besides furnishing many of the ingredients.[2]

The very interweaving of natural and human energies was what made the garden so important. Rather than inert materials understood solely through positivist means, garden nature was intersubjective. The garden was forceful and dynamic, not simply an object for use but a way to express one's humanity. Nor was it only suburban women of the Northeast who expressed this sentiment. Consider Booker T. Washington's description of his garden from his best-selling autobiography *Up from Slavery:*

> My garden . . . is another source of rest and enjoyment. Somehow I like as often as possible, to touch nature, not something that is artificial or an imitation, but the real thing. When I can leave my office in time so that I can spend thirty or forty minutes in spading the ground, in planting seeds, in digging about the plants, I feel that I am coming into contact with something that is giving me strength for the many duties and hard places that await me out in the big world. I pity the man or woman who has never learned to enjoy nature and to get strength and inspiration out of it.[3]

Teaching us how to respect nature's limits and love the outdoors while providing a place for the spiritual and physical revitalization of self is a trait gardens share with the wilderness, and in so doing, they help us recover a more nuanced and wide-ranging conservation movement.

This legacy is an important topic for the history of environmental reform because it demonstrates the more popular and socially inclusive roots of environmentalism. Critics of the history of environmentalism have used the fascination with wilderness among the privileged classes of the Progressive Era to implicate the ostensibly elitist beginnings of environmental reform. For example, in his justly celebrated essay "The Trouble with Wilderness," William Cronon argued, "It is not too much to say that the modern environmental movement is itself a grandchild of romanticism and post-frontier ideology, which is why it is no accident that so much environmentalist discourse takes its bearings from the wilderness these intellectual movements helped create." Moreover, these intellectuals were "elite urban tourists and wealthy sportsmen" who "projected their leisure-time frontier fantasies onto the American landscape and so created wilderness in their own image." In short, wilderness was a place without history and without people—except for the wealthy sportsmen who vacationed there. This vision of wilderness was one that ignored most of the democratic populace and hence infused environmentalism with the preconceptions of Theodore Roosevelt and other members of his social class. Cronon was certainly correct to point out that wilderness advocates have sometimes lacked social compassion and, in support of their cause, have employed a macho, strident language—verbiage rooted in the Progressive Era's intertwining of masculinity with frontier nature—that has been alienating to many. Other historians have criticized Cronon's approach, both for its own assumptions and for its reconstruction of the history of the wilderness idea, which turns out to be more interesting and inclusive than previously thought.[4] My purpose here is to use the progressive embrace of gardening to widen how scholars and activists view the progressive championing of nature and the social roots of the love for nature that nourishes environmentalism.

School gardens solved two problems for the nature study movement. They were accessible to all, even to urban children, and they provided for a practical, results-oriented pedagogy that appealed to teachers and parents alike. School gardens were supported by government agencies, a variety of civic organizations, conservationists, social reformers, and prominent figures such as Frederick Law Olmsted, Jacob Riis, and Woodrow Wilson. Moreover, in a reflection of the progressive ideology they embodied, gardens broke down barriers between theoretical and applied work, beauty and science, preservation and use, and household and school. Gardens were both democratic and pragmatic. They were used to instill the values of hard work, and children sometimes reaped financial rewards when they sold their vegetables and flowers. Nature study advocates held that gardens fought juvenile delinquency; beautified urban, rural, and school environments; and taught the invaluable lessons of conservation. In short, gardening was a great way to create productive and responsible citizens. "The very fact that a child finds himself a producer, providing something of value for the family or the community," averred one school garden supporter, created in the child "self-respect and a self-reliance that is a great asset in the character of any citizen of a democracy."[5]

As with other aspects of the nature study movement, school gardening drew on European theorists of education—including Friedrich Froebel—whose romantic inclinations included the benefits of school gardens. As early as 1691 George Fox, founder of the Religious Society of Friends, willed a tract of land near Philadelphia "for a playground for the children of the town to play on, and for a garden to plant with physical [medicinal] plants."[6] A variety of schools followed up on Fox's idea during the nineteenth century, but the widespread creation of gardens in schools and vacant lots did not emerge until the 1890s.

The social purposes of gardens were popularized when Detroit's fiery mayor Hazen Pingree used community gardening to alleviate the economic suffering caused by the panic of 1893. Putting idle labor and vacated city lands together, Mayor Pingree initiated a garden program variously known as "Potato Patch Farms" or "Pingree's potato patches." Despite considerable controversy, 450 acres of donated land were cultivated. The city printed gardening instructions in three languages, and the gardeners both consumed and sold their products. Soon, even the program's critics acknowledged its success, noting that it provided work and produced more money than it cost to implement.[7] If gardening helped unemployed labor, why not schoolchildren? Soon innovative schools in Boston, New York City, and Philadelphia planted gardens, and the idea spread across the nation, with glowing reports of gardening success appearing in Cleveland, Dayton, St. Louis, Minneapolis, and throughout California.

Observing this trend, prominent theorists of progressive education agreed that gardening could have tremendous educational value, and they made the school garden a part of their curricula. Reporting on the work of his Laboratory School, John Dewey argued that the school garden achieved a plethora of social ends:

> The [school] work is given a civic turn; that is to say, the value of the gardens to the child and to the neighborhood is demonstrated: to the child as a means of making money or helping his family by supplying them with vegetables, to the community in showing how gardens are a means of cleaning up and beautifying the neighborhood. . . . Starting with the interest and effort of the children, the whole community has become tremendously interested in starting gardens, using every bit of available ground.[8]

Moreover, Dewey found that gardening performed the basic nature study function of preparing students for more advanced scientific work. Gardens "are a means for making a study of the facts of growth, the chemistry of soil, the role of light, air, moisture, injurious and helpful animal life, etc." The social and educational ends of gardening quickly coalesced. Rather than cordoning knowledge into a discrete field, "it will belong to life . . . [and find] its natural connectedness with the facts of soil, animal life, and human relations."[9] The nature of the garden made it a social and natural tool, one that cultivated community cohesion as well as a knowledge of nature.

School and neighborhood beautification was of primary importance to garden advocates. Like many other progressives, these educators were firm believers in what historian Paul Boyer termed "positive environmentalism," which he defined as "the attempt to elevate the moral character of city dwellers by transforming the physical conditions of their lives."[10] The concrete and clutter of urban life shocked conservationists. Fannie G. Parsons, a pioneer of school gardens in the United States, described urban children as living "encased amid bricks, stone, concrete, trolleys, trucks, and automobiles . . . the blue sky overhead is seldom seen. . . . City children are alienated from their human birthright of trees, fields, and flowers."[11] Similarly, Margaret Knox of New York City reported that when asked by a teacher to name a sign of spring, one child replied, "Yes ma'am, I know when spring is here because the saloons put on their swinging doors."[12] Such children lost their human birthright to experience nature as well as the social values accrued from interacting with the green world. Moreover, progressives believed that such alienation from nature brought about profound social malaise: juvenile delinquency and myriad other social ills arose because "men, women and children cannot be well as long as their home conditions are exposed to disease breeding and fly breeding streets, alleys and back yards. A man cannot be moral on an empty stomach. Dyspepsia is not conducive to the highest moral and spiritual growth."[13] Parsons reasoned that lack of contact with nature made children "hard and unfeeling." Deprived of their "natural lives," children became callous, finding "the only diversion possible . . . vice and crime."[14] The remedy was environmental reform.

Although Boyer emphasized the coercive aspects of positive environmentalism, much of it, including the school garden movement, was decentralized, engendered broad public support, instilled the values—especially the work ethic—of the Protestant middle classes, and agitated for lasting social betterment. Positive environments meant better housing, parks and playgrounds (many of which began adding gardens to complement their play equipment), attractive and well-equipped schools, and progressive support for a variety of public institutions such as libraries. For nature study advocates, positive environmentalism necessarily included unfettered contact with the natural world.

All these rich environments produced rich experiences for those who interacted with them. Finally, gardens were democratic. Accessible to all, gardens depressed social distinction. One study of school gardens in Michigan, for example, emphasized the social equality fostered by work with nature:

> While the children of the rich and of the poor sit side by side in the same schoolroom and receive the same instruction from the same teacher, they do not necessarily learn the great lesson of social equality, but when they stand side by side and engage in tilling the soil they learn that "in work there is no shame" and that the real man is the same, whether clad in overalls or in broadcloth. These are the lessons in my judgment that the children of America cannot learn too early.[15]

Working in gardens instilled social equality; they were, as Neltje Blanchan put it, "of the million as well as the millionaire."[16] Positive environments would change the culture to a democratic one that valued the richness of experience gained from the social and natural worlds.

Gardening enthusiasts agreed that city environments stunted the growth of children and nature. Urban conditions prevented children from developing their "innate love" for "growing things, a love which cannot be gratified in the lives of the great majority of the children of the cities."[17] The problem was a profound one, and one that intersected with pedagogy. Professor B. M. Davis, writing in *Nature-Study Review,* noted that urban children have "little or no opportunity for acquiring new experiences" with the natural world. Because natural "objects have not really entered into the child's active life," the "natural method of acquiring knowledge by direct experience is suddenly dropped and an entirely new method substituted—the book method. Learning words takes the place of real knowledge." Garden plots provided the natural objects that ensured real knowledge. Through active, hands-on pedagogy, they counteracted the limited experiential possibilities of the urban landscape and promoted the "general human interests" that fostered "human sympathy and a truer democracy." As an example, Davis cited conservation: "The value of irrigation and conservation of water cannot be appreciated by talking about it. But actual experience in the practice of irrigation in which the principles are involved should go a long way in making the child a citizen who, whatever his business or profession may be, will have an intelligent interest in the subject."[18] To drive such lessons home, Davis suggested that children use their gardens to perform experiments on packed and loose dirt to understand how farmers might best conserve water in arid soils.[19]

As a rule, nature study advocates conflated personal and social growth. Arguing, like Jacob Riis, that ruffians were made, not born, garden advocates believed that transforming "what had been a repellent yard" into a "luxuriant garden" that produced vegetables and "gladden[ed] the eye" would help create responsible citizens rather than criminals.[20] Giving students the kind of environments that fostered wholesome personal development would foster wholesome societies. This approach was moral and effective: "Prevention," argued nature study advocate B. J. Horchem of Dubuque, Iowa, "is better than vain attempts at the cure of society's evil. The wholesome continuance of inspiring, enjoyable, and profitable living for twelve months in the year is the true antidote to progressive vice and criminality."[21] In Dubuque, prevention took the form of what Horchem described as "park life." Progressive reform in Dubuque aimed to provide "people with homes of their own, with little parks around these, and with surely an ideal place to live. They will live 'Park Life,' not slum or tenement life." Park life also enhanced "the vitality of the child." Vitality was inseparable from interaction with nature, which allowed "the charm, the dignity, the wholesomeness of out door life" to foster children's social development into citizens. Moreover, park life created "an interest in public affairs," such as "the conservation of the water supply . . . so that all who have homes can have all the water necessary for irrigation, which, together with fertilization, can bring returns that are profitable and enjoyable."[22]

Enthusiasm for the positive environmentalist approach colored almost all the activities of school garden supporters. Constructive labor in healthy environments would create responsible and active citizens. The straight rows of a proper garden were a popular metaphor for the straight and narrow moral life that gardening inculcated. Belief in the positive results derived from gardening was so powerful that Worcester, Massachusetts, termed its Garden City Plan the "Good Citizens' Factory."[23] The Garden City Plan, initiated by the Worcester Social Settlement, consisted of transforming unsightly dumps (including the dead cat dump) and vacant lots into a series of gardens organized, tended, and governed by schoolchildren. Schoolchildren thus built the positive environments that would help them develop into productive citizens. The Garden City Plan included rules that instilled a strong social ethic: each child was required to work ten hours helping to tend someone else's plot.

Gardening taught the children of Worcester the "grit, thrift, [and] self-reliance" needed for democratic vitality as well as a respect for nonhuman life. In describing the work of the Good Citizens' Factory, R. J. Floody reported in *Nature-Study Review* that before the gardening program began, "Cruelty to animals was quite common . . . I personally know of a little boy driving nails through a kitten's paws and nailing it to a board and then stoning it." Rather than simply reprimanding the ruffian—"What are you going to do with a boy of that kind? Tell him he is a very bad boy?"—the Garden City Plan formed a zoo consisting of "rabbits, guinea pigs, foxes, coon, white mice, white rats, pigeons, etc." Boys cared for these animals, and doing so transformed their attitudes toward them. Soon these burgeoning good citizens formed "a Band of Mercy 800 strong. . . . There has not been a single case of cruelty to animals for months and months in the whole district."[24] For progressive reformers, responsibility and nature combined to bring about the moral transformation of urban children.

Despite the use of vacant lots and home gardens, many city teachers still had to confront the vexing problem of finding nature with which their charges could interact. At times teachers simply brought nature to the children. One such teacher was Alice Rich Northrop. Born and raised in New York City, Northrop studied botany at Hunter College and worked as a substitute teacher in the New York City schools before becoming a professor of botany at Hunter. During her stint in the public schools she was horrified to realize how little contact city children had with the natural world. "Nature has no press agent," lamented Northrop, "and her marvels are unheralded."[25] One teacher confided to Northrop that she was sure many of her pupils had never seen growing grass. The lack of contact with flora and fauna revealed itself in the students' ignorance of the natural world. Children could not identify common plants or animals, even when school lessons had imparted facts about them.[26] Determined to rectify the situation, Northrop committed to deliver the things of nature into New York City classrooms, "bringing the mountain to Mohammed." "If we cannot take the children of New York City to the country," asserted Northrop, "we must bring all the country that is transportable to the children."[27]

Northrop brought the country to city children through flower shows. After attending a flower show in Cornwall, New York, Northrop resolved to organize similar shows as a pedagogical tool for the teachers of city children. The first show in 1894 featured more than a hundred species, both wild and cultivated, with each specimen classified and labeled. Students and teachers responded to the initial flower shows with great enthusiasm, and teachers began to incorporate flower shows into the curriculum. Soon three flower shows were being held over the course of the year. The first took place in early May so that Arbor Day celebrations could be included with the exhibit, the second was held in late May, and the last occurred during the fall and featured a variety of fruits and vegetables and late-blooming flowers. The shows met with great success and became a regular part of the curriculum; by 1917, city children had attended fifty flower shows. Writing in *Natural History,* Northrop reported, "In 1919 about 10,000 children visited the flower shows. There may be two hundred different kinds of plants exhibited. The wild flowers and the garden flowers are arranged separately, each distinctly labeled with its common name."[28] The flowers, always fresh, came from wealthy benefactors with country estates, personal friends, and children enrolled in the very popular Junior Naturalist Clubs in upstate New York, which, under the direction of Cornell University's "Uncle" John Spencer, collected plants for the city children. In this manner, the flower shows connected rural and urban children. Northrop took pains to ensure that the schools were not sent rare specimens or flowers that had been uprooted rather than cut.

In 1897 Northrop founded the School Nature League, an organization that provided flowers and other natural objects that teachers could use in their classrooms. In 1919 the School Nature League "supplied 576 teachers representing 26 different schools with such things as fruits and seeds, autumn foliage, winter bouquets, birch bark (taken from 'down timber' only), mosses, lichens, fungi, cones, frog spawn, birds' and wasps' nests, [and] shells."[29] Schools often displayed the objects in a single classroom that functioned as a miniature museum. The exhibits, dubbed "nature rooms," proved to be a great success, and the School Nature League adopted "A Nature Room in Every School" as its slogan. Nature rooms contained many natural phenomena—puffballs "that the children never tire of 'making smoke,'" "caterpillar corners," or even a "miniature swamp" complete with "pitcher plant, cranberry vines and sphagnum moss" surrounding a "tiny pool . . . in which a small turtle and some tadpoles disported themselves."[30] Twenty-four New York City schools adopted nature rooms. "The teachers are grateful for the help," wrote Northrop, "and tell us their classes often talk of the visits to the nature room for weeks afterward."[31] To keep the students talking about nature, Northrop advised that they needed to view "the flowers two or three times and have an opportunity to talk them over with each other and with their teachers. At the first visit they are too much overwhelmed to take in the details."[32]

Recognizing that public schools had few employees trained in science, Northrop endeavored to instruct teachers as well as students in nature study. Beginning in 1892 she led teachers on a series of weekly field trips, usually on Wednesdays or Saturdays, under the auspices of the Hunter College Normal School's Alumnae.[33] Using the trolley system, she took twenty schoolteachers on springtime nature study visits to parks in and around the metropolitan area. Eventually, she added a Wednesday class to meet the increasing demand for her program. Nature study, she argued, would enhance the health, intellect, and morals of students; likewise, it "cannot fail to awaken sympathy with these humble neighbors of ours, and kindness will take the place of thoughtless cruelty." Northrop also connected her nature study work to the country life movement. "The awakening of a general interest in nature," argued Northrop, "will have a tendency to counteract the strong drift city-ward, which is one of the country's greatest problems."[34] Wielding nature study as a pedagogical tool, teachers could help alleviate the metropolitan provincialism that tied urban children to the city.

The city of St. Louis provided nature study materials to its teachers through a traveling museum. Specimens available through the Educational Museum of the St. Louis Public Schools (its official title) included "most of the common cereals, grains and other food products, the various vegetable and animal fibers . . . minerals, rocks and ores of many varieties; woods, plants, and models and charts of plants; specimens of sea life; hundreds of mounted birds and small mammals; [and] thousands of stereoscopic views." The horse-drawn museum saved the energy of transporting classes to a museum and focused "the child's attention . . . on one collection instead of being distracted by the innumerable variety presented in a museum." The idea proved popular; in the 1908–1909 school year, "22,042 collections were delivered to schools, while for more than a year past twenty wagon loads per week have been carried to and from the schools."[35] The system also provided teachers with books on natural history and pedagogy, which they could check out as they would from a library.

Nature study instructors were also supported by a variety of civic and governmental organizations that saw school gardens as an opportunity to abet city beautification or instill sound business practices in young entrepreneurs. Gardens proved so popular with city and civic organizations that many became directly involved in the school garden movement. Although the garden movement in Cleveland began with reforms initiated by the Goodrich Social Settlement, the municipality quickly became involved. The city of Cleveland distributed seeds in penny packages to schoolchildren. Other private organizations chipped in; the Home Gardening Association cooperated with the city's Slavic Alliance to sell schoolchildren seeds for use in home and neighborhood gardens. The city sold 140,000 seed packages in 1904 and more than twice that number in 1905. By 1905 sixty-five thousand Cleveland children had gardens either at home or at school.[36]

Other governmental and private organizations embarked on similar programs. Many organizations awarded prizes to schools with the best gardens; for example, the City Federation of Women's Clubs of Saginaw, Michigan, presented the school that grew the best garden with a $25 banner flag. The Evansville, Indiana, *Courier* sponsored a prize for the best garden produced by schoolchildren, as well as a prize for the best student essay on gardening. *Garden Magazine* sponsored a children's garden contest. Winnebago County, Illinois, formed a Farmer's Boys Experiment Club that included 350 members who used their gardens to further instruction in agriculture. The U.S. Department of Agriculture (USDA) dedicated an acre and a greenhouse to school gardening for the Franklin Normal School in Washington, D.C. Indeed, the USDA's response to school gardens was enthusiastic, and it quickly created programs to support the school garden movement. "Its publications, its seeds, its slides, its advice are yours. Use them," urged Susan B. Sipe in *Nature-Study Review*.[37] Prodded by such an enthusiastic reception, the school garden idea spread throughout the country and beyond, from the industrial Midwest to the island of Grenada in the West Indies. By 1906 more than a hundred cities had gardens connected to their schools.[38] A year later the USDA estimated the number of school gardens at seventy-five thousand.[39] Two organizations with the express intent of spreading the school garden movement formed in 1910: the School Garden Association of America and the International Children's School Farm League.[40]

Part of the widespread appeal of the garden derived from its flexibility, allowing it to satisfy different pedagogical purposes. Many nature study advocates cited garden work as a way to promote aesthetic and utilitarian conservation. But the vocational implications of garden work—many teachers pictured their students as young farmers—also heightened the sense that education should turn children into productive workers. Yet gardening was more than an example of the progressive credo of learning by doing. The moral values associated with sustained labor swept into the nature study rhetoric of gardening. Teachers justified school gardening with the common nature study goals of enhancing the moral relationship between nature and people or developing a sympathetic connection between children and their environment, but also with the popular language of character development through the ennobling processes of labor. "The school-garden," asserted H. D. Hemenway, "creates a love for industry, a love for the country, for nature and things beautiful and makes boys and girls stronger, more intelligent, truer men and women."[41] Indeed, another writer claimed that "many nature study advocates overlook the utilitarian idea," but gardening could overcome this oversight because it developed a "socially efficient citizen." Social efficiency was especially enhanced when gardening was tied to vocational training such as "industrial and commercial geography."[42] The only failed children's gardens, wrote another teacher, were those whose gardeners "have not the moral stamina to push on to a completed result."[43] Adults felt free to pass such judgments because children laboring in a garden were in a safe environment—unlike the troublesome notion of children laboring in the factory system.

Despite their flexibility, school gardens were confined by the academic year, which then as now conformed to the agricultural calendar. Thus teachers faced the continuing problem of planting a spring garden with a classroom full of enthusiastic students, only to have no one to tend the garden or harvest its products. Indeed, teachers and students often returned from summer break to find "scrawny plants, growing in a weedy, neglected school garden." Such a sight was a "daily reminder to the effect that the school garden is a failure and the promoter of it a weak organizer, an inefficient supervisor, a faddist, an imbecile, or a misguided enthusiast."[44] Teachers and students embraced a number of strategies to counteract this problem: home and community gardens, committees of students to tend the garden over the summer, even paid supervisors to look after the garden during summer vacation. Some school districts increased teachers' salaries to compensate for supervising gardens during the summer months; other districts hired full-time garden curators. One of the reasons gardens were so strongly integrated into community life was to avoid the constraints of the academic year.

Alternatively, students could simply plant radishes. A hearty vegetable, radishes grow well in cool temperatures and thrive even when neglected. As the *Cornell Rural School Leaflet* advised, "Radishes will certainly grow in your garden." Most important, radishes grow rapidly, so children could plant them in early spring and harvest them before school let out. Impatient younger students, in particular, could see the results of their gardening efforts before the semester ended. Accordingly, radish harvests were vast. In 1914 children harvested 11,940 radishes from New York City's Rockefeller garden. School garden advocate Dora Williams believed that growing radishes gave children the satisfaction of being producers as well as the keen enjoyment of a "handful for breakfast."[45] The course of study for the Baltimore schools suggested that students celebrate their home gardens with a "Bread, Butter and Radish Party" in June.[46] The humble radish gave young gardeners the satisfaction of seeing their work come to fruition.

The rhetoric of character building through practical labor was also deployed by school garden advocates in the service of the "Americanization" of immigrant children. Bertha Chapman, supervisor of nature study in Oakland, California, proudly described the "earnest, delightful [gardening] work" of Portuguese, Irish, and Jewish children living in refugee camps following the San Francisco earthquake of 1906. Entranced by the mix of languages and the exuberance of children at the camps, Chapman viewed her work as helping "these people learn how to live." The necessity of measuring precise plots and the labor involved in tilling the soil not only occupied the unruly immigrant children but also taught them the moral principles of work and thrift. Indeed, the gardens were so successful at transmitting bourgeois values that the earthquake and subsequent fire may have "prove[d] a blessing rather than a calamity" for the young gardeners.[47]

In the application of gardening to immigrant children, nature study advocates were as concerned with conserving the dominant values of Protestant respectability as they were with conserving nature. Thus, when nature study was brought to bear on American Indian children, who, ostensibly, were already "accustomed to out-of-door life," it remained useful because they were unfamiliar with "the lucrative results from . . . cultivation" and "individuality." Inculcating individuality would help Indian children "see the possibilities in their land, and give them a practical knowledge that will enable them to obtain the most lucrative results from its cultivation."[48] Gardens could cultivate cultural assimilation as easily as vegetables. The physical activity of gardening made nature studies a particularly fruitful way to transmit dominant values because of the twice ennobling factors of physical work and the touch of nature.

Despite such rhetoric, most nature study advocates were far less interested in Americanizing their charges than in using nature study to inculcate the values that created the foundation for personal growth and sympathy with the social and natural worlds. Biologist Clifton Hodge of Clark University in Worcester displayed the evangelical tone of nature study advocates when he pondered the life of children deprived of contact with nature. "To allow a child to grow up without planting a seed or rearing a plant is a crime against civilized society," proclaimed Hodge. "Our armies of tramps and hordes of hoodlums are among the first fruits of an educational system that slights this important matter." To counteract destructive urban environments, "within the limits of every town or city there ought to be a game preserve." Moreover, Hodge advocated that households plant trees that were beneficial to avian life and control their bird-killing cats.[49] Indeed, Hodge's noisy campaign against the cats of Worcester provoked much controversy.[50]

As Hodge's efforts show, progressive educators believed that gardens could do much more than produce healthier, conservation-minded citizens; they could be directly involved in conservation through the preservation of birds and wildflowers. *Nature-Study Review* noted that the need for wildflower gardening arose because "the development of the country over large areas . . . is of such a nature that no natural refuges are being left for the wild flowers, and unless they are given a place in our private gardens and public parks, they are doomed to follow the pigeon into oblivion." To avoid such a fate, "wild flowers should be established and maintained permanently wherever possible." If "nature lovers who have gardens" grew and shared wildflowers, "their chance of survival [would be] greatly enhanced."[51] Thus school gardening could be actively incorporated into the crusade to preserve biodiversity.

Garden ethics extended to flowers encountered in the wild. Worried that "excessive picking" contributed to the decline of native flora, *Nature-Study Review* concurred with the Wild Flower Preservation Society of America that cultivated flowers should decorate the home because, unlike delicate wildflowers, they "do not soon fade." The *Cornell Rural School Leaflet* agreed. While noting that it was "fortunate" that flowers grow in easily reached areas, accessibility meant "that flowers are so attractive to passers-by that their numbers are being greatly reduced."[52] To combat the mindless collecting of threatened wildflowers, nature study teachers were urged to teach that what one picks cannot be enjoyed by others, wildflowers wither quickly, and, "worst of all, there will not be enough flowers left in that place to go to seed and make it beautiful again next year."[53] In this way, the garden united the ethical duties owed to domestic and wild environments.

Other threats to wildflowers demanded the attention of teachers and students. Motorists traveling "far afield to the natural reserves" were a particular threat because these excited urbanites, overcome by the sheer amount of vegetation, heedlessly picked the available wildflowers. The lack of nature in urban areas allowed people to forget how fragile nature could be. Hence the Society for the Preservation of New England Plants wanted children to understand which flowers "are not to be picked, no matter how pretty they look and how much the children want to make big bunches for their parents or teachers." Teachers, meanwhile, should encourage the "awakening of a wide ideal of the conservation of our natural forms" by using the flowers students did pick to impart lessons in sensible conservation. The flowers were a "text" that instructed which "should never be picked at all" and which could be "picked more freely." All people needed to study "local conditions" so they could "use judgment" in their relations with wildflowers.[54] Wildflower ethics were a means to activate children's moral development. Conservation would be the result.

No educator did more to incorporate children into the conservation movement than Mabel Osgood Wright, who was a founder and first president of the Connecticut Audubon Society, a leader of the National Association of Audubon Societies, and associate editor of and frequent contributor to *Bird Lore*. Wright's career coincided with and expanded the school gardening movement. As argued in the excellent work by Daniel J. Philippon, Wright's conservation "grew out of the ethics and aesthetics of suburban life." By championing suburban nature as the locus of environmental change, Wright "helped to broaden the audience for environmental reform and deepen the arguments used by its reformers, moving the focus of conservation away from the disappearing frontier of the sportsman and into the backyard gardens of suburban America."[55] By examining nature close to home, Wright's activism focused on women and children and the nature they encountered daily: gardens and the birds that visited them.

In addition to focusing on the nature that children encountered, Wright's activism was built on the idea that a broad campaign of public education must serve as the foundation for conservation efforts. Much of this work—and of the early Audubon movement more broadly—occurred in reaction to the brutal impact on bird populations by the millinery industry, which supplied the then-fashionable birds and feathers that women wore on their hats. The toll on avian life was tremendous: contemporary ornithologists estimated that 5 million domestic and 200 million foreign birds were sacrificed for fashion annually.[56] White herons and egrets, in particular, were hunted mercilessly, most often during the breeding season, when their bright plumage shone most vividly. Wright did not blame the milliners for responding to an economic opportunity (though she reviled their anticonservationist propaganda); rather, effective conservationists needed to stop the demand, and hence the market, for bird feathers.

To accomplish this, conservationists must "educate the moral nature [of the public] so that it will not desire to do the wrong act." Consequently, Wright argued that conservationists must change the culture that viewed birds as mere ornaments. This cultural transformation was crucial due to the limits of the law. Laws were not always enforced, and Wright correctly noted that the American public found "something disagreeably coercive . . . in signing, or promising away, even the smallest fraction of its liberty of action." Yet there remained a role for statutory penalty. Conservationists should agitate for "the establishment and enforcement of laws that shall punish those who do the wrong."[57] Indeed, education and the law must work together to protect nature: "The bird protective societies are tireless, but the ground must be prepared for the message they send forth."[58]

Wright's strategy was widely copied. Ornithologist Edward Howe Forbush, a founder of the Massachusetts Audubon Society, argued:

> The first and most important step in protecting birds from their human enemies is to create a public sentiment in favor of birds by teaching their value and the necessity for conserving them. This is legitimate work for State

boards of agriculture and State boards of education. . . . There is ample reason for introducing economic nature study into the schools. . . . The boy who learns to feed birds and to furnish them with houses will always be their friend.[59]

Wright expounded on the idea that education could turn American culture in a nature-friendly direction as the editor of *Bird Lore*'s Education Department. Her concerns were long-standing; in 1895 she published *Birdcraft*, a taxonomic handbook of birds that featured her short essays and personal anecdotes about them. *Birdcraft* was hugely successful and remained the most widely used field guide until Roger Tory Peterson's *Field Guide to the Birds* appeared in 1934. Moreover, Wright produced a stream of fiction for children, including the notable titles *Tommy-Anne and the Three Hearts* and *Citizen Bird*. Although these books anthropomorphized their animal characters, they did so in a manner consistent with scientific facts and the animals' known behaviors. Wright also combined her literary and activist efforts by championing Bird Day celebrations for Connecticut schoolchildren.

Despite her literary accomplishments, Wright was in unreserved agreement with the central proposition of the nature study movement that to understand the natural world, children must interact with actual wild things instead of representations of them. And gardens could contain actual wild things—including endangered ones. Wright believed that gardens could be sites of practical conservation. She noted that private and public efforts at preservation and education "may be able to preserve certain great stretches of forest lands and by educational propaganda . . . curb the indiscriminate gathering of attractive, but very perishable, wild flowers." Yet such efforts were not enough; the conservation of nature needed to enter daily life. Endangered plants, for example, could be integrated into gardens: "If we would preserve the wild things in their haunts, let us re-create these haunts upon soil that is still under private control and intelligently remove the vanishing wild species to it." Gathering and caring for such plants saved them from being doomed by development or by faddist "'back to nature' squads of automobilists."[60]

In making such suggestions, Wright followed the logic of the garden itself. Rather than bifurcating nature and humans into separate realms, the garden united human and natural processes in ways that benefited both. Wright's multifaceted use of the garden reflected the unique properties of cultivated space and its wild denizens. As Philippon argued, "Wright sought not merely to celebrate the domestic landscape but also to depict its nonhuman inhabitants as members of a living ecological community, members deserving the same moral citizenship granted to members of the living social community."[61] When wild things were brought into gardens, they entered the realm of social and moral consequence. Furthermore, making the garden the locus of the social community necessarily included citizens who were not often associated with conservationist concerns: women and schoolchildren. In this sense, the garden was a deeply democratic space, one that united the sundry concerns of conservationists and provided a means for a variety of citizens to bridge their personal and political commitments. Though very often private, the garden was simultaneously a social, female, democratic, and conservationist place.

Wright's entwining of education and conservation pushed her to create the nation's first privately owned songbird garden and sanctuary in her hometown of Fairfield, Connecticut, in 1914. She named it the Birdcraft Museum and Sanctuary, after her classic field guide, and envisioned the ten acres as providing visitors "an oasis in a desert of material things [so that] . . . the bird may lead its own life for that life's sake, and [so that] the joy of many such lives [will] overflow all arbitrary boundaries in its ethical benefit to the community and state."[62]

The idea of making urban sanctuaries for birds had long intrigued Wright. In creating her new sanctuary, she demanded that it feature native species of trees and shrubs, a practice now known as "birdscaping." Nor was the sanctuary meant to keep people out; it included a museum and walking trails for visitors. Indeed, Wright intended the sanctuary to be a welcoming place for all those who "crave a place to rest, watch and wait surrounded by the philosophy of nature." Rather than traipsing off to the wilderness, people could appreciate birds in a natural habitat close to home. It was an idea whose time had arrived; in his book on "useful birds," Forbush claimed, "Some of the most successful bird colonies have been established in city gardens. Birds about the home can be readily watched and protected at all seasons."[63] Wright's sanctuary made that vision a reality. Ornithologist Frank Chapman of the American Museum of Natural History concluded that the sanctuary was "an object lesson in conservation and museum methods." Despite the relative smallness of the reserve's ten acres, the "idea which they embody can reach to the ends of the earth."[64]

The idea that Birdcraft embodied was widely popular during the early twentieth century. Gardening was a genuine craze, and planting a "wild garden"—a garden of native plants, friendly to other wild things—swept the nation. "Wild" gardeners contributed to conservation by preserving wildflowers. "Each year the woods recede," noted one wild garden supporter. "The town reaches out and seizes land, and the haunts of wildflowers are plowed and paved."[65] One answer was to propagate endangered wildflowers in home and public gardens. Wild gardeners went so far as to advocate the planting of wildflowers along roadsides to beautify travel routes and to help propagate native species. Many articles encouraged the use of seeds to avoid transplanting wild species, so the ethics of wildland preservation extended to the garden. That ethic embraced the entire ecological community: much of the rhetoric surrounding wild gardens was decidedly ecological, focusing on such matters as the positive role of insects.[66]

Despite Wright's ecological perspective, some of the early management practices at Birdcraft might shock contemporary sensibilities. "If you would keep the wild birds in your garden," advised Wright, "you must exclude from it four things: English sparrows, the usual gardeners, cats, and firearms."[67] Birdscaping attracted native birds but also invasive species such as English sparrows and European starlings, and in its early years, the Birdcraft staff killed impressive numbers of them. More important, Wright's anxieties over nonnative species corresponded with her nativist concerns about the "usual gardeners"—specifically, the ostensibly uncultured immigrants (often Italians) who, in her mind (and in the minds of some other leading conservationists), posed a threat to American wildlife. Wright worried that an inability to read English prevented "the newly arrived foreign element," who, "together with cats, are the birds' worst enemies," from being swayed by the reasoned appeals of conservationists.[68] Furthermore, in educating "the average child of the public school," Wright advised teachers to remember the "many races [of which] this average child is compounded,—races with instincts concerning what are called lower animals, quite beyond the moral comprehension of the animal-loving Anglo Saxon."[69] Wright clearly conflated invasive species with "invasive" immigrants. Although Wright's strategy of cultural change toward conservation remained sound, it could also devolve into reactionary assumptions about which cultures could enact such newfound sympathies.

At the time, the majority considered black Americans to be incapable of the higher moral sentiments supposedly characteristic of Anglo-Saxons, and many people who are now recognized as heroic fought throughout their lifetimes to reverse such insidious and false assumptions. Among those with the most controversial legacy was Booker T. Washington, whose famous public feud with W. E. B. DuBois still defines much of his reputation. He is often remembered as the "great accommodator" due to his provisional acceptance of the existing social hierarchy. In the most common view, Washington's theories of education supported his supposed acceptance of racial segregation. Yet a closer examination of Washington's pedagogy, especially his support of gardening as a way to unify the theory and practice of agricultural nature study, reveal that his nature study was propagated for social development, not to acquiesce to existing hierarchies.

Most of Washington's ecological critics focus on his privileging of agricultural production as a means of rural uplift and interracial economic cooperation at the expense of sustainability. Washington certainly shared the dominant belief in transforming nature for the end of human production. Calling on whites to cast down their buckets among those who have "tilled your fields, cleared your forests . . . and brought forth treasures from the bowels of the earth," Washington emphasized material advancement through wiser, more efficient exploitation of the natural world. Yet his utilitarian views were tempered by an abiding, genuine, effusive enthusiasm for nature, particularly the garden. For Washington, nature was a storehouse of materials awaiting capitalist transformation as well as an invaluable site of intellectual and spiritual refuge. As an example, Washington described his family outings on Sunday afternoons as an enjoyable escape "into the woods, where we can live for a while near the heart of nature, where no one can disturb or vex us, surrounded by pure air, the trees, the shrubbery, the flowers, and the sweet fragrance that springs up from a hundred plants, enjoying the chirp of the crickets and the songs of the birds. This is solid rest."[70]

Like other nature study enthusiasts, Washington found in the natural order a place that allowed for recuperation and aesthetic enjoyment. Furthermore, nature consented to these expressions precisely because it did not enact social claims on people—in nature, "no one can disturb or vex us"—a trait that, given the violent, racially heated atmosphere of the fin de siècle South and the taxing demands of Washington's career, he likely found especially appealing.

Washington enjoyed a lifelong love of nature. He had "always been intensely fond of outdoor life," a quality he attributed to having "had many close and interesting acquaintances with animals" during his enslaved childhood. In adult life, Washington liked to tend to his barnyard animals early in the day, hunting for freshly laid eggs and offering a hearty "'Good morning' to my pigs, cows, and horse." He bred chickens and "was deeply interested in the different kinds of fowls," although "the pig, I think, is my favorite animal." This cheery bonhomie extended to all of rural life. Yet Washington held "little respect for the farmer who is satisfied with merely 'making a living.'" Such farmers were not really living, in that they did not appreciate their surroundings and deprived themselves of the pleasures of knowing nature. The best farmer, then, must prosper and have "time for study and investigation" as well as access to the arts and travel. Moreover, Washington's emphasis on the pleasures and possibilities of rural life led him to an ecological critique of tenant farming and monoculture. Lack of property encouraged shortsightedness, an attitude that extended to the land itself: "Instead of returning the cotton-seed to the ground to help enrich the soil, [the tenant farmer] sold this valuable fertilizer. The land, of course, was more impoverished each year. Ditching and terracing received little attention."[71] Tools and animals were treated poorly as well.

Wise farming methods could also exert a positive effect on race relations. Washington famously believed that the key to social equality was for "the Negro, when given a chance, to help himself, and make himself indispensable to the community." Knowing how to prosper was a sure way to make oneself indispensable. To illustrate, Washington wrote about black sweet potato farmers who gained great yields, and hence great profits, by applying the methods of scientific agriculture developed by George Washington Carver. "The deep interest shown by the neighboring white farmers has been most gratifying," reported Washington. "I do not believe that a single white farmer who visited the field to see the unusual yields ever thought of having any prejudice or feeling against this colored man . . . there were, on the other hand, many evidences of respect."[72] Washington's attitude entailed much more than capitulation to the dominant social order; it embodied the progressive belief that schools imparted the knowledge that regenerated the social order and hence could be key institutions in the democratization of society. Education would simultaneously alleviate black rural poverty and develop the mutual regard that would assuage the race problem.

Though concerned primarily with public matters such as racial uplift, Washington did not subsume his love of nature into social affairs; his enthusiasm for his garden, for example, was unbounded. "I do not believe that any one who has not worked in a garden can begin to understand how much pleasure and strength of body and mind and soul can be derived from one's garden, no matter how small it may be." When a garden thrived, "a feeling of kinship [arose] between the man and his plants." The growth of cultivated plants—the "newness" and "expectancy" of "the appearance of bud, or blossom or fruit"— brought to Washington not only kinship but also a "daily inspiration whose sympathetic significance it is impossible to convey in words." Indeed, the garden was so important because "I feel a nearness and kinship to the plants which makes them seem to me like members of my own family." The pleasures were numerous. When he ate the products of his garden, he felt as if he were "getting near to the heart of nature." The taste of vegetables one had raised made the "dishes found in the most expensive restaurants seem flavorless." And no matter how demanding his work, he was able to persevere through a long day "because of the delightful anticipation of another half hour or so in my garden." Because he derived "so much pleasure" from time spent in his garden plot, "I frequently find myself beseeching Mrs. Washington to delay the dinner hour that I may take advantage of the last bit of daylight for my outdoor work."[73]

Washington's views of the natural world were thoroughly articulated through his educational philosophy. Like John Dewey and other nature study proponents of the garden, Washington sought to reconcile the split between subject and object, mind and body—or, in the more tangible terms of his educational philosophy, the divide between mental and physical labor. "While I have never wished to underestimate the awakening power of purely mental training," wrote Washington, "I believe that . . . visible tangible contact with nature gave me inspirations and ambitions." From his own experience—and from the European theorists of education he studied—Washington drew a universal lesson: "I favor the most thorough mental training and the highest development of mind, but I want to see these linked with the common things of the universal life about our doors." The split between theory and practice was also manifest in the attitudes of his students. They believed "that school was a place where one was expected to do nothing but study books; where one expected not to study things, but to study about things. Least of all did the students feel that a school was a place where one would be taught actually to *do* things."[74] For many students, education meant no longer having to work with their hands, an attitude that thwarted the application of scientific agriculture.

Washington was shocked to find how little the development of the mind was linked to the outdoors. In the agriculturally abundant South, whose residents should be dining on local foods such as "pigs, chickens, ducks, geese, berries, peaches, plums, vegetables, [and] nuts," teachers and students settled for "salt pork from Chicago" or "canned chicken and tomatoes from Omaha." Nor was this just a utilitarian (and epicurean) issue: the natural beauty of the landscape did not enter into local consciousness. Locally abundant shrubs and wildflowers, for example, never "found their way into the houses or upon the dinner tables."[75] All the textbooks Washington surveyed depicted the good life as an urban life, effectively divorcing students and teachers from their environs.

Because educators traditionally separated practice from theory, students became engulfed in the frustration of having "an awakened mind" but no functional way to realize their new knowledge. "The result," concluded Washington, "is that the young man, instead of being educated to love agriculture, is educated out of sympathy with it."[76] Because he believed in the basic pragmatic assumption that human intelligence is developed through interaction with environments, Washington concluded that education without tangible application estranged students from their surroundings. Alienated by the split between theory and practice, rural denizens decamped for the city. This depopulation of the countryside removed citizens from the ennobling touch of nature. Life in urban environments exacted a physical and moral toll. "How many times I wished . . .

that by some power of magic I might remove the great bulk of these [urban] people into the country districts and plant them upon the soil, upon the solid and never deceptive foundation of Mother Nature."[77] To Washington, farmers were "real," a distinct contrast to the "artificial" world of urban pretense.

Washington sought to use education to combat urbanization and alienation, but he understood that pedagogy must not replicate the culture that had created the problems in the first place. Washington thus called for an educational philosophy of "Head and Hands Together," a union of mind and body manifested in a variety of subjects such as trigonometry and basic engineering, which were taught by taking students outside to survey lots and roads. Most important, Washington made nature study a central component of his Tuskegee Institute's educational work. Nature study had both its practical side—to "train the faculty of observation," "gain knowledge," and "cultivate a practical interest in agriculture"—and its less tangible but equally important goal of creating "an interest in and love of nature." Tuskegee prioritized the local before the universal: Washington wished to impart "a clear and definite acquaintance with home surroundings (plants, animals, minerals, natural phenomena, and the human body)" before moving on to "things more distant." Moreover, teachers determined the specific subject matter, depending on the needs of the students and "according to the seasons." This pedagogical emphasis on the local included gardens, which were "prominent features of the courses in Nature Study."[78]

Crucially, immersion in nature could teach people real happiness—a lesson Washington strove to impart to his students. While lecturing at Tuskegee he described the beauty one could find in the "common things" of life—even in such ostensibly uninteresting things as a mud puddle. "You would be surprised if you were to make a careful investigation," averred Washington, "how many really charming things you can find in a stagnant pool of water." The point was to find beauty and intellectual stimulation by immersing oneself in the nearby things of nature. This approach to life created happiness. Thus education was training to "get real happiness out of the common things of life—everything: out of grass, out of trees, out of animals."[79] Moreover, Washington intended this to be an ongoing process: "in connection with Nature Study . . . the pupils are urged to be on the alert to detect something new, something which they have seen often, but can afterward view in a new light because of the information obtained."[80] The goal was to cultivate curious individuals who found in science the ability to see anew the places they inhabited. Finding joy in common things also included finding joy in work, such as the labor in his garden that Washington so cherished.

Like other nature study advocates, Washington emphasized the importance of students interacting with actual things instead of representations. "I have seen teachers keep children caged up on a beautiful bright day in June . . . making them learn . . . about lakes, or islands, by means of a map or globe." Rather than trying to explain such abstract concepts with symbols, the teacher should have walked the students to "a brook not a mile away," where they could "pull off their shoes and stockings and wade through the water" and experience "real islands, peninsulas and bays." "Besides the delight of wading through the water, and of being out in the pure bracing air," declared Washington, "they would learn by this method more about these natural divisions of the earth in five minutes than they could learn in an hour in books."[81]

Much of the agricultural training adopted by Washington focused on the immediate improvement of agricultural productivity: animals were studied for their practical uses and to improve their breeding, soils for "the increase of fertility," with the overarching aim of "the general development of agriculture." Yet even at his most expedient, Washington promoted gardening to cultivate "a sense of the beautiful" that is also "given expression in floriculture, to the end that more of nature's beauty shall pervade the home and its surroundings."[82] For Washington (like Dewey), cultivating the beautiful was an instrumental end in itself, because people required nature's beauty in their lives. Nature study could help farmers prosper both financially and spiritually.

Those instrumental ends of nature study included social reform. Tuskegee attempted to unite the everyday experiences of students with their educational activities and their social lives. This pedagogy was a bridge between specialized knowledge and practical problems and a way to integrate educational praxis in the remaking of communities and the society at large. Washington thus stressed that his students embrace "the power of doing things." Knowledge of chemistry, for example, could be applied to important questions facing developing communities: "Is this fertilizer of high grade? How shall the sick-room be disinfected? How shall we destroy the cabbage-devouring worm?"[83] The interests of individuals were stimulated by the needs of the community, and meeting those needs created pragmatic intelligence—the ability to solve problems and develop deeper and wider thought. Scientifically based vocational education, in an era in which only 5 percent of the public had high school diplomas, was a means to widen intellectual life and foster social development. Rather than compartmentalizing information, it was a way to democratize the production and utilization of knowledge and hence society.

Washington explicitly included women among those who needed to combine practical knowledge with nature's touch. It was "unwise in a climate like ours in the South to narrow the work of our girls, and confine them to indoor occupations." The idea that women belonged inside was a legacy of "the period of slavery," when the prevailing notion was that "women . . . should do as little work as possible with their hands." As it had with men, urban industrialism blunted women's human qualities until they became "little more than a machine." Under the yoke of supervisors, a woman's "planning and thinking is done for her." Yet outdoor occupations such as raising poultry demanded patience and planning and hence developed "self reliance, independence and initiative." Life in the "sweet, pure, bracing air" was morally and physically superior to being confined in the "factory or store."[84] According to Margaret Murray Washington, "gardening and greenhouse work" was so popular among female Tuskegee students that "there are constant applications for transfers from the sewing divisions to this outside work."[85] Like their male counterparts, women thrived when in contact with the green world of nature.

Using contact with nature to improve life also fit with the larger strategy of the country life movement, whose goal was to create an interest in rural life among children. Such enlightened children would choose to continue to farm for their livelihood. Washington was intent on "making the farm home the most attractive spot on earth." The "trained and educated" rural women who were "enthusiastically taking up the profession of farming" would bring "new charms" to country life, and the "exodus of young men to cities will be materially lessened." By imparting the latest science of agriculture—making it more profitable—and by developing an appreciation for nature—making rural living more enjoyable—rural communities could counteract the cultural attractions of the city and thereby enhance the desirability of farm life. In this manner, education was a primary weapon in the battle to revitalize rural life.

Another potential weapon in the battle to revitalize country life was the rural church. In advocating reform of this key institution, Washington was again in keeping with the mainstream country life movement, which gave considerable attention to the travails of the rural church. But like so many educators, the church missed the necessary connection between rural people and the land. Because "the Negro minister is trained to meet conditions which exist in New York or Chicago," he scarcely attends to the concerns of rural people. The church was yet another social institution that failed to address the immediate, concrete concerns of rural people. To combat this problem, Washington wished the rural minister "could be taught to get the larger portion of his own living from the soil—to love outdoor work, and to make his garden, his farm, and his farmhouse object lessons for his people."[86] Such a situation would ground the minister in the concerns of his congregation, guarantee his independence, and prevent the idleness that might enhance temptation.

Washington's goal for reforming the rural ministry exemplified the larger goals of the school gardening movement. The garden was used to engender love for and sympathy with nature. It was also an explicit means of reforming social life. This idea united school gardeners, Mabel Osgood Wright, Booker T. Washington, and countless other Americans who saw the garden as a means to re-think and re-create the social sphere. The garden was central to the personal and political strategies of Progressive Era conservationists. In its imagining of the social sphere, the garden was no different from any other human construc-tion of the natural world, which we always and inevitably understand through the lens of culture. But in the garden, activists found an explicit way to use na-ture while thinking about the social order, including the social order's malad-justment to the natural world. In this manner, conservationists confounded the split between nature and culture and embraced social reform as part of their agenda.

In his critique of wilderness, William Cronon correctly warns us, "Wilderness gets us into trouble only if we imagine that this experience of wonder and oth-erness is limited to the remote corners of the planet, or that it somehow depends on pristine landscapes we ourselves do not inhabit."[87] Insofar as this critique extends to the founding of environmentalism, the history of Progressive Era gardening suggests that he need not worry. The positive environments that pro-gressives sought could come in the form of a distant wilderness or a garden in a vacant lot. Conservationists understood that the garden, like wilderness, is a cultural as well as a natural artifact. They found purpose, meaning, and spiritual enlightenment ("I seem to know the mind of the Creator better for my garden-ing," wrote one reflective gardener[88]) in this most quotidian example of nature: the schoolyard and neighborhood garden. Spiritual enlightenment does not free one from the deep problems of the culture itself. Cronon is correct to warn us of unexamined assumptions that feed into our understandings of the green world, and as the nativist rhetoric surrounding gardening shows, no cultural construction of nature is immune from the problems that plague the culture at large.

Despite such universal troubles, the garden and its progressive champions have two important lessons to teach us. The first is the garden's specificity. Notwithstanding the lofty rhetoric surrounding the values of gardening, the garden itself is always rooted in a place. And gardens exist because of the culti-vation of the people who tend them. The fact that they can thrive in grounds not usually thought of as natural—schoolyards, urban lots—demonstrates that the very location of the garden undermines the duality that supposedly debases the wilderness idea and, with it, the moral vision of conservation. Moreover, the places gardens inhabit are social as well as natural. Progressives championed gardens because they cultivated social relationships along with wildflowers. Community gardens have always been just that—communities. Gardens are places of repose—and places of entrepreneurship and of learning. The environmental imagination has always been rooted in specific places; the history of school gardens shows how flexible and ingenious that imagination has been. Rather than a legacy to lament, the conservationist understanding of nature has much to offer the present day.

Last, gardens themselves undermine the bifurcation of wilderness and civilization and hence the dualism that ostensibly informs environmentalist discourse. The landscapes that conservationists cared for were diverse and elicited diverse responses from their caretakers. Gardens demonstrate the varieties of nature valued by conservationists, and they show that the conservation movement often eschewed simple and unthinking dualisms that divided nature from civilization. Indeed, some theorists have proposed that the garden is a "third nature": not the "first nature" (wilderness) of the earth untouched by people or the "second nature" of the built environment, but a third nature that combines first and second natures.[89] This characteristic is especially important, given the powerful symbolic importance of the garden in Western culture. Third nature is not nature "out there," removed from prosaic experience, but the embodiment of humanity embedded in the natural order. Insofar as school gardens imparted this lesson, they demand a more prominent place in the history of conservation and contemporary environmental discourse.

Nature study advocates credited Louis Agassiz with inspiring their bedrock pedagogic principle: that people should study actual nature, not representations of it. (Library of Congress, LC-USZ62-103949)

Anna Botsford Comstock was among the greatest of nature study's practitioners and theorists. Her *Handbook of Nature Study* remains in print. From the *Nature-Study Review,* vol. 11, no. 2 (February 1915).

Nature study advocates considered direct interaction with nature the foundation for all higher learning and moral development. From Alice G. McCloskey, "Nature Study," chap. 1 of *Public School Methods,* new ed., vol. 2 (Chicago: School Methods Co., 1921).

The outdoors, where children could romp, explore, and discover, was the ideal classroom for nature study because students interacted with nature, not words on a page. From Adeline F. Schively, "The Nature-Study Course of the School of Observation and Practice," *Nature-Study Review* 10, no. 9 (December 1914): 351.

Nature study advocates believed that if children made friends with nature—like this young girl and her bobwhite "chum"—they would work to protect it, like the children advocating on behalf of street trees with their "shade tree protectors' league." From C. F. Hodge, "Nature-Study and the Bobwhite," *Nature-Study Review* 6, no. 3 (March 1910): 57, and Agnes V. Luther, "The Shade Trees Protectors' League of Newark, N. J.," *Nature-Study Review* 7, no. 2 (February 1911): 29.

Children participated in a wide variety of nature study activities. Here the Bird Lover's Club of Peru, Nebraska, shows off well-crafted birdhouses. From B. Clifford Hendricks, "News and Notes for September," *Nature-Study Review* 11, no. 6 (September 1915): 300.

Millions of schoolchildren once commemorated Bird Day—a day devoted to celebrating birds and nature. Here, children in Carrick, Pennsylvania, receive bird boxes to post and cherry trees to plant. The best nature study activities made children active participants in their learning. From William T. Hornaday, *Our Vanishing Wild Life: Its Extermination and Preservation* (New York: Charles Scribner's Sons, 1913), 381.

Ernest Thompson Seton believed in recapitulation—that children repeated the evolutionary history of the human race. He thus insisted that children emulate, through woodcraft, the lives of American Indians, which he considered more physically and spiritually free than the lives of industrial citizens. In this photo, Seton (*back and right*) is banging the drum. (Library of Congress, LC-DIG-ggbain 01502)

Booker T. Washington was a staunch advocate of using nature study to give children an intellectual, economic, and spiritual investment in rural life. In this photograph, Washington is to the right. From Booker T. Washington, *Working with the Hands: Being a Sequel to "Up from Slavery" Covering the Author's Experience in Industrial Training at Tuskegee* (New York: Doubleday, Page & Co., 1904).

Booker T. Washington was a vociferous proponent of gardening, which provided
him close communion with nature and spiritual fulfillment. *Top*, Washington
feeding his chickens. *Middle*, Washington in his onion patch. *Bottom*, Washington
in his lettuce bed. From Emmett J. Scott and Lyman Beecher Stowe, *Booker T.
Washington: Builder of a Civilization* (New York: Doubleday, Page & Co., 1916).

Gardening could fit with age-appropriate pedagogy. Nature study advocates felt
that it taught students the values of thrift and hard work as well as basic natural
history. Clockwise from top left: the kindergarten harvest; the first-grade radish
harvest; seventh-grade experimenters; and gathering peas for the luncheon.
From Laura E. Woodward, "The Uses of the School Garden Harvest," *Nature-
Study Review* 6, no. 8 (November 1910): 223.

Many nature study advocates used gardens to bring nature into the lives of urban children. Gardens were also useful tools for imparting basic scientific ideas, such as pollination. From Louise Klein Miller, "School-Gardens of Cleveland, Ohio," *Nature-Study Review* 4, no. 3 (March 1908): 79.

Nature study advocates often pictured school gardeners as young farmers. Gardening provided them the twice-ennobling factors of contact with the soil and hard work. From E. A. Howes, "The School-Garden at Bowesville, Canada," *Nature-Study Review* 2, no. 2 (February 1906): 48.

The city schools of Los Angeles used live animal exhibits to help generate interest in nature study. All 127 Los Angeles grammar schools organized nature clubs that went on field trips and collected specimens for school museums. From Charles Lincoln Edwards, "The Los Angeles Nature-Study Exhibition," *Nature-Study Review* 10, no. 7 (October 1914): 268.

Nature study teachers often integrated nature study with other areas of progressive reform. Gardening not only taught basic botany and hard work but could beautify urban areas and provide otherwise bored children with purposeful recreation. From Emilie Yunker, "School Gardens in Louisville, KY.," *Nature-Study Review* 6, no. 4 (April 1910): 97.

Many teachers used the things of nature in art class. Copying from specimens taught students to observe closely. "The pencil," counseled Louis Agassiz, "is one of the best of eyes." (Quoted by Mary Mapes Dodge in "Essay on Agassiz," *St. Nicholas* 10, no. 9 [July 1883]: 718.) From J. Liberty Tadd, *New Methods in Education: Art, Real Manual Training, Nature Study* (Springfield, Mass.: Orange Judd Co., 1904), 49.

If children could not get to nature, nature could be brought to children. School teachers in New York City organized thousands of flower shows so students could learn from actual nature, not representations of it. From Delia Isabel Griffin, "Nature-Study in a Museum," *Nature-Study Review* 5, no. 2 (February 1909): 61.

CHAPTER SIX

The Art of Life

Nature Study, Photography, and

Conservation in the Progressive Era

To many the camera has been the companion that has led
them out, and little by little awakened an appreciation of
the beauties of nature.

—Arthur H. Farrow, "Nature Photography"

In September 1905 the *School Arts Book* published an address by Harvard University president Charles W. Eliot in which he vigorously promoted the need for the citizens of democratic societies to cultivate a sense of beauty. Though most often remembered as a robust proponent of a "new education" based on the theoretical and applied sciences, Eliot also advocated "public happiness" by increasing the "number, variety and intensity of those sensations and emotions which give innocent and frequently recurring pleasure." Eliot's plan to help citizens develop innocent pleasure consisted of adding reverence for beauty to the Puritan tradition of learning. Beyond enhancing individual happiness, the cultivation of beauty would aid society by restraining the eager drive for "material possessions and coarser bodily satisfactions." Like many educators steeped in the classical tradition of learning, Eliot assumed that enlightened self-constraint could overcome the troublesome impulses of the body. And like many progressive moralists, he looked to formalized education to fulfill his goals: "The best place to inculcate the love of the beautiful," he concluded, "is in the schoolroom" through aesthetic education.[1]

Although the schoolroom was the best place to instill a love of beauty, the best place to encounter it was in nature. Eliot instructed his readers to habitually observe the "heavens" and "landscape," for they included "beauty of form, of texture, of color and of luster." Niagara Falls, Colorado's Garden of the Gods, and Yosemite National Park exemplified public landscapes that enhanced happiness. Eliot also understood that public happiness demanded political engagement. To continue granting innocent pleasure, landscapes needed to be preserved and available to the public. Social well-being demanded access to the beauty of unspoiled nature; in short, it required conservation. Eliot viewed conservation as one of the best ways to cultivate "democratic happiness." Although aesthetic pleasure derived from great works of art remained the privilege of the elite, almost any American could experience beauty through contact with the untrammeled outdoors. The "public ownership" of land, asserted Eliot, "will provide in our country the forests, parks, river banks, and beaches which will give the urban and suburban population access to landscape beauty."[2]

The only problem Eliot perceived with the promotion of beauty was the mistaken belief that "the beautiful is an effeminate sentiment." Eliot countered such notions with the assertion that the sense of beauty was a manly attribute. "Love of the beautiful is not inconsistent with reverence for honor, justice and faithfulness," lectured Eliot. Indeed, many "beautiful objects are coarse, rough, stern, or fierce, like the sea, the thunderstorms, or the bare mountain crag."[3] Although beauty could promote conservation, it remained fraught with the complex politics of culture and sensibility.

Eliot's support of public lands through an ideological mix of aesthetic pleasure, democratic principle, and public education offered a new path into the thickets of Progressive Era conservation. Conservationists recognized that they lived in a society badly out of step with ecological realities. Concern over nature's intangible qualities such as beauty pushed the politics of conservation beyond resource use and into cultural criticism. Longing for aesthetic splendor was frequently attached to a critique of modern industrial culture. Nature study conservationists deplored the instrumental values that accompanied the rapid industrialization of the late nineteenth century. They believed that Americans, especially the workaday masses, needed outlets for their creativity to enhance their spiritual and physical health. Popular essayist and poet Bliss Carman vividly expressed their perspective when he warned, "with the body made a slave to machinery, the spirit defrauded of any scope for its pent up force, we have nothing to hope for in the industrial world." To counteract such despair, one must make "an art of life"; that is, labor must be modified so that "it provides . . . expression of the spirit."[4]

Concern with expressions of the spirit—or, in Eliot's words, "democratic happiness"—and resource scarcity doubled the conservationist critique of industrial society. Resources were necessary not only for wise industrial use but also for the health of the human psyche. In this manner, conservationists yoked resource protection and cultural preservation together. Yet embracing aesthetic motivations for the protection of public lands brought conservationists into troubled cultural waters. Those waters were roiling with the gender expectations that so troubled Eliot, and as we shall see, aesthetic experience itself, such as knowing nature through the lens of a camera, was bound up in contradictory ways with the critique of industrial civilization that fueled the conservation movement.[5]

The camera provides an excellent means of testing my thesis. If conservationists were scientifically minded proponents of bureaucratic effectiveness, it follows that they should welcome the camera as a new tool to further efficiency. New technologies such as photography embodied the official pieties of industrial progress, and their wise use (that was the essential battle—to use them properly) should appeal to conservationists. Technologies were mere tools to be utilized for socially benign purposes. Conversely, if conservationists were steeped in romantic feelings, harboring deep criticisms of modernity, they should receive new technologies with substantial skepticism and wariness.

As we shall see, conservationists levied a number of critiques at photography. These criticisms did not reflect mere anxiousness about technology disrupting the pastoral countryside, the ideological ideal favored by romantic conservation advocates. Rather, conservationists employed two general lines of critique: First, they worried that the camera was another mechanism that debilitated physical vitality. Time spent with machines eroded the vigorous natural forces that fueled human energy, whereas time spent with nature enhanced vivacity. The question was whether the camera might become another industrial product whose use mediated the relationship between humans and nature and depressed the powerful currents of natural vitality. Second, nature study conservationists worried about the moral uses of the camera. If it worked to estrange people from the natural world, alienating sympathy, it contributed to the destruction of nature. Thus photography met with a moral critique as conservationists worked to make sure this new technology united people with the natural world rather than separating them from it. In these and other ways, aesthetic concerns played a central role in the cultural politics of conservation and education.

The nature study movement provided thinkers such as Eliot with a working model for using education to inculcate the public with aesthetic sensibilities and a consciousness for conservation. One result of sympathetic contact with nature was to bring beauty into people's lives. Nature study advocates disavowed the idea that the experience of beauty should be a distinct and specialized component of a well-rounded education. They preferred to see beauty as continuously integrated into all parts of life. Sympathy with nature and the aesthetic pleasure derived from it affected every part of being. Rather than existing in things, aesthetic pleasure arose from human experience—especially experience with nature.[6] People only needed to open themselves to nature to experience beauty. Yet in an industrialized culture, many people missed this part of life.[7] This recognition led to one of the most common conservationist (and later, environmentalist) tropes: once people sympathetically experience the green world, they will be moved to protect it. "The generations growing up to-day have in their hands the future of our forests and of our wild-life," wrote Ralph Hoffmann in the *School Arts Book.* "If they can be taught to love birds, flowers and trees, the love of these simple and beautiful things will leave less room in their hearts for the greed of gain and the pursuit of worldly pleasures."[8] For nature study thinkers such as Hoffmann, the cultivation of a sense of beauty combated the "coarser bodily satisfactions" while enhancing "innocent pleasures" such as the love of nature that promoted a conservation ethic.

Aesthetic education, then, was another tool to combat the rationalizing forces that desensitized the human relationship with the natural world. Philosophers such as John Dewey provided the nature study movement with an intellectual justification for this approach to aesthetic experience. Dewey recognized that cognitive and aesthetic experiences were qualitatively different, but he flatly rejected the compartmentalization of existence that separated aesthetic experiences from daily life. For Dewey, the source of art derived from the individual's striving for continuity. Put another way, art derived from the desire to break free of reified life. Aesthetic experience thus accomplished many of the same things as interaction with the natural world. "The function of art," argued Dewey, "has always been to break through the crust of conventionalized and routine consciousness. Common things, a flower, a gleam of moonlight, the song of a bird, not things rare and remote, are the means with which the deeper levels of life are touched so that they spring up as desire and thought. This process is art."[9] Aesthetic appreciation resulted from the immediate appreciation of things—and the appreciation of immediate things. Whether art or nature, the place to encounter it was close to home.

Like nature study's insistence on finding the natural world in daily life, Dewey's aesthetic principles insisted that beauty was not rarefied but an everyday, if special, occurrence. Aesthetic experience was accessible to anyone who sought it. But conventionalized life dampened that ability; hence interaction with varied natural and social environments was key to experiencing aesthetic pleasure.

> To grasp the sources of esthetic experience it is . . . necessary to have recourse to animal life below the human scale. The activities of the fox, the dog, and the thrush may stand as reminders and symbols of that unity of experience

which we so fractionalize when work is labor, and thought withdrawals from the world. The live animal is fully present, all there, in all of its actions: in its wary glances, its sharp sniffings, its abrupt cocking of ears.[10]

Aesthetic experience confounded rationalized existence. But without recourse to those experiences that broke through the integument of convention, "mankind might become a race of economic monsters, restlessly driving hard bargains with nature and with one another, bored with leisure or capable of putting it to use only in ostentatious display and extravagant dissipation."[11] The same forces that saved nature prevented humans from degenerating into blind cogs of mindless consumption.

Yet those forces could also work together for human betterment. Nature study advocates believed that aesthetic appreciation could contribute to the scientific worldview that made technology possible. Progressive advocates of school arts programs held that, like nature study, art instruction promoted skills in observation, analysis, and representation, which inspired artistic expression and fostered scientific investigation. Writing in *Education,* University of Wisconsin professor M. V. O'Shea concluded, "Drawing bears a very vital relation to nature-study; skill in representation may be secured by such a relation; science receives invaluable aid thereby, and drawing is really thus its handmaid, whatever else it may be in addition."[12] Similar sentiments existed throughout the history of the nature study movement. Nature study patriarch Louis Agassiz counseled that the "pencil is one of the best of eyes."[13] One contributor to the *School Arts Book* bluntly asserted that "the pen becomes a dissecting instrument, tracing carefully the flower, leaf, stem, or their parts."[14] Aesthetic appreciation cultivated essential countermodern attributes and prepared students for the rigors of scientific observation.

Drawing promoted the critical skills in accurate observation and representation necessary for analytic reflection as well as for material success in the modern world. As an editorial in the *Nation* put it, both nature study and artistic seeing "have the same enemy—lazy and abbreviated habits of vision; both fight the same battle—to intensify the powers of observation."[15] Many educators felt that enhancing the public's capacity for critical and aesthetic observation was supremely important; as one frankly stated, "The average man sees imperfectly and images dimly."[16] Moreover, accurate observation rooted people in the details of time and place that were so easily displaced by the bustle of industrial life. The *Nation* argued that critical observation and aesthetic sensibility combated the modern feeling of "homelessness" by promoting "intimacy with all that is beautiful, interesting and instructive in one's natural surroundings," a practice that can "create the sense of home."[17] Natural and man-made beauty grew from each other and granted the possibilities for human satisfaction that industrial life alone could not match.

Other commentators furthered the *Nation*'s view, urging Americans to discover in nature the satisfactions that industrial society suppressed. Critic, columnist (for *Ladies' Home Journal*), and editor Hamilton Wright Mabie wrote extensively on this theme, recommending that Americans find in the outdoor world the "delight" of the naturalist, the "sense of exhilaration" of the scientist, and the "deepening beauty" of the artist. The ineffable gifts that nature provided its admirers were "more vital and important than any of these special knowledges," yet "accessible" to the "multitude." Open conversance with nature granted to people "a resource of inexhaustible delight and enrichment." To establish intimacy with nature, then, "ought to be as much a part of every education as the teaching of the rudiments of formal knowledge."[18]

Rather than cultivating such consciousness through education, industrial civilization inhibited the realization of nature's spiritual power. Mabie thus urged citizens to awaken "to the wonder of the world" and "feel afresh its subtle and penetrating charm. From that moment the familiar earth and sky become miracles once more." The way to ensure the miracle was to be "constantly in the presence and company of Nature." People needed to seize opportunities to get to the "woods," "fields," "streams," and "most secluded places." Nature would revitalize the pilgrim who sought its charms; "the beautiful order of seasons, stars and flowers and verdure which surround us, and which most of us barely notice, become a constant companionship in their most secret thoughts and in their daily occupations."[19] Mabie's message resonated widely; he published his meditations in such outlets as the *Christian Union* and *Outlook* and was received "as Emerson's most popular successor on the Chautauqua circuit."[20]

The appreciation of natural beauty thus fulfilled the fundamental drives that propelled nature study conservation: it promoted science while simultaneously engaging the romantic longings of turn-of-the-century nature lovers. The development of aesthetic sensibilities became one way for nature study advocates to promote their discipline and a methodology by which they taught children to know nature. Those who had close contact with nature—a place unburdened by industrial regimentation—could express spirit and thereby receive the gifts of "health" and "sanity" that nature provided.

Progressive educators theorized art as a way to promote democratic happiness as well as a way to prepare students for science and conservation. Given this harmony of interests, the merging of art education with popular and curricular nature study was inevitable. Both took contact with nature as the best way to educate the young. As Royal B. Farnum asserted in the *School Arts Book:*

> To the painter, the designer, the sculptor, and the poet, no less than to the botanist, the biologist, and the zoologist, nature is ever the chief source of inspiration. . . . For this reason, perhaps more than any other, nature study found its way into the curricula of our public schools. . . . Nature, like art, is so full of the larger, the nobler meaning of life, that we can-not afford to do without it.[21]

The ideology of using art as a bulwark against routine, mind-numbing labor was most widely expressed in turn-of-the-century America as the revival of handicrafts, known as the arts and crafts movement. Like its cousins in the nature study and school arts movements, arts and crafts ideology mixed a progressive belief in science and technology with a deeply felt anxiety about the place of creativity in a mechanized world. Arts and crafts aficionados embraced technical accuracy yet longed for the idiosyncrasies of the unique craftsman. Politically, the arts and crafts movement was similarly mixed. Arts and crafts enthusiasts often combined patrician disdain for commonplace labor with utopian longings for alternatives to the modern busywork that reduced skilled labor to bland, perfunctory repetition. However, the movement, often drawing on Henry Thoreau, kept its critical and utopian edge, as Jackson Lears demonstrated in his authoritative discussion of arts and crafts.[22] Yet the most visible political outcomes of the movement occurred within the realm of education. Nearly all proponents of arts and crafts embraced educational reform as the solvent for the social tensions they bewailed. Arts and crafts enthusiasts held that individuals could revitalize their creativity through artistic expression. They also agreed that the best means of ensuring that such expression was unique was direct observation and interaction with the primordial world of nature.

Like nature study, the arts and crafts movement drew inspiration from prominent nineteenth-century European intellectuals. British poet, craftsman, and socialist agitator William Morris (1834–1896) popularized the idea that craftsmanship might be a way to ease the drudgery of industrial production. Morris hated the capitalism of his day for its "crude utilitarianism, its mass production, its compulsory labor and its machine dominated mind." Seeking to combine his vision of craft revitalization with libertarian socialism, Morris bewailed what he viewed as the aesthetic impoverishment of capitalist production. In turn, he championed the medieval guild as an example of the communal production of goods for use that resisted both feudal and capitalist oppression alike. The core of Morris's critique focused on the right of workers to joyful and productive labor rather than the excessive rationalization that incapacitated creativity and turned workers into what Morris called "wretched, lopsided creatures."[23]

Morris's elevation of the aesthetic into a political position took into consideration the product of the worker and the worker's natural surroundings. Indeed, like Charles Eliot, Morris explicitly linked the degradation of aesthetic pleasure to the degradation of nature. In a lecture titled "Art under a Plutocracy" delivered on 14 November 1883 before the liberal Russell Club in Oxford, Morris intoned:

> To keep the air pure and the rivers clean, to take some pains to keep the meadows and tillage as pleasant as reasonable use will allow them to be; to allow peaceable citizens freedom to wander where they will, so they do no hurt to garden or cornfield; nay, even to leave here or there some piece of waste or mountain sacredly free from fence or tillage as a memory of man's ruder struggles with nature in his earlier days: is it too much to ask civilization to be so far thoughtful of man's pleasure and rest, to help so far as this her children to whom she has most often set such heavy task of grinding labor? Surely not an unreasonable asking. But not a whit of it shall we get under the present system of society.[24]

Morris continued by deploring the squalid degradation of urban and suburban sprawl, which he contended was ruining the peaceful and once beautiful countryside. Like the nature study and school arts proponents his work helped inspire, Morris repeatedly emphasized that the degradation of the outdoor world produced indifference to aesthetic pleasure, for "the well of art is poisoned at its spring."[25] Artists could not produce works of beauty if they had to live in an ugly and debased physical environment.

Morris directly affected the nature study and school arts movements through his influence on educator Henry Turner Bailey. Bailey's career mirrored the rise of art education in America. Public art education surged in the late nineteenth century following Massachusetts' passage of the 1870 drawing act, which required that free drawing classes be offered in every town with a population in excess of ten thousand. Like the arts and crafts movement, the campaign for school arts stressed the practical as well as aesthetic values gained from art instruction. One widely read book claimed that "drawing has its practical uses in every occupation. It opens inexhaustible sources of utility."[26] Another work assured farmers that drawing "assists the farmer to arrange with taste and beauty his grounds."[27] More broadly, periodicals observed that workers who learned to draw could plan more carefully, avoid waste, and produce saleable ideas for their bosses or clients.

Henry Turner Bailey, the son of a New England Baptist clergyman, grew up in Scituate, Massachusetts. A devout Baptist like his father, Bailey believed that nature was part of God's revelation to humankind. Like Morris, he championed with evangelical zeal the power of art to counteract the ugliness of industrial life. Unlike Morris, Bailey never carried his ideas to a radical political conclusion. He taught for a short period in the public schools of Boston and Lowell before being appointed in 1887, at age twenty-one, Massachusetts' supervisor of drawing. He held this position until 1903, when he devoted himself full-time to the editorship of the *School Arts Book*. Eventually, Bailey took a position as dean of the Cleveland School of Art before retiring in 1930. Throughout his life he traveled in the United States and Europe spreading the school arts gospel. Among other duties, he served in 1898 as the official U.S. representative to the First International Conference on Art Education, held in Brussels. Despite these travels, he also maintained a base in his hometown of North Scituate. His estate, "Trustworth," served as a Mecca for artists and art teachers throughout the nation.

Bailey's writings revealed his countermodern attitude through his forthright, if evangelical, criticism of industrial life, especially urban life. He hated factories, railway lines, and cities above all because they were monstrously ugly. For Bailey, like Eliot, ugliness was an aesthetic crime and a spiritual one as well. Bailey argued that the possibility of encountering beauty needed to exist so that "when the child becomes a man, though shut in a factory by day, and lodged in a city of bricks by night, he will know that Yon ridge of purple landscape, / Yon sky between the walls, / holds all the hidden wonders / in scanty intervals."[28] Art made it possible to appreciate nature as a refuge from industrial blight.

Bailey also believed wholeheartedly in the spiritual mission of those who introduced students to nature: "What a privilege is Ours!" wrote Bailey of teachers. "To free the spirit of a single child is to do a divine thing."[29] Indeed, teachers were "blessed," for they could pass to children the "keys to the celestial city, that dream city more real than all our New Yorks and Chicagos, to which in all ages the human spirit has looked for satisfaction."[30] Thus, in Bailey's view, the "love of beauty" that derived from love of nature would enable the student to live a full life and battle "against superficiality, sham, and shortcut" in the design, creation, production, and consumption of industrial products.[31]

The school arts movement grew tremendously during the late nineteenth and early twentieth centuries with Bailey editing its primary theoretical and practical journal, the *School Arts Book*. By 1912 between thirty thousand and forty thousand teachers relied on the advice it offered. Bailey hailed manual arts such as drawing and draftsmanship as exemplars of the dignity of manual labor.

More broadly, the *School Arts Book* concurred that manual training or "integral education" could remove wealthy children from fruitless and parasitical leisure, prepare middle-class children with a variety of skills required for the professional world, and save poor children from tenement life.[32] Like contact with nature, the development of aesthetic sensibility could ennoble the denizens of industrial society.

Bailey used his editorship of the *School Arts Book* to champion the aesthetic lessons derived from the close observation of nature. He advised students to "study nature for materials and principles. Study historic ornaments to see how these have been applied."[33] Like Hamilton Wright Mabie, he held that aesthetic instruction would help students find God's beauty "in the ordinary surroundings of life—in crystals of the rocks, in humble grass, and modest flowers, in air and sea and stars."[34] Above all, Bailey loved nature's cycles and encouraged art teachers to organize lessons around the changing seasons.

Bailey's injunctions about drawing from nature were widely followed. Like other nature study advocates, he insisted that students encounter directly the objects they represented in art. Thus he encouraged teachers to bring nature into the classroom. Subjects for instruction frequently included plant fronds, tree branches, seedpods, bunches of long grasses, or flowers. Utilizing nature as the raw material of their lesson plans, Bailey and his followers bolstered and reinforced the nature study movement. Bailey hoped that the love of beauty would revolutionize the dreary site of education. "The day cannot be far," wrote Bailey, "when every school-room shall have beautiful pictures upon its walls, sculpture in its halls, and, as material for constant reference and inspiration, photographs of the master pieces of Greek and Italian art, casts of design and decoration from the great temples and public buildings of the works, and colored prints from that highly artistic nation, Japan. Meanwhile the rich and varied lavishness of nature is ours."[35] Bailey intended art to do for humans what nature had always done—break routine and provide beauty and relief from workaday concerns.

Bailey summarized his thought in a series of articles published in the 1920s. Most fundamentally, he maintained that the "education that will banish ugliness must begin with nature study." Citing the history of Western art from the Greeks to the Impressionists, he argued that "nature study clears the eye, reveals the elements of beauty, fires the imagination." Thus all children must have the right "to see the country—the house his Heavenly Father made for him—unobstructed by brick walls, unspoiled by filth and undimmed by smoke."[36] Enacting such an education required the complete reversal of standard practices. "When we are wiser" counseled Bailey, "we will not run the busses . . . to bring rural children into city schools, but to take city children into the country that they may learn to know and love God's first revelations to man, and feel at home in the natural world because [they are] well acquainted with it."[37]

Bailey concurred with Eliot about the importance of access to landscape beauty because it enhanced democratic happiness against the ugliness of industrial society. Yet at times, industrial technology could help create beauty. A newly popular invention like the camera, for example, could be used to promote an aesthetic connection with nature or contribute to the dull, instrumental precision of industrial processes. Nature study advocates embraced the camera but debated whether it would be a craftsman's tool that enhanced the aesthetic knowledge of nature or a blunt instrument that interfered with the direct experience of the outdoor world. Cameras might provide accurate representations of the outdoor world but replace people's conscious interaction with nature with a fascination for technology.

The debate over the use of cameras illustrates the complications and contradictions inherent to a conservation movement that was progressive yet romantic, scientific and aesthetic. Did photography promote superficial appearances at the cost of the deep meanings of nature? As with all ideological uses of nature, aesthetic orientations toward the nonhuman world were filled with cultural meaning, most significantly the gender norms that so concerned Eliot. As he feared, the standards for masculine behavior hampered men from appreciating the beauty in nature. Women had to struggle with another set of expectations, ones that subordinated feminine sentiment and appreciation of beauty to scientific learning and thus assumed that aesthetic nature study was superfluous and unprofessional.

As suggested by Peter Schmitt, nature study enlarged a well-established relationship between Americans and nature photography.[38] The great Civil War photographers such as Mathew Brady, Alexander Gardner, and George S. Cook all practiced landscape photography, especially when their rudimentary equipment failed to adequately depict battlefield chaos. The photographs of William Henry Jackson, along with the magnificent paintings of Thomas Moran, provided a visual record of the Hayden survey that helped convince Congress, beginning in 1872, to set aside the most spectacular of America's scenic wonderlands and protect them from development.[39] Soon the idea that average Americans might experience landscape through photography seized the popular imagination.

During the late nineteenth century, photography became a professional endeavor as well as a widespread craze. The small handheld camera, and the Kodak in particular, represented a triumph of technology and clever marketing. Photography became a widespread pastime, and amateur photographers were often known by the slang term "Kodakers."[40] In 1889 the *New York Tribune* reported that "amateur photography is rapidly approaching, if it has not already reached, the dignity of a 'craze.'"[41] At times the promise of photography was overblown; for instance, the pleasures of photography were said to cure neurasthenia and prevent suicide.[42] Innovations in photographic technology created moderately priced cameras, including such novelties as the Folding Pocket Kodak and the Bicycle Kodak, designed to fit on handlebars. This popularized picture taking and made photography a common way for Americans to appreciate the natural world.[43]

Like professional landscape photographers, amateurs sought to capture nature's beauty on film. The connection between photography and nature was repeatedly emphasized in advertisements for Kodak; "All out-doors invites your Kodak" was a prominent selling point.[44] Yet nature study enthusiasts and art educators worried that the active interest in photography might degenerate into routine function or a fascination with photographic technology rather than nature. What was supposed to fire the aesthetic imagination might devolve into manual training. Students trained in this manner might "become simply machines, thoughtless mechanisms."[45] And mechanisms could not evoke the wonders of the natural order. Successful photographers were aware of this problem; the widely published Herbert Job hoped his photographs could transfer the "spirit" of nature "to the printed page."[46]

The literature on cameras assumed that photography could provide an aesthetic activity for the masses while it simultaneously worried about the intrusion of technology into nature study. Many nature study articles about photography focused on providing readers with practical instruction in picture taking, particularly the technical aspects of camera use and film developing.[47] Much of that same literature was ethically charged with debate over whether photographs represented truthful representations of nature. Some writers upheld the Aristotelian tradition, arguing that photographs could hold a mirror up to nature, capturing its truth through exact representation. Nature photographer Radclyffe Dugmore insisted that the camera "was of great scientific value, for it cannot lie, and it records in an unmistakable form every detail presented."[48] Mimesis also echoed the popular idea that honest intentions were best represented through plain speech.

Yet nature study and school arts advocates worried about the sincerity of mass production and doubted that the exact representation of nature in photographs equaled truth. Working from the fundamental nature study dictum of direct contact with living nature, Dugmore railed against his early use of stuffed specimens for photos. They were "unsympathetic. . . . The likeness was there, but the *life* was lacking."[49] It was a common sentiment. One contributor to *Nature-Study Review* noted that "a good landscape picture must not only show certain definite things, but must at the same time be artistic."[50] Art revealed the truths of nature better than mechanical reproduction. "By truth I mean the eternal verities of nature," wrote C. H. Robinson in *Nature-Study Review,* "not photographic reproduction, which is sometimes very inartistic."[51] Just underneath the critiques of emotionally stale photographs, then, was the artisan's yearning that self-expression not be sacrificed to the rigid demands of technical precision and representational verisimilitude.

Nature study conservationists noted that cameras were the products of the same industrial technology that eliminated the spiritual value of nature. Given that modern life seemed to separate people from nature, why did the camera not heighten the sense of technology mediating, and thus fabricating, human contact with nature? Nature study enthusiasts intuited that technologies such as the camera might either enhance or retard sympathetic attachments to nature. The technology itself was neutral; what mattered were the uses to which it was put. Such thinking allowed nature study advocates to maintain progressive pieties about the beneficence of material and scientific progress while simultaneously criticizing the mania for technological industrialization that often seemed independent of and superior to human will. "See how willingly Nature poses herself upon photographer's plates," wrote John Muir, a fan of landscape photography. Yet the relative sympathy of the photographer determined the quality of the experience: "No earthly chemicals are so sensitive as those of the human soul. All that is required is exposure, and purity of material. The pure in heart shall see God!'"[52]

Nature study advocates mixed countermodern anxiety with hopefulness about the aesthetic promise of the camera. These concerns pervaded the larger culture as well. Even as it was fast becoming a craze, many Americans felt considerable anxiety about photography. Cameras were often described as "deadly weapons" or "deadly little boxes." The click of the shutter produced an "ominous" or "dreadful" feeling.[53] Rather than a joyous means of promoting aesthetic wonder, many nineteenth-century Americans regarded the camera with deep suspicion.

The fact that photography became an essential tool in the rationalization of industrial production furthered such apprehensions.[54] Photography served the regimentation of a wide range of bourgeois culture, including manufacturing. Taylorist managers deployed the camera in their time and motion studies. It supported the very uniformity and regimentation that nature study aesthetes sought to combat. Moreover, as Nancy Martha West demonstrated in her provocative study of Kodak, photographs granted the American public the ability to organize and collect its memories.[55] This rationalization of experience potentially interfered with the continuity between nature's beauty and the individual's unique sympathy that nature study conservationists championed. Americans' ambivalent relationship with technology heightened the need to attach innovations such as photography to moral purposes. How could technology bring people into closer communion with the natural world?

To combat the feeling that photography was a mere species of technocracy, nature study enthusiasts emphasized its potential outdoor uses and the physical struggles necessary to take the best pictures of wild nature. The camera was a machine, but one that people controlled; those who invested their picture taking with moral clarity would transform this new species of technology into a means of gaining access to nature. Ornithologist Frank Chapman, for example, argued that using cameras would grant the outdoorsman the healthful, masculine vigor of the hunter. Indeed, photography promised greater physical and mental benefits than hunting:

> Camera-hunting fulfills all the essential requirements of true sport. It is infinitely more difficult than hunting with the gun, and makes far greater demands on the patience, perseverance, strength and ingenuity of the hunter. The apparatus is interesting in its manipulation; its use implies no restriction of place or season, and once its results become as desirable as those to be obtained with rod or gun, the latter will be used by sportsmen only to supply the larder.[56]

The photographer's equipment, claimed Chapman, was rapidly replacing the rifle as the outdoorsman's primary tool: "Among sportsmen a photograph of a wild animal in its haunts is beginning to be more highly prized than the animal itself."[57] Gentlemen best experienced nature through the sophisticated practices of the photographer rather than the blunt methods of the gun-toting hunter.

An even more potent means to link vigor and morality with picture taking was to enlist photography in the cause of conservation. Indeed, photography enthusiasts enjoined their hobby to the conservation crusade with a moral fervor that belied the evangelical nature of their beliefs. In his guide to nature photography, Herbert Job asserted that opposing the "slaughter of white herons" for millinery purposes is "one of the moral questions—to be classed with the opium traffic and the slave trade—to which there is but one side."[58] Professional nature photographer Radclyffe Dugmore compared the unwise killing of birds to the history of fratricidal Christianity. "How often do we see people kill hawks, thinking they are doing a good deed," observed Dugmore, "just as various

Christian sects burned or otherwise killed one another in days gone by, fully believing that such acts were for the good of the world."[59] Linking photography with conservation provided an outlet for vivid but plainspoken Protestant moral instruction, which many felt was losing power in the secular modern world.

Nature study advocates heartily concurred with Chapman's injunction that wildlife photographers experience rugged outdoor life. Conservationists thus enlisted the camera to advance the moral righteousness of their cause and the manly preoccupation with healthy vitality and spiritual strength. Photography could promote both physical power and strength of character—the primary sources of masculine identity.[60] "In this age of strain and stress some pleasant incentive is needed to drive us from our toil and give the exercise in the pure open air which is absolutely essential to health and vigor," explained Job. "Added years and serenity of soul are the reward."[61]

Nature study advocates linked photography to the cause of conservation in a number of ways. First, nature photography required close observation outdoors and thus brought people into sympathetic contact with the natural world. Photographers insisted that the intimate contact with nature necessary for good photographs promoted conservation. "If a close-up camera acquaintance with wild birds and beasts will not transform a destroyer into a preserver of wild life, nothing ever will," argued conservation evangelist William T. Hornaday (former director of the New York Zoological Park), "not even the chastening and refining influence of old age."[62]

More immediately, photographer-conservationists held that the camera could replace the gun as the hunter's way to interact with nature. "All animals are the camera's game," claimed Dugmore. Sadly, few "sportsmen appreciate the amount of sport which may be had when the camera takes the place of the rifle."[63] Photography granted the same satisfactions as sport hunting and, like hunting, forced participants to learn about nature. "Even a moderately successful bird-photographer must have an intimate knowledge of the subject," argued Dugmore in the *World's Work*. "The camera, in teaching us to know the birds, must of necessity stimulate our affection for these useful and defenseless creatures."[64]

Given that camera hunting could unite moral and physical ideals, it is not surprising that Theodore Roosevelt would lend his support to the idea. "A true democracy really alive to its opportunities, will insist upon game preservation because it is in the interest of our people as a whole," wrote Roosevelt.

More and more, as it becomes necessary to preserve the game, let us hope that the camera will largely supplant the rifle. . . . The shot is after all, only a small part of the free life of the wilderness. The chief attractions lie in the physical hardihood for which the life calls, the sense of limitless freedom which it brings, and the remoteness and wild charm and beauty of primitive nature. All of this we get exactly as much in hunting with the camera as in hunting with the rifle.[65]

Roosevelt's comments also conveyed a sense of the class dimensions of the hunting issue. Roosevelt excused settlers from the occasional kill, though he hoped to educate them to the potentially more bountiful economic possibilities of using big game to attract tourist dollars. Professional game hunters, however, "have no excuse of any kind," for they killed only for the "hide and for the flesh."[66] Those whose livelihood depended on resource extraction sacrificed their moral standing.

In his introduction to a volume of nature photography, Roosevelt called for a new organization modeled on the Audubon Society to fight decorations and clothing made from the hide or bones of wild game animals. As it had with regard to the collecting of bird eggs, popular education could help instill conservation ethics. It might not be easy to replace the rifle and the thrill of the killing shot, however. Roosevelt confessed as much in a note he wrote to Job that was reproduced in *Wild Wings*; in it Roosevelt confessed that he was "still something of a hunter, although a lover of wild nature first!"[67]

Conservationists also found ways to elide Charles Eliot's concern that an interest in beauty was thought to be exclusively feminine. A variety of prominent conservationists championed beauty as a public good because it enhanced patriotism—an example of the allegedly manly qualities of honor and justice. One defense of beauty as an essential component of conservation came from J. Horace McFarland, president of the American Civic Association. Like Eliot, he believed that a desire for beauty implied a conservation ethic. Writing on the question of "Shall We Have Ugly Conservation?" he tied "our great scenic possessions" to the "pure love of country" that "alone makes for patriotism."[68] McFarland thus followed the common progressive rhetorical maneuver of attaching the individual's moral growth to national purposes. So did the crusading editor of *Century*, Robert Underwood Johnson, who argued that "there is no more popular and effective trumpet-call for the conservation movement than the appeal to the love of beautiful natural scenery." But again, such love was not mere fancy, because if "*beauty as a principle*" were inculcated, citizens would "love their country more devotedly the more loveable it is made."[69] Beauty might remain an effeminate concern, but put into the service of patriotism, it functioned safely within the confines of masculine, reformist rhetoric.

Although much of the language surrounding nature photography emphasized masculine moral injunction and outdoor vigor, the amateur spirit of the venture and the lack of gatekeeping mechanisms, such as professional credentialing, made outdoor photography an option for women. Restrictive gender conventions influenced how women might act as outdoor photographers, however. While Eliot despaired that beauty was considered effeminate, female photographers had to overcome the notion that the rugged outdoor experiences inherent in nature photography were unladylike. Advice to female photographers thus emphasized such concerns as field clothing that was both practical and presentable. The author of one such piece, Miss E. L. Turner, described how she used gender to her advantage as a photographer, in that she was given access to protected areas from which men were excluded because "every man is a possible collector."[70] Overzealous hunting had recently wiped out the passenger pigeon and nearly exterminated the American bison. Game reserve managers had reason to be wary of the masculine ethos of hunting, which focused on the kill rather than the ostensibly effeminate activities of observation and communion with nature's beauty.

Turner approached her avocation in the spirit of nature study. The camera was primarily a means to engage nature rather than another industrial mechanism that distanced people from the outdoor world. "To me," wrote Turner, "the pleasure of securing a good photograph is not to be compared with the delight of getting in close touch with these beautiful and shy wild things [birds], whose emotions and actions are so akin to our own." For Turner, avian behavior revealed fascinating domestic dramas that the hunter, intent on the kill, could never discover. Bird photography was thus "the highest form of sport," for its end was "not death, but life and a fuller knowledge of the life history of nature's elusive and perhaps most beautiful children."[71] The assumed sympathetic interconnection between women and nature thus served Turner's desire to legitimate the outdoor activities of women.

Other women used photography to burnish their credentials as nature study professionals, turning assumptions about the sophisticated and sympathetic emotional lives of women to their advantage. This was a well-established strategy in literary nature study. Works by authors such as Olive Thorne Miller and Florence Merriam were replete with metaphors of domesticity. Miller's *In Nesting Time*, for example, excoriated the killing, dissecting, and stuffing of specimens in favor of the "infinite patience, perseverance, untiring devotion ... and ... sympathetic heart" needed for field study. Such attributes, concluded Miller, were "particularly suited to woman with her great patience and quiet manners."[72] In this way, some women were able to use ostensibly domestic virtues to enter the masculine world of science. The connection between nature and sentiment could open otherwise closed doors for ambitious women who wished to make nature study a career.

The most prominent example of such a woman was Gene Stratton Porter. Born into rural poverty in Wabash County, Indiana, she married a local druggist and moved to nearby Geneva, Indiana, adjacent to Limberlost Swamp. When developers discovered valuable trees (and eventually oil) in the swamp, Porter used their newly built roads to enter the swamp and observe its mammalian and avian residents in close proximity. Limberlost Swamp eventually furnished Porter with the setting for her phenomenally successful novels *Freckles* (1904) and *Girl of the Limberlost* (1909).[73] Although some critics panned Porter's fiction as sentimental and derided her nature study as unscientific, her enormous and enthusiastic audience prompted Yale professor of literature William Lyon Phelps to dub her "a public institution, like Yellowstone Park."[74]

Porter was shaped by the gender stereotypes of her day and, like her fictional characters, used ingenuity and perseverance to work around them. Unlike others who advocated aesthetic pleasure as a way to bring people into contact with nature, Porter was not plagued by antimodern doubt. Rather, she used entrepreneurial drive to capitalize on the cultural assumptions that linked women and the aesthetic appreciation of nature. The connections between nature and gender, then, affected different individuals in vastly different ways. For elite professional men such as Charles Eliot, the sense that "the beautiful is an effeminate sentiment" merely needed logical refutation to make the pursuit of beauty an acceptable goal for men. Yet for women such as Gene Stratton Porter, the assumed connection among femininity, beauty, and nature presented a different set of cultural and professional problems that Porter turned to her advantage.

Fiction provided Porter with financial success, but it was nature photography that allowed her to enter the world of published, and thereby professional, work on nature study. Her uncanny ability to obtain close-up photographs of birds in their natural habitats led to a series of columns titled "Camera Notes" in the outdoor magazine *Recreation*. Editors and readers marveled at Porter's ability to capture birds on their nests, seemingly undisturbed by the photographer's presence. Porter agreed that she had "reproduced birds in fear, anger, greed, pride, surprise, in full tide of song, while dressing the plumage, taking a sun bath, courting, brooding, and carrying food to their young." She believed that photographs—when taken by a sympathetic observer—best represented the vitality of nature. The masculine ethos of physical power did not promote authentic representations of nature. As an example, Porter cited the illustrations of John James Audubon, which she disparaged as inauthentic and stiff, "as if they had been cut out with a scroll saw."[75] Audubon's paintings failed the test of accuracy despite his practice of killing birds to study them closely. She described the method that allowed her to create lively images as the victory of patience and communion with nature rather than technical expertise. "My procedure was merely to turn child's play into women's work," wrote Porter. "My methods must be followed by any one who desires to accustom wild creatures to a state of fellowship with humanity."[76]

That method included what Porter termed "a mute contract between woman and bird." That contract was one of respect for wild things: "Your nest and young will be touched as I would wish some giant, surpassing my size and strength as I surpass yours, to touch my cradle and baby."[77] The intimacy of the mute contract produced photographs that depicted "the thing as it is," unlike paintings that contained "inaccuracies [when] depicting anatomy, feathering, and other characteristics." Rather than using one animal to portray an entire species, Porter's photographs showed unique individuals. "One bird no more represents the whole of his species," claimed Porter, "than one man represents the whole of his race." Thus, while it is "right to give all the art and beauty possible," the naturalist photographer's first duty is "to truth and accuracy."[78] Her methods worked. Her photographs were exceptionally popular, prompting Kodak to send representatives to her home to learn her methods firsthand.[79]

As nature study aesthetes claimed, Porter's method also supported conservation. She lambasted "one writer who complacently states that he shot fifty-eight rose-breasted grebes" during "breeding season" to "make a record of the contents of their crops." Multiply this example by "the host of workers" who are "gathering scientific details for their volumes," and one can accurately gauge what "happened to millions of our most precious birds."[80] Science unchecked by sympathy could be destructive indeed. Other methods of obtaining photos also infuriated Porter. She railed against those who insisted on "cutting down, tearing out and placing nests . . . for your own convenience." A picture so gathered had "no earthly value."[81] Only mimetic aesthetic experience that accurately depicted nature could develop sympathy and its concomitant dedication to conservation.

Like Turner, Porter attributed her success at nature photography to skills developed in and appropriate to the domestic sphere: patience, sympathy, and attentiveness to routine household business. In this way, Porter translated the assumption that women were the emotional caretakers of the home into a sympathetic interconnection with the outdoor world. She wrote of her method in explicitly gendered terms: "No man ever has had the patience to remain with a bird until he secured a real character study of it."[82] Conversely, feminine understanding allowed her to capture intimate images of wild nature. Her pictures of birds on their nests—that is, of birds in a "domestic" setting—emphasized the intuitive qualities of her nature study. Only a woman's sympathy could guide the photographer to take such candid photographs of wild nature.

Despite Porter's success as a nature photographer, her spectacular popularity derived mainly from her work as an author. Her longtime career ambition was to become a popular writer of nature study texts like those of John Burroughs or Ernest Thompson Seton. Her break came in 1905 when she accepted a commission to write a series of articles on birds, illustrated with her photographs, for *Ladies' Home Journal*. Those articles formed the basis of Porter's book *What I Have Done with Birds*, which carried the cumbersome subtitle: *Character Studies of Native American Birds which through Friendly Advances I Induced to Pose for Me, or Succeeded in Photographing by Good Fortune, with the Story of My Experiences in Obtaining the Pictures*. She turned photography into "women's work," sweetly enticing birds to pose for her. Porter hoped to make a living from such straightforward nature study works, but her publishers preferred the market for sentimental domestic fiction authored by a woman.

Porter struck an agreement with Doubleday, Page & Company, which stipulated that for every sentimental novel she produced, it would publish a work of her nature study. The deal worked for both parties. The sentimental fiction sold hugely and allowed Porter to pursue her interests in nature study. Doubleday, Page also burnished its reputation as a home for nature study, symbolized by its move from New York City to Garden City on Long Island, where it continued "to foster a love of the wide outdoors."[83] Yet even her sentimental fiction displayed Porter's devotion to popular nature study. Her books may have been hackneyed, Algeresque, rags-to-riches stories populated with characters who overcame hard knocks through pluck, courage, and good luck, but they also contained a good deal of nature study, featuring characters who, for example, puzzled over the nesting patterns of the turkey vulture. Even some of Porter's detractors admitted that her digressions into nature study were well executed and authoritative.[84] Porter claimed that her novels were simply nature study texts "sugarcoated with fiction."[85]

Although her texts might have been "sugarcoated," it was Porter's carefully crafted tomboy persona that fostered her success as a writer and her authority as a naturalist. The fact that she had to transgress traditional femininity demonstrated how deeply ingrained was the idea that men—or boys—appropriately experienced rugged nature. She bristled at one critic who accused her of writing from the comforts of a "modern mansion" when she was actually "dressed in green khaki" and "sunburned, scratched, and that day blistered with sumac poison" from her excursion into a nearby swamp.[86] She acknowledged that the "hardships" she endured as a field photographer—which included "wading, swimming, climbing," and confronting "hidden dangers"—were emphatically "*not* a woman's work."[87] Yet the flexible gender identity of the tomboy allowed her to embrace such hardships.

Moreover, the "finesse" and "limitless patience" required of camera hunting was "not a man's work."[88] Women needed outdoor life because civilization engendered overly "delicate women" as well as "puny children" while, more broadly, creating "narrowed minds."[89] And narrow minds denied the importance of wild things. Civilization's "revolt against the forest" resulted in a loss of vitality and a culture that "wantonly sacrificed" its "wild life." Porter therefore viewed her career as attempting to inculcate sympathy with nature into "every human being I could influence" so that "the devastation [of nature] would not be ultimately complete."[90] Like male nature photographers, Porter tied her work to the moral imperative of conservation.

The tomboy persona allowed Porter to achieve success as a popular naturalist in two ways. One, she could display the physical vitality that the luxuries of industrial living abated. Women as well as men could turn to outdoor life to recapture the exuberance of bodily vivacity. Second, she could criticize in explicitly gendered terms the male ethos of the kill and its implied disavowal of the patience and sympathy needed to know nature. Women had skills that readily transferred to the world of the professional naturalist. They only needed to understand that immersion in nature was not for men alone and that the search for natural beauty demanded toughness. The complexities of these gender constructions allowed Porter to appeal to both men and women and ensured her popular approval and professional success.

Porter turned commonly held assumptions about nature and gender to her advantage and used them with tremendous entrepreneurial success. Five of her novels sold more than a million copies each, and Porter also ventured into the field of moviemaking. She despised an early film version of *Freckles,* so she decided to oversee subsequent adaptations herself. In 1919 Porter made Los Angeles her permanent home, and in 1924 she incorporated her own film production company that produced four films adapted from her books. She died shortly thereafter when her chauffeured Lincoln limousine collided with a trolley car. Despite this sudden end, Porter's foray into the wilderness of Hollywood anticipated the centrality of a variety of visual media to the environmental politics of the twentieth century.

As scholars from a variety of disciplines have long argued, representations tell us a great deal about how society perceives itself. Yet this simple insight is rarely attached to the representation of nature. Indeed, the idea that nature is intrinsically beautiful is so ordinary that it rarely elicits analysis. Progressive Era conservationists, however, considered it an essential tool in their crusade for environmental reform. Yet historians have mostly failed to examine how ideals of beauty affected the progressive conservation movement. It was not only aesthetes such as John Muir who were moved by natural beauty. Through the nature study and school arts movements, we can see that the regard for nature's beauty was one of the most widespread ideals of progressive conservation.

The concept of aesthetic pleasure was (and remains) central to the conservationist critique of industrial society. Conservation always implied, and often expressed, a profound dissatisfaction with industrial culture. Conservationists worried about wise resource use and the essential humanity of people who were disconnected from contact with the green world. Interaction with nature could foster beauty, joy, and intellectual passion—all qualities endangered by the mechanical mind-set of industrial society. Moreover, championing the need for beauty helped ensure support for public lands. Reverence for beauty was a powerful motivation for conservation. This strategy lasted throughout the twentieth century and continues to the present day. Indeed, aesthetics remain central to the environmental movement, and the idea that the camera can replace firearms as the mark of an outdoorsman is still a common environmentalist trope.[91] Despite its contradictions and difficulties, the politics of beauty played a central role in the politics of progressive conservation.

CHAPTER SEVEN

The Science and Poetry of the Soil

Nature Study and Country Life

How many a farm boy in his solitary wanderings through
woods and fields is . . . questioned by nature, and stifles a
heart hunger to get at the meaning of the things he sees,
but cannot rightly understand!
—Sidney Morse, "The Boy on the Farm"

What is the relationship between farmers and science? Americans living at the
turn of the twentieth century were keenly interested in this question, despite its
many perplexing dimensions. Complicating the response to urban issues were
the widely held values of Jeffersonian agrarianism—independence, thrift,
courage, moral integrity, and a healthy relationship with nature—which seemed
threatened by industrial agriculture. If farmers succumbed to industrial monotony, where would other principles arise from? Rural life was especially important to the larger society because in the cultural imagination, farmers
provided both food and the values that caused America to flourish. "If we apply
our science constructively here [to rural life]," wrote Liberty Hyde Bailey, "as it
must necessarily be applied in the main, we shall have a vast foundational element to hold us in check."[1]

These dilemmas suggested that nature study was as necessary and vital to
rural denizens as was exposing urban children to nature. Just because farmers
were physically close to nature did not guarantee that they would use it wisely
or remain untainted by industrial prerogatives. Industrialism revolutionized
the entire country, not just the cities; farm children needed nature study as
much as their counterparts in the city did. As the country debated the future of
rural America, nature study became central to the conversation. When the government proposed remedies to the problems facing agriculture, nature study
was a prominent solution. Most broadly, nature study advocates believed they

could increase farm efficiency by instilling the methods of scientific agriculture while at the same time revitalizing rural culture by helping country residents gain intellectual and cultural satisfaction from their relationship with nature. Only nature study could respond to both the institutional and the cultural crises that seemed to define rural America in the early decades of the twentieth century.

The nature study concern with country life was typical of fin de siècle America. Indeed, as America became increasingly urban during the late nineteenth century, the cultural significance of farmers and rural life increased considerably. Urbanites, newly anxious about the state of farmland America, devoted unprecedented attention to rural affairs and rural people. This concern was often economic, as the farm economy remained vital to overall commercial health. More important, the concern was social and cultural, for many Americans worried that the nation was becoming unmoored from the vital qualities of rural life that, mixed with moral individualism, accounted for the best components of the American character.

Such anxieties were expressed by a bevy of progressive professionals—educators, religious leaders, politicians, and social scientists—who believed that the promise of urban cultural opportunity was drawing people of the best character to the city. Such professionals, united by their concern for country life, worried that a blighted countryside would harm the economy and deplete the natural conditions that fostered the moral development of the American people. Even confirmed urbanites such as Frederic C. Howe, an ardent social reformer who helped found the National Progressive Republican League and authored *The City: The Hope of Democracy*, warned of the debilitating effects of a civilization deprived from contact with the green world. "Human life seems to require a ground wire to the sod," argued Howe, "a connection with Mother Earth to maintain its virility."[2] Other reformers worried that the depopulated countryside would no longer provide the "fresh blood" that would "repair the physical, mental and moral waste" of the city.[3] Nature itself was the key to these feelings. "Trees everywhere exert a moral influence," declared California's superintendent of public instruction Ira G. Hoitt, "that fact we know and feel in our every day's experience."[4] For many of these reformers, nature was a primary source of moral conviction; thus, urban life by definition veered away from virtuous action.

Such attitudes reflected tremendous wariness toward industrial, urban life. Bailey characterized the city as "a parasite, running out its roots into the open country and draining it of its substance." He concluded that the urban parasitoid "takes everything to itself—materials, money, men—and gives back only what it does not want."[5] The substances that cities depleted were also moral—the community bonds that tied human interests together. Although the values championed tended to replicate the concerns of middle-class Anglo-Saxons—thrift, hard work, stability—they were promoted for the cause of democratic flourishing. "The farmer is the fundamental fact in democracy," argued Bailey, "not merely because he produces supplies, but because to him is delegated the keepership of the earth."[6] Bailey viewed this "keepership"—he termed the farmer a "trustee"—as an intensely moral endeavor. The farmer was responsible for ensuring the fertility of the land so that its "productiveness ... must increase from generation to generation. He must handle all his materials, remembering man and remembering God. A man cannot be a good farmer unless he is a religious man."[7] The keepership worked both ways. By handling God's materials, the farmer was imbued with moral clarity; by providing the moral bedrock of society, the farmer was the indispensable foundation of democratic society.

Many reformers thus tried to reconstruct in the city the feeling of community ostensibly present in the country. Community-oriented settlement houses and churches, as well as neighborhood reform initiatives, tried to bring the culture of rural America to the city. Many supporters of urban gardens viewed gardeners, especially school gardeners, as little farmers, thus bringing the virtues of rural labor to urban denizens. For progressives, so appalled by the corrupt and debasing features of industrial society, the tenets of agrarianism seemed, by comparison, not merely benign but laudable.

Concern for country life was also intensely economic. As agricultural historian David Danbom demonstrated, country life enthusiasts who concerned themselves with economic backwardness rather than moral decay found plenty of worrisome trends in rural life. Rural economists and sociologists held that relatively inefficient production might not disable America's farmers in the near term, but it could undermine the entire economy. In the short run, they worried about the rising price of food. Over the longer term, they surmised that if agricultural production fell behind population growth, living standards would decline. Such a decline would likely foment further labor unrest; in turn, this would price American industrial exports out of the increasingly competitive world market. Eventually, American farmers would be squeezed out of global markets—a dangerous development for a debtor nation in need of gold and other foreign goods. Agricultural products were America's only reliable export of significant size. Should the country's agricultural production falter, capital flight and economic depression would become real possibilities.[8] Farmers, then, needed to utilize the best agricultural methods to support a robust yet perilously fragile economic structure that depended on their contributions.

Concerns over the rural culture and economy manifested themselves in a variety of rural reform initiatives, including progressive education and a presidential delegation, the Country Life Commission, created to investigate the crisis in rural America. The nature study movement was intimately bound up with these expressions of country life reform. Educators felt that nature study held the answer to economic quandaries by imparting scientific methods of agricultural production. Nature study could also assuage the cultural crisis of agrarian America by instilling a love of nature in rural children, encouraging them to appreciate their surroundings and develop an abiding commitment to rural living. As Bailey argued, "The real solution of the agricultural problem—which is at the same time the national problem—is to give the countryman a vital, intellectual, sympathetic, optimistic interest in his daily life."[9] No longer would the best and brightest young people decamp for the city; once they were properly trained, they would find intellectual and spiritual satisfaction in their interactions with nature. In short, country life advocates championed the study of nature as a means to modernize the agricultural economy and revitalize rural culture.

The country life movement thus hoped to alter rural life so that it would produce good citizens, men and women of character who would temper degenerate (most often urban) social habits and transform antiquated agricultural practices. At the center of the country life movement, then, was an essential contradiction: country lifers wished to modernize the countryside while revitalizing many established aspects of its culture. Deeply concerned with tradition, but also committed to the progressive improvement of social institutions, country life reformers attempted to control social change by tempering it with moral regeneration. For them, scientific agriculture had to harmonize with moral belief. Put another way, country life reformers believed that the modernization of rural life needed to occur without the ostensibly corrupting influences of modern culture. Behind the country life movement was an intellectual suspicion of modern culture yoked to a zest for progressive social transformation and an embrace of science and technology that ensured modern culture would thrive.

The goal of reforming rural institutions brought the disparate concerns of country life advocates together. School reform united country life theorists because education addressed both the moral and sociological quandaries that drove country life reform efforts. Education could enhance rural culture and thus help rural life maintain its role as the developer of the American conscience. Moreover, rural children could learn the fundamentals of modern science and its application to agriculture. No part of the school curriculum promised to address the disparate concerns of country life activists more than nature study. Nature study promised contact with the soil, which assured proper moral development, while also nurturing the curious and analytic habits of the scientific worldview, which fostered agricultural efficiency.

Nature study thus appeared to be the one subject that could meet the goals of those who called for moral regeneration as well as those who wished to modernize the countryside through science. Indeed, nature study advocates wanted to make it clear that modern life was dependent both morally and physically on the premodern countryside. Many intellectuals perpetuated the idea that exposure to country life was essential to building an admirable character. As one educator at the annual meeting of the National Education Association put it, "The strong and independent men of our nation . . . [have been] born and bred in village communion with nature in her grand and ennobling forms."[10] Moreover, urban areas remained dependent on the physical resources of rural America. "Cities cannot build cities," asserted Bailey, "the country builds the cities. The cities only handle and transform what the country produces." Despite these criticisms and his love of farmers and country life, Bailey was no one-note antiurbanist. "The countryman needs the city," argued Bailey in 1911. The country "does not need the city man so much to teach the countryman farming, as to touch and elevate the general currents of all country life. The city man goes to the country with new and large ideas, active touch with great affairs, keen business and executive ability, generosity, altruism, high culture."[11] Bailey and other country life reformers understood that the attractions of the city were not chimerical temptations but tangible realities.

Given metropolitan appeal, it was not difficult to understand why people left the country for the city. Moreover, some commentators felt that the industrialization of the countryside contributed to the exodus to the city: "The first effect of farm machinery," argued Wilbert L. Anderson, "is the hastening of the departure of the farmer's boy from the home."[12] To stem the flood of urbanization, Bailey and many other country life reformers recommended nature study as a means to enhance rural vitality, for a "sympathetic knowledge of nature will in the end be more satisfying than much of the amusement that the town has to offer."[13] Country life advocates championed a variety of educational efforts intended to vitalize rural culture. As Sidney Morse, writing in *Craftsman,* contended, "the interrelation of scientific thought and intellectual culture with the physical contact of Nature robs the latter of its monotony and instills into it the supremest joy: all of these are lessons which the farmer's boy of our day and his children are to learn."[14] The goal of the country life movement was to inculcate in rural people an educational system that imparted lessons in scientific efficiency and an abiding, sympathetic appreciation of nature as manifested in rural landscapes.

This goal has befuddled most historians investigating the country life movement. Seeing the movement either as romantic and impractical or, conversely, as an attempt by scientifically minded technocrats to impose modernization on a reluctant rural populace, historians have found little to praise in it. Both lines of criticism assumed that the concerns of country life advocates stemmed from a zeal for social engineering among urban elites.[15] Rather than romantic or technocratic, the country life movement might be better described as holistic. Its proponents' concerns were disparate and contradictory because that was the nature of the reality they faced. Moreover, country life reform enacted real improvements and, as we shall see, articulated an important vision of sustainable agriculture and the general belief that rural people—not urban sophisticates— should control the reform of their own lives.

One thing that almost all reformers and almost all rural residents could agree on was the desperate need to reform rural schools. The actual structures that housed rural schools—often consisting of a single room—were unfit for barnyard fowl, let alone learning. Children either froze near drafty windows or baked near a single pot-bellied stove. The slab seats induced blisters, as did the birch rods the teachers wielded to maintain discipline. Teachers were often poorly trained, and their classroom curricula were subject to the whims and biases of the communities they served. Schoolchildren in the primary grades were usually lumped together in one large group, with older children given the task of instructing the younger ones. School attendance was often voluntary, and children attended classes only when their farm families could spare the labor. Moreover, rural people tended to view formal education as impractical "book learning" that made little pragmatic difference to their lives. In rural communities, education occurred as part of children's socialization by their families, neighbors, and churches; schools needed to demonstrate practical results if they were to be accepted into this process.[16]

Various forms of practical education had long been part of the rural scene. Indeed, nature study was not the first attempt to use education to reform rural life; for years, rural vocational education had been used to impart social as well as practical lessons. Beginning in Massachusetts in 1852, several states—at least thirteen—created farmers' institutes intended to apply academic endeavor to the practical problems of farmers. This idea was at least partially responsible for the Morrill Act. Officially known as the Federal Land Grant Act of 1862, the Morrill Act, named for Vermont congressman Justin Smith Morrill, provided federal monies for states to establish institutions of higher education to train citizens in agriculture, home economics, the mechanical arts, and other practical professions. More than any other federal initiative of the nineteenth century, the Morrill Act established the practice of using federal expertise and federal monies to combat the problems of agricultural America.

Importantly, farmers themselves embraced the idea of using education to reform rural life. The Grange was a good example. Oliver H. Kelley founded the National Grange in 1867 for "the resuscitation of the country and recuperation of its farmers." In 1874 the Grange announced its interest in the teaching of "practical agriculture, domestic science, and all the arts which adorn the home."[17] Two years later the Grange created a standing committee on education to deliberate on matters of pedagogy as they affected rural populations; the committee then directed its findings to the state Granges. Congress recognized these concerns in the Hatch Act of 1887, which provided monies to disseminate information on agricultural subjects to the people of the United States. Later, such enthusiasm for rural education was carried forward by people such as Henry Wallace, who used his influential magazine *Wallace's Farmer* to champion the improvement of rural life by fusing the interests of teachers and farmers.

One example of the successful dissemination of agricultural knowledge to farmers was the agricultural extension service, pioneered in Texas by scientist and entrepreneur Seaman Knapp in 1902. Remembered as the "schoolmaster of American agriculture," Knapp discovered that the best way to institute progressive change in agricultural practices was through practical demonstrations intended to conciliate a wary agricultural workforce.[18] The essential idea behind Knapp's program was for the Department of Agriculture to send extension personnel, who became known as "county agents," to work with willing farmers, institute progressive agricultural practices, and then offer successful outcomes as examples to nearby farmers who remained cautious about governmental interference with their livelihood. Knapp thus emphasized the progressive education credo of learning by doing, correctly assuming that farmers would be more impressed with real-world results than with theoretical information.

Knapp's programs gained great renown in the early years of the twentieth century when the Mexican cotton boll weevil created a national panic. The boll weevil, or snout beetle, arrived in America from Mexico around 1892 and promptly devastated cotton crops because its larvae fed on the seed-bearing capsule in the middle of the plant—the cotton boll.[19] To various public officials, the epidemic highlighted the precarious nature of single-crop farming, and they sought a way to diversify the southern agricultural economy beyond cotton. They seized on Knapp's extension service as a way to spread new agricultural methods. Congress voted to fund Knapp's enterprise, and he quickly organized the Farmer's Cooperative Demonstration Work. Such initiatives made Knapp a legendary figure in Texas. As the president of Texas A&M University quipped, "There are two universities here in Texas, one is at Austin; the other is Dr. Knapp."[20] Following Knapp's successes, the federal government offered substantial subsidies for extension work, beginning with the 1914 Smith-Lever Act.

The nature study movement quickly took up the cause of implementing this new agricultural education. The fifth volume of *Nature-Study Review* initiated a "Department of School Agriculture" that mixed reports on agricultural education with theoretical examinations of the relationship between nature study and agriculture. In a typical article, Dick Crosby of the U.S. Office of Experiment Stations asserted that nature study "is both more and less than agriculture, and agriculture, even in the elementary school, includes much which cannot properly be termed nature-study." The practicalities of agriculture were not, by themselves, components of nature study, but agricultural education needed nature study to broaden the curriculum and impart a love of nature—and thus a love of learning—to enhance the culture of rural America. Crosby continued by repeating the nature study mantra: that nature study's ability to minister to the spiritual and intellectual freedom of youth made it essential to agricultural education. "What we need in this country is not *more* farmers, but *better* farmers," stressed Crosby. Schools should not attempt to make farmers; they should "stop unmaking them." Educators would cease to unmake farmers if they worked "to open the boy's mind to see and understand himself and to see and understand the nature and social environment in which he lives."[21]

The country life emphasis on agricultural education and rural cultural reform highlighted the difficulties of teaching nature study to urban children. One teacher, Anna Wright, lamented in *Nature-Study Review* that teachers could not expect city children "to hear the small voices of nature." Urban life—as country life reformers were quick to point out—disguised its "dependence on the country." Thus city children grew up failing to understand that "sardines do not always live in flat tins, nor do peas grow in the cans on the grocer's shelf." Such remarks presaged Aldo Leopold's dictum that the greatest spiritual malady plaguing modern American civilization was the belief that food comes from the supermarket. For Wright, the preeminence of environment in shaping the worldview of children meant that urban students must begin to know nature through the commodity form. Children should thus learn about nature by way of "the fish of the market or wharf, the fruits or nuts of the store." Wright was a typical Progressive Era educator, in that she believed that knowledge must "be linked with [students'] own observations." Observations of nature in its commodity form would act "as a stepping stone to knowledge of the real things of the surrounding country."[22]

Educators were convinced that rural children as well as their urban counterparts needed to be introduced to the real things of the country. Cornell University attempted to do this through its extension work, but under the direction of Liberty Hyde Bailey, it also carried on a more socially ambitious program that aimed to modernize agriculture and enhance the culture of rural life. The difficulties of modernizing agricultural technology while revitalizing the culture of rural peoples were reflected in the institutional history of Cornell itself. The legislature of the state of New York was initially unsure how to use its share of Morrill Act land grants. New York had an established tradition of using public monies to endow private colleges, and many legislators favored selling the land-grant acreage and transferring the profits to established private schools. That plan was challenged when wealthy industrialist Ezra Cornell proposed that the Morrill Act proceeds be used to endow a new university, adding to his initial contribution of $500,000. After a "rather violent" legislative battle, the state accepted Cornell's plan and chartered the new university in 1865.[23] This unique legislative situation endowed a private school, Cornell University, as New York State's sole land-grant institution.

The early history of Cornell University reflected the tensions between the public and private goals of its founding. The Morrill Act required instruction in agriculture in its beneficiary institutions, but as was the case at many other land-grant institutions, instruction in agriculture remained weak at Cornell. The university had always focused on teaching the classical liberal arts curriculum rather than imparting practical or vocational knowledge. That tradition reflected the biases of most elite educators. Faculty at Cornell and elsewhere tended to view instruction in farming as unworthy of higher learning.[24] Moreover, the farming community itself remained wary of the universities' intentions. The situation improved somewhat with the influx of monies from the Hatch Act of 1887 and the Second Morrill Act of 1890, both of which appropriated resources for agricultural research and teaching; however, agriculture remained little valued by the university community. Into this tension between theoretical and applied knowledge walked a young horticulturist from the Michigan State Agricultural College: Liberty Hyde Bailey.

Although Bailey was a prominent intellectual who was widely known and widely read during his lifetime, he is now largely overlooked in the history of progressive conservation.[25] Dubbed by one historian the "philosopher of country life," Bailey was a remarkable figure—perspicacious, wide ranging in his academic interests and achievements, a passionate philosopher of not only country life but also conservation and nature study.[26] His abiding interests in conservation, rural life, and education were forged through his childhood experiences on the family farm in South Haven, Michigan, located about one mile inland from Lake Michigan. Named "Liberty" after his father, to express the strong antislavery views of his family, Bailey grew up on a working farm that was well known for its apple orchards and innovative horticultural techniques. Despite the death of his mother when he was five, Bailey led a happy childhood absorbed in observing the local flora and fauna as he explored nearby streams and woodlands.

A signal event of his childhood was the rapid disappearance of passenger pigeons.[27] As with many Progressive Era conservationists, the extermination of passenger pigeons—once easily the most numerous birds on the North American continent—transformed Bailey into a conservationist who defended nature for both utilitarian and aesthetic reasons. At age fifteen he read an essay on birds to the State Pomological Society at South Haven that asked farmers: what "is more useful [than birds] in destroying the myriads of insects which infest our vegetation?" He noted that thousands of "noxious insects . . . are destroyed by these harmless songsters, yet the selfish man dooms them to destruction." Furthermore, he emphasized that birds "have powers of music unequaled by works of art," qualities that "lend life and vivacity to the dullest place."[28]

Bailey continued stumping for aesthetic and practical conservation in his rural Michigan community. He was influenced in his outreach to rural people by the farmers' cooperative known as the Grange, using it as a model of rural engagement to broach his aesthetic and conservation concerns. Delivering a paper before the Michigan State Horticultural Society in 1885 that advocated the preservation of natural stream banks and other wild places, Bailey called on farmers to preserve native trees and to adapt wild shrubs and flowers to the farm and garden landscape. All these measures would help farm efficiency as well as give a face-lift to the surrounding countryside. Moreover, Bailey advocated planting trees and shrubs to provide a border for wetlands and to beautify untillable areas such as roadsides.[29]

Bailey's activism and academic interests led him to invite Professor William James Beal of the Michigan Agricultural College to lecture in South Haven. Beal and Bailey impressed each other, and Bailey enrolled at Michigan Agricultural College the following year. Beal, a follower of Louis Agassiz, instructed Bailey in scientific methodology and botany by using live plants rather than preserved specimens. Upon graduation Bailey apprenticed with the nation's leading botanist, Harvard's Asa Gray.

A mere year later, in 1884, Bailey received an offer to become a professor of horticulture at Michigan Agricultural College. Gray advised his student against taking the position, arguing that botany was science, whereas horticulture was mere gardening. Bailey, however, was already chafed by such hierarchies of knowledge and by distinctions between pure and applied science. This was a view that Bailey maintained throughout his life. He asserted that there was "as much culture in the study of beet roots as in the study of Greek roots."[30] According to Bailey, the split between theory and practice divided disciplines that should be allied. He bemoaned what he perceived as the needless prejudice embodied by Gray that separated the botanist from the horticulturist. Bailey accepted the position at Michigan. Four years later, when Cornell University offered Bailey a professorship, he accepted it on the condition that he could develop horticulture as he saw fit. Beginning at Cornell in 1888, Bailey tried to unify theory and practice through his horticultural research and his support of the nature study movement.

The merging of the country life and nature study movements came about due to a severe economic depression that ravaged the rural economy of New York State during the early 1890s. That crisis did for Bailey's Cornell nature study program what the Mexican boll weevil epidemic did for Seaman Knapp's Texas extension work. Beginning in 1893, rural economic refugees flooded urban areas. Taking notice of this development, charity organizations such as the Association for Improving the Condition of the Poor developed an interest in rural affairs, which was formalized as the Committee for the Promotion of Agriculture. In addition to wealthy urban capitalists such as Jacob Schiff and William E. Dodge, committee members included George T. Powell, director of the Farmers' Institutes for the state of New York. Powell created an experimental program in nature study for the suburban Westchester schools. The success of that program prompted him to recommend that the study of nature be used to promote rural children's interest in farming.[31] The idea was to educate rural children in efficient agriculture so that rural economies would be less susceptible to commercial turmoil. Moreover, by learning about the beauties and intricate wonders of nature, rural people could combat the intellectual isolation and ostensible cultural impoverishment that marked country life as inferior to urban sophistication.

The Arbor Day movement also helped establish nature study as a method to improve country life. Like nature study, Arbor Day grew from both utilitarian and aesthetic concerns. Groups such as the American Forestry Association were formed in the late nineteenth century to combat wasteful forestry practices as well as to emphasize the aesthetic appreciation of trees. The American Forestry Association pushed for Arbor Day celebrations as a way to further its aims.[32] The specific impetus behind Arbor Day came from Secretary of Agriculture J. Sterling Morton, who introduced Arbor Day in Nebraska as a tree-planting movement. Many states quickly followed Nebraska's example. New York established Arbor Day in 1888, declaring that each May schools should "encourage the planting, protection and preservation of trees and shrubs."[33] The state of New York issued leaflets that included directions on how to plant trees as well as literary selections that might accompany tree-planting celebrations. The state issued new, enlarged pamphlets each year, and eventually they featured contests to determine the state tree and state flower and included directions for collecting and preserving herbarium specimens, insects, and other items of interest to amateur naturalists. In 1895, in his annual report to the legislature, the state superintendent described the fusion of practical and aesthetic interests that promoted Arbor Day as a way to fuel interest in nature study and country life:

> There is a practical as well as sentimental side to Arbor Day. It had its inception in a commendable movement looking to the protection of our forest trees and what may be called the making of new forests on the vast plains of the West. The sentimental feature attached to its observance has been in the development of a love for nature and her wonderful works, and in the encouragement to delightful study of trees, plants, flowers and birds. There is no doubt that in hundreds of thousands of the children of our country there has been awakened a deep interest in the attractive study of how plants grow, of the use and abuse of trees, and of the relations which birds and flowers bear to the problem of nature and to human happiness. A child who learns to love trees and flowers, and who derives happiness from them, can never go entirely wrong. . . . The study of nature can be turned to practical use, and be made of lasting benefit to many thousands of the world's workers, especially to those whose privilege it is to till the soil. . . . We may give those who go from the schools back to the farms a knowledge which shall arouse a love and an enthusiasm for agricultural pursuits which they could never otherwise obtain. This love would do more than any other influence to keep our boys on the farm. . . . Arbor Day should give us educated farmers.

These educated farmers would find and develop the cultural as well as economic pleasures of rural life. The superintendent concluded that there is "profit as well as poetry in 'a little farm well tilled.'"[34]

The idea of using education to combat rural social and economic difficulties was also finding friends in the New York State legislature. One such legislator was S. F. Nixon, a grape grower from Chautauqua County who was chairman of the Ways and Means Committee. Nixon converted to the gospel of rural education when Bailey and other Cornell faculty helped save Nixon's vineyards from "black rot" through the inventive use of chemical pesticides. The legislator responded by shepherding through the legislature the State Experiment Station

Extension Bill of 1893, colloquially known as the Nixon bill. The bill funded a series of outreach programs in the form of two- or three-day "Schools of Horticulture" that promulgated "horticultural knowledge" throughout upstate New York. Bailey spearheaded the effort, and soon the roving seminars reflected his interests in social and cultural issues as well as experimental agriculture. One flyer confirmed the school's intention "to awaken an interest in rural affairs and to inspire correct methods of observation and thinking, quite as much as to give explicit direction for horticultural work."[35] For Cornell nature study advocates, the study of nature implied social and cultural revitalization as well as agricultural efficiency.

The Cornell extension work was an immediate success. Fifty-eight students attended the first School of Horticulture held at Fredonia in Chautauqua County; nearly twice as many attended the second school at Jamestown. The pedagogical methods were derived from the early instruction in nature study popularized by Louis Agassiz at Penikese Island. To develop skills in observation, each student was given a twig, fruit, flower, or other common natural object and was then asked to explain what he or she had seen. Afternoons were given over to the study of fundamental topics, with evenings devoted to lectures illustrated with lantern slides, still a distinctive treat in the 1890s. In 1895 the Cornell agricultural outreach program initiated a series of "spring rallies" led by two or three Cornell faculty members. Bailey averred that the purpose of such rallies was "to send the farmer into season's work with such an initial velocity that he could not stop himself before harvest time." Bailey remembered the rallies as containing "plain direct talks about philosophy of tillage, fertilizing the land, conservation of moisture, and the like, instructions about spraying, and sometimes talks about insects. An orchard was generally sprayed for the purpose of explaining the operation." The interest generated by such lectures was phenomenal. Bailey was soon speaking to crowds of three thousand to four thousand farmers. As with the new education he was working so hard to develop, he sensed a pent-up demand for rural reform. "Surely," he wrote, "the time is ripe for sowing the seeds of a new agriculture."[36]

One spring rally attendee proved to be vital in establishing nature study as a strategy for rural revitalization. John W. Spencer, another fruit grower from Chautauqua County, was, according to Bailey, "one of the most progressive and intelligent farmers I have ever met." Born in 1843 at Cherry Valley, New York, Spencer had been an active farmer for thirty years. Fascinated by the natural principles underlying agriculture, Spencer was equally motivated by the idea that children should be well grounded in such principles. A man of warm bearing and natural pedagogical skills, Spencer was added to the Cornell team in

1896. Thousands of schoolchildren in upstate New York soon knew Spencer as "Uncle John"; his popularity was such that Bailey confided, "the man really behind this [nature study] movement is John W. Spencer."[37] In 1896 Spencer visited fifty-four public schools, attempting to interest teachers in nature study involving direct interaction with natural objects. He applied the methods he witnessed in the farmers' institutes to childhood education. Teachers were eager to participate, but they loudly proclaimed their own need for nature study education. To meet that need, Bailey wrote *How a Squash Plant Gets Out of a Seed*, the first in a long series of *Cornell Nature Study Leaflets*.

Funds for agricultural education continued to flow from federal and, more importantly, state coffers. In June 1898 the Faculty of Agriculture divided the work stemming from the Nixon appropriation into two coordinating bureaus, with Bailey the chief and Spencer the deputy chief of the Bureau of University Extension of Agricultural Knowledge. Bailey and Spencer quickly made the expertise of the Cornell faculty available to any schoolteacher, rural or urban, who wished to develop nature study as part of the curriculum. They theorized that nature study was the best way to attack both practical and cultural problems. "As with all education," wrote Bailey, the "central purpose" of nature study "is to make the individual happy; for happiness is nothing more nor less than pleasant and efficient thinking." The same efficiency that produced greater agricultural output would create the mental satisfaction that came from the cultivation of knowledge. Such knowledge would create satisfaction and also build on itself because the farmer would become interested in the things and processes of nature. "The person who actually knows a pussy-willow will know how to become acquainted with the potato-bug," declared Bailey. "He will introduce himself."[38]

Bailey's philosophy assumed that the modernization of the countryside would stabilize the rural economy and alleviate the alienation that came from the narrow instrumentalism inherent in the market mentality. The farmer who sees in his crops "only clods and weeds, and corn," wrote Bailey, leads an "empty and a barren life." Conversely, the "knowledge of soil and atmosphere, of plant and animal life that makes [the farmer] an intelligent producer, puts him in sympathetic touch with these activities of nature." For nature study advocates, such sympathy created happiness. Thus Bailey asserted that nature study must begin with "an interest in the things with which the farmer lives and has to do, for a man is happy only when he is in sympathy with his environment."[39] Thus Bailey emphasized that the countryman needed an "intellectual horizon. He needs something else [besides money] to think of. He needs to have a real personal sympathy with the natural objects in his environment. He needs the nature study outlook."[40]

Bailey also supported the nature study outlook because it addressed the larger problem of individuality and independent judgment among the citizenry. He argued that as society became more bureaucratized—or, in Alan Trachtenberg's brilliantly telling phrase, "incorporated"—it became "more difficult . . . for the person to find himself."[41] The remedy came from "contact with the earth," because interaction with nature tended "to make one original or at least detached in one's judgments and independent of group control." Independent judgment formed the basis of democratic decision making: "We can never successfully substitute bookkeeping for men and women. We are more in need of personality than of administrative regularity." In short, "we must protect the person from being submerged in the system."[42]

Contact with nature reinvigorated the bureaucratically stamped individual because nature, almost by definition, is unique, thus allowing authentic experience to thrive. Of the many kinds of interactions with nature sought by the nature study movement, they all had in common the essential trait of individuals developing personal skills and sympathies—hence the long tradition of using contact with the natural world to live, as Thoreau stated, "deliberately." Unlike society, natural environments did not make social claims on people; thus interactions with nature helped produce distinctive and sovereign individuals. In this manner, farmers produced the cultural as well as the material building blocks of democracy. But this process worked only if the farmer remained independent. "When the farmer is a free land-owner and is not a peasant," noted Bailey, "he resists the standardizing process."[43]

For Bailey, the renewal of country life must therefore start with a spiritual rather than economic revitalization. Much extension work in agriculture missed this point. "The burden of the new agricultural teaching has been largely the augmentation of material wealth," wrote Bailey. "Hand in hand with this new teaching, however, should go an awakening in the less tangible but equally powerful things of the spirit." In the last analysis, Bailey would "make farm life interesting before I made it profitable."[44] Bailey's close colleague at Cornell, Anna Botsford Comstock, concurred with Bailey's position. "The ideal farmer is not the man who by hazard and chance succeeds," wrote Comstock. "He is the man who loves his farm and all that surrounds it because he is awake to the beauty as well as the wonders which are there; he is the man who understands as far as may be the great forces of nature which are at work around him, and therefore he is able to make them work for him."[45]

For Bailey, the tensions and contradictions within country life ideology were not constraining but an opportunity to implement many reforms. "It is a public duty . . . to train the farmer [so] that he shall appreciate his guardianship," asserted Bailey. This duty focused the entire society's attention on the farmer and thus opened avenues for civically mature and responsible democratic change. "The farmer cannot keep the earth for us without an enlightened and very active support from every other person," wrote Bailey. That support included "safeguards from exploitation and from unessential commercial pressure." Key to social health was landownership. Persons who work the land "should have the privilege of owning it." The trend in tenant occupancy was dangerous, according to Bailey, "because the practice in tenancy does not recognize the public interest in fertility ... [it] is largely an arrangement for skinning the land." Beyond ecological considerations, "the aristocracy of land is a very dangerous power in human affairs. It is all the more dangerous when associated with aristocracy of birth and of facetious social position." Again the situation of the farmer spoke to the health of the entire democracy, because if "rigid aristocracy in land connects itself with the close control of politics, the subjugation becomes final and complete."[46] Bailey insisted that great aggregations of wealth corrupted democracy. Genuine self-government relied on the democratic social control of natural wealth and beauty.

Nature study advocates across the country reacted to the rural crisis and the demand for agricultural education by arguing that only the unique capabilities of nature study pedagogy could answer the disparate demands of country life reformers. They were equally adamant that if agricultural education consisted only of dry instructions—yet another subject that required students to memorize sets of facts—it would fail students and subvert its stated purposes by driving rural people to the city. As Comstock noted in her presidential address to the American Nature Study Society, "corn, potato or tomato growing will never induce the army of youth to be satisfied with the tillage of the land." But the intellectual curiosity aroused by a love for and interest in nature would give agricultural knowledge "permanent value," because "in nature-study the child finds the answer of the 'why' of agriculture." Indeed, "the following up of this 'why' broadens out in so many directions that there is no chance of the agricultural processes becoming an old story." Comstock cited lessons about soil that enabled the child-farmer to rightly judge its fertility, thus forming "an interest and a respect for the soil which is the first requisite of a good farmer; faith in soil without knowledge is a broken reed on which to lean." Comstock concluded that "knowledge of the kind of soil is the first step to the right treatment of it." The moral and ecological approach of nature study would give the child "confidence of his own powers in dealing with nature, and ... give him courage to attack any problem that requires investigation."[47]

Education was the ammunition farmers needed for a successful attack. By

April 1898, six different Cornell authors had prepared eleven different nature study leaflets for teachers. In 1907 the effort became the *Cornell Rural School Leaflet*. Soon leaflets reached 25,111 junior naturalists as well as 26,839 home study subscribers. By 1914 the leaflets reached 155,000 people in both urban and rural areas.[48] The leaflets varied greatly in style and intended audience. Some were written for teachers, others for the students themselves. The leaflets demonstrated the spirit of progressive education that nature study embodied. In "An Appeal to the Teachers of New York State," Bailey decried that the common schools were largely "undemocratic" institutions that "teach out of books" that are unrelated to the child's life. As a result, the "child lives in one world and goes to school in another."[49] Education was thus meeting neither the child's practical needs nor his spiritual ones. Such criticisms demonstrated the connections between progressive education and the country life movement that made curricular reform such a vital part of turn-of-the-century politics.

Conservation was an important and frequently recurring theme in the Cornell leaflets. The expedient concerns of rural residents drove conservation education as it appeared in the leaflets. E. Laurence Palmer described the leaflets' commitment to conservation in this way:

> The leaflets definitely focused on conservation were, for the most part, concerned with the management of environments or environmental factors. There were units on saving the soil, on vermin, on cover, on winter food for wildlife, on hedgerows, on wildfire, on fish bait, on fish and fishing, and on the management of waterways. At least four of the annual teachers' numbers have been given wholly to the teaching of conservation.[50]

The leaflets also theorized how to instill the conservation ethic. Because opposition to conservation arose "largely from ignorance and greed," educators needed to emphasize how "we are all dependent upon nature." Despite that dependency, we failed to understand that "nature is a wheel many of whose spokes are worm-eaten by thoughtless acts of human beings." People would repair the spokes only when they had "gained an interest" in nature's workings: "The game laws so often misunderstood are the natural out growth of the observations of those who had the vision to see that unless protected these animals would not be able to survive the conditions imposed upon them by the increasing population of human beings." Without the nature study vision, interest in and understanding of conservation would decline. But stressing the interdependence of humans and the things of nature would "lead to a realization that each part of the landscape has a particular form dependent upon it or vice versa each part of the landscape is dependent upon a definite form to control its enemies. This principle influences all agricultural practices, and conservation." The "real results" would be seen "when we can educate the every day man and woman to see the justice of the [conservation] movement."[51]

The Cornell nature study program did more than create pedagogical tools such as pamphlets; it institutionalized nature study by organizing Junior Naturalist Clubs. "Uncle John" Spencer spearheaded the club effort. His personal magnetism and children's genuine affection for him, combined with his ability to successfully present Cornell's programs to wary farmers, made him perfect for the role. One writer remembered that "Uncle John ... made him feel kindly toward a university not wholly admired by his deeply religious relatives because of the early and widespread rumors of its 'godlessness.'"[52] The Junior Naturalist Clubs were easy to form. After a group of children signed membership lists and elected officers, Spencer sent them a charter and badges for each member. Membership dues took the form of letters sent to Cornell describing what the children had learned about nature during the previous week. In return, the children received badges or buttons. "Do not worry about your spelling and punctuation," Spencer counseled Junior Naturalists, "for these will improve as you develop your ideas and powers of observation. Please do not be afraid of us, but write us as you would to an old friend of whom you are very fond."[53] Periodicals such as the *Chautauquan* regularly promoted the clubs. By May 1899 at least 135 clubs had formed. Many were located in larger cities, and forty-five were located outside New York State, some as far away as California. Spencer also attended ordinary farmers' institutes, where he organized special sessions for children that investigated elementary aspects of farming.[54]

The nature study advocates at Cornell also continued to educate teachers. Cornell extension faculty issued four leaflets for teachers each year. By June 1899 twenty-five thousand teachers regularly received the leaflets. Cornell faculty also produced another series of publications directed specifically to the Junior Naturalist Clubs, including a monthly newsletter titled *Junior Naturalist*. The genuine enthusiasm of the Cornell faculty energized their work; nature study supporter and professor of agriculture Isaac P. Roberts characterized the faculty's attitude toward nature study as one of "true missionary spirit." Bailey emphasized the collaborative and entrepreneurial zeal of the Cornell nature study faculty when speaking to rural audiences: "We appeal to every person who loves his kind and his country to help us. We need the cooperation. We can do nothing alone. We want to know the shortcomings and mistakes. We want to reach every child in the New York State; and we hope that others will carry the movement beyond our boundaries and make it better."[55] The combination of evangelical and entrepreneurial drive spread the Cornell program not only to other states but also abroad. Junior Naturalist Clubs appeared in England, France, Egypt, India, and Japan.

The Junior Naturalist Clubs served as one of the precursors to present-day 4-H Clubs. The idea of encouraging educators to tailor their lessons to the practical concerns of rural children remains the essence of 4-H Club work. Franklin M. Reck, historian of 4-H, attributed this concern for the welfare of rural youth to the nature study attitude spread by Bailey and others who built on the Cornell program. "In the inspired, creative [nature study] programs introduced by these scattered schoolmen," argued Reck, "may be found the materials out of which modern 4-H Club work was built."[56]

As Reck implied, the success of the Cornell nature study program drew nationwide attention. A letter from A. E. Winship, editor of the *Journal of Education,* accurately represented the impact of the Cornell program. Winship wrote to Bailey to profess his admiration for the nature study movement:

> Permit me, in thanking you for a set of the Nature-Study Leaflets, to say, from a fairly complete knowledge of what is being done educationally throughout the country, that there is no attempt through the schools to give knowledge of nature and love for it that will compare for a moment in efficiency with the New York plan. It is intelligent, comprehensive, practical. The information is reliable—which is of prime importance—the presentation is interesting, and everything is adapted to the schools, even to untrained teachers. The influence of this work is being felt in the teaching of other subjects, so that Nature Study under the patronage of the State, has a mission in many phases of school work.[57]

Cornell's nature study work and agricultural outreach made it the center of nature study activity during the height of the nature study movement.

The Cornell faculty also continued to reach farmers with practical advice geared toward improving the efficiency of their operations. They sought to inculcate a scientific outlook, which they understood as the key to the future. Secretary of Agriculture James Wilson warned in 1904, "It is becoming increasingly clear that the results of the work of this Department and the experiment stations can not be most effectively and widely utilized by our farmers unless in early life they are taught to think and act along the lines in which the application of scientific principles and discoveries is made to appear theoretically rational as well as practically used."[58]

Despite the prodigious outreach efforts of Cornell faculty, it was not always easy to induce a scientific mind-set from a distance. Previously, Cornell had suggested a series of books that farmers should read, but farmers did not generally view books as a source of knowledge suitable to the practicalities of farming operations. Indeed, many farmers still refused to send their children to school, viewing their farm labor as more valuable than a formal education. Cornell responded with a series of leaflets geared toward issues in practical conservation that interested most farmers. Attempting to resolve seemingly perennial problems regarding the return of spent land to fertility, the first two lessons explicated the principles involved in the formation and tillage of soil, while a third lesson considered the meaning of fertility. A list of questions accompanying each lesson urged farmers to form study groups to share local knowledge gained firsthand. Cornell promised faculty visits to large study groups that explored in detail the questions attached to the lessons. Cornell eventually hired some farmers to help organize study clubs in their neighborhoods. In 1897 nature study literature reached seventy-five hundred farmers enrolled in the reading course; by 1900 that number topped twenty thousand.

An important part of the success of nature study as a strategy for rural outreach was its flexibility. Nature study attempted to teach people about their local environment and thus altered its focus to fit the particular circumstances of the place where it was being implemented. Instruction in agricultural nature study could thereby be adjusted to address fruit growers in New York or wheat farmers in Kansas. By aiming to place people in the context of their local ecology—what nature study advocates described as placing people in "sympathy" with their environment—nature study could meet local needs and elide excess bureaucratic centralization of the curriculum.

Sensing the curricular possibilities of nature study, other institutions around the country copied the Cornell program. Significantly, these included schools that served rural African Americans (in the late nineteenth century, African Americans were overwhelmingly rural southerners) such as the Hampton and Tuskegee institutes. In 1901 both schools opened extension bureaus that produced nature study leaflets modeled after Cornell's publications. Thousands of requests for the leaflets poured into the offices at Hampton and Tuskegee. African American teachers and farmers responded specifically to nature study; they also desperately needed instructional materials for schools that were, as a rule, vastly underfunded. The Hampton and Tuskegee leaflets were distributed at school conventions and country fairs. Some were reproduced in southern newspapers, multiplying their circulation. Hampton Institute also created more than fifty traveling libraries of nature study and agriculture books that supplemented the meager libraries of schools that served African Americans in the rural South.[59]

The most famous scientist working at Tuskegee, George Washington Carver, spearheaded the school's nature study efforts. Carver, a member of the editorial board of *Nature-Study Review,* insisted that farmers must understand the deep processes of nature to fully comprehend the dynamics of agriculture. As Carver wrote in one of his many pamphlets, the study of nature "is the only true method that leads up to a clear understanding of the great natural principles which surround every branch of business in which we may engage."[60] Carver, however, was no single-minded empiricist. Like other nature study advocates, he contended that if nature study were properly presented, it could not fail to both entertain and instruct. Carver's classes at Tuskegee entertained and instructed students about the marvels of the natural world; as one historian wrote, whether "his course was labeled botany, chemistry, or agriculture, what he taught was an appreciation of the miracles and beauties of nature."[61] Moreover, Carver held that nature study education should correlate with "composition, spelling, reading, arithmetic, geography and history classes." Nature study had such wide applicability because it "helps to develop and round out a beautiful character and fit the individual for filling in the best possible manner the great object for which God brought him into existence."[62] For Carver, like other progressive educators, the study of nonhuman nature ministered to spiritual as well as practical matters.

Carver, however, spent much of his tenure at Tuskegee focusing on practical matters. In the farmlands near Tuskegee he encountered landscapes severely taxed by cotton monoculture and degraded by erosion. "Where the land is rolling (and most of it is)," observed Carver, "it washes badly . . . leaving great ditches, gutters and bald places."[63] Carver believed that the introduction of environmentally sound scientific agriculture would alleviate such ecological destruction and lift poor farmers from poverty. By learning about the processes and limits of nature, rural farmers could alleviate erosion, forgo costly fertilizers, spare expenses such as store-bought foods, and generally improve the efficiency and output of their operations. Education was the key to rural uplift, and Carver, like his nature study colleagues at Cornell, threw himself into extension work with true missionary zeal.

Nature study fit the goals of reformers such as Carver especially well because it attempted to develop the entire person—a radical program in white southern society, which viewed blacks, at best, as fit for only manual labor. Thus progressive educators such as W. E. B. DuBois and Kelly Miller, dean of Howard University, insisted on holistic education. "The negro is a man and is entitled to all the privileges of mankind," wrote Miller. "Why should the larger elements of his nature be left unnurtured while the mechanical side only is developed?"[64] By developing all aspects of the human mind, nature study fit the ideology of efficient professionalism and character development and the evangelical sense of righteousness characteristic of white and black progressive educators.

The nature study work of the Tuskegee and Hampton institutes suggests the need to revise one assumption common to Progressive Era historiography on education. Most historians have seen progressive reform in agriculture and outreach programs as emphasizing scientific efficiency, hierarchical management, and organized economic development at the expense of the local knowledge and traditions of African Americans.[65] Although scientific efficiency was undoubtedly a prominent theme of nature study efforts, rural reformers such as Carver encouraged creativity and aesthetic appreciation as well as economic innovation. Moreover, as historian Dianne D. Glave argued, African Americans responded to progressive initiatives by combining them with existing traditions.[66] The humanist and creative side of nature study tempered and localized the drive for scientific and economic efficiency that imposed order on rural agriculture and its peoples.

The nationwide concern for country life also elicited a federal response, one initiated, appropriately enough, with a speech given by Liberty Hyde Bailey. In 1907 the Michigan Agricultural College invited Bailey, one of its most prominent graduates, to deliver the keynote speech at its semicentennial celebration. Bailey seized the opportunity to expound on the crisis in rural life and his proposed remedies. Michigan Agricultural College was an appropriate venue for Bailey's remarks; the school had previously hosted conferences on the rural life crisis, including one in 1902 headed by prominent sociologist Kenyon Butterfield. Among the audience at Bailey's speech was President Theodore Roosevelt. A year later Roosevelt asked Bailey to chair the Commission on Country Life. Roosevelt later recalled, "I doubt if I should have undertaken to appoint a commission if I had not been able to get Director Bailey for its head, and no man in our country did better work for the country than he did on that commission."[67] The Russell Sage Foundation funded the commission with a grant of $5,000.

The commission consisted of a who's who of country life intellectuals, including sociologist Kenyon Butterfield, conservationist and head of the U.S. Forest Service Gifford Pinchot, *World's Work* editor Walter Hines Page, and Henry Wallace of *Wallace's Farmer* (the father and grandfather of future secretaries of agriculture). To gain knowledge about the country life crisis, the committee sent out questionnaires to roughly 550,000 rural residents; more than 115,000 responded. Butterfield conducted research into the country church, and Wallace inquired into farm labor tenancy. The commission also encouraged country people to hold meetings to examine rural problems and then forward their ideas to the commission. Thousands of such meetings were held. Bailey in particular wanted rural people to lead the reform of their lives and institutions, and the commission's report reflected his democratic orientation. "The forces that make for rural betterment must themselves be rural," emphasized the report. "Care must be given in all the reconstructive work to see that local initiative is relied on to the fullest extent, and that federal and even state agencies do not perform what might be done by the people in the communities."[68]

The commission submitted its final report, written by Bailey, to the president on January 23, 1909. Roosevelt forwarded the report to Congress, but the legislators, aggrieved at not being consulted about the commission, refused to fund printing of the document and ordered the commission to desist its activities. Congressional hostility, along with a lack of interest in the commission by President William Howard Taft (who took office shortly after the report was completed), ended its work.

Despite the lack of congressional response, the Commission on Country Life prompted legislation that led to the U.S. Parcel Post System, federally funded rural electrification, and a nationwide extension service. Indeed, the commission focused a great deal of its efforts on the reform of education—not a surprising outcome, given that several members were professors. One question from the commission's questionnaire, "Are the schools in your neighborhood training boys and girls satisfactorily for farm life," elicited a resoundingly negative response. The commission noted, "Everywhere there is demand that education have relations to living, that the schools should express the daily life, and that in rural districts they should educate by means of agriculture and country life subjects." The kind of education the commission envisioned extended well beyond technical instruction in agriculture. "As a pure matter of education," its report stated, "the countryman must learn to love the country and to have an intellectual appreciation of it." The commission cited nature study, among other curricular possibilities, as a way to ensure that agriculture "color the work of rural public schools."[69] Progressive nature study would impart the latest methods of scientific agriculture and bestow the moral foundation that country life reformers, also quick to bring reform to rural churches, wished to impart.[70]

Nature study could also help implement conservation, a key recommendation in the commission's report. Indeed, the report is an overlooked minor classic of progressive conservation. Most important, the report called for a "system of self-sustaining agriculture." Conservationist agriculture would consist of "a system of diversified and rotation farming, carefully adapted in every case to the particular region. Such systems conserve the resources of the land, and develop diversified and active institutions." Conventional agriculture was so wasteful owing to its "lack of appreciation of our responsibility to society to protect and save the land."[71] Like other aspects of country life, moral reform was central to the commission's understanding of the need to implement conservation.

Crucially, the findings of the report did not remove conservation from social conditions; rather, the commission viewed conservation and social reform as intertwined. Writing about the "monopolistic control of streams," which it perceived as a "real and immediate danger," the commission recommended a new governmental body charged with "protecting the people in their ownership" and "reserving to agriculture" appropriate amounts of water. "Waterlordism," argued the commission, "is as much to be feared as landlordism." Thus the role of the government was to help farmers own "both the land and the water," which was crucial if the farmer "is to be a master of his own fortunes." Those fortunes included the entire system of agricultural production and distribution. The commission thus excoriated the "injustice, inequalities, and discriminations on the part of transportation companies and middlemen," recommending a "searching inquiry" into these "grave abuses."[72]

The commission also coupled watershed conservation with forest conservation: "The loss of soil in denuded areas increases the menace of flood." Additionally, the "reckless destruction" of forests has "ruined streams for navigation, power, irrigation [and] common water supplies." Clearly forest and stream must be preserved together. The commission cited "communal forests in Europe" that "yield revenue to the cities and towns by which they are owned and managed" as a model for how the United States might mitigate the destruction of its own forests. The commission reported that it had "heard strong demand from farmers for the establishment" of similar reservations.[73]

As with waters and forests, soil conditions also worried the commission. Soil depletion was so serious that it constituted an "acute national danger." The danger threatened both the land and the social world. With the depletion of "virgin fertility . . . a system of tenantry farming has gradually developed." Tenant farmers—a "pathetic social condition"—"have little interest in the land." Tenancy was worst in areas dominated by single-crop agriculture. The commission insisted that new social institutions must arise to assuage the intertwined fates of nature and rural social life. "The hope for the future" came from the work of "public institutions that are devoted to the new agriculture." That work had already begun. New institutions such as land-grant colleges and experiment stations were "teaching the people how to diversify their farming and to redeem themselves from the bondage of a hereditary system."[74]

As difficult as creating those new institutions may have been, it was not as great a challenge as reforming rural schools while retaining core components of their provincial character. Nature study and agricultural education could assuage but could not overcome the heavy contradictions that fostered the country life movement. The country life reformers' emphasis on education caused them to slight other social factors that contributed to the urbanization of America. Some reformers stubbornly refused to acknowledge that, despite reforms, farming remained a demanding, difficult way of life. Moreover, revolutions in farmland technologies improved agricultural efficiency and reduced the need for manual labor, thus contributing to the exodus to the city. The relationship between education and new technologies also remained a difficult one. Education could impart knowledge of new technologies and could even place them in the context of the greater workings of nature. But education alone could not sufficiently abate the power of technological change to foment a revolution in the manners and morals of rural life. The modern values represented by updated agricultural technology both eased the manual labor associated with an agricultural livelihood and encased rural people in modern values and patterns of living. Technologies expressed the cultural changes demanded by scientific innovation and economic efficiency that were incompatible with traditional rural values.

Though it could change culture and enhance worldviews, education could not combat high land prices or the lure of easier work at higher wages in some urban occupations. Education could do much to enrich rural culture, but through its promotion of science and scientific thinking, it also enhanced the forces of industrial capitalism that were remaking the structure and culture of rural communities. Education reformers in the country life movement thus struggled with the same issues that define much of the debate on education today. Although country life reformers such as Liberty Hyde Bailey wished to preserve local control and the regional character of the countryside school, they also understood the need for the professional standards that inevitably imposed curricular norms on all schools. Local culture could not be modernized and still retain the values it once promoted. Given that both local and federal control could impose unwise standards on the schools, nature study—with its flexible curriculum meant to serve local needs and its ethical as well as scientific basis—met the challenges of the rural problem as well as any other curricular initiative did.

Conclusion

The Decline and Rebirth
of Nature Study

Nature-study will endure, because it is natural and of
universal application. Methods will change and will fall into
disrepute; its name will be dropped from the curriculums;
here and there it will be encased in the school master's
"method" and its life will be smothered; now and then it
will be overexploited; with many persons it will be a fad:
but the spirit will live.
—Liberty Hyde Bailey, *The Nature Study Idea*

As with all the disparate parts of Progressive Era reform, nature study was greatly affected by World War I. The war haunted nature lovers. *Nature-Study Review* asserted that the "appalling loss of life" caused by the war "must over-shadow all else," but its writers were also cognizant of the "added destruction of Nature that has been fiendish." For nature lovers, the destructive power of war and the beauties of nature were inextricably linked. "To study and to admire nature in these coming days when she appears in her most charming garb," continued the *Review* in the spring of 1918, "is to be saddened by the obtrusion of the vision of whole countrysides laid in waste, of shrines of nature-lovers in all parts of the world violated or obliterated."[1]

Because the tranquility encountered in nature sharply contrasted with the devastation caused by war, nature study advocates found in the green world a refuge from thoughts of the ongoing destruction. During times "when cares and anxieties weigh heavily upon us," editorialized Anna Botsford Comstock, "diversion is often attained most easily by going to the fields and woods."[2] Just as nature study advocates used immersion in the things of nature to combat the general malaise arising from modern life, so too could nature assuage the specific spiritual crisis engendered by the war. Comstock and other nature lovers worried that such an attitude might appear selfish. She argued that only by maintaining mental strength through abandoning themselves in the common things of nature could people summon the necessary resources to face the daunting challenges of the day. Retreat to nature was not a flight from responsibility but a therapeutic recharging that allowed the grand struggle to enact a better world to continue.

Other writers in *Nature-Study Review* understood the war as typifying the very traits of modern life against which nature lovers rebelled. Cora A. Smith of Erie, Pennsylvania, argued that nature study helped create the "Army of Future Defense," a revivification of spirit and a rededication to human decency and progress as defined by those who knew "man's place in nature." Yet the knowledge of man's place in nature had to include the spiritual basis of human endeavor. Indeed, "our present enemies"—those who deny the spiritual basis of human existence—do not know of the victory "by Love over Might, by spirit over body," despite the fact that "they have penetrated nature's cold, material facts." The nature study debate with modernity extended to the restrictive, technocratic rationality that unlocked the secrets of nature but also organized the means for efficient warfare. Nature study advocates responded by continuing to insist on the need to surround science with ethical deliberation and to enrich the modern relationship between people and nature. "We might say that to teach nature-study is to humanize science, giving it the warmth of the child's interest," asserted Smith. "It is to create a background against which lives may be built with knowledge of the Divine plan."[3] Nature study rhetoric connected the war to the mechanistic, unfeeling character of modern society.

The use of nature to reinforce political resolve in the troubled times of war fit with the larger progressive belief in using a variety of means—such as propaganda—to ensure proper morale in the home-front population. Preparing people for war combined the progressive concerns over individual reform with social betterment. If morality involved obeying laws originating from outside the self, then morale, the innate strength of the individual, consisted of adapting the inner resources of the self to a larger cause. The psychic health of the individual thus influenced the social health of the nation. Progressive social scientists and supporters of nature study such as G. Stanley Hall and Luther Gulick embraced this view, finding a compelling connection between the reform of individuals and the greater social needs of the nation. By theorizing nature as a means of enhancing psychic health in order to steel the individual to the ugly necessities of war, nature study advocates contributed to the larger progressive program of a (supposedly) benign mobilization of people for the greater good.

Yet this confident engagement of individual and social power in the cause of war foreshadowed the decline of progressivism and, with it, the nature study movement. The loftiest rhetoric of progressive reformers always paled against their real-world achievements, as deeply impressive as those were. The rhetoric of war was especially susceptible to overblown pronouncements, and the resulting Great Crusade, despite a solid military victory, could not compete with the public dreams of its most fervent supporters. After two decades of constant work, the gap between dreams and reality sapped the drive and moral vision of progressive leaders and their publics. Moreover, many progressives such as John Dewey immediately regretted the use of propaganda to sway public opinion; connections between the mobilization of individuals and social improvement turned out to be more difficult to make than many progressive activists initially believed. The intellectual basis that connected individual and social reform yielded to easier, more personalized concerns. The war itself did not end the drive for progressive reform—indeed, progressive reform continued throughout the 1920s—but it heralded the revival of deep social divisions and the growing intellectual malaise toward social betterment. After the war, the propensity for organized, ameliorative reform yielded to the corporate values of mass consumption and commercialized leisure that became the popular ethos of the 1920s.

The war also greatly impacted one of the prime motivations for nature study—the conservation of nature. The United States' entry into the war, and especially the homeland preparations for it, significantly altered the public perception of conservation. Conservation was a prominent part of home-front war activities. With the greater demand for food and materials, conservation came to signify maximum effectiveness of resource exploitation. Waste, like the kaiser, was an enemy to be vanquished. No longer prioritizing human moral duty to the green world or wildlife viability, the conservation crusade became much more instrumental, development oriented, and tied to industrial and national priorities. The uneasy and constantly shifting alliance between science and sentiment tipped toward the zeal for efficient production.

A good example of this transition can be found in school gardening. The rhetoric of nature study gave way to the expedient language of economic expansion. The Department of Education viewed children and their gardens in the nationalized and militarized language of "the United States School Garden Army." The army's goal was to vanquish waste: unused soil was "slacker land"; newspaper headlines demanded that citizens "Make Use of Your Waste Land and Be Patriotic" and reminded readers that "Grass and Weeds Won't Feed an Army." Young gardeners became "soldiers of the soil."[4] This ideology led to more gardens, but it tied gardening to wartime expediency, leaving science and sentiment behind.

The mobilization for war also emphasized the progressives' ambitious program to reconstruct the private behavior of the individual. As socialist clergyman Walter Rauschenbusch asserted, "the greatest contribution which any man can make to the social movement is the contribution of a regenerated personality."[5] Well-regarded Congregational minister Washington Gladden concurred, maintaining that business and government reform represented only the surface of the needed transformation. "What we have got to have," wrote Gladden, "is a different kind of men and women."[6] Nature study, though not as intrusive as other progressive programs, did try to produce the kind of people who were at once scientifically minded and sympathetically connected to nature.

Reforming the core morality of human beings naturally pointed to the importance of education, helping to explain the ardent progressive faith in the revolutionary possibilities of curricular change. Those who championed the innovative pedagogy that made up the "new education" were never solely concerned with how children best learned; they were also thinking about the kind of person and citizen such an education could create. This is one reason nature study advocates rejected the memorization of facts and other traditional pedagogical methods used to introduce science to children. Nature study advocates focused not on the fact but on the meaning of the fact and thus its importance to individual personality. As Liberty Hyde Bailey asserted, nature study "is the full expression of personality." This flowering of individuality will "reach the masses and revive them."[7] Charles Scott also highlighted the transformation of the individual in his popular textbook *Nature Study and the Child*. Asserting that "nature study . . . aims to develop each child as an individual," Scott argued that the ultimate aim of nature study was to lead the child "up from nature to the Author of nature."[8] Contact with nature was part of the larger progressive ideal of national betterment through the transformation of individuals.

Yet over the years, this bold attempt to reshape individuals wore thin, and with the progressive enthusiasm for war, individuals were less sure where such reforms might lead. Moreover, newly available consumer goods provided an easier route to personal revitalization than the more difficult work of learning about nature.[9] Even Comstock could proclaim the joys of "Nature-Study from a Car Window" without questioning how automobiles might fit into the enduring nature study method of direct contact with the natural world.[10] As with so much of American life, the potent pleasures of consumerism trumped the more difficult work of intellectual and spiritual insight. As with progressivism as a whole, much of the reforming energy had left the nature study movement.

Just as individualized consumption trumped the push for social regeneration, the rhetorical justification of nature study as immersing young minds in the workings of the author of nature lost its power as science became increasingly secular in the twentieth century. No longer could scientists confidently expound on the ways science contributed to religious and moral development. Natural theology gave way to secular precision. The First World War exacerbated these trends because of the vital need to emphasize the physical sciences to combat the enemy's poison gas and submarines. The biological sciences, though important, took a backseat to the pressing concerns of the physical sciences. The Wilson administration created the National Research Council, and the physical and chemical sciences dominated research. The halcyon days of natural history and its higher spiritual purpose had long departed.[11]

Perhaps most important to the decline of nature study was that after two solid decades of reform efforts, the difficulties of establishing nature study in the schools remained unresolved. Chief among these difficulties was the recruitment and training of teachers. Charles Eliot summarized the problem in a short defense of nature study. "To my thinking," he argued, "the real reason for the unsatisfactory condition of nature-study in American schools is that it is practically impossible in many places to find teachers who are competent to direct the study in an intelligent manner."[12] Qualified teachers were so rare that one textbook written for classroom instruction bluntly suggested how science teachers might conceal their own ignorance.[13] Training teachers who were pedagogically competent for the varied purposes of nature study was particularly demanding. The nature study movement required teachers who were knowledgeable in basic science and also able to introduce children to the spiritual benefits of contact with nature. Successful nature study teachers, explained Mary C. Dickerson in *Nature-Study Review*, "should have felt the influence of nature. She must at some time in her life have felt sympathy not only with man but with all life."[14] In a country where such ideas were radical and where teacher training in basic science was rare, nature study advocates envisioned a kind of teacher that scarcely existed. Like progressive education more broadly, many nature study ideas were wonderfully innovative yet impractical, given the insufficient resources available to educators who wished to implement them.

In 1909 Arthur S. Dewing surveyed teachers to determine the practical obstacles that impeded effective nature study. Thirty-seven percent cited the difficulty of securing appropriate study materials, 30 percent worried over their own lack of knowledge, and 18 percent confessed to a lack of time for nature study.[15] The multiple purposes of and justifications for nature study also confused teachers. A 1925 study by Christine Hartley described nineteen different objectives cited as the "real purpose" of nature study. The most widely given justifications were "to obtain knowledge of and interest in the world about us, to cultivate the habit of observing and interpreting what is seen, to regulate human conduct by understanding nature, to provide a source of happiness throughout life, to help one better enjoy leisure time, to acquire facts, and to love nature."[16] Such a varied list of outcomes must have been daunting for even the most seasoned teacher, let alone the nature study novice. The same diversity and flexibility that allowed nature study to fulfill local purposes in a wide-ranging and interdisciplinary manner also created confusion and a lack of focus among many of its practitioners.

For those instructors who could teach nature study and teach it well, there was still the daunting task of transporting urban children to the countryside. School gardens could achieve a great deal, but they did not fulfill the entire mandate of nature study. "The teacher in the densely populated areas of great cities," averred Stanley Coulter, "works at a disadvantage."[17] Other writers agreed. "The intelligent observation of nature seems very desirable," stressed one group of educators, "but to secure it under the ordinary limitations of the schools has proved to be one of the most elusive tasks that teachers have ever undertaken."[18] Nature study teachers faced a difficult dilemma. They believed that the conditions of city life justified, even demanded, that nature study become part of the curriculum, yet the very conditions of urban life made enacting their remedy all but impossible. Even Comstock came to believe that nature study would survive not in schools but in camps, vacations, leisure time, and youth organizations.

Faced with the practical challenges and the vague goal of securing students' "sympathetic" interaction with nature, many teachers, especially those not deeply schooled in nature study, turned to the old enemy of Louis Agassiz: books. Literature, rather than the things of nature, became the source material for many nature study classrooms. Dallas Lore Sharp's *Ways of the Woods,* for example, was required reading for eighth-grade nature study students in New York City. Teachers who substituted books for contact with nature could find intellectual justification from Edward Thorndike, a man who hated nonhuman nature but advised teachers that using literature to give students insight into the only nature he cared about—human nature—was excellent pedagogy.[19] Even Bailey supported the use of textbooks—after students had encountered nature firsthand and thus formed original impressions of it. If nature study differed from science in its attention to questions of meaning, then many teachers felt that they could safely use literature to begin nature study before moving students toward experimental science.

Yet books used to promote an interest in nature could promote instead the mawkish sentimentalism that nature study critics associated (at times correctly) with the movement. If not leavened with science, literary nature study could devolve into a quest for superficial emotional satisfaction. Comstock described such growing pains as the "cute and fluffy" stage of nature study, one that resulted from the "imagination and enthusiasm of those teachers trained in pedagogy but utterly untrained in science."[20] The sympathy that nature study proponents sought was not mere tender sentiment but an emotional and intellectual understanding of the interconnectedness of life. Teachers found it difficult to develop in their students a relationship with nature that was not characterized by one of two extremes: disaffected scientific detachment or maudlin sentiment. The teacher's challenge was to translate the child's enthusiastic interest in the outdoor world into the acquisition of knowledge and a mature appreciation of the wonders of nature.

Moreover, "cute and fluffy" coded as feminine (although male nature study proponents also engaged in weepy sentiment), and the postwar backlash against female teachers was another factor in the decline of nature study. In the politically reactionary aftermath of the war, dozens of authorities either decried the "man shortage" in education or claimed that professional status hurt women, causing such supposed problems as "female burnout" or even infertility. And those women who were not suffering due to their professional status were assumed to be incapable of advanced reason. This new backlash highlighted the long-standing, deeply gendered criticism of nature study as too sentimental. Quantitative science was cloaked in presumably masculine traits. The qualities that ensured sound experimentation—reason, adherence to method, objectivity, and quantification—coded as masculine. Sentiment and a feeling of interconnectedness with the natural world implied a female and thus unscientific mind-set.[21]

Nature study pedagogy exacerbated these gender stereotypes in two ways. First, by emphasizing the student's active engagement with the subject matter, nature study undermined the traditional authority of the teacher. No longer did the instructor possess passive knowledge that was imparted to the learner. Rather, in nature study and the best of progressive education, the teacher became a facilitator and molder of innate student interest. The initiative to learn came from the student as well as the instructor—a troubling development for traditionalists who wished to maintain the masculine hierarchy of the conventional student-teacher relationship. Many experts argued that, deprived of masculine authority, male students suffered. "Women teachers do not appeal in any way to the virile or feral qualities" of boys, wrote educator William Lee Howard in the *Arena*. "The want of rapport naturally causes the boys to remain indifferent in their lessons."[22] Botanist John Coulter agreed: "The foolish and forced sprightliness of many [female] teachers" had a propensity to "repel rather than attract strong children."[23]

Second, nature study's conservation ethic did not fit with the ostensibly objective standards of scientific investigation. Advocacy was not supposed to impinge on science—especially the advocacy for "soft" concerns such as birds, gardens, trees, and spiritual interaction with nature. The difficult relationship between nature study and science was thus infused with gender ideology that reinforced critical suspicions that nature study was not sound pedagogy but sentimental faddishness. G. Stanley Hall, for example, criticized many nature study textbooks because they were insufficiently scientific and suffered from what he described as "effeminization."[24] Caring for nature was female sentiment, not sound science.

All these factors combined to emphasize order and discipline instead of student-centered learning in the new education of the postwar years. The progressive goal of establishing science in schools succeeded; the goal of child-centered, progressive pedagogy did not. One history of education summarized the legacy of progressivism in education in this way: "pedagogical progressives lost out to the administrative progressives."[25] Nature study advocates had long feared that the disciplinary impetus of organized science would crowd out broad education in basic natural history. Moreover, as nature study advocates also feared, disciplinary spirit impinged on pedagogy. The teacher-dominated, subject-centered curriculum became part of the bureaucratic public school system. Child-centered learning in the outdoors did not fit the new curriculum.

Yet despite these very real difficulties, nature study thrived in many ways. One of its lasting achievements is that it helped institute science as an important part of the primary school curriculum. But the difficulty of finding a pedagogy that increases rather than retards children's interest in science continues to vex educators. Just as nature study methods were subject to fierce debate, teachers today still struggle with how to introduce science to young minds in a way that stimulates a love for learning as well as an ethical responsibility to nonhuman nature. During its heyday, nature study advocates claimed that their pedagogy was reaping benefits, in that students were becoming more attuned to the possibilities of learning from and about their environment rather than merely memorizing scientific facts. For example, James Needham, a professor at Cornell, scorned the lingering influence of memorization and recitation among his freshman charges. "Words," complained Needham, "are symbols of experience only to those who know their content. Words express concepts derived from things. It is the study of things that puts meaning into them." Yet the study of words was yielding to the more meaningful study of things: "The leaven of the nature-study movement is working." Needham could make that claim because the students in his freshman laboratory increasingly "know things out of doors" and "are interested in the world they live in and in all their fellow creatures, and . . . want to handle the raw materials and build up from them. Fewer come who are satisfied with the shadow of knowledge, not knowing its substance."[26]

Whatever the merit of such claims, what remains striking about the nature study movement is that, as Liberty Hyde Bailey predicted, it has thrived as an ideal in different times and under different names. Like progressivism more broadly, nature study went into decline in the years following World War I, only to reemerge in many different guises of contemporary life.

One way that nature study ideals persevered was through the wilderness movement. Although the nature study emphasis on local nature, gardens, and schoolchildren might at first glance seem anathema to wilderness advocacy, the two phenomena in fact overlapped a great deal. Wilderness advocacy stemmed from the same critique of the shallowness and conformity of modern life that drove nature study. As shown by Paul Sutter in his pathbreaking study of inter-war wilderness advocacy, much of the wilderness ideal derived from moral revulsion with the expansive drive and clutter of modern life. Both nature study and wilderness advocacy sought to use nature to accommodate values that commercialism could not meet. Moreover, wilderness advocacy shared with nature study uneasy accommodations with modern life. The designation of untrammeled nature as wilderness areas became a bureaucratic means to protect lands from recreational overuse. But the fact that modern bureaucracy could be used to preserve wilderness does not negate the critique of materialism that helped make wilderness important to so many people.[27]

Many of the activists who worked for wilderness also worked for education reform, and the two issues were often intertwined. As we shall see, Aldo Leopold, a founder of the Wilderness Society, was immersed in nature study during childhood and, as an adult, levied a similar critique against the education system of his day. Another founder of the Wilderness Society, Robert Sterling Yard, also turned to education and wilderness advocacy to combat the rampant commercialization of national parks. The Park Service, like the nature study movement, was active in spreading a variety of educational materials. Yard was one of its most successful proponents, helping to distribute numerous books and articles on the park ideal. But the promotional aspects of his work did not sit well with Yard. Indeed, the tensions between genuine education and his job as an advocate of national parks drove Yard toward wilderness advocacy. Last, with the growing awareness of ecology and the role of wilderness areas in providing researchers access to ecological systems unimpeded by industrial processes, wilderness became important for scientific research, once again overlapping with nature study as an educational institution.

As wilderness areas, national forests, and reclamation districts became important parts of the federal bureaucracy, the government moved to create well-trained workers to staff its land management agencies. Conservation education emerged in the 1920s and 1930s to meet this need. By the 1930s, educational journals regularly carried articles about conservation and education. These articles, however, did not include the subjective and sympathetic side of nature study conservation—only science and its practical application. Most conservation education focused on the technical skills associated with regional planning, forest management, or other practical matters of utilitarian conservation. Conservation education thus differed from nature study because the expedient development of resources rather than the sympathetic interconnection of people and nature characterized the new course of study.[28] Yet the idea of immersing students in applied science to further conservation was a direct continuation of one important goal of nature study.

Another of the lasting pedagogical legacies of nature study is its role as a precursor to environmental education. Environmental education surged to prominence due to the environmental activism of the 1960s and was codified by the Environmental Education Act of 1970. The early leaders of the environmental education movement noted nature study's legacy. Charles Roth, in his capacity as educational director of the Massachusetts Audubon Society, suggested that environmental education attempted to bring together the philosophies of the American Nature Study Society, the Conservation Education Association, and the Outdoor Education Association.[29] Similarly, Malcolm Swan cited nature study, and especially its insistence on direct experience with nature, as a forerunner of environmental education.[30]

Examining the theoretical basis of their shared pedagogy reveals the connection between progressive nature study and contemporary environmental education. In defining environmental education, John F. Disinger of the Ohio State University cited the goals put forward by the United Nations Educational, Scientific, and Cultural Organization (UNESCO), which included fostering awareness of the ecological interdependence of urban and rural areas, providing each person with opportunities to acquire knowledge and values about local environments, and changing behaviors that exploited the environment.[31] Surely Anna Botsford Comstock, Liberty Hyde Bailey, and their nature study cohorts would wholly embrace these objectives, finding in them the goals of the nature study movement stated in contemporary language. Indeed, environmental education is merely nature study in an age defined by ecology and environmental crisis. The primary differences are nature study's belief in pedagogy as a way to instill character reform and improve the lives of students, and the modern understanding of ecology that infuses the environmental education movement. Moreover, the contemporary jargon of "learner-centered" and "interdisciplinary" environmental education also describes nature study, indicating the ongoing influence of nature study in particular and progressive education more broadly. The stunning variety of publications, camps, organizations, school gardens, and other innovative and successful efforts at contemporary environmental education evoke the tradition of nature study.

Even though nature study did not use the language of scientific ecology that was just being formulated at the turn of the twentieth century, the contemporary reader is nevertheless struck with nature study's ecological orientation. Nature study advocates constantly argued that the things of nature must be studied in their natural setting and in their relationship with other things of nature. For example, Charles B. Scott, instructor of nature study at the State Normal School in Oswego, New York, declared that nature study is "nature studied in its relations. Every phenomenon in nature stands in relation to a host of other phenomena." If the things and processes of nature were not studied in their totality, "we study only a part of nature, and that side of it which is least adapted to our elementary schools, and of least value to our pupils."[32] Cornell University's E. Laurence Palmer put the matter this way: "In Nature-Study the important thing is not the name of the individual forms of life but an understanding of their relation to other forms of life." But nature study pedagogy did not ignore facts; the narrative that evoked such relationships was such that "no child can help but get the name . . . with a little assistance."[33] The best of nature study rejected the mere cataloging of nature for the more interesting and ecological work of learning how various parts of the natural world interacted. Nature study insisted on the interconnection of human and nonhuman life, a theme that continues in modern-day environmental education.

Nature study advocates also explicitly adopted the science of ecology as the professional extension of nature study. "Ecology," declared Comstock, "is merely nature-study grown to robust middle age." She made this assertion with confidence because ecologists "took their results into the field . . . and used them in discovering how manifold life was affected in its development and habits by its environment." In short, "the Ecologist was fired with the nature-study idea." She placed the development of ecology and its comparatively slow acceptance by the broad scientific community within the debate between nature study and laboratory science. "It took too much time [for scientists] to work out the problems of the interdependence of life; it was much easier to catch something, chloroform it, and cut it into sections." Like other nature study advocates, Comstock fervently desired that the public embrace ecology through their own investigations into natural history. In Comstock's ideal world of popular nature study, "even those who never come to universities" would "be able to go out into the fields and without the aid of books or teachers read the lessons in God's great laboratory."[34]

Most important, the science of ecology implies the kind of moral lessons that nature study advocates strived to impart. Ecology is the study of the relationships between an organism and its environment. It shows how deeply and systematically intertwined living things are with one another and with their environment: in short, ecology demonstrates that, as the popular phrase puts it, "everything's connected." Like any science, ecology does not proffer moral lessons, and like nature study, ecology has veered between romantic nature love and imperial, utilitarian concerns. Nevertheless, the basic idea of the mutual fate of people and their environments implies such obvious moral instruction that nature study activists could embrace the science of ecology as an expression of nature study morality. Ecology demonstrates humanity's inevitably intertwined ties to all of life and thus holds our collective actions responsible for the fate of nature—and ourselves. It also points to the future: as an example of deeply historical thinking, ecology demonstrates how the future arises from the present, emphasizing the importance of our actions today. The moral concerns of the natural theology tradition found new expression in the staunchly secular science of ecology. It is ecology that translates Progressive Era nature study and conservationist concerns into modern environmentalism. Rather than an acute break between conservation and environmentalism, we can see a united tradition that merged science and moral suasion in the service of environmental reform.

The most important lesson that Comstock's "God's great laboratory" imparted to its students was the need for wildlife and wildland conservation. Nature study was central to environmental reform. Comstock was quick to credit nature study with spreading the conservation gospel:

Note the great work done through the nature-study idea in the conservation of wild life. With fatuity that our descendants of three centuries hence will characterize [as] a criminal stupidity we have exterminated many species of birds, destroyed many interesting and harmless wild animals, hacked down our trees ruthlessly and cleared our streams of valuable fish. . . . It was not until the nature-study movement permeated the people throughout the land that they came to resent this extermination.[35]

Nature study does not deserve sole credit for this resentment, but it does demand a place in this tradition. By stressing the interdependence of humans and nature and a sympathetic attitude toward the environment, nature study was able to nurture what Comstock described as "a sufficiently strong popular opinion . . . to establish and carry out protective laws."[36] Conservation—what Cornell nature study professor Laurence Palmer called "science with a conscience"—remains one of the legacies of the nature study movement.[37]

The ideology of nature study conservation—that people must develop an emotional connection with nonhuman nature so they will be moved to save it—is a common theme in environmentalist thought. Writer and conservationist Joseph Wood Krutch is but one example of an important modern figure from the history of environmental activism who explicitly linked aesthetic and emotional interests to the conservation crusade. In 1967 Krutch argued that the decline in natural history—as opposed to specialized, disinterested science—was a "calamity to those of us whose attitude toward nature is both esthetic and emotional as well as scientific, and to whom, for that reason, conservation is a primary concern." For Krutch, mechanistic interpretations of the green world stymied the sympathetic interconnection with nature that promoted a conservationist ethic. To combat the idea that nature can be known only through quantification, Krutch hoped that schools might teach "natural history as well as laboratory biology." Closely echoing the nature study movement, Krutch concluded that students needed to learn not only about nature but also about "the perennial joy and consolation which nature can provide."[38] More recently, ecologist Stephen Kellert put the matter this way: "When people are not emotionally and intellectually attached to buildings, landscapes, and places around them, they will rarely be motivated to commit the resources and energies needed to sustain [them]."[39] Nature study is not the only source of these ideas, but due to the great number of people it affected, it is arguably the most important.

Nature study also exerted a decisive influence on some of the great conservationists of the twentieth century. Examining the legacy of nature study provides a final chance to test my thesis: the mature thought of environmentalists raised in nature study should reflect its attitudes about the need for spiritual interaction with nature and the need to inform science with ethical commitment. To analyze this idea, I briefly examine the thought of Aldo Leopold and Rachel Carson.

The great wildlife ecologist Aldo Leopold is best known as author of the seminal *A Sand County Almanac*. Leopold's family encouraged his childhood interest in the outdoors, and he spent a great deal of time exploring the lands near Burlington, Iowa, where he grew up. At age eleven he wrote in his school composition book that his favorite class was "bird study." At age thirteen his parents gave him a copy of nature study advocate Frank M. Chapman's *Handbook of Birds of Eastern North America,* a book that exerted a lifelong influence on the young conservationist. He also read Ernest Thompson Seton and Liberty Hyde Bailey. "As a boy, I . . . read with intense sympathy, Seton's masterly biography of a lobo wolf," wrote Leopold.[40] He went on to decry his early attitude toward predators—most famously in his short essay "Thinking Like a Mountain"—recognizing that his mature thought was more closely aligned with Seton's than with that of the predator control advocates formulating federal policy. Like Seton, Leopold came to value predators and their role in nature's economy. Likewise, Bailey's moral ecology informed Leopold's belief in the need for a conservation ethic. As shown by Thomas Dunlap, Leopold's articulation of ethical values regarding the land drew "most clearly from Liberty Hyde Bailey." In 1915 Leopold copied quotations from Bailey's *The Holy Earth* into a notebook—and undoubtedly Bailey's emphasis on a "biocentric" world impressed Leopold.[41] "Time was," wrote Leopold in very Baileyesque language, "education moved toward soil, not away from it." Not surprisingly, Leopold quoted Bailey in his classic textbook *Game Management.*[42]

Most important, Leopold exemplified the nature study attitude in his mature writings. He spent a great deal of time thinking about education—Leopold was sharply critical of dominant modes of pedagogy—and he posited the study of natural history as an antidote to overspecialized education. "The Ph.D.," wrote Leopold, "may become as callous as an undertaker to the mysteries at which he officiates." This ignorance arose from the conditions of modern life. "Civilization has so cluttered this elemental man-earth relation with gadgets and middlemen," asserted Leopold, "that awareness of it is growing dim."[43] Natural history could be cluttered too, advancing a taxonomic rather than ecological understanding of the natural order. Leopold criticized "labeling species and amassing facts" when such classification came at the expense of considering the relationship of "plants and animals" to "each other," "to the soil and water," and to "human beings."[44] In contrast, Leopold echoed the common nature study theme that the awakened mind could find "real treasures" with an ecological view of common objects such as "the weeds in a city lot" or a "cow pasture"; one need not traipse off to the "South Seas" for ecological enlightenment.[45]

A central part of Leopold's idea of constructive natural history education was a careful examination of humans' ethical responsibilities toward nature, responsibilities that arose from the human consciousness of being part of an ecological community.[46] In his essay "The Land Pyramid," Leopold argued, "An ethic to supplement and guide the economic relation to land presupposed the existence of some mental image of land as a biotic mechanism. We can be ethical only in relation to something we can see, feel, understand, love or otherwise have faith in."[47] It was precisely ethical "content" that Leopold found lacking in conservation education: "It defines no right or wrong, assigns no obligation, calls for no sacrifice, implies no change in the current philosophy of values." The "net result" of such education is that "we have more education but less soil" and "fewer woods."[48]

Leopold also extended his analysis of science education to the omission of actual nature in the science classroom. Echoing the critique of zoologists made by Hornaday and Adams nearly a half century earlier, he criticized the "typical zoology department" because "the living animal is virtually omitted from the present system of zoological education." The exclusion of animals and the human relationship with them prompted the skeptical Leopold to wonder whether "the educated citizen" can know that he or she is merely a "cog in an ecological mechanism." "Perhaps the most serious obstacle impeding the evolution of a land ethic," continued Leopold, "is the fact that our educational and economic system is headed away from rather than toward, an intense consciousness of land." Science was a "sharpener of [humankind's] sword" rather than "the searchlight on his universe."[49] An educational searchlight, however, could reveal unpleasant truths. In one of his most famous formulations, Leopold argued:

> One of the penalties of an ecological education is that one lives alone in a world of wounds. Much of the damage inflicted on land is quite invisible to laymen. An ecologist must either harden his shell and make believe that the consequences of science are none of his business, or he must be the doctor who sees the marks of death in a community that believes itself well and does not want to be told otherwise.[50]

The history of environmentalism might be thought of as teaching people to see the wounds that, if sympathetically motivated, they might heal.

Even more than Leopold, Rachel Carson embraced the nature study ideal. Perhaps the central figure in the history of modern environmentalism, Carson was reared in an environment of nature study. Her mother, Maria Carson, was, according to Rachel Carson's biographer Linda Lear, "the perfect nature-study teacher." Comstock's *Handbook of Nature Study* provided outdoor activities that guided Maria and her children in the woodlands near their Pennsylvania home. Every day, weather permitting, the Carson family could be found enjoying the outdoors, Comstock's book in hand, studying birds and natural history, particularly botany. This upbringing was apparent in young Rachel's early literary efforts. A book of pictures for her father depicted a variety of animal "friends" and otherwise "reflected the influence of the nature-study movement in the Carson household."[51] Soon Rachel was writing and publishing her own stories in such periodicals as *St. Nicholas* magazine, a popular outlet for children's nature study work. When not working on her own stories, she absorbed popular nature study literature such as the novels of Gene Stratton Porter and the essays of Dallas Lore Sharp. Prodded by her mother, Rachel clearly modeled her writing career on that of such pioneering and popular female nature study authors as Porter and Mabel Osgood Wright.

The nature study movement also figured in Carson's writings that urged parents to immerse their children in nature. Carson's piece "Help Your Child to Wonder" appeared in the July 1956 issue of *Woman's Home Companion*. The article urged its readers to feel rather than merely intellectualize their knowledge of nature. In her notes for the article, Carson advanced the idea that "once you are *aware* of the wonder and beauty of earth you will want to learn about it."[52] The article beautifully expressed the nature study worldview and its reform agenda:

A child's world is fresh and new and beautiful, full of wonder and excitement. It is our misfortune that for most of us that clear-eyed vision, that true instinct for what is beautiful and awe-inspiring is dimmed and even lost before we reach adulthood. If I had influence with the good fairy who is supposed to preside over the christening of all children I should ask that her gift to each child in the world be a sense of wonder so indestructible that it would last through life, as an unfailing antidote against the boredom and disenchantment of later years, the sterile preoccupation with things that are artificial, the alienation from the sources of our strength.[53]

Properly instilled by immersing children in nature, an intellectual curiosity for nature's workings would enrich life and maintain an abiding sense of wonder. Carson argued in classic nature study fashion, "Once the emotions have been aroused—a sense of the beautiful, the excitement of the new and the unknown, a feeling of sympathy, pity, admiration or love—then we wish for knowledge about the object of our emotional response."[54]

Carson furthered these observations in a speech before a thousand members of Theta Sigma Phi, the sorority of women journalists. Announcing that "a large part of my life has been concerned with some of the beauties and mysteries of this earth," she described her worldview as one that provoked "deep thoughts," "unanswerable questions," and a "certain philosophy." Nature lovers are "never bored," for "there is always something new to be investigated." Like her nature study forerunners, she believed that these pleasures were open to all. "The values of contact with the natural world are not reserved for the scientists," declared Carson. "They are available to anyone . . . who will stop to think about so small a thing as the mystery of a growing seed."[55] As someone who grew up without means, Carson understood both the popularity of natural history and that it was accessible to all who could wander in the local forest.

For Carson, exploring local environments was perfect pedagogy. Children's education needed to stem from interaction with nature, not from systematic inquiry. "It is essential that the beginning student should first become acquainted with the true meaning of his subject through observing the lives of creatures in their true relation to each other and to their environment," wrote Carson in an introduction to a booklet for the Animal Welfare Society. If such students observed "artificial conditions," they would develop "distorted conceptions" and a thwarted emotional response to the lifeworld. Like her nature study forebears, Carson worried about the emotional effects of modern life on the moral development of children. "Only as a child's awareness and reverence for the wholeness of life are developed can his humanity to his own kind reach its full development."[56]

Nor did Carson the scientist shy away from the emotional and ethical implications of her worldview. "I am not afraid of being thought a sentimentalist," she declared, because "I believe natural beauty has a necessary place in the spiritual development of any individual or society." As with nature study, the spiritual development of humans implied a conservation ethic. "Whenever we destroy beauty, or whenever we substitute something man-made and artificial for a natural feature of the earth, we have retarded some part of man's spiritual growth." Carson suggested that an affinity for the outdoor world stemmed from human nature and thus could not be described as a mere by-product of modern living: "I believe this affinity of the human spirit for the earth and its beauties is deeply and logically rooted."[57]

Carson's criticisms of the artificial conditions that warped human intellectual and spiritual development point to another lasting legacy of nature study. Environmentalism, along with its embrace of science, is simultaneously infused with criticisms of modern life. Indeed, the insightful, vociferous, and scathing indictment of industrial modernity remains one of environmentalism's most important contributions to public discourse. The narrow instrumentalism and blind consumerism that crowd out other, more fully human ways of being in the world remain a staple object of environmental criticism.

Criticisms of the modern estrangement of people from nature have recently taken some surprising turns that might unite such critiques with scientific findings. Scholars are examining the older nature study idea that human feeling for the earth is deeply and logically rooted; this new concept updates and human-izes the older theory of recapitulation. Called the "biophilia hypothesis," the theory holds that humans, having evolved in a state of nature, contain a funda-mental, genetically based need to affiliate with nonhuman life. Celebrated nat-uralist Edward Wilson defined biophilia as "the innate tendency to focus on life and lifelike processes" and noted, "to the degree that we come to understand other organisms, we will place greater value on them, and on ourselves."[58] Though not yet widely accepted by the scientific community, there is a growing body of evidence that the biophilia hypothesis might represent a way for scien-tists to further investigate the relationship between human and nonhuman na-ture. The key link between the theory of recapitulation and the biophilia hypothesis is that both ideas posit that contact with nature enriches human life and, conversely, that separation from nature diminishes the potential for satis-factory human experience.

Unlike recapitulation, the biophilia hypothesis is a cross-cultural idea that rejects the idea that human civilizations can be ranked hierarchically, based on their technological sophistication. Like recapitulation, the biophilia hypothesis contains important implications for our view of childhood and education. Writ-ing on "The Coming Biophilia Revolution," educational theorist David W. Orr concludes that children require contact with nature or, in his words, "places of mystery and adventure where children can roam, explore, and imagine." Ac-cording to Orr, the education system should not continue its current preoccu-pations with preparing children for "upward mobility" but instead should nourish the nature study value of "a reverence for life" that "would occur more often out-of-doors and in relation to the local community."[59] In Orr's system of education, children would be trained in the biological sciences and engage in meaningful debate about human responsibilities toward nature.

A growing body of scientific evidence suggests the importance of outdoor life for the lives and education of children. Children who roam the outdoors are healthier and happier, and they have better psychological and cultural lives. Moreover, research indicates that children who experience the outdoors become more caring, grounded adults. These ethics extend to the treatment of nature. Thus contemporary research, though not conclusive, seems to validate the na-ture study intuition that children need to experience nature in order to care for it and for their fellows.[60] The biophilia hypothesis may gain its strongest support from scientific research that attempts to understand the relationship between childhood development and immersion in the green world.

Contemporary thinkers such as Orr who connect the ecological crisis to the faulty, nature-hating ideals of our current education system build on the legacy of the nature study movement. Particularly important in this regard is the insistence that scientific education should tackle questions of meaning and the ethical implications of human interaction with nature. This line of thinking understands the wisdom in Stephen J. Gould's observation that "we cannot win this battle to save species and environments without forging an emotional bond between ourselves and nature . . . for we will not fight to save what we do not love."[61] For Orr and Gould, as for Carson and the turn-of-the-century nature study advocates who nurtured her values, interacting with nature is nothing short of a vehicle for human redemption and the good fight to stop the destruction of nature.

Orr and other proponents of ecological education have also built on the insight of progressive nature study advocates when they urge that nature studies correlate with all facets of education. They build on a key insight that all educators must embrace: all education is environmental education. Most education, including the writing and teaching of history, imparts a crucial lesson about the environment: it is so unimportant that it can be entirely ignored. Rather than tying the human relationship with the earth to all disciplines, as it is in reality and as nature study advocates wished, rigid disciplinary boundaries combine with the lack of a broad ecological education to ghettoize "the environment" as little more than another intellectual or disciplinary subspecialty. Part of our current ecological crisis arises from the fact that we have not made the human relationship with nonhuman nature a central part of all learning.

Happily, there are signs of renewed public interest in the relationship among children, education, and nature. Journalist Richard Louv sounds the alarm against what he terms "nature deficit disorder" in his best-selling book *Last Child in the Woods*. Louv elucidates the physical and psychological ill effects of lack of contact with the outdoors and raises the chilling prospect that this distance from the natural world is thwarting the future stewards of the planet. Most important, Louv connects many of the contemporary maladies discussed in the public sphere—childhood obesity, depression, attention-deficit disorder—to a lack of exposure to nature. By tying the common concerns of parents with the protection of nature, Louv and like-minded authors and activists open up new avenues for our culture to address this pressing issue. Louv believes we are at the beginning of a genuine movement to reconnect children with nature, a movement he is furthering through his organization, the Children and Nature Network.[62]

But if we are to address the problem of children suffering from nature-deficit disorder, we must continue to think deeply about science education. Philosopher Bertrand Russell also worried about the consequences of scientific education unleavened with spiritual and aesthetic concern. Such a system of education will never "question the value of science." It will thwart students who "coquette with the idea that perhaps poetry is as valuable as machinery, or love as good a thing as scientific research." If such ideas are aired, "they will be received in a pained silence, and there will be a pretence that they have not been heard." The hierarchy of such education was especially worrisome to Russell, who felt that even scientific investigation would diminish in the long run, because "discovery will be killed by respect for authority." The problems of an instrumentally based scientific society and the fears it engenders, then, are the same ones recognized by nature study. When science "takes out of life the moments to which life owes its value, science will not deserve admiration" but instead will diminish our "heritage of culture and beauty."[63]

The ongoing attempt to institutionalize the insight that an open and loving knowledge of nature is a necessary part of becoming fully human is the greatest legacy of nature study. It is this part of the nature study movement that, working alongside Richard Louv and others, we need to resuscitate today. If society is to bequeath to our children a world worth living in, we need to increase our ecological knowledge and enact a cultural revolution that recognizes when we enrich our relationship with nature, we enrich our very selves.

Educators thus need to forge a system of learning that rejects narrow expediency as its highest value and the best way to know nature. Put another way, we should not turn our children into youthful technocrats but rather help them develop an intertwined and interconnected curiosity, a love of learning and a love for nature. If we continue to impart to our children the narrow understanding of the human relationship with nature inherent in much of modern science and capitalist economics, we will exacerbate—perhaps fatally—the ecological crisis and continue to restrict what it means to be human. As Bertrand Russell wrote:

> It is only insofar as we renounce the world as its lovers that we can conquer it as its technicians. But this division in the soul is fatal to what is best in man. . . . The power conferred by science as a technique is only obtainable by something analogous to the worship of Satan, that is to say, by the renunciation of love. . . . The scientific society in its pure form . . . is incompatible with the pursuit of truth, with love, with art, with spontaneous delight, with every ideal that men have hitherto cherished.[64]

The sympathetic interconnection with nature was a strategy to impart a conservation ethic and the beginnings of scientific inquiry, as well as a means to become wholly human. The recognition of our joyful embeddedness in nature enriches our deepest selves; the false idea that all of life can be quantified is the enemy of human and nonhuman nature. In our contemporary era of efficiency worship and denatured technical discourse, a loving relationship with nature is one value we most urgently need to revive.

Notes

INTRODUCTION: NATURE, SCIENCE, AND SYMPATHY IN THE PROGRESSIVE ERA

1. Liberty Hyde Bailey, *The Nature Study Idea: Being an Interpretation of the New School Movement to Put the Child in Sympathy with Nature* (New York: Doubleday, Page, 1903), 31.
2. Mabel Osgood Wright, *The Friendship of Nature: A New England Chronicle of Birds and Flowers* (1894; reprint, Baltimore: Johns Hopkins University Press, 1999), 86.
3. Horace H. Cummins, *Nature Study by Grades* (New York: American Book Company, 1909), 21.
4. C. W. G. Eifrig, "A Practical Angle in the Aesthetic Side of Nature Study," *Nature-Study Review* 17, no. 8 (November 1921): 327.
5. Robert Wiebe, *The Search for Order, 1877–1920* (New York: Hill & Wang, 1967), 111.
6. Jacob Riis, "What Ails Our Boys?" *Craftsman* 21, no. 1 (October 1911): 6.
7. Anna Botsford Comstock, "Nature Study and Agriculture," *Nature-Study Review* 1, no. 4 (July 1905): 145.
8. Alice Jean Patterson, "A Survey of Twenty Years Progress Made in the Course of Nature Study," *Nature-Study Review* 17 (February 1921): 62.
9. Wilbur S. Jackman, *Nature Study for the Common Schools* (New York: Henry Holt, 1891), 4.
10. William A. McKeever, "A Better Crop of Boys and Girls," *Nature-Study Review* 7 (December 1911): 266.
11. Theodore Roosevelt, "Men Who Misinterpret Nature," in "Roosevelt on the Nature Fakirs," *Everybody's Magazine* 16 (June 1907): 770–774.
12. Gifford Pinchot, *The Fight for Conservation* (New York: Doubleday & Page, 1910), 107–108.
13. David I. Macleod, *The Age of the Child: Children in America, 1890–1920* (New York: Twayne, 1998); Daniel T. Rodgers, "Socializing Middle-Class Children: Institutions, Fables, and Work Values in Nineteenth Century America," in *Growing Up in America: Children in Historical Perspective,* ed. Ray Hiner and Joseph M. Hawes (Urbana: University of Illinois Press, 1985), 128.
14. Liberty Hyde Bailey, *The Nature Study Idea,* 31.
15. John Ruskin, *Fors Clavigera: Letters to the Workmen and Labourers of Great Britain* (Sunnyside, Calif.: George Allen, 1873), letter XXXIV, 5.

16. Charles B. Scott, *Nature Study and the Child* (Boston: D. C. Heath, 1902), 123, 124.

17. Ibid., 126–127, 124.

18. Mabel Osgood Wright, "Fees and Pledges," *Bird Lore* 2, no. 2 (April 1900): 64.

19. Mabel Osgood Wright, *Gray Lady and the Birds: Stories of the Bird Year for Home and School* (New York: Macmillan, 1917), xii.

20. Anna Botsford Comstock, *Handbook of Nature Study* (Ithaca, N.Y.: Comstock Publishing Co., 1911), 5.

21. Ibid., 21.

22. Samuel P. Hays, *Conservation and the Gospel of Efficiency: The Progressive Conservation Movement, 1890–1920* (Cambridge, Mass.: Harvard University Press, 1959), 2.

23. The most prominent proponent of this argument is J. Leonard Bates, who concluded that conservation "was an effort to implement democracy for twentieth-century America, to stop the stealing and exploitation, to inspire high standards of government, to preserve the beauty of mountain and stream, to distribute more equitably the profits of this economy." Despite this brief concern with "beauty," Bates's account accepts the supposedly wholly utilitarian character of conservation. See J. Leonard Bates, "Fulfilling American Democracy: The Conservation Movement, 1907 to 1921," *Mississippi Valley Historical Review* 44, no. 1 (June 1957): 57. Clayton R. Koppes also develops this theme in "Efficiency, Equity, Esthetics: Shifting Themes in American Conservation," in *The Ends of the Earth: Perspectives on Modern Environmental History*, ed. Donald Worster (Cambridge: Cambridge University Press, 1988).

24. The most well-known figure in the history of the conservation movement who might be fairly characterized in the terms Hays ascribes to it was John Wesley Powell, who received only passing mention in Hays's work. For a full explication of Powell and his legacy, see Donald Worster, *A River Running West: The Life of John Wesley Powell* (New York: Oxford University Press, 2002).

25. Hays, *Conservation and the Gospel of Efficiency*, 265.

26. See, for example, Roderick Nash, *Wilderness and the American Mind*, 3rd ed. (New Haven, Conn.: Yale University Press, 1982). For a recent retelling of this fascinating story, see Robert W. Righter, *The Battle over Hetch Hetchy: America's Most Controversial Dam and the Birth of Modern Environmentalism* (New York: Oxford University Press, 2005).

27. Char Miller, *Gifford Pinchot and the Making of Modern Environmentalism* (Washington, D.C.: Shearwater Books, 2004).

28. Char Miller, "A Sylvan Prospect: John Muir, Gifford Pinchot, and Early Twentieth-Century Conservationism," in *American Wilderness: A New History*, ed. Michael Lewis (New York: Oxford University Press, 2007), 144.

29. For the local effects of conservation policy, see Mark David Spence, *Dispossessing the Wilderness: Indian Removal and the Making of the National Parks* (New York: Oxford University Press, 1999); Karl Jacoby, *Crimes against Nature: Squatters, Poachers, Thieves and the Hidden History of American Conservation* (Berkeley: University of California Press, 2001); Louis Warren, *The Hunter's Game: Poachers and Conservationists in Twentieth-Century America* (New Haven, Conn.: Yale University Press, 1997). For an examination of the rural origins of conservation and the impact of federal policy on localities, see Richard Judd, *Common Lands, Common People: The Origins of Conser-*

vation in Northern New England (Cambridge, Mass.: Harvard University Press, 1997). For urban conservation, see David Stradling, *Smokestacks and Progressives: Environmentalists, Engineers, and Air Quality in America, 1881–1951* (Baltimore: Johns Hopkins University Press, 1999). For conservation's ambiguous legacy to the resources themselves, see Nancy Langston, *Forest Dreams, Forest Nightmares: The Paradox of Old Growth in the Inland West* (Seattle: University of Washington Press, 1995); Joseph E. Taylor III, *Making Salmon: An Environmental History of the Northwest Fisheries Crisis* (Seattle: University of Washington Press, 1999).

30. Jacoby, *Crimes against Nature*, 6. Jacoby was making the important point that conservation had profound social implications. The idea that conservationists were dispassionate technicians was widely held. Another author argued that "conservation came to mean the proper use of the nation's natural resources as determined by the scientific standards of the times and regulated by objective bureaucrats." Benjamin Klein, *First along the River: A History of the U.S. Environmental Movement* (Lanham, Md.: Rowman & Littlefield, 2007), 53.

31. W. J. McGee, "The Conservation of Natural Resources," *Proceedings of the Mississippi Valley Historical Association* 3 (1911): 376. For more on McGee, see Whitney R. Cross, "WJ McGee and the Idea of Conservation," *Historian* 15, no. 2 (spring 1953).

32. Walter Lippmann, *Drift and Mastery* (1914; reprint, Englewood Cliffs, N.J.: Prentice-Hall, 1961), 92, 91, 92.

33. Edward Alsworth Ross, *Social Control: A Survey of the Foundations of Order* (1901; reprint, Cleveland, 1969), 428, cited by Michael McGerr, *A Fierce Discontent: The Rise and Fall of the Progressive Movement in America, 1870–1920* (New York: Free Press, 2003), 107.

34. Leo Marx, *The Machine in the Garden: Technology and the Pastoral Ideal in America* (New York: Oxford University Press, 1967), 11.

35. Peter J. Schmitt, *Back to Nature: The Arcadian Myth in Urban America* (1969; reprint, Baltimore: Johns Hopkins University Press, 1990).

36. Ralph Waldo Emerson, *The Prose Works of Ralph Waldo Emerson* (Boston: James R. Osgood, 1875), 222.

CHAPTER 1. "NATURE STUDY IS AN AMERICAN HABIT"

1. Louise Hall Tharp, *Adventurous Alliance: The Story of the Agassiz Family of Boston* (Boston: Little, Brown, 1959), 234. The standard intellectual biography of Agassiz is Edward Lurie, *Louis Agassiz: A Life in Science* (Chicago: University of Chicago Press, 1960). For his work on Penikese Island, see Report of the Trustees for 1873, in *The Organization and Progress of the Anderson School of Natural History at Penikese Island* (Cambridge, Mass.: Welch, Bigelow, 1874).

2. Albert Hazen Wright and Anna Allen Wright, "Agassiz's Address at the Opening of Agassiz's Academy," *American Midland Naturalist* 43, no. 2 (March 1950): 504.

3. James David Teller, *Louis Agassiz, Scientist and Teacher* (Columbus: Ohio State University Press, 1947).

4. David Starr Jordan, "Agassiz at Penikese," *Popular Science Monthly* (April 1892): 722.

5. Ibid., 721.

6. Quoted in John F. Woodhull, "The Educational Value of Natural Science," *Educational Review* (April 1895): 370.

7. A. E. Dolbear, "The Disappointing Results of Science Teaching," *Educational Review* (December 1894): 488.

8. J. S. Kingsley, "How a Naturalist Is Trained," *Popular Science Monthly* 30 (1886–1887): 631–632.

9. Burt G. Wilder, "Agassiz at Penikese," *American Naturalist* 32 (March 1898): 190.

10. Both the popular and the scientific press tended to slight Shaler's contribution, but Agassiz continually acknowledged Shaler's inspiration. In a letter to U.S. Fish Commissioner Spencer Fullerton Baird, Agassiz wrote, "The plan is to be carried out under my supervision whether Shaler comes back in time for it or not. [Shaler was in Europe.] But I want it should be known that the first suggestion was his." This point is made by Keith R. Benson, "Laboratories on the New England Shore: The 'Somewhat Different Direction' of American Marine Biology," *New England Quarterly* 61, no. 1 (March 1985).

11. Wilder, "Agassiz at Penikese," 190. Also quoted in Edward S. Morse, "Agassiz and the School at Penikese," *Science* 58, no. 1502 (12 October 1923): 273.

12. Quoted in Louis C. Cornish, "Agassiz's School on Penikese," *Scientific Monthly* 57, no. 4 (October 1943): 316.

13. "Agassiz's Academy," *New York Tribune*, 9 July 1873. For an example of laudatory coverage, see "Penikese Island," *Harper's Weekly*, 9 August 1873, 701–702.

14. Nathaniel Shaler, "Chapters from an Autobiography II: A Pupil of Agassiz," *Atlantic Monthly*, February 1909, 221–222.

15. Samuel H. Scudder, "How Agassiz Taught Professor Scudder," in Lane Cooper, *Louis Agassiz as a Teacher: Illustrative Extracts on His Methods of Instruction* (Ithaca, N.Y.: Comstock Publishing Co., 1945), 56, 61; originally published as "In the Laboratory with Agassiz," *Every Saturday*, 4 April 1874, 369–370.

16. Helen B. C. Beedy, "Reminiscences of Penikese," *Education* 13 (February 1893): 340.

17. William James, "Louis Agassiz," in *Memories and Studies* (1911; reprint, New York: Greenwood Press, 1968), 11–12, 14.

18. Beedy, "Reminiscences of Penikese," 346.

19. "Penikese Island," *Frank Leslie's Illustrated Newspaper,* 23 August 1873, 378.

20. Ibid., 339.

21. Quoted in Cornish, "Agassiz's School on Penikese," 320.

22. E. Ray Lankester, "An American Sea-side Laboratory," *Nature,* 25 March 1880, 498.

23. Alexander Agassiz, "The Abandonment of Penikese," *Popular Science Monthly* 42 (1892): 123.

24. Ralph Dexter, "From Penikese to the Marine Biological Laboratory at Woods Hole—the Role of Agassiz's Students," *Essex Institute Historical Collections* 100 (1974): 151–161; Jane Maienschein, "Agassiz, Hyatt, Whitman, and the Birth of the Marine Biological Laboratory," *Biological Bulletin* 168 (June 1985 supplement): 26–34.

25. David Starr Jordan, *Science Sketches* (Chicago: A. C. McClurg, 1887), 242–243.

26. Ibid., 151–152.

27. Liberty Hyde Bailey, *The Outlook to Nature* (New York: Macmillan, 1911), 95.

28. Elizabeth Cabot Agassiz, *First Lesson in Natural History* (1859; reprint, Boston: D. C. Heath, 1886), 7. For more on Elizabeth Cabot Agassiz, see Vera Norwood, *Made from This Earth: American Women and Nature* (Chapel Hill: University of North Carolina Press, 1993), 22–24. Elizabeth Agassiz (1822–1907) also published *Seaside Studies in Natural History* in 1865; it was dedicated to Louis Agassiz and taken from his notes. Though published in the hope of attracting a general audience, the book used Latin names and was fairly technical, making it less engaging as popular natural history.

29. Jordan, "Agassiz at Penikese," 727.

30. Ned Harland Dearborn, *The Oswego Movement in American Education* (New York: Teacher's College, Columbia University, 1925); Will S. Monroe, *History of the Pestalozzian Movement in the United States* (Syracuse, N.Y.: C. W. Bardeen, 1907).

31. John Dewey, *The School and Society* [1899], in *John Dewey: The Middle Works*, vol. 1, ed. Jo Ann Boydston (Carbondale: Southern Illinois University Press, 1976), 8.

32. Lloyd E. McCann, "Henry Harrison Straight, Educator," *Nebraska History Magazine* (1954): 59–71.

33. H. H. Straight, "A 'Complete Life' the Foundation of a True Philosophy of Education," *Nebraska Teacher* (March 1873): 62–66.

34. Ibid., 65.

35. Dewey, *School and Society*, 98.

36. William J. Reese, "The Origins of Progressive Education," *History of Education Quarterly* 41, no. 1 (spring 2000): 18.

37. Louisa Parsons Hopkins, *The Spirit of the New Education* (Boston: Lee & Shepard, 1892), 9, 20–21.

38. Ibid., 255.

39. Lynn Barber, *The Heyday of Natural History 1820–1870* (London: Jonathan Cape, 1981), 159.

40. John Muir, *John of the Mountains: The Unpublished Journals of John Muir*, ed. Linnie Marsh Wolfe (Madison: University of Wisconsin Press, 1979), 79.

41. My information on Phelps derives from Norwood, *Made from This Earth*.

42. Richard Wightman Fox, "The Culture of Liberal Protestant Progressivism, 1875–1925," *Journal of Interdisciplinary History* 23, no. 3 (winter 1993): 639–660.

43. Thorstein Veblen, *The Theory of the Leisure Class* (New York: Macmillan, 1899).

44. Thorstein Veblen, "The Place of Science in Modern Civilization," *American Journal of Sociology* 11, no. 5 (March 1906): 585, 609.

45. Muir, *John of the Mountains*, 320.

46. Liberty Hyde Bailey, *The Nature Study Idea: Being an Interpretation of the New School Movement to Put the Child in Sympathy with Nature* (New York: Doubleday, Page, 1903), 4.

47. T. J. Jackson Lears, *No Place of Grace: Antimodernism and the Transformation of American Culture, 1880–1920* (Chicago: University of Chicago Press, 1981); Max Weber, *The Protestant Ethic and the Spirit of Capitalism*, trans. Talcott Parsons (New York: Charles Scribner's Sons, 1958), 182; Theodore Roosevelt, *The Strenuous Life: Essays and Addresses* (New York: Century Company, 1900). For more on antimodernism, see James Clifford, *The Predicament of Culture: Twentieth Century Ethnography, Literature and Art* (Cambridge, Mass.: Harvard University Press, 1988); Theodore W. Adorno and

Max Horkheimer, *Dialectic of Enlightenment,* trans. John Cumming (New York: Continuum, 1993).

48. Theodore Roosevelt, *A Book-Lover's Holidays in the Open* (New York: C. Scribner's Sons, 1916), viii, quoted in Peter J. Schmitt, *Back to Nature: The Arcadian Myth in Urban America* (1969; reprint, Baltimore: Johns Hopkins University Press, 1990), 14.

49. Karl Marx and Frederick Engels, *Manifesto of the Communist Party,* ed. and annot. Frederick Engels (Chicago: Charles H. Kerr, 1906), 16.

50. Weber, *Protestant Ethic,* 181–182; Nietzsche quoted in Karl Jaspers, *Nietzsche and Christianity,* trans. E. B. Ashton (Chicago: Henry Regnery, 1961), 14; Ralph Waldo Emerson, "Fate" [1852], in *Collected Works,* Century ed. (Boston, 1903), 6:9, quoted in Lears, *No Place of Grace,* 34.

51. Lears, *No Place of Grace,* 32.

52. Ralph Waldo Emerson, *The Collected Works of Ralph Waldo Emerson* (Cambridge, Mass.: Harvard University Press, 1971–1987), 1:14, 17, 40.

53. Dallas Lore Sharp, "The Nature Student," in *The Lay of the Land* (Boston: Houghton Mifflin, 1908), 73.

54. Quoted in Bradley P. Dean, "Natural History, Romanticism, and Thoreau," in *American Wilderness: A New History,* ed. Michael Lewis (New York: Oxford University Press, 2007), 77.

55. Henry David Thoreau, *The Writings of Henry David Thoreau,* vol. 2 (New York: Houghton Mifflin, 1906), 232.

56. Henry David Thoreau, *Journal,* vol. 3, *1848–1851,* ed. Robert Sattelmeyer, Mark R. Patterson, and William Rossi (Princeton, N.J.: Princeton University Press, 1990), 380.

57. Quoted in John Burroughs, "Another Word on Thoreau," in *The Last Harvest* (Boston: Houghton Mifflin, 1922), 121.

58. Henry David Thoreau, *Journal,* vol. 4, *1851–1852,* ed. Leonard N. Neufield and Nancy Craig Simmons (Princeton, N.J.: Princeton University Press, 1992), 31.

59. Thoreau, *Journal,* 3:184.

60. Henry David Thoreau, *The Journal of Henry David Thoreau,* 14 vols., ed. Bradford Torrey and Francis Allen (Boston: Houghton Mifflin, 1906), 14:119–120.

61. Thoreau, *Journal,* 4:163.

62. Thoreau, *Journal of Henry David Thoreau,* 1:89–90.

63. Henry David Thoreau, "The Natural History of Massachusetts," in *The Natural History Essays,* ed. Robert Sattelmeyer (Salt Lake City: Peregrine Smith, 1980), 29.

64. John Dewey, *Experience and Nature* [1929], in *John Dewey: The Later Works,* vol. 1, ed. Jo Ann Boydston (Carbondale: Southern Illinois University Press, 2008), 12–13.

65. Bailey, *Nature Study Idea,* 157.

66. Editorial, "Specialization in Scientific Study," *Science,* 11 July 1884, 35–36.

67. Dorthea Lange, "Nature Study in the Public Schools," *National Education Association Proceedings* (1900): 407.

68. C. A. McMurray and Lida B. McMurray, *Special Method in Natural Science* (Bloomington, Ill.: Public School Pub. Co., 1896), 32.

69. Clifton Hodge, *Nature Study and Life* (Boston: Ginn, 1902), vii.

70. Anna Botsford Comstock, "Editorial," *Nature-Study Review* 7, no. 9 (December 1911): 278.

71. Bailey, *Outlook to Nature,* 6.

72. Charles Eliot Norton to S. G. Ward, 19 September 1900, in *Letters of Norton,* 2:300, quoted in Lears, *No Place of Grace,* 34–35.

73. Mary C. Dickerson, "Nature-Study in City Primary Schools," *Nature-Study Review* 2, no. 3 (March 1906): 100.

74. Bailey, *Outlook to Nature,* 91–92.

75. Miles Orvell, *The Real Thing: Imitation and Authenticity in American Culture, 1880–1940* (Chapel Hill: University of North Carolina Press, 1989).

76. Ralph Waldo Emerson, *Nature* (Boston: James Munroe, 1836), 1.

77. John Burroughs, "Nature Study," *Outlook* 61 (4 February 1899): 326.

78. John Burroughs, "Science and Sentiment," *Independent,* 15 February 1912, 360.

79. Bliss Carman, *The Making of Personality* (Boston: Page Co., 1908), 315, 317.

80. Bliss Carman, *The Kinship of Nature* (Boston: L. C. Page, 1903), 143.

81. Carman, *Making of Personality,* 313.

82. "Back to Nature," *Outlook* 74, no. 6 (6 June 1903): 305.

83. Dallas Lore Sharp, "The Nature Movement," in *The Lay of the Land* (Boston: Houghton Mifflin, 1908), 124.

84. *Nature-Study Review* 3, no. 6 (September 1907): 190.

85. Quoted in Mark Hamilton Lytle, *The Gentle Subversive: Rachel Carson, Silent Spring, and the Rise of the Environmental Movement* (New York: Oxford University Press, 2007), 31.

86. Sharp, "The Nature Student," 56, 68.

87. Sharp, "The Nature Movement," 124.

88. Ibid., 118.

CHAPTER 2. "A LIVING SYMPATHY WITH EVERYTHING THAT IS"

The quote in the chapter title is from G. Clarke Nuttall, "An American Scheme of Nature Study," *Journal of Education* (May 1899): 337.

1. Benjamin O. Flower, "The Great Mother as an Educator; or, the Child in Nature's Workshop," *Arena* 38 (September 1907): 311–313.

2. Benjamin O. Flower, "The New Education and the Public Schools," *Arena* 8 (October 1893): 511–528. For scholarship on Flower and *Arena,* see Allen J. Matusow, "The Mind of B. O. Flower," *New England Quarterly* 34, no. 4 (December 1961): 492–509. See also Frank Luther Mott, *A History of American Magazines,* vol. 4 (Cambridge, Mass.: Harvard University Press, 1957), 401–416.

3. Van Evrie Kilpatrick, *Nature Education in the United States* (New York: School Garden Association of America, 1923), 7.

4. The literature on educational progressivism is vast. Interested readers should begin with Lawrence A. Cremin, *The Transformation of the School: Progressivism in American Education, 1876–1957* (New York: Vintage Books, 1964); Herbert Kliebard, *The Struggle for the American Curriculum, 1893–1958* (Boston: Routledge & Kegan Paul, 1986);

William J. Reese, *Power and the Promise of School Reform: Grassroots Movements during the Progressive Era* (Boston: Routledge & Kegan Paul, 1986); and Diane Ravitch, *Left Back: A Century of Failed School Reforms* (New York: Simon & Schuster, 2000). Two important essays are Timothy L. Smith, "Progressivism in American Education, 1880–1900," *Harvard Educational Review* 31, no. 2 (spring 1961): 168–193, and William J. Reese, "The Origins of Progressive Education," *History of Education Quarterly* 41, no. 1 (spring 2001): 1–24.

5. Reese, "Origins of Progressive Education," 3.

6. Cremin, *Transformation of the School*, viii–ix.

7. "Editorial," *Nature-Study Review* 11, no. 1 (January 1915): 4.

8. Liberty Hyde Bailey, *The Nature Study Idea: Being an Interpretation of the New School Movement to Put the Child in Sympathy with Nature* (New York: Doubleday, Page, 1903), 41.

9. Morse Peckham, "Toward a Theory of Romanticism," *PMLA* (March 1951): 11–12. For this quote and his discussion of romanticism, I am indebted to Colin Campbell's excellent *The Romantic Ethic and the Spirit of Modern Consumerism* (Oxford: Blackwell, 1987).

10. Donald Worster, *Nature's Economy: A History of Ecological Ideas*, 2nd ed. (Cambridge: Cambridge University Press, 1994), 82.

11. Comenius quoted in Bogan Suchodolski, "Comenius and Teaching Methods," in *Comenius and Contemporary Education*, ed. C. A. Dobinson (Hamburg: UNESCO Institute for Education, 1970), 35. For his discussion of Comenius, I am indebted to Tyree G. Minton, "The History of the Nature-Study Movement and Its Role in the Development of Environmental Education" (Ed.D. diss., University of Massachusetts, 1980).

12. S. S. Laurie, *John Amos Comenius, Bishop of the Moravians: His Life and Educational Works* (Cambridge: Cambridge University Press, 1893).

13. Quoted in Dora Otis Mitchell, "A History of Nature-Study," *Nature-Study Review* 19 (September 1923): 261.

14. Quoted in Laurie, *John Amos Comenius*, 37. The lasting impact of Comenius can be seen in his influence on such thinkers as psychologist and theorist of childhood education Jean Piaget. Writing in 1967, Piaget highlighted the comprehensiveness of Comenius's thought in its attempt to fuse philosophic and didactic aims. That fusion required the theorization of the relationship between humans and nonhuman nature—"a synthesis," in Piaget's words, "linking man with nature so as to show why the educative process is the keystone of this philosophy." See Jean Piaget, "The Significance of John Amos Comenius at the Present Time," in *John Amos Comenius on Education* (New York: Teachers College Press, 1967), 4.

15. Jean-Jacques Rousseau, *Emile or On Education* [1762], trans. Allan Bloom (New York: Basic Books, 1979), 37.

16. Grace G. Roosevelt, *Reading Rousseau in the Nuclear Age* (Philadelphia: Temple University Press, 1990), 151. My discussion of Rousseau follows Roosevelt's format.

17. Rousseau, *Emile or On Education*, 344–345.

18. Johann Heinrich Pestalozzi, *How Gertrude Teaches Her Children* [1801], ed. Daniel N. Robinson (Washington, D.C.: University Publications of America, 1977), 131–132.

19. Ibid., 321. See also Gerald Lee Gutek, *Pestalozzi & Education* (New York: Random House, 1968).

20. Quoted in Mitchell, "History of Nature-Study," 270.

21. Quoted in William Heard Kilpatrick, *Froebel's Kindergarten Principles Critically Examined* (New York: Macmillan, 1916), 189.

22. Quoted in Barbara Beatty, *Preschool Education in America: The Culture of Young Children from the Colonial Era to the Present* (New Haven, Conn.: Yale University Press, 1997), 41.

23. Ralph Waldo Emerson, *The Essays of Ralph Waldo Emerson*, ed. Alfred Kazin (Cambridge, Mass.: Belknap Press, 1987), 5.

24. Ralph Waldo Emerson, "The Fortune of the Republic," in *The Collected Works of Ralph Waldo Emerson* (Cambridge, Mass.: Harvard University Press, 1971–1987), 11:527.

25. John Dewey, *The Collected Works of John Dewey*, ed. Jo Ann Boydston (Carbondale: Southern Illinois University Press, 1969–1991), cited as *The Early Works, The Middle Works*, and *The Later Works*. Quotes from *Middle Works*, 12, 199.

26. Henry David Thoreau, *The Journal of Henry David Thoreau*, ed. Bradford Torrey (Mineola, N.Y.: Dover Publications, 1962), 83.

27. Amos Bronson Alcott, *Essays on Education*, ed. Walter Harding (Gainesville, Fla.: Scholars' Facsimiles, 1960), 174.

28. Bailey, *Nature Study Idea*, 7.

29. Geraldine Jonçich Clifford, "Man/Woman/Teacher: Gender, Family and Career in American Educational History," in *American Teachers: Historians of a Profession at Work*, ed. Donald Warren (New York: Macmillan, 1989). See also Jill Conway, "Perspectives on the History of Women's Education in the United States," *History of Education Quarterly* (spring 1974): 1–13; Myra H. Strober and Audri Gordon Lanford, "The Feminization of Public School Teaching: Cross-sectional Analysis, 1850–1880," *Signs: Journal of Women in Culture and Society* 11, no. 2 (1986): 212–235.

30. For more on Parker, see Jack K. Campbell, *Colonel Francis W. Parker, the Children's Crusader* (New York: Teachers College Press, 1967).

31. For Parker's own account of Cook County, including his support of nature study, see Francis Parker, "An Account of the Work of the Cook County and Chicago Normal School from 1883 to 1899," *Elementary School Teacher and Course of Study* (June 1902): 752–780.

32. Mitchell, "History of Nature-Study," 298.

33. Orville T. Bright, "Jackman," *Elementary School Teacher* 7 (April 1907): 433–438.

34. Wilbur S. Jackman, *Nature Study for the Common Schools* (New York: Henry Holt, 1891), 11.

35. Wilbur S. Jackman, "What Has Been Accomplished in Co-ordination in the Field of Natural Sciences," *Journal of the Proceedings of the National Education Association* 34 (1895): 98, 99.

36. Jackman, *Nature Study*, 3.

37. Cremin, *Transformation of the School*, 135.

38. Ida B. DePencier, *The History of the Laboratory Schools: The University of Chicago 1896–1965* (Chicago: Quadrangle Books, 1967), 18.

39. Ibid., 28.

40. In my view, Ravitch made this mistake in *Left Back*. For a defense of Dewey, see Robert B. Westbrook, *John Dewey and American Democracy* (Ithaca, N.Y.: Cornell University

Press, 1991). See also Alan Ryan, "Deweyan Pragmatism and American Education," in *Philosophers on Education: New Historical Perspectives,* ed. Amélie Oksenberg Rorty (New York: Routledge, 1998), 394–410, as well as Cremin, *Transformation of the School.* On Dewey's Laboratory School pedagogy, see Kliebard, *Struggle for the American Curriculum.* See also Laurel N. Tanner, *Dewey's Laboratory School: Lessons for Today* (New York: Teachers College Press, 1997).

41. Westbrook, *Dewey and American Democracy,* 100.

42. Dewey, *Later Works,* 5:324–325.

43. For the history of the Laboratory School, see Katherine Camp Mayhew and Anna Camp Edwards, *The Dewey School* (1936; reprint, New York: Atherton Press, 1965); see also DePencier, *History of the Laboratory Schools;* Cremin, *Transformation of the School.* A brief account of the Dewey and Jackman relationship can be found in Jay Martin, *The Education of John Dewey* (New York: Columbia University Press, 2002), 203–205.

44. For Jackman adopting Deweyan pedagogical ideas, see Wilbur S. Jackman, "Correlation of Science and History," *Educational Review* (May 1895): 464–471, and "Relation of Arithmetic to Elementary Science," *Educational Review* (January 1893): 35–51.

45. John Dewey, "The University Elementary School, Studies and Methods," *University Record,* 21 May 1897.

46. Quoted in Mayhew and Edwards, *Dewey School,* 78.

47. Dewey, *Early Works,* 5:199.

48. John Dewey, *Democracy and Education: An Introduction to the Philosophy of Education* (1916; reprint, New York: Free Press, 1997), 211.

49. Dewey, *Middle Works,* 9:219.

50. Ibid., 9:221, 8:272, 271.

51. Maurice A. Bigelow, "Correlation of Nature-Study and Manual Training," *Nature-Study Review* 2, no. 3 (March 1906): 91.

52. Margaret W. Morley, "Nature Study and Its Influence," *Outlook* 68 (27 July 1901): 739, 738.

53. L. H. Baekeland, "The Danger of Overspecialization," *Science* 25, no. 648 (31 May 1907): 853–854, 849.

54. John M. Coulter, "Nature Study and Intellectual Life," *Science* 4, no. 99 (20 November 1896); C. P. Snow, *The Two Cultures and the Scientific Revolution* (New York: Cambridge University Press, 1963).

55. Coulter, "Nature Study and Intellectual Life," 744, 743.

56. Edward Thorndike, "Sentimentality in Science Teaching," *Educational Review* (January 1899): 57, 50, 60–61. On Thorndike, see Cremin, *Transformation of the School,* 110–115.

57. Thorndike, "Sentimentality in Science Teaching," 63, 61–62.

58. See, for example, John F. Woodhull, "The Educational Value of Natural Science," *Educational Review* (April 1895): 368–376.

59. W. M. Davis, "What Is Nature Study?" *Science* 16, no. 414 (5 December 1902): 911.

60. Anna Botsford Comstock, *Handbook of Nature Study* (1911; reprint, Ithaca, N.Y.: Comstock Publishing Associates, 1986), 6.

61. William Sedgwick, "Educational Value of the Methods of Science," *Educational Review* (March 1893): 250, 251.

62. Bailey, *Nature Study Idea,* 15.

63. Quoted in Philip Dorf, *Liberty Hyde Bailey: An Informal Biography* (Ithaca, N.Y.: Cornell University Press, 1956), 112.

64. E. R. Whitney, "Nature Study as an Aid to Advanced Work in Science," *Proceedings of the National Education Association* (1904): 891.

65. Otis Caldwell, untitled essay, *Proceedings of the National Education Association* (1904): 895.

66. Richard R. Olmsted, "The Nature-Study Movement in American Education" (Ed.D. diss., Indiana University, 1967).

67. M. A. Bigelow, "Interest of Men of Science in the Nature-Study Society," *Nature-Study Review* 4, no. 1 (January 1908): 4.

68. For example, see Davis, "What Is Nature Study?" and Harold W. Fairbanks, "Nature Study and Its Relation to Natural Science," *Nature-Study Review* 1, no. 1 (January 1905): 2–18.

69. John Burroughs, "Nature Study," *Outlook* 61 (4 February 1899): 326.

70. Bailey, *Nature Study Idea*, 14.

71. Ibid., 20.

72. Fairbanks, "Nature Study and Its Relation to Natural Science," 6.

73. Nathaniel S. Shaler, "Faith in Nature," *International Quarterly* 6 (December 1902): 281, 304.

74. Quoted in Ralph H. Lutts, *The Nature Fakers: Wildlife, Science and Sentiment* (Golden, Colo.: Fulcrum Publishing, 1990), 30.

75. David Starr Jordan, "Nature Study and Moral Culture," *Science* 4, no. 84 (7 August 1896): 153.

76. Ibid., 154.

77. There is a good deal of secondary literature on Anna Botsford Comstock from which the following portrait derives. See Edward H. Smith, "Anna Botsford Comstock: Artist, Author, Teacher," *American Entomologist* 36, no. 2 (summer 1990): 105–113; James G. Needham, "The Lengthened Shadow of a Man and His Wife," *Scientific Monthly* 62, pts. 1 and 2 (1946): 140–150, 219–229; Marcia Myers Bonta, *Women in the Field: America's Pioneering Naturalists* (College Station: Texas A&M University Press, 1991), 154–166; Pamela M. Henson, "The Comstocks of Cornell: A Marriage of Interests," in *Creative Couples in Science,* ed. H. Pycior et al. (New Brunswick, N.J.: Rutgers University Press, 1995); Pamela Henson, "'Through Books to Nature': Anna Botsford Comstock and the Nature Study Movement," in *Natural Eloquence: Women Reinscribe Science,* ed. B. T. Gates and Ann B. Shteir (Madison: University of Wisconsin Press, 1998), 116–143; Pamela M. Henson, "Comstock, Anna Botsford," American National Biography Online, http://www.anb.org/articles/13/13-01944.html.

78. Bonta, *Women in the Field*, 159.

79. Anna Comstock, *Ways of the Six Footed* (1903; reprint, Ithaca, N.Y.: Cornell University Press, 1977), 56, 71.

80. Amy Green, "Two Woman Naturalists and the Search for Autonomy: Anna Botsford Comstock and the Producer Ethic; Gene Stratton-Porter and the Gospel of Wealth," *Women Studies Quarterly* (spring–summer 2001).

81. Quoted in Bonta, *Women in the Field*, 164.

82. Comstock, *Handbook of Nature Study*, 2, 17.

83. Quoted in Bonta, *Women in the Field*, 164.

84. "Topics of the Times," *New York Times*, 8 May 1923, 16.

CHAPTER 3. "THE CHILD IS BORN A NATURALIST"

1. John Dewey, "How Much Freedom in New Schools?" *New Republic* 63 (9 July 1930): 204; Francis Parker, "The Child," *Proceedings and Addresses of the National Education Association* (1889): 479.

2. Parker, "The Child," 481, 480; emphasis in original.

3. Recapitulation was also commonly referred to as the "cultural epoch" theory of human development. For more on the history of recapitulation, see Stephen Jay Gould, *Ontogeny and Phylogeny* (Cambridge, Mass.: Belknap Press, 1977); Cynthia Eagle Russett, *Sexual Science: The Victorian Construction of Womanhood* (Cambridge, Mass.: Harvard University Press, 1989).

4. Katherine E. Dolbear, "Nature Study for the Graded Schools," *Proceedings and Addresses of the National Education Association* (1900): 601.

5. Cyril A. Stebbins, "Growing Children in California Gardens," *Nature-Study Review* 8, no. 2 (February 1912): 67–68.

6. The idea that children needed to leave the classroom and experience nature firsthand to develop sympathy with it was a controversial one. See, for example, the criticism of nature study leveled by renowned psychologist Edward Thorndike, "Sentimentality in Science Teaching," *Educational Review* (January 1899).

7. G. Stanley Hall, *Adolescence*, vol. 1 (1904; reprint, New York: Arno Press, 1969), xi, xv.

8. Louis Agassiz, *Contributions to the Natural History of the United States of North America* (Boston: Little, Brown, 1857). The standard intellectual biography of Agassiz is Edward Lurie, *Louis Agassiz: A Life in Science* (Chicago: University of Chicago Press, 1960).

9. For Agassiz's racism, see Louis Menand, *The Metaphysical Club* (New York: Farrar, Straus & Giroux, 2001), 103–116.

10. For a close study of Hall, see Dorothy Ross, *G. Stanley Hall* (Chicago: University of Chicago Press, 1972).

11. The notion that there is a connection between the evolution of species and the development of individuals is once again the rage in the biological sciences. This area of research is known as evolutionary developmental biology, or "evo devo" for short. For an entertaining overview of evo devo written for nonspecialists, see Sean Carroll, *Endless Forms Most Beautiful: The New Science of Evo Devo* (New York: W. W. Norton, 2005).

12. E. M. Robinson of the YMCA argued that "the higher Christian values are built on savage virtues." See David Macleod, *Building Character in the American Boy: The Boy Scouts, YMCA, and Their Forerunners, 1870–1920* (Madison: University of Wisconsin Press, 1983), 99.

13. Hall, *Adolescence*, 1:xiii.

14. Macleod, *Building Character*, 100.

15. G. Stanley Hall, untitled essay, *Proceedings and Addresses of the National Education Association* (1904): 443.

16. G. Stanley Hall, untitled essay, *Proceedings and Addresses of the National Education Association* (1896): 157.

17. Hall, *Adolescence*, 1:x.

18. "Use and Abuse of America's Natural Resources," in *Report of the National Conservation Commission* (1909; reprint, New York: Arno Press, 1972), 637. Yale economist Irving Fisher wrote this section of the report. Fisher, an advocate of eugenics and health-food diets, made a fortune with his index card system—known today as the Rolodex—and advocated the establishment of a 100 percent reserve requirement in the banking system. He lost his fortune and his reputation when, just days before the 1929 Wall Street crash, he reassured investors that stock prices were not overinflated but had achieved a permanent plateau. For more on Fisher, see Robert Loring Allen, *Irving Fisher: A Biography* (Cambridge, Mass.: Harvard University Press, 1993).

19. "Use and Abuse," 630. For more on the National Conservation Commission, see Samuel P. Hays, *Conservation and the Gospel of Efficiency: The Progressive Conservation Movement, 1890–1920* (Cambridge, Mass.: Harvard University Press, 1959), 129–140.

20. Charles Lincoln Edwards, "Nature-Play," *Popular Science Monthly* 84 (April 1914): 330.

21. Ibid., 342–343.

22. On this point, see Russett, *Sexual Science.*

23. Harold W. Fairbanks, "The Relation of Geography to Nature-Study in the Elementary School," *Nature-Study Review* 1 (September 1905): 175, 177.

24. N. Cropsey, "The Higher Use of Nature Studies," *Proceedings and Addresses of the National Education Association* (1894): 199, 201.

25. W. A. Hoyt, "Children's Love of Nature," *Proceedings and Addresses of the National Education Association* (1894): 1013.

26. Advocates of nature study even bolstered the recapitulation rationale through their own research findings in evolutionary psychology. They attempted to correlate data obtained from questionnaires to childhood affinities for nature. See Laura Emily Mau, "Some Experiments with Regard to the Relative Interests of Children in Physical and Biological Nature Materials in the Kindergarten and Primary Grades," *Nature-Study Review* 8 (November 1912): 285–291; Elliot R. Downing, "Children's Interest in Nature Material," *Nature-Study Review* 8 (December 1912): 334.

27. Maurice A. Bigelow, "Are Children Naturally Naturalists?" *Nature-Study Review* 3 (November 1907): 236, 238.

28. Willard N. Clute, letter, *Nature-Study Review* 4, no. 1 (January 1908): 30.

29. Clayton F. Parker, "Are Children Naturally Naturalists?" *Nature-Study Review* 4, no. 1 (January 1908): 29.

30. Steven L. Schlossman, "G. Stanley Hall and the Boy's Club: Conservative Applications of Recapitulation Theory," *Journal of the History of the Behavioral Sciences* 9, no. 2 (April 1973): 140–141.

31. Joseph Lee, *Play in Education* (New York: Macmillan, 1915), 218.

32. Theodore Roosevelt to G. Stanley Hall, 29 November 1899, cited in both Ross, *G. Stanley Hall,* 318, and Gail Bederman, *Manliness & Civilization: A Cultural History of Gender and Race in the United States, 1880–1917* (Chicago: University of Chicago Press, 1995), 100–101.

33. H. Allen Anderson, *The Chief: Ernest Thompson Seton and the Changing West* (College

Station: Texas A&M University Press, 1986), 131. On Seton, see also John Henry Wadland, *Ernest Thompson Seton: Man and Nature in the Progressive Era, 1880–1915* (New York: Arno Press, 1978). For Seton as an antimodernist and appropriator of Indianness, see Philip J. Deloria, *Playing Indian* (New Haven, Conn.: Yale University Press, 1998), 95–128.

34. John Burroughs, among others, criticized Seton's fanciful stories for their lack of veracity. Seton thus became entangled in the "nature faker" debate. See Ralph H. Lutts, *The Nature Fakers: Wildlife, Science and Sentiment* (Golden, Colo.: Fulcrum Publishing, 1990).

35. Forbush, a Congregational minister, was a staunch proponent of recapitulation and of character building in the American boy. He also found in recapitulation theory a justification for contact with nature: "The infant," wrote Forbush, "is like the wild creature of the wood, and it is as cruel to confine the physical activities of young children as those of squirrels and swallows." William Byron Forbush, *The Boy Problem: A Study in Social Pedagogy* (Boston: Pilgrim Press, 1901), 10. Forbush recommended nature study, school gardening, the Agassiz Association science club, and summer camps to put boys in contact with nature.

36. Robert H. MacDonald, *Sons of Empire: The Frontier and the Boy Scout Movement* (Toronto: University of Toronto Press, 1993). For a clear elaboration of his theory of instincts, see Ernest Thompson Seton, "The Woodcraft League or College of Indian Wisdom," *Homiletic Review* (June 1931): 434–439.

37. Ernest Thompson Seton, "The Boy Scouts in America," *Outlook*, 23 July 1910, 630.

38. Parker, "The Child," 480.

39. Ernest Thompson Seton, *Gospel of the Red Man: An Indian Bible* (1936; reprint, Santa Fe, N.M.: Seton Village, 1966), 105.

40. Seton, "Boy Scouts in America," 630.

41. Seton, "Woodcraft League," 435.

42. Ernest Thompson Seton, "Organized Boyhood: The Boy Scout Movement, Its Purpose and Laws," *Success Magazine* (December 1910): 804.

43. Ibid.

44. Seton, "Boy Scouts in America," 630.

45. For romantic intellectuals' attachment to medieval tropes, see T. J. Jackson Lears, *No Place of Grace: Antimodernism and the Transformation of American Culture, 1880–1920* (Chicago: University of Chicago Press, 1981), 141–182.

46. Seton, "Boy Scouts in America," 630.

47. Seton, "Woodcraft League," 435. Although Seton clearly romanticized his depiction of Native Americans, he also had a good deal of contact with actual native peoples and was an ardent critic of governmental relations with Indians. Seton attended the organizing meeting of the Sequoya League in 1901, cementing his friendship with Charles Eastman. Seton remained a reformer for decades, eventually endorsing John Collier's Indian New Deal.

48. Hall, *Adolescence*, 1:x.

49. Ernest Thompson Seton, *How to Play Indian: Directions for Organizing a Tribe of Boy Indians and Making Their Teepees in True Indian Style* (Philadelphia: Curtis, 1903), 3.

50. Deloria, *Playing Indian*, 95–128.

51. Seton, *Gospel of the Red Man,* 108. For antimodernism, see Lears, *No Place of Grace;* James Clifford, *The Predicament of Culture: Twentieth Century Ethnography, Literature and Art* (Cambridge, Mass.: Harvard University Press, 1988); Theodore W. Adorno and Max Horkheimer, *Dialectic of Enlightenment,* trans. John Cumming (New York: Continuum, 1993).

52. Andreas Huyssen, "Mass Culture as Woman: Modernism's Other," in *After the Great Divide* (Bloomington: Indiana University Press, 1987), 44–64. For a discussion of authenticity and mass culture, see T. J. Jackson Lears, "Sherwood Anderson: Looking for the White Spot," in *The Power of Culture: Critical Essays in American History,* ed. Richard Wightman Fox and T. J. Jackson Lears (Chicago: University of Chicago Press, 1993), 13–38. See also David E. Shi, *Facing Facts: Realism in American Thought and Culture, 1850–1920* (New York: Oxford University Press, 1995).

53. Quoted in Bederman, *Manliness & Civilization,* 95. My discussion is indebted to Bederman, who further investigates the relationship between gender and dominant understandings of civilization.

54. Ernest Thompson Seton, *Two Little Savages: Being the Adventures of Two Boys Who Lived as Indians and What They Learned* (New York: Doubleday, Page, 1903). According to Macleod (*Building Character,* 132), *Two Little Savages* was one of "the most widely read and widely remembered boys' books of its generation." For one memory of the book, see Brooks Atkinson, "A Puritan Boyhood," *Massachusetts Review* 15 (1974): 353; some boys even copied the book by hand.

55. Seton, *Two Little Savages,* 326.

56. Ibid., 375–376.

57. Ibid., 56.

58. Richard Slotkin, "Nostalgia and Progress: Theodore Roosevelt's Myth of the Frontier," *American Quarterly* 33 (winter 1981): 619.

59. Seton, "Organized Boyhood," 804. See also Anderson, *The Chief,* 138–142.

60. The 200,000 number comes from Seton's biographer, who cited Seton's own estimates; see Anderson, *The Chief,* 148. Journalist McCready Sykes estimated the number as between 150,000 and 200,000; see McCready Sykes, "Let's Play Indian: Making a New American Boy through Woodcraft," *Everybody's Magazine* (October 1910): 481.

61. Macleod, *Building Character,* 130–132.

62. Burroughs to Roosevelt, 2 July 1906, quoted in Peter J. Schmitt, *Back to Nature: The Arcadian Myth in Urban America* (1969; reprint, Baltimore: Johns Hopkins University Press, 1990), 107.

63. Muir to Daniel Beard, April 1907, cited in Donald Worster, *A Passion for Nature: The Life of John Muir* (New York: Oxford University Press, 2008), 369.

64. Roosevelt to West, 30 November 1915, quoted in Anderson, *The Chief,* 174.

65. "Seton Still Insists on Quitting Scouts," *New York Times,* 6 December 1915, quoted in Anderson, *The Chief,* 174.

66. For more on the Camp Fire Girls, see Mary Jane McCallum, "'The Fundamental Things': Camp Fire Girls and Authenticity, 1910–1920," *Canadian Journal of History* (April 2005): 45–66.

67. William Gould Vinal, "The Call of Girls' Camps," *Nature-Study Review* 15, no. 5 (May 1919): 201, 202.

68. Quoted in Helen Buckler, *Wo-He-Lo; The Story of Camp Fire Girls, 1910–1960* (New York: Holt, Rinehart & Winston, 1961), 22–23.

69. Quoted in Deloria, *Playing Indian,* 96.

70. Ernest Thompson Seton, "On Nature-Study," in *Library of Natural History I* (New York: Saalfield, 1904–1910), iii.

71. Quoted in Nancy Bell, "The Work of Ernest Thompson Seton," *Humane Review* (April 1903): 18–19.

72. Quoted in Sykes, "Let's Play Indian," 481. Sykes was especially impressed with the way Seton's Indians replaced the idea of competition as something coming at the expense of another with the woodcraft view of competition as the betterment of one's self.

73. Quoted in Bell, "Work of Ernest Thompson Seton," 14, 11.

74. Russett, *Sexual Science,* 157.

75. Seton, "Woodcraft League," 435, 436.

76. John Burroughs, "Nature Study," *Outlook* 61 (4 February 1899): 328.

CHAPTER 4. BIRD DAY FOR KIDS

1. William Temple Hornaday, *Our Vanishing Wildlife: Its Extermination and Preservation* (New York: New York Zoological Society, 1913), 377; emphasis in original. For more on Hornaday, see Gregory John Dehler, "An American Crusader: William Temple Hornaday and Wildlife Protection in America, 1840–1940" (Ph.D. diss., Lehigh University, 2001); William C. Sharp, "In Search of a Preservation Ethic: William Temple Hornaday and American Environmental Education" (Ph.D. diss., University of Kansas, 1997); James Andrew Dolph, "Bringing Wildlife to Millions: William T. Hornaday, the Early Years, 1854–1896" (Ph.D. diss., University of Massachusetts, 1975).

2. For a critical examination of Arbor Day, see Shaul E. Cohen, *Planting Nature: Trees and the Manipulation of Environmental Stewardship in America* (Berkeley: University Press of California, 2004), especially 34–39. See also Nathaniel H. Egleston, *Arbor Day: Its History and Observance* (Washington, D.C.: Department of Agriculture, Government Printing Office, 1896).

3. Charles Babcock, *Bird Day: How to Prepare for It* (New York: Silver, Burdett, 1901), 20.

4. William Temple Hornaday, *Wild Life Conservation in Theory and Practice* (New Haven, Conn.: Yale University Press, 1914), 188, 184.

5. Hornaday, *Our Vanishing Wildlife,* 386.

6. Hornaday, *Wild Life Conservation,* 184.

7. Nature study proponents wanted to ensure that Bird Day programs did not devolve into a mere literary appreciation for birds but "consist[ed] of actual work out-of-doors in keeping with the day." See "Programs for Arbor and Bird Day," *Nature-Study Review* 6, no. 4 (April 1910): 107. For an example of the many articles that gave advice about incorporating Bird Day into an ongoing program of nature study, see Robert W. Hegner, "Nature-Studies with Birds for the Elementary School," *Elementary School Teacher* 5, no. 7 (March 1905): 408–419; Robert W. Hegner, "Nature-Studies with Birds for the Elementary School [Continued]," *Elementary School Teacher* 5, no. 8 (April 1905): 462–472.

8. T. S. Palmer, "Object of Bird Day," in *Bird Day in the Schools*, U.S. Department of Agriculture Circular no. 17 (Washington, D.C.: Government Printing Office, 1896), 3.

9. Babcock, *Bird Day*, 21, 20.

10. For more on Dutcher, see Oliver H. Orr, *Saving American Birds: T. Gilbert Pearson and the Founding of the Audubon Movement* (Gainesville: University Press of Florida, 1992).

11. Frank Graham Jr., *The Audubon Ark* (New York: Alfred A. Knopf, 1990), 83.

12. The problem of reconciling science and sentiment arose in many contexts. One that environmental historians have thoroughly examined is the effort by writers of popular nature stories to reconcile sympathy for animals with Darwinian natural selection. On this topic, see Lisa Mighetto, "Science, Sentiment, and Anxiety: American Nature Writing at the Turn of the Century," *Pacific Historical Review* 54 (February 1985): 33–50. For the expanded argument, see Lisa Mighetto, *Wild Animals and American Environmental Ethics* (Tucson: University Press of Arizona, 1991), especially 9–26. See also Thomas R. Dunlap, *Saving America's Wildlife: Ecology and the American Mind, 1850–1990* (Princeton, N.J.: Princeton University Press, 1988), especially 18–33.

13. Hornaday, *Wild Life Conservation*, 194, 186.

14. Hornaday, *Our Vanishing Wildlife*, 388, 392. Because science is multifaceted, it is important to emphasize the kind of science Hornaday and his allies in the nature study movement were critiquing. Hornaday and other conservationists promoted popular natural history but were greatly concerned with the relentless drive for quantification and reproducibility that typified modern scientific inquiry. Whereas the older tradition of natural history investigation had room for moral deliberation, modern experimental science eschewed any form of subjectivity. Many conservationists worried about what moral deliberation's elimination from science meant for progressive conservation. Bird Day and nature study were attempts to reconcile support for modern science with the belief that conservation stemmed from a love of nature. One relatively little studied part of this tradition is that of the naturalist-conservationist. See Mark V. Barrow Jr., "Naturalists as Conservationists: American Scientists, Social Responsibility and Political Activism before the Bomb," in *Science, History and Social Activism: A Tribute to Everett Mendelsohn*, ed. Garland E. Allen and Roy M. MacLeod (Dordrecht: Kluwer Academic Publishers, 2001). Barrow examines three leading conservationist-scientists, two of whom, David Starr Jordan and Frank Michler Chapman, were strong supporters of nature study. For more on the tensions between natural history and experimental laboratory science, expressed as the divide between the field and the laboratory, see Robert E. Kohler, *Landscapes & Labscapes: Exploring the Lab-Field Border in Biology* (Chicago: University of Chicago Press, 2002). Kohler concludes that the divide was not merely physical but was "a cultural zone with its own complex topography of practices and distinctions" (xiv).

15. Charles Adams, "Zoologists, Teachers and Wild Life Conservation," *Science* 41, no. 1065 (28 May 1915): 790–791. For more on Adams, see Paul B. Sears, "Charles C. Adams, Ecologist," *Science* 123, no. 3205 (1 June 1956): 974; Hugh M. Raup, "Charles C. Adams, 1873–1955," *Annals of the Association of American Geographers* 49, no. 2 (June 1959): 164–167. Adams spent much of his early career working on the methodology of ecology. Adams insisted on a historicized understanding of evolutionary processes and thus viewed ecology as allied with anthropology and geology. See Juan Ilerbaig, "Allied

Sciences and Fundamental Problems: C. C. Adams and the Search for Method in Early American Ecology," *Journal of the History of Biology* 32 (1999): 439–463.

16. Herbert Smith, "Preservation of the Natural Resources of the United States," *National Education Association Journal of Proceedings and Addresses* (1908): 994. For more on Smith, see Henry Clepper, "Herbert A. Smith, 1866–1944," *Journal of Forestry* 42, no. 9 (September 1944): 625–627.

17. J. Sterling Morton to Charles Babcock, reprinted in Babcock, *Bird Day*, 10.

18. Quoted in Babcock, *Bird Day*, 10, 11, 12. For more on Burroughs, see Edward J. Renehan Jr., *John Burroughs: An American Naturalist* (Post Mills, Vt.: Chelsea Green Publishing Co., 1992). For more on Miller, see Florence Merriam Bailey, "Olive Thorne Miller," *Condor* 21, no. 2 (March 1919): 69–73. For more on Morton, see James C. Olson, *J. Sterling Morton: Pioneer, Statesman, Founder of Arbor Day* (Lincoln: University Press of Nebraska, 1942).

19. Quoted in Palmer, "Object of Bird Day," 2.

20. *Journal of Education*, 24 May 1894, quoted in Palmer, "Object of Bird Day," 2.

21. "Bird Day for Children," *New York Times*, 21 April 1901, 20.

22. "'Bird Day' for Nebraska," *Omaha Sunday World-Herald*, 15 January 1899, 4.

23. *North Dakota Special Day Programs* (Bismarck, N.D.: Department of Public Instruction, 1913), 43.

24. C. G. Lawrence, "A Letter to the Teachers of South Dakota," in *South Dakota Arbor and Bird Day Annual* (Pierre, S.D.: Superintendent of Public Instruction, 1914), 3.

25. Frank O. Lowden, "By the Governor of Illinois—A Proclamation," in *Arbor and Bird Days*, Illinois Department of Public Instruction Circular no. 134 (1919), 2.

26. Augustus E. Willson, "Arbor Day Proclamation," in *Kentucky Arbor and Bird Day* (1910), 3.

27. Mrs. P. S. Peterson, "Nature Lover's Creed," in *Kentucky Arbor and Bird Day* (1910), 12.

28. Eva Shelley Voris, "Who Love the Birds," in *Kentucky Arbor and Bird Day* (1910), 84.

29. For examples, see Margaret M. Withrow, "Program for Bird Day," *Virginia Journal of Education* 3, no. 6 (March 1910): 384–387; "Bird Day Exercises," *Werner's Magazine* 28, no. 6 (February 1902): 917–926; "Bird Day Exercises," *Journal of Education* 45 (1 April 1897): 209–210; E. V. Brown, "A Bird Day Program," *Bird Lore* 1, no. 2 (April 1899): 52.

30. Frederick Leroy Sargent, "Wings at Rest: A Bird Day Tragedy in One Act," *Journal of Education* 47 (24 March 1898): 180–182.

31. Grace B. Faxon, *Mother Earth's Party, and a Bird Day Exercise* (New York: F. A. Owens Publishing Co., 1903).

32. "Birds and Men," *Advocate of Peace* 68, no. 3 (March 1906): 63–64.

33. For example, see Amos M. Kellogg, *Primary Recitation: Short Bright Selections for Thanksgiving, Washington's Birthday, Arbor Day, May Day, Memorial Day, Flag Day, Closing Exercises, Nature Recitations, Patriotic and General Occasions* (1897; reprint, Freeport, N.Y.: Books for Libraries Press, 1971).

34. "Without Birds Agriculture Would Be Impossible," in *Arbor and Bird Day Manual* (Ohio Department of Education, 1912), 16. The field of "economic ornithology" was an important one in the Progressive Era. See Matthew D. Evenden, "The Laborers of Nature: Economic Ornithology and the Role of Birds as Agents of Biological Pest Con-

trol in North American Agriculture, ca. 1880–1930," *Forest & Conservation History* 39 (October 1995): 172–183. See also W. L. McAtee, "Economic Ornithology," in *Fifty Years' Progress of American Ornithology 1883–1933: Published by the American Ornithologists' Union, on the Occasion of Its Semi-centennial Anniversary, New York, N.Y., November 13–16, 1933* (Lancaster, Pa.: American Ornithologists' Union, 1933).

35. B. M. Davis, "Birds and Their Relation to Insects," in *Arbor and Bird Day Manual* (Ohio Department of Education, April 1914), 21.

36. "Great Work of the Bob Whites," in *West Virginia Arbor and Bird Day Manual* (1906), 30–31.

37. Edward Hyatt, "Conservation, Bird and Arbor Day," in *Conservation, Bird and Arbor Day in California* (Sacramento, Calif.: Superintendent of Public Instruction, 1916), 1.

38. "Man and Nature," in *Arbor Day Bird Day* (Harrisburg: Commonwealth of Pennsylvania Department of Public Instruction, 1934), 7.

39. "The Birds' Declaration of Dependence," in *Arbor and Bird Day Bulletin* (Olympia: State of Washington, 1917), 5.

40. "Our Patriots Were Nimrods," in *Bird Day Book* (Montgomery, Ala.: Department of Education, 1915), 8. The idea that outdoor activity accounted for the skills that could lead to victory in war occurred to other conservationists. See, for example, the writings of Ernest Thompson Seton, who argued, "The drilled soldier is a piece of admirable mechanism—mechanically brave, mechanically obedient—an able fighting machine." But the outdoorsman "is one of all-round development; a man who can ride, shoot, plan, go ahead, and take care of himself in the woods." Seton used this idea to explain the victory of the Continental army over the British in the Revolutionary War. See Ernest Thompson Seton, "Organized Boyhood: The Boy Scout Movement, Its Purpose and Laws," *Success Magazine* (December 1910): 804.

41. "The Preservation of the Wild Life of Alabama," in *Bird Day Book* (Montgomery, Ala.: Department of Education, 1910), 10, 12.

42. William T. Hornaday, "Duty of the Citizen toward Life," in *Bird Day Book* (Montgomery, Ala.: Department of Education, 1915), 92.

43. Harry Gunnels, foreword to *Bird Day Book* (Montgomery, Ala.: Department of Education, 1910), 5.

44. Sam Walter Foss, "The Bloodless Sportsman," in *Bird Day Book* (Montgomery, Ala.: Department of Education, 1910), 6.

45. "Bird Minstrelsy," in *Bird Day Book* (Montgomery, Ala.: Department of Education, 1915), 23.

46. Joe Kosack, *The Pennsylvania Game Commission, 1895–1995: 100 Years of Wildlife Conservation* (Harrisburg: Pennsylvania Game Commission, 1995), 132.

47. Hornaday, *Our Vanishing Wildlife*, 381.

48. "Tener Talks to Carrick Tots on Bird Day," *Pittsburgh Gazette Times,* 12 April 1912, 1.

49. Quoted in Hornaday, *Our Vanishing Wildlife*, 380, 381.

50. *Arbor and Bird Day* (Ohio Department of Education, March 1911), 6. See also "Duty of Teachers," in *Arbor Day* (Springfield, Ohio: State Commissioner of Common Schools, 1903), 7.

51. "Results of Wildlife Conservation Contest," *Arizona Bird Day Annual,* 4 May 1916, 24.

52. Library of Congress American Memory Collection, *To Elevate Morals. Bird Day.*

Animal Day (Milwaukee, 1894), http://memory.loc.gov/cgi-bin/query/D?rbpebib:9:./temp/~ammem_iPWe:: (accessed 18 July 2006).

53. "Bird Club Suggestions," *Colorado Arbor Day Notes with Suggestions for Bird Day,* 20 April 1900, 25.

54. "News and Notes for September," *Nature-Study Review* 11, no. 6 (September 1915): 300.

55. Emelyn Clark, "Bird Study in the Grades," *Nature-Study Review* 11, no. 4 (April 1915): 208, 209.

56. R. E. Wager, "Editorial," *Nature-Study Review* 11, no. 4 (April 1915): 211.

57. Frank Luther Mott, *A History of American Magazines 1865–1885* (Cambridge, Mass.: Harvard University Press, 1957), 505.

58. Robert Henry Welker, *Birds and Men: American Birds in Science, Art and Conservation, 1800–1900* (Cambridge, Mass.: Belknap Press of Harvard University Press, 1955).

59. Edward Bigelow, "Nature and Science for Young Folks," *St. Nicholas* 29, no. 8 (June 1902): 745, 747.

60. Edward Bigelow, "Nature and Science for Young Folks" *St. Nicholas* 38, no. 2 (December 1910): 173–174.

61. Edward Bigelow, "The Passenger-Pigeon," *St. Nicholas* 27, no. 4 (February 1900): 359.

62. Mabel Osgood Wright and Elliott Coues, *Citizen Bird: Scenes from Bird-Life in Plain English for Beginners* (New York: Macmillan, 1897), 90.

63. Daniel J. Philippon, introduction to *The Friendship of Nature: A New England Chronicle of Birds and Flowers* by Mabel Osgood Wright (1894; reprint, Baltimore: Johns Hopkins University Press, 1999). Philippon is the best scholar on Wright. See his *Conserving Words: How American Nature Writers Shaped the Environmental Movement* (Athens: University of Georgia Press, 2004), especially 72–105. For more on women and the conservation movement, see Carolyn Merchant, "The Women of the Progressive Conservation Crusade, 1900–1915," in *Environmental History: Critical Issues in Comparative Perspective,* ed. Kendall E. Bailes (Lanham, Md.: University Press of America, 1985), 153–170.

64. C. A. Babcock "Suggestions for Bird-Day Programs in the Schools," *Bird Lore* 1, no. 2 (April 1899): 49.

65. Marianne Gosztonyi Ainley, "The Contribution of the Amateur to North American Ornithology: A Historical Perspective," *The Living Bird: Eighteenth Annual of the Cornell Laboratory of Ornithology* (1979–1980). The best treatment of modern ornithology is Mark V. Barrow Jr., *A Passion for Birds: American Ornithology after Audubon* (Princeton, N.J.: Princeton University Press, 1998). Barrow emphasizes the tensions between amateur and professional ornithologists.

66. Frank M. Chapman, "The Educational Value of Bird-Study," *Educational Review* (March 1899): 246, 247.

67. Orr, *Saving American Birds,* 124.

68. William Dutcher, "Education as a Factor in Audubon Work—Relation of Birds to Man," *Bird Lore* 11, no. 6 (1 December 1909): 287.

69. Olive Thorne Miller, "The Study of Birds—Another Way," *Bird Lore* 2, no. 5 (October 1900): 153.

70. Mabel Osgood Wright, "A Little Christmas Sermon for Teachers," *Bird Lore* 7, no. 6 (December 1910): 253, 254.

71. Considering the role of nature writing in the conservation movement is an extremely complex endeavor that requires the resolution of thorny theoretical issues. Readers interested in examining these issues can consult several excellent studies of nature writing and American conservation, beginning with Philippon, *Conserving Words*. See also Paul Brooks, *Speaking for Nature: How Literary Naturalists from Henry Thoreau to Rachel Carson Have Shaped America* (Boston: Houghton Mifflin, 1980); Lawrence Buell, *The Environmental Imagination: Thoreau, Nature Writing, and the Formation of American Culture* (Cambridge, Mass.: Belknap Press, 1995).

72. Welker, *Birds and Men,* 189; Mabel Osgood Wright, *Tommy-Anne and the Three Hearts* (New York: Macmillan, 1896), front matter.

73. For more on Hoar's political career, see Richard E. Welch Jr., *George Frisbie Hoar and the Half-Bred Republicans* (Cambridge, Mass.: Harvard University Press, 1971).

74. George F. Hoar, "The Birds' Petition," *Educational Gazette* (May 1904): 145.

75. *Current Literature* 22, no. 3 (September 1897): 210.

76. Anna Botsford Comstock, "The Growth and Influence of the Nature-Study Idea," *Nature-Study Review* 11, no. 1 (January 1915): 11.

77. Anna Botsford Comstock, "Conservation and Nature-Study," *Nature-Study Review* 18, no. 7 (October 1922): 300.

78. William T. Hornaday, "The Right Way to Teach Zoology," *Outlook,* 11 June 1910, 256; emphasis in original. For more on Hornaday's pedagogy, see William T. Hornaday, "Educational Value of Popular Museums," in *The Twelfth Celebration of Founder's Day* (Pittsburgh: Carnegie Institute, 1908), 42–50.

79. Alexandra Oleson and John Voss, eds., *The Organization of Knowledge in Modern America, 1860–1920* (Baltimore: Johns Hopkins University Press, 1979).

80. For a discussion of the tensions between secular modernity and ethical conviction, see T. J. Jackson Lears, *No Place of Grace: Antimodernism and the Transformation of American Culture, 1880–1920* (Chicago: University of Chicago Press, 1983); David Danbom, *"The World of Hope": Progressives and the Struggle for an Ethical Public Life* (Philadelphia: Temple University Press, 1987).

81. Hornaday, "The Right Way to Teach Zoology," 263.

CHAPTER 5. STICKING A FINGER INTO NATURE'S PIE

1. Alice J. Patterson, "Educational Value of Children's Gardens," *Nature-Study Review* 12, no. 3 (March 1916): 128, 125.

2. Mabel Osgood Wright, *The Garden of a Commuter's Wife* (New York: Macmillan, 1901).

3. Booker T. Washington, *Up from Slavery: An Autobiography* (New York: Doubleday, Page, 1901), 154.

4. William Cronon, "The Trouble with Wilderness; or, Getting Back to the Wrong Nature," *Environmental History* 1, no. 1 (January 1996): 7–28. See also Samuel P. Hays, "Comment: The Trouble with Bill Cronon's Wilderness," *Environmental History* 1, no. 1 (January 1996): 29–32. Highlights of the debate include Michael P. Cohen, "Comment: Resistance to Wilderness," *Environmental History* 1 (1996): 33–42; Thomas R. Dunlap, "Comment: But What Did You Go Out into the Wilderness to See?" *Environmental*

History 1 (1996): 43–46; William Cronon, "The Trouble with Wilderness: A Response," *Environmental History* 1 (1996): 47–55; J. Baird Collect and Michael P. Nelson, eds., *The Great New Wilderness Debate* (Athens: University of Georgia Press, 1998). The best recent book-length examination of the history of wilderness in the United States is Paul Sutter, *Driven Wild: How the Fight against Automobiles Launched the Modern Wilderness Movement* (Seattle: University of Washington Press, 2002). The best critique in article form remains Donald Worster's "The Wilderness of History," *Wild Earth* 7 (fall 1997): 9–13. A terrific overview is Michael Lewis, ed., *American Wilderness: A New History* (New York: Oxford University Press, 2007).

5. Patterson, "Educational Value of Children's Gardens," 127. Despite their popularity, school gardens have generated little scholarship. See Sally Gregory Kohlstedt, "'A Better Crop of Boys and Girls': The School Gardening Movement, 1890–1920," *History of Education Quarterly* 48, no. 1 (February 2008): 58–93; Laura J. Lawson, *City Bountiful: A Century of Community Gardening in America* (Berkeley: University of California Press, 2005), especially 51–92; E. Backert, "History and Analysis of the School Garden Movement in America, 1890–1910" (Ph.D. diss., Indiana University, 1977). See also Constance Carter's Web site on school gardens: http://www.loc.gov/rr/program/journey/school gardens.html.

6. Attributed to George Fox by James Ralph Jewell, *Agriculture Education Including Nature Study and School Gardens,* Bulletin 2, Department of Interior, Bureau of Education (Washington, D.C: Government Printing Office, 1907), 30, quoted in Lawson, *City Bountiful,* 51.

7. For more on Pingree's potato patches, see Lawson, *City Bountiful,* 24–27.

8. John Dewey, *Schools of To-Morrow* [1915], in *John Dewey: The Middle Works,* vol. 8, ed. Jo Ann Boydston (Carbondale: Southern Illinois University Press, 1979), 266.

9. John Dewey, *Democracy and Education: An Introduction to the Philosophy of Education* (1916; reprint, New York: Free Press, 1997), 200.

10. Paul Boyer, *Urban Masses and Moral Order in America, 1820–1920* (Cambridge, Mass.: Harvard University Press, 1978), 179.

11. Fanny Griscom Parsons, *The First Children's Farm School in New York City, 1902, 1903, 1904* (New York: DeWitt Clinton Farm School, 1904), n.p.

12. Margaret Knox, "The Function of a School Garden in a Crowded City District," in *Second Annual Report* (New York: School Garden Association of New York, 1910), 33, quoted in Lawson, *City Bountiful,* 55.

13. Louise Klein Miller, "The Civic Aspect of School Gardens," *Nature-Study Review* 8, no. 2 (February 1912): 75.

14. Parsons, *First Children's Farm School.*

15. Michigan State Superintendent of Public Instruction, *A Study of School Gardens,* 56, cited in Lawson, *City Bountiful,* 79.

16. Neltje Blanchan, "The Garden Anyone Can Have," *Ladies' Home Journal* 25 (January 1908): 44.

17. H. M. Benedict, "Will School-Gardening Survive?" *Nature-Study Review* 9, no. 8 (November 1913): 261.

18. B. M. Davis, "School Gardens," *Nature-Study Review* 2, no. 3 (March 1906): 84.

19. B. M. Davis, *School Gardens for California Schools: A Manual for Teachers* (Chico, Calif.: Publications of the State Normal School, 1905), 76, 77.

20. Jacob Riis, "What Ails Our Boys?" *Craftsman* 21, no. 1 (October 1911): 10.

21. B. J. Horchem, "School Gardening, a Fundamental Element in Education," *Nature-Study Review* 8, no. 2 (February 1912): 63.

22. Ibid., 64, 65, 66.

23. R. J. Floody, "Worcester Garden City Plan; or, The Good Citizens' Factory," *Nature-Study Review* 8, no. 4 (April 1912): 145.

24. Ibid., 148.

25. Alice R. Northrop, "Nature and the Child," in *The Uplift Book of Child Culture* (Philadelphia: Uplift Publishing Co., n.d.), 253.

26. Alice Rich Northrop, "Flower Shows in City Schools," *Nature-Study Review* 1, no. 3 (May 1905): 104–109.

27. Mrs. John I. Northrop, "Nature and the City Child," *Natural History* (April 1920): 268.

28. Ibid., 273.

29. Ibid., 275.

30. Northrop, "Flower Shows in City Schools," 106.

31. Northrop, "Nature and the City Child," 267.

32. Northrop, "Flower Shows in City Schools," 106.

33. Northrop Papers, box 3, cited in Dawn Chávez, "A Naturalist in New York City: The Story of Alice Rich Northrop" (paper presented at the annual meeting of the American Association for Environmental History, Providence, R.I., March 2003).

34. Northrop, "Nature and the Child," in *The Uplift Book of Child Culture,* 255.

35. "The Educational Museum of the St. Louis Public Schools and its Relation to Gardening and Nature-Study," *Nature-Study Review* 6, no. 4 (April 1910): 102, 100.

36. Lucy C. Buell, "Home Gardens in Cleveland," *Nature-Study Review* 3 (February 1907): 38.

37. Susan B. Sipe, "Practical Aid to the School Garden Movement by the United States Department of Agriculture," *Nature-Study Review* 8, no. 2 (February 1912): 53.

38. H. D. Hemenway, "School Garden Notes," *Nature-Study Review* 1, no. 5 (September 1905): 218–219.

39. Jewel, *Agriculture Education, 37.*

40. According to Laura J. Lawson in *City Bountiful,* the School Garden Association of America grew out of the New York School Garden Association. It met in conjunction with the National Education Association until 1939, when it became the Department of Garden Education of the National Education Association. The International Children's School Farm League was founded due to requests for information about school gardening submitted to the DeWitt Clinton Farm School.

41. H. D. Hemenway, "School Gardens at the School of Horticulture, Hartford Connecticut," *Nature-Study Review* 1, no. 1 (January 1905): 36.

42. Amos W. Farnham, "The Relation Which School-Gardens May Bear to Industrial and Commercial Geography," *Nature-Study Review* 3, no. 3 (March 1907): 85.

43. Edna R. Thayer, "Children's Gardens at Downing Street School, Worcester, Mass.," *Nature-Study Review* 1, no. 2 (March 1905): 64.

44. E. C. Bishop, "The School-Home Garden," *Nature Study Review* 8, no. 5 (May 1912): 170.

45. Cited in Christine B. Damrow, "'Every Child in a Garden': Radishes, Avocado Pits, and the Education of American Children in the Twentieth Century" (Ph.D. diss., University of Wisconsin–Madison, 2005), 2; Dora Williams, *Gardens and Their Meaning* (Boston: Ginn, 1911), 2.

46. Lida Lee Tall and Isobel Davidson, *Course of Study: Baltimore County Maryland Public Schools Grades I to VIII* (Baltimore: Warwick & York, 1919), 228.

47. Bertha Chapman, "School Gardens in the Refugee Camps of San Francisco," *Nature-Study Review* 2, no. 7 (October 1906): 229. For more on nature study and Americanization, see Christena Fear, "Nature and Americanization as Allies," *Nature-Study Review* 19 (January 1923): 2; Amy Green, "'The Good Citizen's Factory': Americanization through School Gardening, 1890–1915" (paper presented at the annual meeting of the American Association for Environmental History, Providence, R.I., March 2003).

48. "Nature Study and Gardening for Indian Schools," *Nature-Study Review* 2, no. 4 (April 1905): 141, 142.

49. Clifton F. Hodge, *Nature Study and Life* (Boston: Ginn, 1902), 10.

50. "Turning the Partridge into a Quiet Barnyard Fowl," *New York Times,* 26 November 1905, SM3.

51. Frank C. Pellett, "Wild Flower Gardening," *Nature-Study Review* 8, no. 6 (September 1912): 218, 219.

52. E. Laurence Palmer, "Flowers of the Woodlands," *Cornell Rural School Leaflet* 16, no. 4 (March 1923): 33.

53. "Wild Flower Preservation Society of America," *Nature-Study Review* 18, no. 7 (October 1922): 269.

54. "Society for the Preservation of New England Plants," *Nature-Study Review* 18, no. 7 (October 1922): 280, 279, 280.

55. Daniel J. Philippon, *Conserving Words: How American Nature Writers Shaped the Environmental Movement* (Athens: University of Georgia Press, 2004), 73. For a brief overview of Wright's career, see Linda C. Forbes and John M. Jermier, "The Institutionalization of Bird Protection: Mabel Osgood Wright and the Early Audubon Movement," *Organization & Environment* 15, no. 4 (December 2002): 458–465.

56. Robin W. Doughty, "Concern for Fashionable Feathers," *Forest History* 16, no. 2 (July 1972): 6. For more on women, birds, hats, and the early Audubon movement, see Jennifer Price, *Flight Maps: Adventures with Nature in Modern America* (New York: Basic Books, 1999), 57–109.

57. Mabel Osgood Wright, "Fees and Pledges," *Bird Lore* 2, no. 2 (April 1900): 63, 64.

58. Mabel Osgood Wright, *Gray Lady and the Birds: Stories of the Bird Year for Home and School* (New York: Macmillan, 1917), xii.

59. Edward Howe Forbush, *Useful Birds and Their Protection: Containing Brief Descriptions of the More Common and Useful Species of Massachusetts, with Accounts of Their Food Habits, and a Chapter on the Means of Attracting and Protecting Birds* (Boston: Massachusetts State Board of Agriculture, 1907), 413–414. Forbush became the Massachusetts state ornithologist in 1908.

60. Mabel Osgood Wright, "How to Save Wild Flowers: The Transplanting of Wild Plants in General and the Mountain Laurel and Rhododendron in Particular," *American Fern Journal* 13, no. 2 (June 1923): 52, 53, 54.

61. Philippon, *Conserving Words*, 89.

62. Mabel Osgood Wright, "The Making of Birdcraft Sanctuary," *Bird Lore* 17, no. 4 (July–August 1915): 263.

63. Forbush, *Useful Birds and Their Protection*, 372.

64. Quoted in Philippon, *Conserving Words*, 100–101. For more on the making of the Birdcraft Museum and Sanctuary, see ibid., 99–100. The Birdcraft Web site is http://www.ctaudubon.org/visit/birdcraft.htm.

65. Julia E. Rogers, "The Nature Club," *Country Life in America* 16 (May 1909): 62.

66. My discussion of the wild garden derives from Virginia Tuttle Clayton, "Wild Gardening and the Popular American Magazine, 1890–1918," in *Nature and Ideology: Natural Garden Design in the Twentieth Century,* ed. Joachim Wolschke-Bulmahn (Washington, D.C: Dumbarton Oaks Research Library and Collection, 1997), 131–154.

67. Mabel Osgood Wright, *The Friendship of Nature: A New England Chronicle of Birds and Flowers* (1894; reprint, Baltimore: Johns Hopkins University Press, 1998), 96.

68. Mabel Osgood Wright, "Meditations on the Posting of Bird Laws," *Bird Lore* 5 (1903): 205. For more on immigrants and the conservation movement, see Adam Rome, "Nature Wars, Culture Wars: Immigration and Environmental Reform in the Progressive Era," *Environmental History* 13, no. 3 (July 2008): 432–453.

69. Mabel Osgood Wright, "The Law and the Bird," *Bird Lore* 1 (1899): 203.

70. Washington, *Up from Slavery*, 185.

71. Booker T. Washington, *Working with the Hands: Being a Sequel to "Up from Slavery" Covering the Author's Experience in Industrial Training at Tuskegee* (New York: Doubleday, Page, 1904), 151, 156, 154–155, 32, 35.

72. Ibid., 51, 136.

73. Ibid., 153, 157, 156, 157.

74. Ibid., 10–11, 39.

75. Ibid., 14.

76. Ibid., 137.

77. Washington, *Up from Slavery*, 63.

78. Washington, *Working with the Hands*, 92–93.

79. Max Bennett Thrasher, *Tuskegee: Its Story and Its Work* (Boston: Small, Maynard, 1900), 87. Thrasher spends considerable time describing the garden work at Tuskegee.

80. Washington, *Working with the Hands*, 90.

81. Ibid., 159.

82. Ibid., 94.

83. Ibid., 96.

84. Ibid., 107, 116.

85. Margaret Murray Washington, "What Girls Are Taught and How," in *Tuskegee and Its People: Their Ideals and Achievements,* ed. Booker T. Washington (New York: D. Appleton, 1905), 74–75.

86. Washington, *Working with the Hands*, 161, 162.

87. Cronon, "The Trouble with Wilderness," 24.

88. "Gardens Imagined," *Scribner's Magazine* 57 (1915): 778.

89. John Dixon Hart, *Greater Perfections: The Practice of Garden Theory* (Philadelphia: University of Pennsylvania Press, 2000).

CHAPTER 6. THE ART OF LIFE

1. Charles W. Eliot, "Beauty and Democracy," *School Arts Book* 5, no. 1 (September 1905): 1, 72. For Eliot's championing of progressive education, see Charles W. Eliot, "The New Education," *Atlantic Monthly* 22 (1869): 203–220, 358–367; Charles W. Eliot, *Educational Reform* (New York: Century Co., 1898). For Eliot's career, see Hugh Hawkins, *Between Harvard and America: The Educational Leadership of Charles W. Eliot* (New York: Oxford University Press, 1972).

2. Eliot, "Beauty and Democracy," 4–5, 6. The idea that aesthetic pleasure derived from contact with nature remained open to all Americans (unlike fine art) was common in the discourse of progressive conservation. For example, popular novelist and illustrator Ernest Thompson Seton observed that the "well-to-do" spent "enormous sums" on "pictures, music, the drama, and kindred pleasures." Yet nature study, a pleasure "at least worthy to rank with them," remained "within the reach of all." See Ernest Thompson Seton, "On Nature-Study," in *Library of Natural History I* (New York: Saalfield, 1904–1910), iii.

3. Eliot, "Beauty and Democracy," 72.

4. Bliss Carman, *The Kinship of Nature* (Boston: L. C. Page, 1903), 6–8.

5. For a history of the use of images by environmental activists, see Finis Dunaway, *Natural Visions: The Power of Images in American Environmental Reform* (Chicago: University of Chicago Press, 2005). See also Dunaway's essay "Hunting with the Camera: Nature Photography, Manliness, and Modern Memory, 1890–1930," *Journal of American Studies* 34, no. 2 (2000): 207–230. Dunaway examines the Progressive Era in the first chapter of *Natural Visions*. Much of my analysis concurs with Dunaway's, especially regarding the importance of the rhetorical context that surrounded photographs of nature. I place greater emphasis on photography as a widespread phenomenon within the conservation community and highlight the contradictions inherent to the cultural politics of conservationist reform. See also Gregg Mitman, *Reel Nature: America's Romance with Wildlife on Film* (Cambridge, Mass.: Harvard University Press, 1999).

6. In his pragmatist philosophy, nature study supporter John Dewey developed the argument that aesthetics is something one experiences rather than something bound up in objects of aesthetic appreciation. This idea is articulated in much of his work but is most thoroughly investigated in *Art as Experience* [1934], in *John Dewey: The Later Works*, vol. 10, ed. Jo Ann Boydston (Carbondale: Southern Illinois University Press, 1987). For more on Dewey and art, see Thomas M. Alexander, *The Horizons of Feeling: John Dewey's Theory of Art, Experience, and Nature* (Albany: State University of New York Press, 1987); Philip W. Jackson, *John Dewey and the Lessons of Art* (New Haven, Conn.: Yale University Press, 1988).

7. For example, consider naturalist John Muir's devastating diagnosis from 1888: "Most people are on the world, not in it. [They] have no conscious sympathy or relationship

to anything about them—undiffused, separate, and rigidly alone like marbles of polished stone, touching but separate." Quoted in *The Wilderness World of John Muir: A Selection from His Collected Works,* ed. Edwin Way Teale (New York: Mariner Books, 2001), 313.

8. Ralph Hoffmann, "Bird Study in the Schools," *School Arts Book* 4 (6 February 1905): 325.

9. Dewey, *The Later Works,* 2:349.

10. Ibid., 10:24.

11. Dewey, *The Middle Works,* 12:152.

12. M. V. O'Shea, "Drawing and Nature Study," *Education* 17 (October 1896): 97.

13. Quoted in Henry Turner Bailey, "Educative Values of Drawing," *School Arts Book* (February 1910): 577.

14. Royal B. Farnum, "My Work Book Chapter VI—Nature Study," *School Arts Book* 10, no. 8 (1910): 647.

15. Editorial, "A Corollary to Nature Study," *Nation* 75, no. 11 (4 September 1902). For a similar view, see Charles C. Abbott, "The Enjoyment of Nature," *Arena* (June 1904): 611–614. Abbott, an archaeologist and naturalist, despaired that "the art of knowing our own homes is not sufficiently cultivated," a situation remedied through nature study.

16. Bailey, "Educative Values of Drawing," 577.

17. "A Corollary to Nature Study."

18. Hamilton Wright Mabie, *Essays on Nature and Culture* (New York: Dodd, Mead, 1896), 117, 118, 113. For information on Mabie, see David J. Rife, "Hamilton Wright Mabie: A Critical Bibliography" (Ph.D. diss., Southern Illinois University, 1974).

19. Mabie, *Essays on Nature and Culture,* 40, 123, 124.

20. Charles A. Fenton, "The Founding of the National Institute of Arts and Letters in 1898," *New England Quarterly* 32, no. 4 (December 1959): 438.

21. Farnum, "My Work Book Chapter VI," 645.

22. T. J. Jackson Lears, *No Place of Grace: Antimodernism and the Transformation of American Culture, 1880–1920* (Chicago: University of Chicago Press, 1981), 59–96. See also Wendy Kaplan, *"The Art that Is Life": The Arts & Crafts Movement in America, 1875–1920* (New York: Bulfinch Press–Little Brown, 1987).

23. William Morris, *The Collected Works of William Morris,* vol. 22 (London: Routledge/Thoemmes Press, 1992), 346.

24. Quoted in Peter Faulkner, *Against the Age: An Introduction to William Morris* (London: Allen & Unwin, 1980), 114. Those interested in Morris should consult E. P. Thompson, *William Morris: Romantic to Revolutionary* (New York: Knopf Publishing Group, 1977). For Morris as environmentalist, see Peter C. Gould, *Early Green Politics: Back to Nature, Back to the Land, and Socialism in Britain, 1880–1900* (New York: Harvester, 1988).

25. Morris, "Art under Plutocracy" [1884], reprinted in Josephine M. Guy, *The Victorian Age: An Anthology of Sources and Documents* (London: Routledge, 2008), 439.

26. John Gadsby Chapman, *American Drawing-book* (New York: J. S. Redfield, 1847), 4, quoted in Diana Korzenik, "The Art Education of Working Women 1873–1903," in *Pilgrims and Pioneers: New England Women in the Arts,* ed. Alicia Faxon and Sylvia Moore (New York: Midmarch Arts Press, 1987), 40.

27. Benjamin H. Coe, *Easy Lessons in Landscape Drawing* (Hartford, Conn.: Tyler & Potter, 1842), quoted in Korzenik, "Art Education of Working Women," 40.

28. Henry Turner Bailey, *The City of Refuge* (Worcester, Mass.: Davis, 1901), 12.

29. Ibid.

30. Ibid.

31. Eileen Boris, *Art and Labor: Ruskin, Morris, and the Craftsman Ideal in America* (Philadelphia: Temple University Press, 1986), 86–87.

32. My discussion is indebted to Cynthia Watkins Richardson, "Art that Is Nature: Nature Study and the Manual Arts in the Early Twentieth Century" (paper presented at the annual meeting of the American Society for Environmental History, Providence, R.I., March 2003).

33. Eleanor Hyde Beaton, "The Contributions of Henry Turner Bailey to Art Education" (master's thesis, Boston University, 1945), 15.

34. Ibid.

35. *Greenfield Annual Report*, 14, cited in Richardson, "Art that Is Nature."

36. Henry Turner Bailey, "The Child's Birthright in Art," *Proceedings of the National Education Association* (1926): 164–165.

37. Henry Turner Bailey, "Fundamental Values of Life and How to Reach Them," *Proceedings of the National Education Association* (1927): 421.

38. Peter J. Schmitt, *Back to Nature: The Arcadian Myth in Urban America* (1969; reprint, Baltimore: Johns Hopkins University Press, 1990), 147. For the history of wildlife photography, see C. A. W. Guggisberg, *Early Wildlife Photographers* (New York: David & Charles, Newton Abbot, 1977).

39. For more on Jackson, see Peter B. Hales, *William Henry Jackson and the Transformation of the American Landscape* (Philadelphia: Temple University Press, 1988). For other works that consider visual representation and the American relationship with nature, see Barbara Novak, *Nature and Culture: American Landscape Painting, 1825–1875* (New York: Oxford University Press, 1980); Angela Miller, *The Empire of the Eye: Landscape Representation and American Cultural Politics, 1825–1875* (Ithaca, N.Y.: Cornell University Press, 1993); Martha A. Sandweiss, *Print the Legend: Photography and the American West* (New Haven, Conn.: Yale University Press, 2002).

40. George Eastman invented the name "Kodak." He liked it because it was "terse, abrupt to the point of rudeness, literally bitten off by firm and unyielding consonants at both ends, it snaps like a camera shutter in your face. What more could one ask?" Quoted in Beaumont Newhall, *The History of Photography from 1839 to the Present* (Boston: Bulfinch, 1982), 489.

41. *New York Tribune*, 5 September 1889, 6.

42. For example, the *New York Tribune* marveled that "amateur photography has the reputation of possessing in its various forms all those seductive charms in the enjoyment of which the weary, earthbound mortal is released from durance vile and translated, for the time being, into some seventh heaven of bliss. Opium, hasheesh, even the fascinations of Monte Carlo are supposed to pall before its many attractions." Quoted in Robert E. Mensel, "'Kodakers Lying in Wait': Amateur Photography and the Right of Privacy in New York, 1885–1915," *American Quarterly* 43, no. 1 (March 1991): 29.

43. For the history of the Kodak, see Nancy Martha West, *Kodak and the Lens of Nostalgia* (Charlottesville: University of Virginia Press, 2000); Douglas Collins, *The Story of Kodak* (New York: H. N. Abrams, 1990). For general histories of photography in America, see Robert Taft, *Photography and the American Scene: A Social History 1839–1889* (New York: Peter Smith, 1964); Alan Trachtenberg, *Reading American Photographs: Images as History—Mathew Brady to Walker Evans* (New York: Hill & Wang, 1989); Gilles Mora, *Photospeak: A Guide to the Ideas, Movements, and Techniques of Photography, 1839 to the Present* (New York: Abbeville Press, 1998). For a cultural history of photography and realism, see Miles Orvell, *The Real Thing: Imitation and Authenticity in American Culture, 1880–1940* (Chapel Hill: University of North Carolina Press, 1989).

44. West, *Kodak and the Lens of Nostalgia*, 38.

45. J. Liberty Tadd, *New Methods in Education: Art, Real Manual Training, Nature Study* (Springfield, Mass.: Orange Judd Co., 1904), 4.

46. Herbert Keightley Job, *Wild Wings: Adventures of a Camera-Hunter among the Larger Wild Birds of North America on Sea and Land* (New York: Houghton Mifflin, 1905), vii.

47. For example, see E. D. Huntington, "Nature Photography," *Nature-Study Review* 12, no. 4 (April 1915): 169–174.

48. Radclyffe Dugmore, "A Revolution in Nature Pictures," *World's Work* (November 1900): 36.

49. Ibid., 34.

50. Earl D. Huntington, "Landscape Nature Photography II," *Nature-Study Review* 12, no. 5 (May 1915): 194.

51. H. Robinson, "Nature-Study in Art," *Nature-Study Review* 10, no. 6 (September 1914): 207.

52. John Muir, *My First Summer in the Sierra* (New York: Penguin, 1911), 236.

53. Mensel, "Kodakers Lying in Wait," 29.

54. Deborah Bright, "The Machine in the Garden Revisited: American Environmentalism and Photographic Aesthetics," *Art Journal* 51, no. 2 (summer 1992): 60–71. The definitive treatment of rationalization and photography is Elspeth H. Brown, *The Corporate Eye: Photography and the Rationalization of American Commercial Culture, 1884–1929* (Baltimore: Johns Hopkins University Press, 2005). As Brown notes, some Progressive Era efficiency experts conflated wasted labor with wasted resources. Business consultant Frank Gilbreth, for example, maintained that "while the waste from the soil washing to the sea is a slow but sure national calamity, it is of much less importance than the loss each year due to wasteful motions by the workers of this country." Quoted in Brown, *Corporate Eye*, 73.

55. See West, *Kodak and the Lens of Nostalgia*.

56. Frank M. Chapman, "Hunting with a Camera," *World's Work* 6 (June 1903): 3555.

57. Ibid.

58. Job, *Wild Wings*, 144.

59. Radclyffe Dugmore, *Nature and the Camera: How to Photograph Live Birds and Their Nests; Animals, Wild and Tame; Reptiles; Insects; Fish and Other Aquatic Forms; Flowers, Trees and Fungi* (New York: Doubleday, Page, 1903), vi.

60. For more on manliness during the early twentieth century, see Gail Bederman,

Manliness & Civilization: A Cultural History of Gender and Race in the United States, 1880–1917 (Chicago: University of Chicago Press, 1995).

61. Job, *Wild Wings*, viii.

62. William T. Hornaday, *A Wild-Animal Round-up: Stories and Pictures from the Passing Show* (New York: Charles Scribner's Sons, 1925), 332. For more of Hornaday's typical rhetoric on cameras, guns, and preservation, see "The Slaughter of Birds for Food," in *Alabama Bird Day Book* (Alabama Department of Game and Fish, 1913), 38–41.

63. Dugmore, *Nature and the Camera*, 73.

64. Dugmore, "Revolution in Nature Pictures," 36.

65. Theodore Roosevelt, introduction to *Camera Shots at Big Game* by Mr. and Mrs. A. G. Wallihan (New York: Doubleday & Page, 1906), 11–12. Dozens of articles suggested that cameras should replace guns as the hunter's tool of choice. For example, see Frank M. Chapman, "The Camera in Nature Study," *Current Literature* 31 (October 1901): 457–458; George Shiras, "A Harmless Sport—Hunting with the Camera," *Independent* (7 June 1990): 1364–1368; A. G. Wallihan, "Hunting Big Game with the Camera," *Outlook* 71 (1905): 355–365; A. Hyatt Verill, "Hunting with a Camera," *St. Nicholas* 27 (August 1890): 927–929.

66. Roosevelt, introduction to *Camera Shots*, 8. Recently, many environmental historians have examined the class dimensions of hunting. See Karl Jacoby, *Crimes against Nature: Squatters, Poachers, Thieves and the Hidden History of American Conservation* (Berkeley: University of California Press, 2001); Jennifer Price, *Flight Maps: Adventures with Nature in Modern America* (New York: Basic Books, 1999), especially chap. 1; Louis S. Warren, *The Hunter's Game: Poachers and Conservationists in Twentieth-Century America* (New Haven, Conn.: Yale University Press, 1997).

67. Roosevelt, introduction to *Camera Shots;* Theodore Roosevelt, "Letter to Herbert Job," in Job, *Wild Wings*, xii.

68. J. Horace McFarland, "Shall We Have Ugly Conservation?" *Outlook* 91 (13 March 1909): 594. For more on McFarland, see William H. Wilson, *The City Beautiful Movement* (Baltimore: Johns Hopkins University Press, 1989). McFarland's position received strong and consistent support from journals such as *Outlook*. For an early example of support for the conservationists' moral crusade for beauty, see "For the Sake of Posterity," *Outlook* 68 (4 May 1901): 15–16. For specific support of McFarland, see "Value of Natural Scenery," *Outlook* 90 (26 September 1908): 149–151.

69. Robert Underwood Johnson, "The Neglect of Beauty in the Conservation Movement," *Century* 74 (1910): 637, 638; emphasis in original.

70. Miss E. L. Turner, "Bird-Photography for Women," *Bird Lore* 17, no. 3 (May–June 1915): 180.

71. Ibid., 182, 188.

72. Olive Thorne Miller, *In Nesting Time* (Boston: Houghton Mifflin, 1888), 152, cited in Vera Norwood, *Made from This Earth: American Women and Nature* (Chapel Hill: University of North Carolina Press, 1993), 44.

73. Between 1895 and 1945, only fifty-five books sold over a million copies. Gene Stratton Porter wrote five of them, including her Limberlost novels. For Porter's career, see Bertrand Richards, *Gene Stratton Porter* (Boston: Americana Books, 1980); Judith Reick

Long, *Gene Stratton Porter: Novelist and Naturalist* (Indianapolis: Indiana Historical Society, 1990). See also Amy Green, "'She Touched Fifty Million Lives': Gene Stratton Porter and Nature Conservation," in *Seeing Nature through Gender,* ed. Virginia J. Scharff (Lawrence: University Press of Kansas, 2003), 221–241; Cheryl Sahm Birkelo, "Allure and Appreciation of Natural History in the Writings of Gene Stratton Porter" (master's thesis, South Dakota State University, 2000).

74. William Lyon Phelps, "The Why of the Best Seller," *Bookman* 54, no. 5 (1921): 298.

75. Quoted in Long, *Gene Stratton Porter,* 180.

76. Gene Stratton Porter, *Homing with the Birds* (New York: Doubleday, Page, 1919), 53.

77. Gene Stratton Porter, *What I Have Done with Birds: Character Studies of Native American Birds which through Friendly Advances I Induced to Pose for Me, or Succeeded in Photographing by Good Fortune, with the Story of My Experiences in Obtaining the Pictures* (Indianapolis: Bobbs-Merrill, 1907), 2.

78. Gene Stratton Porter, "The Camera in Ornithology," in *The American Annual of Photography and Photographic Times-Bulletin for 1906,* ed. W. I. Lincoln Adams (New York: Styles & Cash, 1905), 53, 56. Decades after her death, critics still adopted Porter's language to describe her candid photographs. "Somehow through a trust nurtured with birds and other wildlife, she got her camera within a few feet (sometimes inches) of some of the most intimate moments in the lives of wild creatures. This achievement is certainly one of the early high points in the history of nature photography." Deborah Dalke-Scott and Michael Prewitt, "A Writer's Crusade to Portray the Spirit of the Limberlost," *Smithsonian* 71 (1976): 65.

79. Jeanette Porter Meehan, *The Lady of the Limberlost: The Life and Letters of Gene Stratton Porter* (New York: Doubleday, Doran, 1928), 121.

80. Porter, "Camera in Ornithology," 52.

81. Porter, *What I Have Done with Birds,* 13.

82. Ibid., 2.

83. Quoted in Long, *Gene Stratton Porter,* 190.

84. Green, "She Touched Fifty Million Lives," 230.

85. Eugene Francis Saxon, *Gene Stratton Porter: A Little Story of the Life and Work and Ideals of "The Bird Woman"* (Garden City, N.Y.: Doubleday, Page, 1915), 22.

86. Gene Stratton Porter, "My Life and My Books," *Ladies' Home Journal* (September 1916): 81; emphasis in original.

87. Porter, *What I Have Done with Birds,* 1. For more on children and the idea of the tomboy, see Owain Jones, "Tomboy Tales: The Rural, Nature and the Gender of Childhood," *Gender, Place and Culture* 6, no. 2 (1999): 117–136.

88. Porter, *What I Have Done with Birds,* 2.

89. Porter, "My Life and My Books," 13. For another example of a nature study advocate who worried that civilization robbed women of physical vitality, see William Gould Vinal, "The Call of Girls' Camps," *Nature-Study Review* 15, no. 5 (May 1919): 201.

90. Porter, "My Life and My Books," 13.

91. Dunaway, *Natural Visions.* See also Mark Neuzil and William Kovarik, *Mass Media and Environmental Conflict: America's Green Crusades* (Thousand Oaks, Calif.: Sage Publications, 1996).

1. Liberty Hyde Bailey, *Universal Service: The Hope of Humanity* (New York: Sturgis & Walton, 1918), 22–23, 26.

2. Frederic C. Howe, *The City: The Hope of Democracy* (New York: Charles Scribner's Sons, 1906), 33.

3. Henry Wallace, "The Socialization of Farm Life," cited in William L. Bowers, *The Country Life Movement in America, 1900–1920* (Port Washington, N.Y.: Kennikat Press, 1974), 36. Other writers claimed that urban life enervated formerly healthy rural people. The urban resident must therefore sleep regularly, eat well, exercise, and get to nature as often as possible. See Ada Patterson, "Country Life in the City," *Pittsburgh Gazette Times*, 16 April 1911, 2.

4. Quoted in U.S. Commissioner of Education, *Annual Report* (1887–1888), 159–160.

5. Liberty Hyde Bailey, *The Country Life Movement in the United States* (New York: Macmillan, 1911), 20.

6. Liberty Hyde Bailey, *What Is Democracy?* (Ithaca, N.Y.: Comstock Publishing Co., 1919), 96.

7. Liberty Hyde Bailey, *The Holy Earth* (New York: Charles Scribner's Sons, 1915), 24.

8. David Danbom, *Born in the Country: A History of Rural America* (Baltimore: Johns Hopkins University Press, 1995).

9. Liberty Hyde Bailey, *The Nature Study Idea* (New York: Doubleday, Page, 1903), 85.

10. Lawton B. Evans, remarks, *National Education Association Proceedings* (1896): 270.

11. Liberty Hyde Bailey, *The Outlook to Nature* (New York: Macmillan, 1911), 53, 86, 73.

12. Wilbert L. Anderson, *The Country Town: A Study of Rural Evolution* (New York: Baker & Taylor Co., 1906), 23.

13. Bailey, *Outlook to Nature*, 86.

14. Sidney Morse, "The Boy on the Farm: And Life as He Sees It," *Craftsman* 16, no. 2 (May 1909): 199.

15. See, for example, Bowers, *Country Life Movement*, and, most importantly, David B. Danbom, *The Resisted Revolution: Urban America and the Industrialization of Agriculture, 1900–1930* (Ames: Iowa State University Press, 1979). A revisionist response can be found in Scott J. Peters and Paul A. Morgan, "The Country Life Commission: Reconsidering a Milestone in American Agricultural History," *Agricultural History* 78, no. 3 (summer 2004): 289–316.

16. The travails of rural education were sufficiently well known to inspire a play by M. R. Orne, *The Country School: An Entertainment in Two Scenes* (Boston: Walter H. Baker, 1890). See David B. Tyack, "The Tribe and the Common School: Community Control in Rural Education," *American Quarterly* 24, no. 1 (March 1972): 3–19. The subject of rural schools and the life of rural children is generally understudied. Some primary sources that investigate the situation of rural schools include Ellwood P. Cubberley, *Rural Life and Education: A Study of the Rural-School Problem as a Phase of the Rural Life Problem* (Boston: Houghton Mifflin, 1914); Clifton Johnson, *The Country School in New England* (New York: D. Appleton, 1895); Marion G. Kirkpatrick, *The Rural School from Within* (Philadelphia: J. B. Lippincott, 1917).

17. National Grange of the Patrons of Husbandry, *Proceedings* (1874): 58, cited in Lawrence

A. Cremin, *The Transformation of the School: Progressivism in American Education, 1876–1957* (New York: Vintage Books, 1964), 42.

18. Joseph Cannon Bailey, *Seaman A. Knapp: Schoolmaster of American Agriculture* (New York: Columbia University Press, 1945). See also O. B. Martin, *The Demonstration Work: Dr. Seaman A. Knapp's Contribution to Civilization* (Boston: Stratford Co., 1921). For more on agricultural extension, see Roy V. Scott, *The Reluctant Farmer: The Rise of Agricultural Extension to 1914* (Urbana: University of Illinois Press, 1970).

19. For more on the boll weevil, see Arvarh E. Strickland, "The Strange Affair of the Boll Weevil: The Pest as Liberator," *Agricultural History* 68 (spring 1994): 166.

20. Quoted in Cremin, *Transformation of the School*, 81.

21. Dick J. Crosby, "The Relation of Nature-Study and Agriculture in Elementary Rural Schools," *Nature-Study Review* 5, no. 4 (April 1909): 95, 94.

22. Anna Allen Wright, "Nature Study for the City Child," *Nature-Study Review* 14, no. 3 (March 1918): 94, 95.

23. Malcolm J. Carron, *The Contract Colleges of Cornell University: A Cooperative Educational Enterprise* (Ithaca, N.Y.: Cornell University Press, 1958), 13.

24. Ibid., 15–18.

25. Bailey is nearly absent from the historiography of progressive conservation. One of the important initial examinations of conservation during the environmental era included a section on Bailey; see Donald Worster, *American Environmentalism: The Formative Period, 1860–1915* (New York: Wiley, 1973), 223–231. Yet few scholars followed Worster's lead.

26. Bowers, *Country Life Movement*, 45. Although Bowers privileged Bailey with the honorific of "philosopher," he was quite dismissive of Bailey, whom he also called an "agrarian sentimentalist" whose "philosophy of country life stemmed from a sensitive response to the forces of nature much more than any deep contemplation of the contemporary problems facing farmers." This is wrong. See, for example, Liberty Hyde Bailey, *The State and the Farmer* (New York: Macmillan, 1908). For biographies of Bailey, see Philip Dorf, *Liberty Hyde Bailey: An Informal Biography* (Ithaca, N.Y.: Cornell University Press, 1956); A. D. Rodgers, *Liberty Hyde Bailey: A Story of American Plant Sciences* (Princeton, N.J.: Princeton University Press, 1949). See also John P. Azelvandre, "Forging the Bonds of Sympathy: Spirituality, Individualism and Empiricism in the Ecological Thought of Liberty Hyde Bailey and Its Implications for Environmental Education" (Ed.D. diss., New York University, 2001). For Bailey as conservationist, see Kevin C. Armitage, "'The Science-Spirit in a Democracy': Liberty Hyde Bailey, Nature Study, and the Democratic Impulse of Progressive Conservation," in *Natural Protest: Essays on the History of American Environmentalism*, ed. Michael Egan and Jeff Crane (New York: Routledge, 2008), 89–116; Ben A. Minteer, *The Landscape of Reform: Civic Pragmatism and Environmental Thought in America* (Cambridge, Mass.: MIT Press, 2006), 17–50.

27. For more on passenger pigeons, see Jennifer Price, *Flight Maps* (New York: Basic Books, 1999), 1–55.

28. Quoted in Margaret Beattie Bogue, "Liberty Hyde Bailey, Jr. and the Bailey Family Farm," *Agricultural History* 63, no. 1 (winter 1989): 39.

29. Ibid., 46.

30. Quoted in O. J. Kern, "The Consolidated School and the New Agriculture," *Journal of the Proceedings and Addresses of the National Education Association* (1907): 278.

31. E. Laurence Palmer, "The Cornell Nature Study Philosophy," *Cornell Rural School Leaflet* 38, no. 1 (September 1944).

32. Samuel P. Hays, *Conservation and the Gospel of Efficiency: The Progressive Conservation Movement, 1890–1920* (Cambridge, Mass.: Harvard University Press, 1959), 27–28.

33. Laws of New York, 1888, chap. 196, cited in James Beckley Palmer, "Causal Factors in the Development of the New York State Elementary Course of Study from 1776 to 1904" (Ph.D. diss., Cornell University, 1930).

34. Annual Report of the State Supt. of New York (1895), 1020, cited in Palmer, "Causal Factors," 248–250.

35. School of Horticulture Flyer, folder "Bailey Miscellany," box 40, Bailey Papers, 1400, cited in Azelvandre "Forging the Bonds of Sympathy," 129.

36. Bailey to Roberts, 23 April 1894, Bailey Papers, cited in Gould P. Colman, *Education & Agriculture: A History of the New York State College of Agriculture at Cornell University* (Ithaca, N.Y.: Cornell University Press, 1963), 123.

37. Cited in Colman, *Education & Agriculture*, 123.

38. Bailey, *Nature Study Idea*, 29, 33.

39. Ibid., 82, 65.

40. Bailey, *State and the Farmer*, 173.

41. Bailey, *Holy Earth*, 88; Alan Trachtenberg, *The Incorporation of America: Culture and Society in Gilded Age America* (New York: Hill & Wang, 1982).

42. Bailey, *Holy Earth*, 89.

43. Bailey, *What Is Democracy?* 99.

44. Bailey, *Nature Study Idea*, 80, 81.

45. Anna Botsford Comstock, *Handbook of Nature Study* (1911; reprint, Ithaca, N.Y.: Comstock Publishing Associates, 1986), 22.

46. Bailey, *Holy Earth*, 26, 37, 36, 33. Bailey broadened the critique to include international relations as well. Peace would result only from the just distribution of land and resources. "Neighborliness," wrote Bailey, "is international."

47. Anna Botsford Comstock, "Nature-Study and the Teaching of Elementary Agriculture," *Nature-Study Review* 10, no. 1 (January 1914): 1, 2, 6.

48. E. Laurence Palmer, "As I Have Known the Cornell Nature Program," *Cornell Rural School Leaflet* 46, no. 1 (fall 1952): 26.

49. Liberty Hyde Bailey, "An Appeal to the Teachers of New York State," reprinted in *Cornell Nature Study Leaflets* (Albany, N.Y.: J. B. Lyon, 1904), 31.

50. Palmer, "As I Have Known," 27.

51. E. Laurence Palmer, "How the Cornell Rural School Leaflet Hopes to Teach Conservation through Nature-Study," *Nature-Study Review* 16, no. 2 (February 1920): 72, 69, 67, 72.

52. Palmer, "Cornell Nature Study Philosophy," 45.

53. *Cornell University Agricultural Experimental Station Bulletin* 159 (1899): 259, quoted in Colman, *Education & Agriculture*, 130.

54. Scott, *Reluctant Farmer*, 147.

55. Quoted in Colman, *Education & Agriculture*, 131, 130.

56. Franklin M. Reck, *The 4-H Story: A History of 4-H Club Work* (Ames: Iowa State College Press, 1951), 10.

57. *Cornell University Agricultural Experiment Station Bulletin* 159 (1899): 264.

58. James Wilson, *Annual Reports of the Department of Agriculture for the Fiscal Year Ended June 30, 1904* (Washington, D.C.: Government Printing Office, 1904), 58.

59. "Travelling Libraries Needed," *New York Daily Tribune*, 18 August 1903, 7.

60. George Washington Carver, *Progressive Nature Studies* (Tuskegee Institute, 1897), 4.

61. Linda Elizabeth Ott Hines, "Background to Fame: The Career of George Washington Carver, 1896–1916" (Ph.D. diss., Auburn University, 1976).

62. George Washington Carver, *Teacher's Leaflet Number 2: Nature Study and Children's Gardens* (Tuskegee Institute, 1910).

63. George Washington Carver, "A Study of the Soils of Macon County, Alabama and Their Adaptability to Certain Crops," *Tuskegee Agricultural Experiment Station Bulletin* no. 25 (October 1913), cited in Mark Hersey, "Hints and Suggestions to Farmers: George Washington Carver and Rural Conservation in the South," *Environmental History* 11, no. 2 (April 2006): 6.

64. Quoted in Harvey Wish, "Negro Education and the Progressive Movement," *Journal of Negro History* 49, no. 3 (July 1964): 192.

65. For example, see James D. Anderson, *The Education of Blacks in the South, 1860–1935* (Chapel Hill: University of North Carolina Press, 1988).

66. Dianne D. Glave, "'A Garden So Brilliant with Colors, So Original in Its Design': Rural African American Women, Gardening, Progressive Reform and the Foundation of an African American Environmental Perspective," *Environmental History* 8, no. 3 (July 2003): 395–411.

67. Quoted in *Cornell Countrymen* 11 (December 1913): 88. Roosevelt's letter praising Bailey can be found online at http://rmc.library.cornell.edu/bailey/commission/commission_8.html#.

68. *Report of the Commission on Country Life* (New York: Van Rees Press, 1911), 47–48, 112–113.

69. Ibid., 121, 123.

70. James H. Madison, "Reformers and the Rural Church, 1900–1950," *Journal of American History* 73, no. 3 (December 1986): 645–668.

71. *Report of the Commission on Country Life*, 84, 90.

72. Ibid., 64, 69, 74, 71, 72, 75, 78.

73. Ibid., 73–74.

74. Ibid., 90, 88–89, 89–90.

CONCLUSION: THE DECLINE AND REBIRTH OF NATURE STUDY

1. John Price Jones, "War and Nature," *Nature-Study Review* 14, no. 4 (April 1918): 165. The best discussion of the decline of nature study is Kim Tolley, *The Science Education of American Girls: A Historical Perspective* (New York: Routledge Falmer, 2003), especially chap. 8. Tolley's work strongly informs my argument here.

2. Anna Botsford Comstock, "Editorial: Vacation, War and Nature-Study," *Nature-Study Review* 14, no. 5 (May 1918): 221.

3. Cora A. Smith, "The Spirit of Nature-Study," *Nature-Study Review* 14, no. 2 (February 1918): 53, 54.

4. Laura J. Lawson, *City Bountiful: A Century of Community Gardening in America* (Berkeley: University of California Press, 2005), 136–137; Hunter Dupree, *Science in the Federal Government: A History of Politics and Activities* (Baltimore: Johns Hopkins University Press, 1986), 322. For more on the United States School Garden Army, see "'Soldiers of the Soil': The Work of the United States School Garden Army during World War I," *Applied Environmental Education and Communication: An International Journal* 6, no. 1 (January 2007): 19–29.

5. Walter Rauschenbusch, *Christianity and the Social Crisis* (1907; reprint, New York, 1964), 352, cited in Michael McGerr, *A Fierce Discontent: The Rise and Fall of the Progressive Movement in America, 1870–1920* (New York: Free Press, 2003), 80. McGerr's work informs my argument.

6. Washington Gladden, *The New Idolatry and Other Discussions* (New York, 1905), 210–211, cited in McGerr, *Fierce Discontent,* 80.

7. Liberty Hyde Bailey, *The Nature Study Idea* (New York: Doubleday, Page, 1903), 18.

8. Charles B. Scott, *Nature-Study and the Child* (Boston: D. C. Heath, 1902), 105, 118.

9. For a discussion of consumerism as a means of self-revitalization, see Colin Campbell, *The Romantic Ethic and the Spirit of Modern Consumerism* (Oxford: Blackwell, 1987); T. J. Jackson Lears, *Fables of Abundance: A Cultural History of Advertising in America* (New York: Basic Books, 1995).

10. Anna Botsford Comstock, "Nature-Study from a Car Window," *Nature-Study Review* 15, no. 2 (February 1919): 78.

11. Hunter Dupree, *Science in the Federal Government: A History of Politics and Activities* (Baltimore: Johns Hopkins University Press, 1986), 302–318.

12. Charles W. Eliot, "Dr. Hornaday's 'Weakness of Nature-Study,'" *Nature-Study Review* 3, no. 2 (February 1907): 52.

13. Barney Standish, *Common Things with Common Eyes: An Illustrated Course of Nature Study for Schools, about Insects, Fishes, Quadrupeds, Flowers, Trees and Birds* (Minneapolis: Standish & Standish, 1897).

14. Mary C. Dickerson, "Nature-Study in City Primary Schools," *Nature-Study Review* 2, no. 3 (March 1906): 108.

15. Arthur S. Dewing, "Some Reasons for Decrease of Interest in Nature Study," *Education* (January 1909): 291–293.

16. Christine Hartley, "Factors Influencing the Teaching of Nature Study," *General Science Quarterly* 9 (January 1925): 86–87, cited in Tyree G. Minton, "The History of the Nature-Study Movement and Its Role in the Development of Environmental Education" (Ed.D. diss., University of Massachusetts, 1980), 131.

17. Stanley Coulter, "The Field Trip in Nature-Study," *Nature-Study Review* 2, no. 7 (October 1906): 231.

18. John M. Coulter, John G. Coulter, and Alice Patterson, *Practical Nature Study and Elementary Agriculture: A Manual for the Use of Teachers and Normal Students* (New

York: D. Appleton, 1909), 12, cited in Peter J. Schmitt, *Back to Nature: The Arcadian Myth in Urban America* (1969; reprint, Baltimore: Johns Hopkins University Press, 1990), 87.

19. Edward L. Thorndike, "Reading as a Means of Nature Study," *Education* (February 1899): 368–371.

20. Anna Botsford Comstock, "The Growth and Influence of the Nature-Study Idea," *Nature-Study Review* 11, no. 1 (January 1915): 11.

21. For information on women and careers in science, see Mable Newcomer, *A Century of Higher Education for American Women* (New York: Harper, 1959); Margaret Rossiter, *Women Scientists in America: Struggles and Strategies to 1940* (Baltimore: Johns Hopkins University Press, 1982).

22. William Lee Howard, "The Feminization of the High-School," *Arena* 35 (June 1906): 595, quoted in Tolley, *Science Education of American Girls*, 183.

23. Coulter et al., *Practical Nature Study and Elementary Agriculture*, 35.

24. G. Stanley Hall, introduction to Clifton Hodge, *Nature Study and Life* (Boston: Ginn, 1902), xv.

25. Wayne J. Urban and Jennings L. Wagoner Jr., *American Education: A History* (New York: McGraw-Hill, 2004), 226.

26. James G. Needham, "College Freshman as an Index of the Progress of Nature-Study," *Nature-Study Review* 11, no. 9 (December 1915): 408, 409.

27. See Paul Sutter, *Driven Wild: How the Fight against Automobiles Launched the Modern Wilderness Movement* (Seattle: University of Washington Press, 2002).

28. For more on conservation education, see Robert Steele Funderburk, *The History of Conservation Education in the United States* (Nashville, Tenn.: George Peabody College for Teachers, 1948).

29. Charles Roth, "A Time-Lapse View of Environmental Education in America," (unpublished manuscript, 1976), 16, cited in Minton, "History of the Nature-Study Movement," 141.

30. Malcolm Swan, "Forerunners of Environmental Education," in *What Makes Education Environmental?* ed. Noel McInnis and Don Albrecht (Washington, D.C.: Data Courier and Environmental Educators, 1975), 6–9.

31. John F. Disinger, "Environment in the K–12 Curriculum: An Overview," in *Environmental Education Teacher Resource Handbook: A Practical Guide for K–12 Environmental Education,* ed. Richard J. Wilke (Millwood, N.Y.: Kraus International Publications in cooperation with National Science Teachers Association, 1993), 35.

32. *Nature Study and the Child*, 98.

33. E. Laurence Palmer, "How the Cornell Rural School Leaflet hopes to Teach Conservation through Nature Study," *Nature-Study Review* 16, no. 2 (February 1920): 67.

34. Comstock, "Growth and Influence of the Nature Study Idea," 10.

35. Ibid.

36. Ibid., 11.

37. E. Laurence Palmer, "Orientation in School," *Nature Magazine* 47, no. 9 (November 1954): 493.

38. Joseph Wood Krutch, "The Demise of Natural History," *Audubon* (September–October 1967): 50, 55.

39. Stephen Kellert, *Building for Life: Designing and Understanding the Human-Nature Connection* (Washington, D.C.: Island Press, 2005), 124.

40. Quoted in Thomas Dunlap, *Saving America's Wildlife: Ecology and the American Mind, 1850–1990* (Princeton, N.J.: Princeton University Press, 1988), 89.

41. Thomas Dunlap, *Faith in Nature: Environmentalism as Religious Quest* (Seattle: University of Washington Press, 2004), 62–63.

42. Aldo Leopold, *A Sand County Almanac and Sketches Here and There* (1949; reprint, New York: Oxford University Press, 1987), 178; Aldo Leopold, *Game Management* (New York: Charles Scribner's Sons, 1948), 21.

43. Leopold, *Sand County Almanac,* 178.

44. Quoted in J. Baird Callicott, "Aldo Leopold on Education: An Educator and His Land Ethic in the Context of Contemporary Environmental Education," *Journal of Environmental Education* 14, no. 1 (fall 1982): 35.

45. Leopold, *Sand County Almanac,* 174.

46. Curt Meine, *Aldo Leopold: His Life and Work* (Madison: University of Wisconsin Press, 1988), 16–17. I also relied on personal correspondence with Curt Meine, in my possession.

47. Leopold, *Sand County Almanac,* 214.

48. Ibid., 207–208, 209.

49. Ibid., 223.

50. Aldo Leopold, *Round River: From the Journals of Aldo Leopold* (New York: Oxford University Press, 1993), 165.

51. Linda Lear, *Rachel Carson: Witness for Nature* (New York: Henry Holt, 1997), 14, 17.

52. Rachel Carson, holograph notes for "Help Your Child to Wonder," cited in Lear, *Rachel Carson,* 284; see 280–285 on the sense of wonder children find in nature.

53. Rachel Carson, "Help Your Child to Wonder," *Woman's Home Companion* 83 (July 1956): 25–27, 46–48, cited in Lear, *Rachel Carson,* 284.

54. Quoted in Paul Brooks, *The House of Life: Rachel Carson at Work* (New York: Houghton Mifflin, 1972), 215–216.

55. Rachel Carson, "The Real World around Us," in *Lost Woods: The Discovered Writing of Rachel Carson,* ed. Linda Lear (Boston: Beacon Press, 1998), 159.

56. Ibid., 193–194.

57. Ibid., 160.

58. Quoted in Scott McVay, "Prelude 'A Siamese Connexion with a Plurality of Other Mortals,'" in *The Biophilia Hypothesis,* ed. Stephen R. Kellert and Edward O. Wilson (Washington, D.C.: Island Press, 1993), 4–5.

59. David W. Orr, "Love It or Lose It: The Coming Biophilia Revolution," in *Biophilia Hypothesis,* 432, 434. See also Peter H. Kahn Jr., "Developmental Psychology and the Biophilia Hypothesis: Children's Affiliation with Nature," *Developmental Review* 17 (1997): 1–61. Paul Shepard is one historically minded scholar who has used biophilia to advance a number of interesting ideas about the relationship between humans and nature. See Paul Shepard, *Nature and Madness* (San Francisco: Sierra Club Books, 1982) and *The Others: How Animals Made Us Human* (Washington, D.C.: Island Press, 1996).

60. Peter H. Kahn and Stephen R. Kellert, eds., *Children and Nature: Psychological, Sociocultural and Evolutionary Investigations* (Cambridge, Mass.: MIT Press, 2002).

61. Stephen J. Gould, "Enchanted Evening," *Natural History* (September 1991): 14.

62. Richard Louv, *Last Child in the Woods* (Chapel Hill, N.C.: Algonquin Books, 2006).

63. Bertrand Russell, *The Scientific Outlook* (New York: W. W. Norton, 1959), 246, 248, 267.

64. Ibid., 264, cited in Orr, "Love It or Lose It," 425.

Bibliography

Abbott, Charles C. "The Enjoyment of Nature." *Arena* (June 1904): 611–614.

Adams, Charles. "Zoologists, Teachers and Wild Life Conservation." *Science* 41, no. 1065 (28 May 1915): 790–791.

Adorno, Theodore W., and Max Horkheimer. *Dialectic of Enlightenment.* Translated by John Cumming. New York: Continuum, 1993.

Agassiz, Alexander. "The Abandonment of Penikese." *Popular Science Monthly* 42, no. 123 (1892).

Agassiz, Elizabeth Cabot. *First Lesson in Natural History.* 1859; reprint, Boston: D. C. Heath, 1886.

Agassiz, Louis. *Contributions to the Natural History of the United States of North America.* Boston: Little, Brown, 1857.

"Agassiz's Academy." *New York Tribune,* 9 July 1873.

Ainley, Marianne Gosztonyi. "The Contribution of the Amateur to North American Ornithology: A Historical Perspective." *Living Bird* 18 (1979–1980): 161–177.

Albanese, Catherine L. *Nature Religion in America: From the Algonkian Indians to the New Age.* Chicago: University of Chicago Press, 1990.

Alcott, Amos Bronson. *Essays on Education.* Edited by Walter Harding. Gainesville, Fla.: Scholars' Facsimiles, 1960.

Alexander, Thomas M. *The Horizons of Feeling: John Dewey's Theory of Art, Experience, and Nature.* Albany: State University of New York Press, 1987.

Allen, Robert Loring. *Irving Fisher: A Biography.* Cambridge, Mass.: Harvard University Press, 1993.

Anderson, H. Allen. *The Chief: Ernest Thompson Seton and the Changing West.* College Station: Texas A&M University Press, 1986.

Anderson, James D. *The Education of Blacks in the South, 1860–1935.* Chapel Hill: University of North Carolina Press, 1988.

Anderson, Wilbert L. *The Country Town: A Study of Rural Evolution.* New York: Baker & Taylor Co., 1906.

Arbor and Bird Day. Ohio Department of Education, March 1911.

Armitage, Kevin C. "Bird Day for Kids: Progressive Conservation in Theory and Practice." *Environmental History* (July 2007): 528–551.

———. "'The Child Is Born a Naturalist': Nature Study, Woodcraft Indians and the Theory of Recapitulation." *Journal of the Gilded Age and Progressive Era* (January 2007): 43–70.

———. "'The Science-Spirit in a Democracy': Liberty Hyde Bailey, Nature Study, and the Democratic Impulse of Progressive Conservation." In *Natural Protest: Essays on the*

History of American Environmentalism. Edited by Michael Egan and Jeff Crane, 89–116. New York: Routledge, 2008.

Atkinson, Brooks. "A Puritan Boyhood." *Massachusetts Review* 15 (1974): 339–381.

Azelvandre, John P. "Forging the Bonds of Sympathy: Spirituality, Individualism and Empiricism in the Ecological Thought of Liberty Hyde Bailey and Its Implications for Environmental Education." Ed.D. diss., New York University, 2001.

Babcock, Charles. *Bird Day: How to Prepare for It.* New York: Silver, Burdett, 1901.

———. "Suggestions for Bird-Day Programs in the Schools." *Bird Lore* 1, no. 2 (April 1899): 49–51.

"Back to Nature." *Outlook* 74, no. 6 (6 June 1903).

Backert, E. "History and Analysis of the School Garden Movement in America, 1890–1910." Ph.D. diss., Indiana University, 1977.

Baekeland, L. H. "The Danger of Overspecialization." *Science* 25, no. 648 (31 May 1907).

Bailey, Florence Merriam. "Olive Thorne Miller." *Condor* 21, no. 2 (March 1919): 69–73.

Bailey, Henry Turner. "The Child's Birthright in Art." *Proceedings of the National Education Association* (1926): 164–165.

———. *The City of Refuge.* Worcester, Mass.: Davis, 1901.

———. "Educative Values of Drawing." *School Arts Book* (February 1910): 577–582.

———. "Fundamental Values of Life and How to Reach Them." *Proceedings of the National Education Association* (1927): 421.

Bailey, Joseph Cannon. *Seaman A. Knapp: Schoolmaster of American Agriculture.* New York: Columbia University Press, 1945.

Bailey, Liberty Hyde. "An Appeal to the Teachers of New York State." Reprinted in *Cornell Nature Study Leaflets.* Albany, N.Y.: J. B. Lyon, 1904.

———. *The Country Life Movement in the United States.* New York: Macmillan, 1911.

———. *The Holy Earth.* New York: Charles Scribner's Sons, 1915.

———. *The Nature Study Idea: Being an Interpretation of the New School Movement to Put the Child in Sympathy with Nature.* New York: Doubleday, Page, 1903.

———. *The Outlook to Nature.* New York: Macmillan, 1911.

———. "A Reverie of Gardens." *Outlook* 68, no. 5 (1 June 1901).

———. *The State and the Farmer.* New York: Macmillan, 1908.

———. *Universal Service: The Hope of Humanity.* New York: Sturgis & Walton, 1918.

———. *What Is Democracy?* Ithaca, N.Y.: Comstock Publishing Co., 1919.

Barber, Lynn. *The Heyday of Natural History, 1820–1870.* London: Jonathan Cape, 1981.

Barrow, Mark V., Jr. "Naturalists as Conservationists: American Scientists, Social Responsibility and Political Activism before the Bomb." In *Science, History and Social Activism: A Tribute to Everett Mendelsohn.* Edited by Garland E. Allen and Roy M. MacLeod. Dordrecht: Kluwer Academic Publishers, 2001.

———. *A Passion for Birds: American Ornithology after Audubon.* Princeton, N.J.: Princeton University Press, 1998.

Bates, J. Leonard. "Fulfilling American Democracy: The Conservation Movement, 1907 to 1921." *Mississippi Valley Historical Review* 44, no. 1 (June 1957): 29–58.

Beaton, Eleanor Hyde. "The Contributions of Henry Turner Bailey to Art Education." Master's thesis, Boston University, 1945.

Beatty, Barbara. *Preschool Education in America: The Culture of Young Children from the Colonial Era to the Present.* New Haven, Conn.: Yale University Press, 1997.

Bederman, Gail. *Manliness & Civilization: A Cultural History of Gender and Race in the United States, 1880–1917.* Chicago: University of Chicago Press, 1995.

Beedy, Mrs. Helen B. C. "Reminiscences of Penikese." *Education* 13 (February 1893): 340.

Bell, Nancy. "The Work of Ernest Thompson Seton." *Humane Review* (April 1903): 18–19.

Benedict, H. M. "Will School-Gardening Survive?" *Nature-Study Review* 9, no. 8 (November 1913): 257–262.

Benson, Keith R. "Laboratories on the New England Shore: The 'Somewhat Different Direction' of American Marine Biology." *New England Quarterly* 61, no. 1 (March 1985): 55–78.

Bigelow, Edward. "Nature and Science for Young Folks." *St. Nicholas* 29 (June 1902): 745, 747.

———. "Nature and Science for Young Folks." *St. Nicholas* 38, no. 2 (December 1910): 173–174.

———. "The Passenger-Pigeon." *St. Nicholas* 27 (February 1900): 359.

Bigelow, M. A. "Interest of Men of Science in the Nature-Study Society." *Nature-Study Review* 4, no. 1 (January 1908): 4.

Bigelow, Maurice A. "Are Children Naturally Naturalists?" *Nature-Study Review* 3 (November 1907): 28–29.

———. "Correlation of Nature-Study and Manual Training." *Nature-Study Review* 2, no. 3 (March 1906): 91.

"Bird Club Suggestions." In *Colorado Arbor Day Notes with Suggestions for Bird Day* (20 April 1900).

"Bird Day." *Forest and Stream* 47, no. 3 (18 July 1896).

"Bird Day Exercises." *Journal of Education* 45 (1 April 1897): 209–210.

"Bird Day Exercises." *Werner's Magazine* 28, no. 6 (February 1902): 917–926.

"Bird Day for Children." *New York Times*, 21 April 1901, 20.

"'Bird Day' for Nebraska." *Omaha Sunday World-Herald*, 15 January 1899, 4.

"Bird Minstrelsy." In *Bird Day Book.* Montgomery, Ala.: Department of Education, 1915.

"The Birds' Declaration of Dependence." In *Arbor and Bird Day Bulletin.* Olympia: State of Washington, 1917.

"Birds and Men." *Advocate of Peace* 68, no. 3 (March 1906): 63–64.

Birkelo, Cheryl Sahm. "Allure and Appreciation of Natural History in the Writings of Gene Stratton Porter." Master's thesis, South Dakota State University, 2000.

Bishop, E. C. "The School-Home Garden." *Nature-Study Review* 8, no. 5 (May 1912): 169–172.

Blake, Henry. "Personal Reminiscences of Professor Louis Agassiz." *Nature-Study Review* (March 1923): 97–103.

Blanchan, Neltje. "The Garden Anyone Can Have." *Ladies' Home Journal* 25 (January 1908): 44.

Bogue, Margaret Beattie. "Liberty Hyde Bailey, Jr. and the Bailey Family Farm." *Agricultural History* 63, no. 1 (winter 1989): 26–48.

Bonta, Marcia Myers. *Women in the Field: America's Pioneering Naturalists.* College Station: Texas A&M University Press, 1991.

Boris, Eileen. *Art and Labor: Ruskin, Morris, and the Craftsman Ideal in America.* Philadelphia: Temple University Press, 1986.

Bowers, William L. *The Country Life Movement in America, 1900–1920.* Port Washington, N.Y.: Kennikat Press, 1974.

Boyer, Paul. *Urban Masses and Moral Order in America, 1820–1920.* Cambridge, Mass.: Harvard University Press, 1978.

Bright, Deborah. "The Machine in the Garden Revisited: American Environmentalism and Photographic Aesthetics." *Art Journal* 51, no. 2 (summer 1992): 60–71.

Bright, Orville T. "Jackman." *Elementary School Teacher* 7 (April 1907).

Brooks, Paul. *The House of Life: Rachel Carson at Work.* New York: Houghton Mifflin, 1972.

———. *Speaking for Nature: How Literary Naturalists from Henry Thoreau to Rachel Carson Have Shaped America.* Boston: Houghton Mifflin, 1980.

Brown, E. V. "A Bird Day Program." *Bird Lore* 1, no. 2 (April 1899): 52.

Brown, Elspeth H. *The Corporate Eye: Photography and the Rationalization of American Commercial Culture, 1884–1929.* Baltimore: Johns Hopkins University Press, 2005.

Buckler, Helen. *Wo-He-Lo: The Story of Camp Fire Girls, 1910–1960.* New York: Holt, Rinehart & Winston, 1961.

Buell, Lawrence. *The Environmental Imagination: Thoreau, Nature Writing, and the Formation of American Culture.* Cambridge, Mass.: Belknap Press, 1995.

Buell, Lucy C. "Home Gardens in Cleveland." *Nature-Study Review* 3 (February 1907): 38.

Bullough, William A. "'It Is Better to Be a Country Boy': The Lure of the Country in Urban Education in the Gilded Age." *Historian,* 35, no. 2 (February 1973): 183–196.

Burroughs, John. *The Last Harvest.* Boston: Houghton Mifflin, 1922.

———. "Nature Study." *Outlook* 61 (4 February 1899): 326.

———. "Science and Sentiment." *Independent,* 15 February 1912.

Caldwell, Otis. Untitled essay. *Proceedings of the National Education Association* (1904): 895.

Callicott, J. Baird. "Aldo Leopold on Education: An Educator and His Land Ethic in the Context of Contemporary Environmental Education." *Journal of Environmental Education* 14, no. 1 (fall 1982): 34–41.

Callicott, J. Baird, and Michael P. Nelson, eds. *The Great New Wilderness Debate.* Athens: University of Georgia Press, 1998.

Campbell, Colin. *The Romantic Ethic and the Spirit of Modern Consumerism.* Oxford: Blackwell, 1987.

Campbell, Jack K. *Colonel Francis W. Parker, the Children's Crusader.* New York: Teachers College Press, 1967.

Carman, Bliss. *The Kinship of Nature.* Boston: L. C. Page, 1903.

———. *The Making of Personality.* Boston: Page Co., 1908.

Carroll, Sean. *Endless Forms Most Beautiful: The New Science of Evo Devo.* New York: W. W. Norton, 2005.

Carron, Malcolm J. *The Contract Colleges of Cornell University: A Cooperative Educational Enterprise.* Ithaca, N.Y.: Cornell University Press, 1958.

Carson, Rachel. "Help Your Child to Wonder." *Woman's Home Companion* 83 (July 1956): 25–27, 46–48.

———. *Lost Woods: The Discovered Writings of Rachel Carson.* Edited by Linda Lear. Boston: Beacon Press, 1998.

Carver, George Washington. *Progressive Nature Studies.* Tuskegee Institute, 1897.

———. "A Study of the Soils of Macon County, Alabama and Their Adaptability to Certain Crops." *Tuskegee Agricultural Experiment Station Bulletin* no. 25 (October 1913).

———. *Teacher's Leaflet Number 2: Nature Study and Children's Gardens.* Tuskegee Institute, 1910.

Champagne, A. B., and L. E. Klopfer. "Pioneers of Elementary School Science: Wilbur Samuel Jackman." *Science Education* 63, no. 2 (August 2006): 145–165.

Chapman, Bertha. "School Gardens in the Refugee Camps of San Francisco." *Nature-Study Review* 2, no. 7 (October 1906): 225–229.

Chapman, Frank M. *Bird Studies with a Camera.* New York: D. Appleton, 1900.

———. "The Camera in Nature Study." *Current Literature* 31 (October 1901): 457–458.

———. "The Educational Value of Bird-Study." *Educational Review* (March 1899): 242–246.

———. "Hunting with a Camera." *World's Work* 6 (June 1903): 3554–3560.

Chapman, John Gadsby. *American Drawing-book: A Manual for the Amateur and Basis of Study for the Professional Artist.* New York: J. S. Redfield, 1847.

Clark, Emelyn. "Bird Study in the Grades." *Nature-Study Review* 11, no. 4 (April 1915): 208–211.

Clayton, Virginia Tuttle. "Wild Gardening and the Popular American Magazine, 1890–1918." In *Nature and Ideology: Natural Garden Design in the Twentieth Century.* Edited by Joachim Wolschke-Bulmahn, 131–154. Washington, D.C.: Dumbarton Oaks Research Library and Collection, 1997.

Clepper, Henry. "Herbert A. Smith, 1866–1944." *Journal of Forestry* 42, no. 9 (September 1944): 625–627.

Clifford, Geraldine Jonçich. "Man/Woman/Teacher: Gender, Family and Career in American Educational History." In *American Teachers: Historians of a Profession at Work.* Edited by Donald Warren. New York: Macmillan, 1989.

Clifford, James C. *The Predicament of Culture: Twentieth Century Ethnography, Literature and Art.* Cambridge, Mass.: Harvard University Press, 1988.

Clute, Willard N. Letter. *Nature-Study Review* 4, no. 1 (January 1908): 30.

Coe, Benjamin H. *Easy Lessons in Landscape Drawing.* Hartford, Conn.: Tyler & Potter, 1842.

Cohen, Michael P. "Comment: Resistance to Wilderness." *Environmental History* 1 (1996): 33–42.

Cohen, Shaul E. *Planting Nature: Trees and the Manipulation of Environmental Stewardship in America.* Berkeley: University Press of California, 2004.

Collins, Douglas. *The Story of Kodak.* New York: H. N. Abrams, 1990.

Colman, Gould P. *Education & Agriculture: A History of the New York State College of Agriculture at Cornell University.* Ithaca, N.Y.: Cornell University Press, 1963.

Comstock, Anna Botsford. "Conservation and Nature-Study." *Nature-Study Review* 18, no. 7 (October 1922): 299–300.

———. "Editorial." *Nature-Study Review* 7, no. 9 (December 1911): 278.

———. "Editorial: Nature-Study from a Car Window." *Nature-Study Review* 15, no. 2 (February 1919): 78–79.

———. "Editorial: Vacation, War and Nature-Study." *Nature-Study Review* 14, no. 5 (May 1918): 221–222.

———. "The Growth and Influence of the Nature-Study Idea." *Nature-Study Review* 11, no. 1 (January 1915): 5–11.

———. *Handbook of Nature Study.* Ithaca, N.Y.: Comstock Publishing Co., 1911.

———. "Nature Study and Agriculture." *Nature-Study Review* 1, no. 4 (July 1905).

———. "Nature-Study and the Teaching of Elementary Agriculture." *Nature-Study Review* 10, no. 1 (January 1914): 1–6.

———. *Ways of the Six Footed.* 1903; reprint, Ithaca, N.Y.: Cornell University Press, 1977.

Conway, Jill. "Perspectives on the History of Women's Education in the United States." *History of Education Quarterly* (spring 1974): 1–12.

Cornell University Agricultural Experiment Station Bulletin 159 (1899).

Cornish, Louis C. "Agassiz's School on Penikese." *Scientific Monthly* 57, no. 4 (October 1943): 315–321.

"A Corollary to Nature Study." *Nation* 75, no. 11 (4 September 1902): 184–185.

Coulter, John M. "Nature Study and Intellectual Life." *Science* 4, no. 99 (20 November 1896): 740–744.

Coulter, John M., John G. Coulter, and Alice Patterson. *Practical Nature Study and Elementary Agriculture: A Manual for the Use of Teachers and Normal Students.* New York: D. Appleton, 1909.

Coulter, Stanley. "The Field Trip in Nature-Study." *Nature-Study Review* 2, no. 7 (October 1906): 23–33.

Cremin, Lawrence A. *The Transformation of the School: Progressivism in American Education, 1876–1957.* New York: Vintage Books, 1964.

Cronon, William. "The Trouble with Wilderness; or, Getting Back to the Wrong Nature." *Environmental History* 1, no. 1 (January 1996): 7–28.

———. "The Trouble with Wilderness: A Response." *Environmental History* 1 (1996): 47–55.

Cropsey, N. "The Higher Use of Nature Studies." *Proceedings and Addresses of the National Education Association* (1894).

Crosby, Dick J. "The Relation of Nature-Study and Agriculture in Elementary Rural Schools." *Nature-Study Review* 5, no. 4 (April 1909): 93–98.

Cross, Whitney R. "WJ McGee and the Idea of Conservation." *Historian* 15, no. 2 (spring 1953): 148–162.

Cubberley, Ellwood P. *Rural Life and Education: A Study of the Rural-School Problem as a Phase of the Rural Life Problem.* Boston: Houghton Mifflin, 1914.

Cummins, Horace H. *Nature Study by Grades.* New York: American Book Company, 1909.

Dalke-Scott, Deborah, and Michael Prewitt. "A Writer's Crusade to Portray the Spirit of the Limberlost." *Smithsonian* 71 (1976): 64–68.

Damrow, Christine B. "'Every Child in a Garden': Radishes, Avocado Pits, and the Education of American Children in the Twentieth Century." Ph.D. diss., University of Wisconsin–Madison, 2005.

Danbom, David. *Born in the Country: A History of Rural America.* Baltimore: Johns Hopkins University Press, 1995.

———. *The Resisted Revolution: Urban America and the Industrialization of Agriculture, 1900–1930.* Ames: Iowa State University Press, 1979.

———. *"The World of Hope": Progressives and the Struggle for an Ethical Public Life.* Philadelphia: Temple University Press, 1987.

Davis, B. M. "Birds and Their Relation to Insects." In *Arbor and Bird Day Manual.* Ohio Department of Education, April 1914.

———. "School Gardens." *Nature-Study Review* 2, no. 3 (March 1906).

———. *School Gardens for California Schools: A Manual for Teachers.* Chico, Calif.: Publications of the State Normal School, 1905.

Davis, W. M. "What Is Nature Study?" *Science* 16, no. 414 (5 December 1902).

Dean, Bradley P. "Natural History, Romanticism, and Thoreau." In *American Wilderness: A New History.* Edited by Michael Lewis. New York: Oxford University Press, 2007.

Dearborn, Ned Harland. *The Oswego Movement in American Education.* New York: Teacher's College, Columbia University Press, 1925.

Dehler, Gregory John. "An American Crusader: William Temple Hornaday and Wildlife Protection in America, 1840–1940." Ph.D. diss., Lehigh University, 2001.

Deloria, Philip J. *Playing Indian.* New Haven, Conn.: Yale University Press, 1998.

DePencier, Ida B. *The History of the Laboratory Schools: The University of Chicago 1896–1965.* Chicago: Quadrangle Books, 1967.

Dewey, John. *Art as Experience* [1934]. In vol. 10 of *John Dewey: The Later Works.* Edited by Jo Ann Boydston. Carbondale: Southern Illinois University Press, 1987.

———. *Democracy and Education: An Introduction to the Philosophy of Education.* 1916; reprint, New York: Free Press, 1997.

———. "How Much Freedom in New Schools?" *New Republic* 63 (9 July 1930).

———. *The School and Society* [1899]. In vol. 1 of *John Dewey: The Middle Works.* Edited by Jo Ann Boydston. Carbondale: Southern Illinois University Press, 1976.

———. *Schools of To-Morrow* [1915]. In vol. 8 of *John Dewey: The Middle Works.* Edited by Jo Ann Boydston. Carbondale: Southern Illinois University Press, 1979.

———. "The University Elementary School, Studies and Methods." *University Record* (21 May 1897): 68–73.

Dewing, Arthur S. "Some Reasons for Decrease of Interest in Nature Study." *Education* (January 1909): 291–293.

Dexter, Ralph. "From Penikese to the Marine Biological Laboratory at Woods Hole—The Role of Agassiz's Students." *Essex Institute Historical Collections* 100 (1974).

Dickerson, Mary C. "Nature-Study in City Primary Schools." *Nature-Study Review* 2, no. 3 (March 1906): 102.

Disinger, John F. "Environment in the K–12 Curriculum: An Overview." In *Environmental Education Teacher Resource Handbook: A Practical Guide for K–12 Environmental Education.* Edited by Richard J. Wilke. Millwood, N.Y.: Kraus International Publications in cooperation with National Science Teachers Association, 1993.

Dolbear, A. E. "The Disappointing Results of Science Teaching." *Educational Review* (December 1894): 485–488.

Dolbear, Katherine E. "Nature Study for the Graded Schools." *Proceedings and Addresses of the National Education Association* (1900): 600–608.

Dolph, James Andrew. "Bringing Wildlife to Millions: William T. Hornaday, the Early Years, 1854–1896." Ph.D. diss., University of Massachusetts, 1975.

Dorf, Philip. *Liberty Hyde Bailey: An Informal Biography.* Ithaca, N.Y.: Cornell University Press, 1956.

Doris, Ellen. "The Practice of Nature-Study: What Reformers Imagined and What Teachers Did." Ed.D. diss., Harvard University, 2002.

Doughty, Robin W. "Concern for Fashionable Feathers." *Forest History* 16, no. 2 (July 1972): 4–11.

Downing, Elliot R. "Children's Interest in Nature Material." *Nature-Study Review* 8 (December 1912): 334–338.

Downs, Robert B. *Friedrich Froebel.* Boston: Twayne, 1978.

Dugmore, Radclyffe. *Nature and the Camera: How to Photograph Live Birds and Their Nests; Animals, Wild and Tame; Reptiles; Insects; Fish and Other Aquatic Forms; Flowers, Trees and Fungi.* New York: Doubleday, Page, 1903.

———. "A Revolution in Nature Pictures." *World's Work* (November 1900): 33–46.

Dunaway, Finis. "Hunting with the Camera: Nature Photography, Manliness, and Modern Memory, 1890–1930." *Journal of American Studies* 34, no. 2 (2000): 207–230.

———. *Natural Visions: The Power of Images in American Environmental Reform.* Chicago: University of Chicago Press, 2005.

Dunlap, Thomas R. "Comment: But What Did You Go Out into the Wilderness to See?" *Environmental History* 1 (1996): 43–46.

———. *Faith in Nature: Environmentalism as Religious Quest.* Seattle: University of Washington Press, 2004.

———. *Saving America's Wildlife: Ecology and the American Mind, 1850–1990.* Princeton, N.J.: Princeton University Press, 1988.

Dupree, Hunter. *Science in the Federal Government: A History of Politics and Activities.* Baltimore: Johns Hopkins University Press, 1986.

Dutcher, William. "Education as a Factor in Audubon Work—Relation of Birds to Man." *Bird Lore* 11, no. 6 (1 December 1909): 281–288.

"The Educational Museum of the St. Louis Public Schools and Its Relation to Gardening and Nature-Study." *Nature-Study Review* 6, no. 4 (April 1910): 99.

Edwards, Charles Lincoln. "Nature-Play." *Popular Science Monthly* 84 (April 1914): 330–344.

Egleston, Nathaniel H. *Arbor Day: Its History and Observance.* Washington, D.C.: Department of Agriculture, Government Printing Office, 1896.

Eifrig, C. W. G. "A Practical Angle in the Aesthetic Side of Nature Study." *Nature-Study Review* 17, no. 8 (November 1921): 327–330.

Eliot, Charles W. "Beauty and Democracy." *School Arts Book* 5, no. 1 (September 1905): 1.

———. "Dr. Hornaday's 'Weakness of Nature-Study.'" *Nature-Study Review* 3, no. 2 (February 1907): 52.

———. *Educational Reform.* New York: Century Co., 1898.

———. "The New Education." *Atlantic Monthly* 22 (1869): 203–220, 358–367.

Emerson, Ralph Waldo. *The Collected Works of Ralph Waldo Emerson.* Cambridge, Mass: Harvard University Press, 1971–1987.

———. *The Essays of Ralph Waldo Emerson.* Edited by Alfred Kazin. Cambridge, Mass.: Belknap Press, 1987.

———. *Nature.* Boston: James Munroe, 1836.

———. *The Prose Works of Ralph Waldo Emerson.* Boson: James R. Osgood, 1875.

Evans, Lawton B. Remarks. *National Education Association Proceedings* (1896): 270.

Evenden, Matthew D. "The Laborers of Nature: Economic Ornithology and the Role of Birds as Agents of Biological Pest Control in North American Agriculture, ca. 1880–1930." *Forest & Conservation History* 39 (October 1995): 172–183.

Fairbanks, Harold W. "Nature Study and Its Relation to Natural Science." *Nature-Study Review* 1, no. 1 (January 1905).

———. "The Relation of Geography to Nature-Study in the Elementary School." *Nature-Study Review* 1 (September 1905): 173–198.

Farnham, Amos W. "The Relation which School-Gardens May Bear to Industrial and Commercial Geography." *Nature-Study Review* 3, no. 3 (March 1907): 76–85.

Farnum, Royal B. "My Work Book Chapter VI—Nature Study." *School Arts Book* 10, no. 8 (1910): 645.

Farrow, Arthur H. "Nature Photography." *American Annual of Photography* 34 (1920): 112–118.

Faulkner, Peter. *Against the Age: An Introduction to William Morris.* London: Allen & Unwin, 1980.

Faxon, Grace B. *Mother Earth's Party, and a Bird Day Exercise.* New York: F. A. Owens Publishing Co., 1903.

Fear, Christena. "Nature and Americanization as Allies." *Nature-Study Review* 19 (January 1923): 2.

Fenton, Charles A. "The Founding of the National Institute of Arts and Letters in 1898." *New England Quarterly* 32, no. 4 (December 1959): 1–20.

Floody, R. J. "Worcester Garden City Plan; or, the Good Citizens' Factory." *Nature-Study Review* 8, no. 4 (April 1912): 145–150.

Flower, Benjamin O. "The Great Mother as an Educator: Or the Child in Nature's Workshop." *Arena* 38 (September 1907): 311–313.

———. "The New Education and the Public Schools." *Arena* 8 (October 1893): 511–528.

"For the Sake of Posterity." *Outlook* 68 (4 May 1901): 15–16.

Forbes, Linda C., and John M. Jermier. "The Institutionalization of Bird Protection: Mabel Osgood Wright and the Early Audubon Movement." *Organization & Environment* 15, no. 4 (December 2002): 458–465.

Forbush, Edward Howe. *Useful Birds and Their Protection: Containing Brief Descriptions of the More Common and Useful Species of Massachusetts, with Accounts of Their Food Habits, and a Chapter on the Means of Attracting and Protecting Birds.* Boston: Massachusetts State Board of Agriculture, 1907.

Forbush, William Byron. *The Boy Problem: A Study in Social Pedagogy.* Boston: Pilgrim Press, 1901.

Foss, Sam Walter. "The Bloodless Sportsman." In *Bird Day Book.* Montgomery, Ala.: Department of Education, 1910.

Fox, Richard Wightman. "The Culture of Liberal Protestant Progressivism, 1875–1925." *Journal of Interdisciplinary History* 23, no. 3 (winter 1993): 639–660.

Fox, Stephen. *John Muir and His Legacy: The American Conservation Movement.* Madison: University of Wisconsin Press, 1981.

Froebel, Friedrich. *Education of Man.* Translated by W. H. Hailman. New York: D. Appleton, 1899.

Funderburk, Robert Steele. *The History of Conservation Education in the United States.* Nashville, Tenn.: George Peabody College for Teachers, 1948.

"Gardens Imagined." *Scribner's Magazine* 57 (1915): 775–778.

Gates, B. T., and Ann B. Shteir, eds. *Natural Eloquence: Women Reinscribe Science.* Madison: University of Wisconsin Press, 1998.

Glave, Dianne D. "'A Garden So Brilliant with Colors, So Original in Its Design': Rural African American Women, Gardening, Progressive Reform and the Foundation of an African American Environmental Perspective." *Environmental History* 8, no. 3 (July 2003): 395–411.

Gould, Peter C. *Early Green Politics: Back to Nature, Back to the Land, and Socialism in Britain, 1880–1900.* New York: Harvester, 1988.

Gould, Stephen J. *Ontogeny and Phylogeny.* Cambridge, Mass.: Belknap Press, 1977.

———. "Unenchanted Evening." *Natural History* 100, no. 9 (September 1991): 4–10.

Graham, Frank, Jr. *The Audubon Ark.* New York: Alfred A. Knopf, 1990.

"Great Work of the Bob Whites." *West Virginia Arbor and Bird Day Manual* (1906): 30–31.

Green, Amy. "'She Touched Fifty Million Lives': Gene Stratton Porter and Nature Conservation." In *Seeing Nature through Gender.* Edited by Virginia J. Scharff, 221–241. Lawrence: University Press of Kansas, 2003.

———. "Two Woman Naturalists and the Search for Autonomy: Anna Botsford Comstock and the Producer Ethic; Gene Stratton-Porter and the Gospel of Wealth." *Women Studies Quarterly* (spring–summer 2001): 145–154.

Guggisberg, C. A. W. *Early Wildlife Photographers.* New York: David & Charles, Newton Abbot, 1977.

Gunnels, Harry. Foreword to *Bird Day Book.* Montgomery, Ala.: Department of Education, 1910.

Gutek, Gerald Lee. *Pestalozzi & Education.* New York: Random House, 1968.

Guy, Josephine M. *The Victorian Age: An Anthology of Sources and Documents.* London: Routledge, 2008.

Hales, Peter B. *William Henry Jackson and the Transformation of the American Landscape.* Philadelphia: Temple University Press, 1988.

Hall, G. Stanley. *Adolescence.* 1904; reprint, New York: Arno Press, 1969.

———. Introduction to *Nature Study and Life* by Clifton Hodge. Boston: Ginn, 1902.

———. Untitled essay. *Proceedings and Addresses of the National Education Association* (1896): 156–158.

———. Untitled essay. *Proceedings and Addresses of the National Education Association* (1904): 443–447.

Hart, John Dixon. *Greater Perfections: The Practice of Garden Theory.* Philadelphia: University of Pennsylvania Press, 2000.

Hartley, Christine. "Factors Influencing the Teaching of Nature Study." *General Science Quarterly* 9 (January 1925): 84–88.

Hawkins, Hugh. *Between Harvard and America: The Educational Leadership of Charles W. Eliot.* New York: Oxford University Press, 1972.

Hayden-Smith, R. "'Soldiers of the Soil': The Work of the United States School Garden Army during World War I." *Applied Environmental Education and Communication* 6, no. 1 (January 2007): 19–29.

Hays, Samuel P. "Comment: The Trouble with Bill Cronon's Wilderness." *Environmental History* 1, no. 1 (January 1996): 29–32.

———. *Conservation and the Gospel of Efficiency: The Progressive Conservation Movement, 1890–1920.* Cambridge, Mass.: Harvard University Press, 1959.

Hegner, Robert W. "Nature-Studies with Birds for the Elementary School." *Elementary School Teacher* 5, no. 7 (March 1905): 408–419.

———. "Nature-Studies with Birds for the Elementary School [Continued]." *Elementary School Teacher* 5, no. 8 (April 1905): 462–472.

Hemenway, H. D. *How to Make School Gardens.* New York: Doubleday, Page, 1903.

———. "School Garden Notes." *Nature-Study Review* 1, no. 5 (September 1905): 218–219.

———. "School Gardens at the School of Horticulture, Hartford Connecticut." *Nature-Study Review* 1, no. 1 (January 1905): 29–36.

Henson, Pamela M. "The Comstocks of Cornell: A Marriage of Interests." In *Creative Couples in Science.* Edited by H. Pycior et al. New Brunswick, N.J.: Rutgers University Press, 1995.

———. "'Through Books to Nature': Anna Botsford Comstock and the Nature Study Movement." In *Natural Eloquence: Women Reinscribe Science.* Edited by B. T. Gates and Ann B. Shteir, 116–147. Madison: University of Wisconsin Press, 1998.

Hersey, Mark. "Hints and Suggestions to Farmers: George Washington Carver and Rural Conservation in the South." *Environmental History* 11, no. 2 (April 2006): 239–268.

Hines, Linda Elizabeth Ott. "Background to Fame: The Career of George Washington Carver, 1896–1916." Ph.D. diss., Auburn University, 1976.

Hoar, George F. "The Birds' Petition." *Educational Gazette* (May 1904): 145–147.

Hodge, Clifton F. *Nature Study and Life.* Boston: Ginn, 1902.

Hoffmann, Ralph. "Bird Study in the Schools." *School Arts Book* 4 (6 February 1905): 325–327.

Holtz, Frederick L. *Nature-Study: A Manual for Teachers and Students.* New York: Charles Scribner's Sons, 1908.

Hopkins, Louisa Parsons. *The Spirit of the New Education.* Boston: Lee & Shepard Publishers, 1892.

Horchem, B. J. "School Gardening, a Fundamental Element in Education." *Nature-Study Review* 8, no. 2 (February 1912): 62–66.

Hornaday, William T. "Duty of the Citizen toward Life." In *Bird Day Book.* Montgomery, Ala.: Department of Education, 1915.

———. "Educational Value of Popular Museums." In *The Twelfth Celebration of Founder's Day.* Pittsburgh: Carnegie Institute, 1908.

———. *Our Vanishing Wildlife: Its Extermination and Preservation.* New York: New York Zoological Society, 1913.

———. "The Right Way to Teach Zoology." *Outlook* (11 June 1910): 256–263.

———. "The Slaughter of Birds for Food." In *Alabama Bird Day Book.* Alabama Department of Game and Fish, 1913.

———. "The Weakness in Teaching Nature Study." *Nature-Study Review* 2, no. 7 (October 1906): 241–243.

———. *A Wild-Animal Round-up: Stories and Pictures from the Passing Show.* New York: Charles Scribner's Sons, 1925.

——. *Wild Life Conservation in Theory and Practice*. New Haven, Conn.: Yale University Press, 1914.

Howard, William Lee. "The Feminization of the High-School." *Arena* 35 (June 1906): 593–596.

Howe, Frederic C. *The City: The Hope of Democracy*. New York: Charles Scribner's Sons, 1906.

Hoyt, W. A. "Children's Love of Nature." *Proceedings and Addresses of the National Education Association* (1894): 1010–1015.

Huntington, E. D. "Landscape Nature Photography II." *Nature-Study Review* 12, no. 5 (May 1915): 194–199.

——. "Nature Photography." *Nature-Study Review* 12, no. 4 (April 1915): 169–174.

Huyssen, Andreas. "Mass Culture as Woman: Modernism's Other." In *After the Great Divide*. Bloomington: Indiana University Press, 1987.

Hyatt, Edward. "Conservation, Bird and Arbor Day." In *Conservation, Bird and Arbor Day in California*. Sacramento, Calif.: Superintendent of Public Instruction, 1916.

Ilerbaig, Juan. "Allied Sciences and Fundamental Problems: C. C. Adams and the Search for Method in Early American Ecology." *Journal of the History of Biology* 32 (1999): 439–463.

Jackman, Wilbur S. "Correlation of Science and History." *Educational Review* (May 1895): 464–471.

——. *Nature Study*. Chicago: University of Chicago Press, 1904.

——. *Nature Study for the Common Schools*. New York: Henry Holt, 1891.

——. "Relation of Arithmetic to Elementary Science." *Educational Review* (January 1893): 35–51.

——. "What Has Been Accomplished in Co-ordination in the Field of Natural Sciences." *Journal of the Proceedings of the National Education Association* 34 (1895).

Jackson, Philip W. *John Dewey and the Lessons of Art*. New Haven, Conn.: Yale University Press, 1988.

Jacoby, Karl. *Crimes against Nature: Squatters, Poachers, Thieves and the Hidden History of American Conservation*. Berkeley: University of California Press, 2001.

James, William." Louis Agassiz." In *Memories and Studies*. 1911; reprint, New York: Greenwood Press, 1968.

Jaspers, Karl. *Nietzsche and Christianity*. Translated by E. B. Ashton. Chicago: Henry Regnery, 1961.

Jewel, James Ralph. *Agriculture Education Including Nature Study and School Gardens*. Bulletin 2, Department of Interior, Bureau of Education. Washington, D.C.: Government Printing Office, 1907.

Job, Herbert Keightley. *Wild Wings: Adventures of a Camera-Hunter among the Larger Wild Birds of North America on Sea and Land*. New York: Houghton Mifflin, 1905.

John Amos Comenius on Education. New York: Teachers College Press, 1967.

Johnson, Clifton. *The Country School in New England*. New York: D. Appleton, 1895.

Johnson, Robert Underwood. "The Neglect of Beauty in the Conservation Movement." *Century* 74 (1910): 637–638.

Jones, John Price. "War and Nature." *Nature-Study Review* 14, no. 4 (April 1918): 164–165.

Jones, Owain. "Tomboy Tales: The Rural, Nature and the Gender of Childhood." *Gender, Place and Culture* 6, no. 2 (1999): 117–136.

Jordan, David Starr. "Agassiz at Penikese." *Popular Science Monthly* (April 1892).

———. "Nature Study and Moral Culture." *Science* 4, no. 84 (7 August 1896): 149–156.

———. *Science Sketches.* Chicago: A. C. McClurg, 1887.

Judd, Richard. *Common Lands, Common People: The Origins of Conservation in Northern New England.* Cambridge, Mass.: Harvard University Press, 1997.

Kahn, Peter H., Jr. "Developmental Psychology and the Biophilia Hypothesis: Children's Affiliation with Nature." *Developmental Review* 17 (1997): 1–61.

Kahn, Peter H., and Stephen R. Kellert, eds. *Children and Nature: Psychological, Sociocultural and Evolutionary Investigations.* Cambridge, Mass.: MIT Press, 2002.

Kaplan, Wendy. *"The Art That Is Life": The Arts & Crafts Movement in America, 1875–1920.* New York: Bulfinch Press–Little, Brown, 1987.

Kellert, Stephen. *Building for Life: Designing and Understanding the Human-Nature Connection.* Washington, D.C.: Island Press, 2005.

Kellert, Stephen R., and Edward O. Wilson, eds. *The Biophilia Hypothesis.* Washington, D.C.: Island Press, 1993.

Kellogg, Amos M. *Primary Recitation: Short Bright Selections for Thanksgiving, Washington's Birthday, Arbor Day, May Day, Memorial Day, Flag Day, Closing Exercises, Nature Recitations, Patriotic and General Occasions.* 1897; reprint, Freeport, N.Y.: Books for Libraries Press 1971.

Kern, O. J. "The Consolidated School and the New Agriculture." *Journal of the Proceedings and Addresses of the National Education Association* (1907).

Kilpatrick, Van Evrie. *Nature Education in the United States.* New York: School Garden Association of America, 1923.

Kilpatrick, William Heard. *Froebel's Kindergarten Principles Critically Examined.* New York: Macmillan, 1916.

Kingsley, J. S. "How a Naturalist Is Trained." *Popular Science Monthly* 30, no. 179 (1886–1887): 631.

Kirkpatrick, Marion G. *The Rural School from Within.* Philadelphia: J. B. Lippincott, 1917.

Klein, Benjamin. *First along the River: A History of the U.S. Environmental Movement.* Lanham, Md.: Rowman & Littlefield, 2007.

Kliebard, Herbert. *The Struggle for the American Curriculum, 1893–1958.* Boston: Routledge & Kegan Paul, 1986.

Knox, Margaret. "The Function of a School Garden in a Crowded City District." In *Second Annual Report.* New York: School Garden Association of New York, 1910.

Kohler, Robert E. *Landscapes & Labscapes: Exploring the Lab-Field Border in Biology.* Chicago: University of Chicago Press, 2002.

Kohlstedt, Sally Gregory. "'A Better Crop of Boys and Girls': The School Gardening Movement, 1890–1920." *History of Education Quarterly* 48, no. 1 (February 2008): 58–93.

———. "Nature Not Books: Scientists and the Origins of the Nature Study Movement in the 1890s." *Isis* (December 2005): 324–352.

Koppes, Clayton R. "Efficiency, Equity, Esthetics: Shifting Themes in American Conservation." In *The Ends of the Earth: Perspectives on Modern Environmental History.* Edited by Donald Worster, 230–251. Cambridge: Cambridge University Press, 1988.

Korzenik, Diana. "The Art Education of Working Women 1873–1903." In *Pilgrims and*

Pioneers: New England Women in the Arts. Edited by Alicia Faxon and Sylvia Moore. New York: Midmarch Arts Press, 1987.

Kosack, Joe. *The Pennsylvania Game Commission, 1895–1995: 100 Years of Wildlife Conservation.* Harrisburg: Pennsylvania Game Commission, 1995.

Krutch, Joseph Wood. "The Demise of Natural History." *Audubon* (September–October 1967): 50–55.

Lange, Dorthea. "Nature Study in the Public Schools." *National Education Association Proceedings* (1900): 404–411.

Langston, Nancy. *Forest Dreams, Forest Nightmares: The Paradox of Old Growth in the Inland West.* Seattle: University of Washington Press, 1995.

Lankester, E. Ray. "An American Sea-side Laboratory." *Nature* (25 March 1880): 497–499.

Laurie, S. S. *John Amos Comenius, Bishop of the Moravians: His Life and Educational Works.* Cambridge: Cambridge University Press, 1893.

Lawrence, C. G. "A Letter to the Teachers of South Dakota." In *South Dakota Arbor and Bird Day Annual.* Pierre, S.D.: Superintendent of Public Instruction, 1914.

Lawson, Laura J. *City Bountiful: A Century of Community Gardening in America.* Berkeley: University of California Press, 2005.

Lear, Linda. *Rachel Carson: Witness for Nature.* New York: Henry Holt, 1997.

Lears, T. J. Jackson. *Fables of Abundance: A Cultural History of Advertising in America.* New York: Basic Books, 1995.

———. *No Place of Grace: Antimodernism and the Transformation of American Culture, 1880–1920.* Chicago: University of Chicago Press, 1981.

———. "Sherwood Anderson: Looking for the White Spot." In *The Power of Culture: Critical Essays in American History.* Edited by Richard Wightman Fox and T. J. Jackson Lears, 13–38. Chicago: University of Chicago Press, 1993.

Lee, Joseph. *Play in Education.* New York: Macmillan, 1915.

Leopold, Aldo. *Game Management.* New York: Charles Scribner's Sons, 1948.

———. *Round River: From the Journals of Aldo Leopold.* New York: Oxford University Press, 1993.

———. *A Sand County Almanac and Sketches Here and There.* 1949; reprint, New York: Oxford University Press, 1987.

Lewis, Michael, ed. *American Wilderness: A New History.* New York: Oxford University Press, 2007.

Lippmann, Walter. *Drift and Mastery.* 1914; reprint, Englewood Cliffs, N.J.: Prentice-Hall, 1961.

Long, Judith Reick. *Gene Stratton Porter: Novelist and Naturalist.* Indianapolis: Indiana Historical Society, 1990.

Louv, Richard. *Last Child in the Woods.* Chapel Hill, N.C.: Algonquin Books, 2006.

Lowden, Frank O. "By the Governor of Illinois—A Proclamation." In *Arbor and Bird Days.* Illinois Department of Public Instruction Circular no. 134, 1919.

Lurie, Edward. *Louis Agassiz: A Life in Science.* Chicago: University of Chicago Press, 1960.

Lutts, Ralph H. *The Nature Fakers: Wildlife, Science and Sentiment.* Golden, Colo.: Fulcrum Publishing, 1990.

Lytle, Mark Hamilton. *The Gentle Subversive: Rachel Carson, Silent Spring, and the Rise of the Environmental Movement.* New York: Oxford University Press, 2007.

Mabie, Hamilton Wright. *Essays on Nature and Culture*. New York: Dodd, Mead, 1896.

MacDonald, Robert H. *Sons of Empire: The Frontier and the Boy Scout Movement*. Toronto: University of Toronto Press, 1993.

Macleod, David. *The Age of the Child: Children in America, 1890–1920*. New York: Twayne, 1998.

———. *Building Character in the American Boy: The Boy Scouts, YMCA, and Their Forerunners, 1870–1920*. Madison: University of Wisconsin Press, 1983.

Madison, James H. "Reformers and the Rural Church, 1900–1950." *Journal of American History* 73, no. 3 (December 1986): 645–668.

Maienschein, Jane. "Agassiz, Hyatt, Whitman, and the Birth of the Marine Biological Laboratory." *Biological Bulletin* 168 (June 1985 supplement): 26–34.

"Man and Nature." In *Arbor Day Bird Day*. Harrisburg: Commonwealth of Pennsylvania Department of Public Instruction, 1934.

Marshall, Peter. *Nature's Web: An Exploration of Ecological Thinking*. New York: Simon & Schuster 1992.

Martin, Jay. *The Education of John Dewey*. New York: Columbia University Press, 2002.

Martin, O. B. *The Demonstration Work: Dr. Seaman A. Knapp's Contribution to Civilization*. Boston: Stratford Co., 1921.

Marx, Karl, and Frederick Engels. *Manifesto of the Communist Party*. Edited and annotated by Frederick Engels. Chicago: Charles H. Kerr, 1906.

Marx, Leo. *The Machine in the Garden: Technology and the Pastoral Ideal in America*. New York: Oxford University Press, 1967.

Matusow, Allen J. "The Mind of B. O. Flower." *New England Quarterly* 34, no. 4 (December 1961): 492–509.

Mau, Laura Emily. "Some Experiments with Regard to the Relative Interests of Children in Physical and Biological Nature Materials in the Kindergarten and Primary Grades." *Nature-Study Review* 8 (November 1912): 285–291.

Mayhew, Katherine Camp, and Anna Camp Edwards. *The Dewey School*. 1936; reprint, New York: Atherton Press, 1965.

McAtee, W. L. "Economic Ornithology." In *Fifty Years' Progress of American Ornithology 1883–1933: Published by the American Ornithologists' Union, on the Occasion of Its Semi-Centennial Anniversary, New York, N.Y., November 13–16, 1933*. Lancaster, Pa.: American Ornithologists' Union, 1933.

McCallum, Mary Jane. "'The Fundamental Things': Camp Fire Girls and Authenticity, 1910–1920." *Canadian Journal of History* (April 2005): 45–66.

McCann, Lloyd E. "Henry Harrison Straight, Educator." *Nebraska History Magazine* (1954): 59–71.

McCombs, W. Douglas. "Therapeutic Rusticity: The Wilderness Vacation in the Northeastern United States, 1869–1915." Ph.D. diss., Kent State University, 2004.

McFarland, J. Horace. "Shall We Have Ugly Conservation?" *Outlook* (13 March 1909): 594–598.

McGee, W. J. "The Conservation of Natural Resources." In *Proceedings of the Mississippi Valley Historical Association for the Year 1909–1910*. Cedar Rapids, Iowa, 1911.

McGerr, Michael. *A Fierce Discontent: The Rise and Fall of the Progressive Movement in America, 1870–1920*. New York: Free Press, 2003.

McInnis, Noel, and Don Albrecht. *What Makes Education Environmental?* Washington, D.C.: Data Courier and Environmental Educators, 1975.

McKeever, William A. "A Better Crop of Boys and Girls." *Nature-Study Review* 7 (December 1911): 266–268.

McMurray, C. A., and Lida B. McMurray. *Special Method in Natural Science.* Bloomington, Ill.: Public School Pub. Co., 1896.

Meehan, Jeanette Porter. *The Lady of the Limberlost: The Life and Letters of Gene Stratton Porter.* New York: Doubleday, Doran, 1928.

Meine, Curt. *Aldo Leopold: His Life and Work.* Madison: University of Wisconsin Press, 1988.

Menand, Louis. *The Metaphysical Club.* New York: Farrar, Straus & Giroux, 2001.

Mensel, Robert E. "'Kodakers Lying in Wait': Amateur Photography and the Right of Privacy in New York, 1885–1915." *American Quarterly* 43, no. 1 (March 1991): 24–45.

Merchant, Carolyn. "The Women of the Progressive Conservation Crusade, 1900–1915." In *Environmental History: Critical Issues in Comparative Perspective.* Edited by Kendall E. Bailes, 153–170. Lanham, Md.: University Press of America, 1985.

Michigan State Superintendent of Public Instruction. *A Study of School Gardens.* Lansing, 1904.

Mighetto, Lisa. "Science, Sentiment, and Anxiety: American Nature Writing at the Turn of the Century." *Pacific Historical Review* 54 (February 1985): 33–50.

———. *Wild Animals and American Environmental Ethics.* Tucson: University Press of Arizona, 1991.

Miller, Angela. *The Empire of the Eye: Landscape Representation and American Cultural Politics, 1825–1875.* Ithaca, N.Y.: Cornell University Press, 1993.

Miller, Char. *Gifford Pinchot and the Making of Modern Environmentalism.* Washington, D.C.: Shearwater Books, 2004.

———. "A Sylvan Prospect: John Muir, Gifford Pinchot, and Early Twentieth-Century Conservationism." In *American Wilderness: A New History.* Edited by Michael Lewis, 131–148. New York: Oxford University Press, 2007.

Miller, Louise Klein. "The Civic Aspect of School Gardens." *Nature-Study Review* 8, no. 2 (February 1912): 74–77.

Miller, Olive Thorne. *In Nesting Time.* Boston: Houghton, Mifflin, 1888.

———. "The Study of Birds—Another Way." *Bird Lore* 2, no. 5 (October 1900): 151–153.

Minteer, Ben A. *The Landscape of Reform: Civic Pragmatism and Environmental Thought in America.* Cambridge, Mass.: MIT Press, 2006.

Minton, Tyree G. "The History of the Nature-Study Movement and Its Role in the Development of Environmental Education." Ed.D. diss., University of Massachusetts, 1980.

Mitchell, Dora Otis. "A History of Nature-Study." *Nature-Study Review* 19 (September 1923): 258–274; (October 1923): 295–321.

Mitman, Gregg. *Reel Nature: America's Romance with Wildlife on Film.* Cambridge, Mass.: Harvard University Press, 1999.

Monroe, Will S. *History of the Pestalozzian Movement in the United States.* Syracuse, N.Y.: C. W. Bardeen, 1907.

Mora, Gilles. *Photospeak: A Guide to the Ideas, Movements, and Techniques of Photography, 1839 to the Present.* New York: Abbeville Press, 1998.

Morley, Margaret W. "Nature Study and Its Influence." *Outlook* 68 (27 July 1901): 737–739.

Morris, William. *The Collected Works of William Morris*. London: Routledge/Thoemmes Press, 1992.

Morse, Edward S. "Agassiz and the School at Penikese." *Science* 58, no. 1502 (12 October 1923).

Morse, Sidney. "The Boy on the Farm: And Life as He Sees It." *Craftsman* 16, no. 2 (May 1909): 195–204.

Mott, Frank Luther. *A History of American Magazines*. Vol. 4. Cambridge, Mass.: Harvard University Press, 1957.

Muir, John. *John of the Mountains: The Unpublished Journals of John Muir*. Edited by Linnie Marsh Wolfe. Madison: University of Wisconsin Press, 1979.

———. *My First Summer in the Sierra*. New York: Penguin, 1911.

———. *The Wilderness World of John Muir: A Selection from His Collected Works*. Edited by Edwin Way Teale. New York: Mariner Books, 2001.

Nash, Roderick. *Wilderness and the American Mind*, 3rd ed. New Haven, Conn.: Yale University Press, 1982.

"Nature Study and Gardening for Indian Schools." *Nature-Study Review* 2, no. 4 (April 1905): 141–143.

"Nature Study and Its Relation to Science." *Nature-Study Review* 1, no. 16 (January 1905): 2–18.

Needham, James G. "College Freshman as an Index of the Progress of Nature-Study." *Nature-Study Review* 11, no. 9 (December 1915): 408–409.

———. "The Lengthened Shadow of a Man and His Wife." *Scientific Monthly* 62, pts. 1 and 2 (1946): 140–150, 219–229.

Neuzil, Mark, and William Kovarik. *Mass Media and Environmental Conflict: America's Green Crusades*. Thousand Oaks, Calif.: Sage Publications, 1996.

Newhall, Beaumont. *The History of Photography from 1839 to the Present*. Boston: Bulfinch, 1982.

North Dakota Special Day Programs. Bismarck, N.D.: Department of Public Instruction, 1913.

Northrop, Alice Rich. "Flower Shows in City Schools." *Nature-Study Review* 1, no. 3 (May 1905): 104–109.

———. "Nature and the Child." In *The Uplift Book of Child Culture*. Philadelphia: Uplift Publishing Co., n.d.

Northrop, Mrs. John I. "Nature and the City Child." *Natural History* (April 1920): 265–276.

Norwood, Vera. *Made from This Earth: American Women and Nature*. Chapel Hill: University of North Carolina Press, 1993.

Novak, Barbara. *Nature and Culture: American Landscape Painting, 1825–1875*. New York: Oxford University Press, 1980.

Nuttall, G. Clarke. "An American Scheme of Nature Study." *Journal of Education* (May 1899).

Oleson, Alexandra, and John Voss, eds. *The Organization of Knowledge in Modern America, 1860–1920*. Baltimore: Johns Hopkins University Press, 1979.

Olmsted, Richard R. "The Nature-Study Movement in American Education." Ed.D. diss., Indiana University, 1967.

Olson, James C. *J. Sterling Morton: Pioneer, Statesman, Founder of Arbor Day.* Lincoln: University Press of Nebraska, 1942.

Orne, M. R. *The Country School: An Entertainment in Two Scenes.* Boston: Walter H. Baker, 1890.

Orr, David W. "Love It or Lose It: The Coming Biophilia Revolution." In *The Biophilia Hypothesis.* Edited by Stephen R. Kellert and Edward O. Wilson, 415–434. Washington, D.C.: Island Press, 1993.

Orr, Oliver H. *Saving American Birds: T. Gilbert Pearson and the Founding of the Audubon Movement.* Gainesville: University Press of Florida, 1992.

Orvell, Miles. *The Real Thing: Imitation and Authenticity in American Culture, 1880–1940.* Chapel Hill: University of North Carolina Press, 1989.

O'Shea, M. V. "Drawing and Nature Study." *Education* 17 (October 1896): 369–373.

"Our Patriots Were Nimrods." In *Bird Day Book.* Montgomery, Ala.: Department of Education, 1915.

Palmer, E. Laurence. "As I Have Known the Cornell Nature Program." *Cornell Rural School Leaflet* 46, no. 1 (fall 1952): 26.

———. "The Cornell Nature Study Philosophy." *Cornell Rural School Leaflet* 38, no. 1 (September 1944).

———. "Flowers of the Woodlands." *Cornell Rural School Leaflet* 16, no. 4 (March 1923).

———. "How the Cornell Rural School Leaflet Hopes to Teach Conservation through Nature-Study." *Nature-Study Review* 16, no. 2 (February 1920): 69–72.

———. "Orientation in School." *Nature Magazine* 47, no. 9 (November 1954).

Palmer, James Beckley. "Causal Factors in the Development of the New York State Elementary Course of Study from 1776 to 1904." Ph.D. diss., Cornell University, 1930.

Palmer, T. S. "Object of Bird Day." *Bird Day in the Schools.* U.S. Department of Agriculture Circular no. 17. Washington, D.C.: Government Printing Office, 1896.

Parker, Clayton F. "Are Children Naturally Naturalists?" *Nature-Study Review* 4, no. 1 (January 1908): 28–29.

Parker, Francis. "An Account of the Work of the Cook County and Chicago Normal School from 1883 to 1899." *Elementary School Teacher and Course of Study* (June 1902): 752–780.

———. "The Child." *Proceedings and Addresses of the National Education Association* (1889): 479–482.

Parsons, Fanny Griscom. *The First Children's Farm School in New York City, 1902, 1903, 1904.* New York: DeWitt Clinton Farm School, 1904.

Patterson, Ada. "Country Life in the City." *Pittsburgh Gazette Times,* 16 April 1911, 2.

Patterson, Alice J. "Educational Value of Children's Gardens." *Nature-Study Review* 12, no. 3 (March 1916): 124–128.

———. "A Survey of Twenty Years Progress Made in the Course of Nature Study." *Nature-Study Review* 17 (February 1921): 55–62.

Peckham, Morse. "Toward a Theory of Romanticism." *PMLA* (March 1951): 5–23.

Pellett, Frank C. "Wild Flower Gardening." *Nature-Study Review* 8, no. 6 (September 1912): 218–220.

"Penikese Island." *Frank Leslie's Illustrated Newspaper,* 23 August 1873, 378.

"Penikese Island." *Harper's Weekly,* 9 August 1873.

Perez, Kimberly E. "Fancy and Imagination: Cultivating Sympathy and Envisioning the Natural World for the Modern Child," Ph.D. diss., University of Oklahoma, 2006.

Pestalozzi, Johann Heinrich. *How Gertrude Teaches Her Children*. Edited by Daniel N. Robinson. Washington, D.C.: University Publications of America, 1977.

Peters, Scott J., and Paul A. Morgan. "The Country Life Commission: Reconsidering a Milestone in American Agricultural History." *Agricultural History* 78, no. 3 (summer 2004): 289–316.

Peterson, Mrs. P. S. "Nature Lover's Creed." In *Kentucky Arbor and Bird Day* (1910).

Phelps, William Lyon. "The Why of the Best Seller." *Bookman* 54, no. 5 (1921): 298–302.

Philippon, Daniel J. *Conserving Words: How American Nature Writers Shaped the Environmental Movement*. Athens: University of Georgia Press, 2004.

———. Introduction to *The Friendship of Nature: A New England Chronicle of Birds and Flowers* by Mabel Osgood Wright. 1894; reprint, Baltimore: Johns Hopkins University Press, 1999.

Pinchot, Gifford. *The Fight for Conservation*. New York: Doubleday, Page, 1910.

Porter, Gene Stratton. "Bird Architecture." *Outing* 38 (July 1901): 437–442.

———. "The Camera in Ornithology." In *The American Annual of Photography and Photographic Times-Bulletin for 1906*. Edited by W. I. Lincoln Adams, 51–68. New York: Styles & Cash, 1905.

———. *Homing with the Birds*. New York: Doubleday, Page, 1919.

———. "My Life and My Books." *Ladies' Home Journal* (September 1916): 80–81.

———. *What I Have Done with Birds: Character Studies of Native American Birds which through Friendly Advances I Induced to Pose for Me, or Succeeded in Photographing by Good Fortune, with the Story of My Experiences in Obtaining the Pictures*. Indianapolis: Bobbs-Merrill, 1907.

———. "What My Lens Sees." In *The American Annual of Photography, 1905 ed.* Edited by W. I. Lincoln Adams and Spencer Hord, 27–33. New York: Styles & Cash, 1906.

"The Preservation of the Wild Life of Alabama." In *Bird Day Book*. Montgomery, Ala.: Department of Education, 1910.

Price, Jennifer. *Flight Maps: Adventures with Nature in Modern America*. New York: Basic Books, 1999.

"Programs for Arbor and Bird Day." *Nature-Study Review* 6, no. 4 (April 1910): 107.

Public School Methods. Vol. 2. Chicago: School Methods Co., 1921.

Raup, Hugh M. "Charles C. Adams, 1873–1955." *Annals of the Association of American Geographers* 49, no. 2 (June 1959): 164–167.

Ravitch, Diane. *Left Back: A Century of Failed School Reforms*. New York: Simon & Schuster, 2000.

Reck, Franklin M. *The 4-H Story: A History of 4-H Club Work*. Ames: Iowa State College Press, 1951.

Reese, William J. "The Origins of Progressive Education." *History of Education Quarterly* 41, no. 1 (spring 2001): 1–24.

———. *Power and the Promise of School Reform: Grassroots Movements during the Progressive Era*. Boston: Routledge & Kegan Paul, 1986.

Renehan, Edward J., Jr. *John Burroughs: An American Naturalist*. Post Mills, Vt.: Chelsea Green Publishing Co., 1992.

Report of the Commission on Country Life. New York: Van Rees Press, 1911.

Report of the National Conservation Commission. 1909; reprint, New York: Arno Press, 1972.

Report of the Trustees for 1873: The Organization and Progress of the Anderson School of Natural History at Penikese Island. Cambridge, Mass.: Welch, Bigelow, 1874.

"Results of Wildlife Conservation Contest." *Arizona Bird Day Annual,* 4 May 1916.

Richards, Bertrand. *Gene Stratton Porter.* Boston: Americana Books, 1980.

Rife, David J. "Hamilton Wright Mabie: A Critical Bibliography." Ph.D. diss., Southern Illinois University, 1974.

Righter, Robert W. *The Battle over Hetch Hetchy: America's Most Controversial Dam and the Birth of Modern Environmentalism.* New York: Oxford University Press, 2005.

Riis, Jacob. "What Ails Our Boys?" *Craftsman* 21, no. 1 (October 1911): 5–6, 11.

Robinson, H. "Nature-Study in Art." *Nature-Study Review* 10, no. 6 (September 1914): 207–210.

Rodgers, Andrew Denny. *Liberty Hyde Bailey: A Story of American Plant Sciences.* Princeton, N.J.: Princeton University Press, 1949.

Rodgers, Daniel T. "Socializing Middle-Class Children: Institutions, Fables, and Work Values in Nineteenth Century America." In *Growing Up in America: Children in Historical Perspective.* Edited by Ray Hiner and Joseph M. Hawes. Urbana: University of Illinois Press, 1985.

Rogers, Julia E. "The Nature Club." *Country Life in America* 16 (May 1909): 62.

Rome, Adam. "Nature Wars, Culture Wars: Immigration and Environmental Reform in the Progressive Era." *Environmental History* 13, no. 3 (July 2008): 432–453.

———. "'Political Hermaphrodites': Gender and Environmental Reform in Progressive America." *Environmental History* 11, no. 3 (July 2006): 440–463.

Roosevelt, Grace G. *Reading Rousseau in the Nuclear Age.* Philadelphia: Temple University Press, 1990.

Roosevelt, Theodore. *A Book-Lover's Holidays in the Open.* New York: C. Scribner's Sons, 1916.

———. Introduction to *Camera Shots at Big Game* by Mr. and Mrs. A. G. Wallihan. New York: Doubleday & Page, 1906.

———. "Letter to Herbert Job." In *Wild Wings: Adventures of a Camera-Hunter among the Larger Wild Birds of North America on Sea and Land* by Herbert Keightley Job. New York: Houghton Mifflin, 1905.

———. "Men Who Misinterpret Nature" from "Roosevelt on the Nature Fakirs." *Everybody's Magazine* 16 (June 1907).

———. *The Strenuous Life: Essays and Addresses.* New York: Century Co., 1900.

Ross, Dorothy. *G. Stanley Hall.* Chicago: University of Chicago Press, 1972.

Ross, Edward Alsworth. *Social Control: A Survey of the Foundations of Order.* 1901; reprint, Cleveland, Ohio: Case Western Reserve Press, 1969.

Rossiter, Margaret. *Women Scientists in America: Struggles and Strategies to 1940.* Baltimore: Johns Hopkins University Press, 1982.

Rousseau, Jean-Jacques. *Emile or On Education* [1762]. Translated by Allan Bloom. New York: Basic Books, 1979.

Rubin, Charles T. *Conservation Reconsidered: Nature, Virtue and American Liberal Democracy.* New York: Rowman & Littlefield, 2000.

Ruskin, John. *Fors Clavigera: Letters to the Workmen and Labourers of Great Britain.* Sunnyside, Calif.: George Allen, 1873.

Russell, Bertrand. *The Scientific Outlook.* New York: W. W. Norton, 1959.

Russett, Cynthia Eagle. *Sexual Science: The Victorian Construction of Womanhood.* Cambridge, Mass.: Harvard University Press, 1989.

Ryan, Alan. "Deweyan Pragmatism and American Education." In *Philosophers on Education: New Historical Perspectives.* Edited by Amélie Oksenberg Rorty, 394–410. New York: Routledge, 1998.

Sandweiss, Martha A. *Print the Legend: Photography and the American West.* New Haven, Conn.: Yale University Press, 2002.

Sargent, Frederick Leroy. "Wings at Rest: A Bird Day Tragedy in One Act." *Journal of Education* 47 (24 March 1898): 180–182.

Saxon, Eugene Francis. *Gene Stratton Porter: A Little Story of the Life and Work and Ideals of "The Bird Woman."* Garden City, N.Y.: Doubleday, Page, 1915.

Schlossman, Steven L. "G. Stanley Hall and the Boy's Club: Conservative Applications of Recapitulation Theory." *Journal of the History of the Behavioral Sciences* 9, no. 2 (April 1973): 140–147.

Schmitt, Peter J. *Back to Nature: The Arcadian Myth in Urban America.* 1969; reprint, Baltimore: Johns Hopkins University Press, 1990.

Schulze, Robin G. "Robin G. Schulze on 'Prize Plants.'" *Environmental History* (July 2003): 474–479.

Scott, Charles B. *Nature Study and the Child.* Boston: D. C. Heath, 1902.

Scott, Emmett J., and Lyman Beecher Stowe. *Booker T. Washington: Builder of a Civilization.* New York: Doubleday, Page, 1916.

Scott, Roy V. *The Reluctant Farmer: The Rise of Agricultural Extension to 1914.* Urbana: University of Illinois Press, 1970.

Scudder, Samuel H. "How Agassiz Taught Professor Scudder." In Lane Cooper, *Louis Agassiz as a Teacher: Illustrative Extracts on His Methods of Instruction.* Ithaca, N.Y.: Comstock Publishing Co., 1945.

Sears, Paul B. "Charles C. Adams, Ecologist." *Science* 123, no. 3205 (1 June 1956).

Sedgwick, William. "Educational Value of the Methods of Science." *Educational Review* 5 (March 1893): 243–256.

Seton, Ernest Thompson. "The Boy Scouts in America." *Outlook* (23 July 1910): 630–635.

———. *Gospel of the Red Man: An Indian Bible.* 1936; reprint, Santa Fe, N.M.: Seton Village, 1966.

———. *How to Play Indian: Directions for Organizing a Tribe of Boy Indians and Making Their Teepees in True Indian Style.* Philadelphia: Curtis, 1903.

———. "On Nature-Study." In *Library of Natural History I.* New York: Saalfield, 1904–1910.

———. "Organized Boyhood: The Boy Scout Movement, Its Purpose and Laws." *Success Magazine* (December 1910): 805–805, 843, 849.

———. *Two Little Savages: Being the Adventures of Two Boys Who Lived as Indians and What They Learned.* New York: Doubleday, Page, 1903.

———. "The Woodcraft League or College of Indian Wisdom." *Homiletic Review* (June 1931).

"Seton Still Insists on Quitting Scouts." *New York Times,* 6 December 1915, 6.

Shaler, Nathaniel S. "Chapters from an Autobiography II: A Pupil of Agassiz." *Atlantic Monthly* (February 1909).

———. "Faith in Nature." *International Quarterly* 6 (December 1902): 281–304.

Sharp, Dallas Lore. *The Lay of the Land.* Boston: Houghton Mifflin, 1908.

———. *Wild Life near Home.* New York: Century Co., 1901.

Sharp, William C. "In Search of a Preservation Ethic: William Temple Hornaday and American Environmental Education." Ph.D. diss., University of Kansas, 1997.

Shepard, Paul. *Nature and Madness.* San Francisco: Sierra Club Books, 1982.

———. *The Others: How Animals Made Us Human.* Washington, D.C.: Island Press, 1996.

Shi, David E. *Facing Facts: Realism in American Thought and Culture, 1850–1920.* New York: Oxford University Press, 1995.

Shiras, George. "A Harmless Sport—Hunting with the Camera." *Independent,* 7 June 1990, 1364–1368.

Sipe, Susan B. "Practical Aid to the School Garden Movement by the United States Department of Agriculture." *Nature-Study Review* 8, no. 2 (February 1912): 51–53.

Slotkin, Richard. "Nostalgia and Progress: Theodore Roosevelt's Myth of the Frontier." *American Quarterly* 33 (winter 1981): 608–638.

Smith, Cora A. "The Spirit of Nature-Study." *Nature-Study Review* 14, no. 2 (February 1918): 53–54.

Smith, Edward H. "Anna Botsford Comstock: Artist, Author, Teacher." *American Entomologist* 36, no. 2 (summer 1990): 105–113.

Smith, Herbert. "Preservation of the Natural Resources of the United States." *National Education Association Journal of Proceedings and Addresses* (1908): 992–998.

Smith, Timothy L. "Progressivism in American Education, 1880–1900." *Harvard Educational Review* 31, no. 2 (spring 1961).

Snow, C. P. *The Two Cultures and the Scientific Revolution.* New York: Cambridge University Press, 1963.

"Society for the Preservation of New England Plants." *Nature-Study Review* 18, no. 7 (October 1922): 278–283.

"Specialization in Scientific Study." *Science,* n.s., 4 (11 July 1884): 35–36.

Spence, Mark David. *Dispossessing the Wilderness: Indian Removal and the Making of the National Parks.* New York: Oxford University Press, 1999.

Standish, Barney. *Common Things with Common Eyes: An Illustrated Course of Nature Study for Schools, about Insects, Fishes, Quadrupeds, Flowers, Trees and Birds.* Minneapolis: Standish & Standish, 1897.

Stebbins, Cyril A. "Growing Children in California Gardens." *Nature-Study Review* 8, no. 2 (February 1912): 67–74.

Stradling, David. *Smokestacks and Progressives: Environmentalists, Engineers, and Air Quality in America, 1881–1951.* Baltimore: Johns Hopkins University Press, 1999.

Straight, H. H. "A 'Complete Life' the Foundation of a True Philosophy of Education." *Nebraska Teacher* (March 1873): 62–66.

Strickland, Arvarh E. "The Strange Affair of the Boll Weevil: The Pest as Liberator." *Agricultural History* 68 (spring 1994): 157–168.

Strober, Myra H., and Audri Gordon Lanford. "The Feminization of Public School Teaching: Cross-sectional Analysis, 1850–1880." *Signs: Journal of Women in Culture and Society* 11, no. 2 (1986): 212–235.

Suchodolski, Bogan. "Comenius and Teaching Methods." In *Comenius and Contemporary Education.* Edited by C. A. Dobinson. Hamburg: UNESCO Institute for Education, 1970.

Sutter, Paul. *Driven Wild: How the Fight against Automobiles Launched the Modern Wilderness Movement.* Seattle: University of Washington Press, 2002.

Swan, Malcolm. "Forerunners of Environmental Education." In *What Makes Education Environmental?* Edited by Noel McInnis and Don Albrecht. Washington, D.C.: Data Courier and Environmental Educators, 1975.

Sykes, McCready. "Let's Play Indian: Making a New American Boy through Woodcraft." *Everybody's Magazine* (October 1910): 473–478.

Tadd, J. Liberty. *New Methods in Education: Art, Real Manual Training, Nature Study.* Springfield, Mass.: Orange Judd Co., 1904.

Taft, Robert. *Photography and the American Scene: A Social History 1839–1889.* New York: Peter Smith, 1964.

Tall, Lida Lee, and Isobel Davidson. *Course of Study: Baltimore County Maryland Public Schools Grades I to VIII.* Baltimore: Warwick & York, 1919.

Tanner, Laurel N. *Dewey's Laboratory School: Lessons for Today.* New York: Teachers College Press, 1997.

Taylor, Joseph E., III. *Making Salmon: An Environmental History of the Northwest Fisheries Crisis.* Seattle: University of Washington Press, 1999.

Teller, James David. *Louis Agassiz, Scientist and Teacher.* Columbus: Ohio State University Press, 1947.

"Tener Talks to Carrick Tots on Bird Day." *Pittsburgh Gazette Times,* 12 April 1912, 1.

Tharp, Louise Hall. *Adventurous Alliance: The Story of the Agassiz Family of Boston.* Boston: Little, Brown, 1959.

Thayer, Edna R. "Children's Gardens at Downing Street School, Worcester, Mass." *Nature-Study Review* 1, no. 2 (March 1905): 61–66.

Thompson, E. P. *William Morris: Romantic to Revolutionary.* New York: Knopf Publishing Group, 1977.

Thoreau, Henry David. *Journal.* Vol. 4, *1851–1852.* Edited by Leonard N. Neufield and Nancy Craig Simmons. Princeton, N.J.: Princeton University Press, 1992.

———. *The Journal of Henry D. Thoreau.* 14 vols. Edited by Bradford Torrey and Francis H. Allen. Boston: Houghton Mifflin, 1906.

———. *The Journal of Henry D. Thoreau.* Vol. 3, *1848–1851.* Edited by Robert Sattelmeyer, Mark R. Patterson, and William Rossi. Princeton, N.J.: Princeton University Press, 1990.

———. *The Journal of Henry David Thoreau.* Edited by Bradford Torrey. Mineola, N.Y.: Dover Publications, 1962.

———. "The Natural History of Massachusetts." In *The Natural History Essays.* Edited by Robert Sattelmeyer. Salt Lake City: Peregrine Smith, 1980.

———. *The Writings of Henry David Thoreau.* Vol. 2. New York: Houghton Mifflin, 1906.

Thorndike, Edward. "Reading as a Means of Nature Study." *Education* (February 1899): 368–371.

———. "Sentimentality in Science Teaching." *Educational Review* (January 1899): 58–62.

Thrasher, Max Bennett. *Tuskegee: Its Story and Its Work.* Boston: Small, Maynard, 1900.

To Elevate Morals. Bird Day. Animal Day. Milwaukee, 1894. Library of Congress American Memory Collection. http://memory.loc.gov/cgi-bin/query/D?rbpebib:9:./temp/ ~ammem_iPWe::.

Tolley, Kim. *The Science Education of American Girls: A Historical Perspective.* London: Taylor & Francis, 2004.

"Topics of the Times." *New York Times,* 8 May 1923, 16.

Trachtenberg, Alan. *Reading American Photographs: Images as History—Mathew Brady to Walker Evans.* New York: Hill & Wang, 1989.

"Travelling Libraries Needed." *New York Daily Tribune,* 18 August 1903, 7.

Turner, Miss E. L. "Bird-Photography for Women." *Bird Lore* 17, no. 3 (May–June 1915): 175–190.

Tyack, David B. "The Tribe and the Common School: Community Control in Rural Education." *American Quarterly* 24, no. 1 (March 1972): 3–19.

Urban, Wayne J., and Jennings L. Wagoner Jr. *American Education: A History.* New York: McGraw-Hill, 2004.

"Value of Natural Scenery." *Outlook* 90 (26 September 1908): 149–151.

Veblen, Thorstein. "The Place of Science in Modern Civilization." *American Journal of Sociology* 11, no. 5 (March 1906): 585–609.

———. *The Theory of the Leisure Class.* New York: Macmillan, 1899.

Verill, A. Hyatt. "Hunting with a Camera." *St. Nicholas* 27 (August 1890): 927–929.

Vinal, William Gould. "The Call of Girls' Camps." *Nature-Study Review* 15, no. 5 (May 1919): 201–204.

Voris, Eva Shelley. "Who Loves the Birds." In *Kentucky Arbor and Bird Day* (1910).

Wadland, John Henry. *Ernest Thompson Seton: Man and Nature in the Progressive Era, 1880–1915.* New York: Arno Press, 1978.

Wallihan, A. G. "Hunting Big Game with the Camera." *Outlook* 71 (1905): 355–365.

Warren, Louis. *The Hunter's Game: Poachers and Conservationists in Twentieth-Century America.* New Haven, Conn.: Yale University Press, 1997.

Washington, Booker T. *Up from Slavery: An Autobiography.* New York: Doubleday, Page, 1901.

———. *Working with the Hands: Being a Sequel to "Up from Slavery" Covering the Author's Experience in Industrial Training at Tuskegee.* New York: Doubleday, Page, 1904.

Washington, Margaret Murray. "What Girls Are Taught and How." In *Tuskegee and Its People: Their Ideals and Achievements.* Edited by Booker T. Washington. New York: D. Appleton, 1905.

Weber, Max. *The Protestant Ethic and the Spirit of Capitalism.* Translated by Talcott Parsons. New York: Charles Scribner's Sons, 1958.

Welch, Richard E., Jr. *George Frisbie Hoar and the Half-Bred Republicans.* Cambridge, Mass.: Harvard University Press, 1971.

Welker, Robert Henry. *Birds and Men: American Birds in Science, Art and Conservation, 1800–1900.* Cambridge, Mass.: Belknap Press of Harvard University Press, 1955.

West, Nancy Martha. *Kodak and the Lens of Nostalgia.* Charlottesville: University of Virginia Press, 2000.

Westbrook, Robert B. *John Dewey and American Democracy.* Ithaca, N.Y.: Cornell University Press, 1991.

"What Is Nature Study?" *Science* 16, nos. 910–913 (5 December 1902).

Whitney, E. R. "Nature Study as an Aid to Advanced Work in Science." *Proceedings of the National Education Association* (1904): 889–894.

Wiebe, Robert. *The Search for Order, 1877–1920.* New York: Hill & Wang, 1967.

"Wild Flower Preservation Society of America." *Nature-Study Review* 18, no. 7 (October 1922): 268–269.

Wilder, Burt G. "Agassiz at Penikese." *American Naturalist* 32 (March 1898): 375.

Williams, Dora. *Gardens and Their Meaning.* Boston: Ginn, 1911.

Willson, Augustus E. "Arbor Day Proclamation." In *Kentucky Arbor and Bird Day* (1910).

Wilson, James. *Annual Reports of the Department of Agriculture for the Fiscal Year Ended June 30, 1904.* Washington, D.C.: Government Printing Office, 1904.

Wilson, William H. *The City Beautiful Movement.* Baltimore: Johns Hopkins University Press, 1989.

Wish, Harvey. "Negro Education and the Progressive Movement." *Journal of Negro History* 49, no. 3 (July 1964): 184–200.

"Without Birds Agriculture Would Be Impossible." In *Arbor and Bird Day Manual.* Ohio Department of Education, 1912.

Withrow, Margaret M. "Program for Bird Day." *Virginia Journal of Education* 3, no. 6 (March 1910): 384–387.

Woodhull, John F. "The Educational Value of Natural Science." *Educational Review* (April 1895): 368–376.

Worster, Donald. *American Environmentalism: The Formative Period, 1860–1915.* New York: Wiley, 1973.

———. *Nature's Economy: A History of Ecological Ideas,* 2nd ed. Cambridge: Cambridge University Press, 1994.

———. *A Passion for Nature: The Life of John Muir.* New York: Oxford University Press, 2008.

———. *A River Running West: The Life of John Wesley Powell.* New York: Oxford University Press, 2002.

———. "The Wilderness of History." *Wild Earth* 7 (fall 1997): 9–13.

Wright, Albert Hazen, and Anna Allen Wright. "Agassiz's Address at the Opening of Agassiz's Academy." *American Midland Naturalist* 43, no. 2 (March 1950): 503–506.

Wright, Anna Allen. "Nature Study for the City Child." *Nature-Study Review* 14, no. 3 (March 1918): 93–100.

Wright, Mabel Osgood. "Bird-Cities of Refuge." *Bird Lore* 12 (1910): 159–160.

———. "A Bird Class for Children." *Bird Lore* 1 (1899): 100–101.

———. *Birdcraft: A Field Book of Two Hundred Song, Game, and Water Birds.* New York: Macmillan, 1895.

———. "Encouraging Signs." *Bird Lore* 3 (1901): 146–147.

———. "Fees and Pledges." *Bird Lore* 2 (1900): 63–65.

———. *The Friendship of Nature: A New England Chronicle of Birds and Flowers.* Edited by Daniel J. Philippon. 1894; reprint, Baltimore: Johns Hopkins University Press, 1999.

———. *The Garden of a Commuter's Wife.* New York: Macmillan, 1901.

———. *The Garden, You and I.* New York: Macmillan, 1906.

———. *Gray Lady and the Birds: Stories of the Bird Year for Home and School.* New York: Macmillan, 1917.

———. "How to Save Wild Flowers: The Transplanting of Wild Plants in General and the Mountain Laurel and Rhododendron in Particular." *American Fern Journal* 13, no. 2 (June 1923): 52–55.

———. "The Law and the Bird." *Bird Lore* 1 (1899): 203–204.

———. "A Little Christmas Sermon for Teachers." *Bird Lore* 7, no. 6 (December 1910): 253–254.

———. "The Making of Birdcraft Sanctuary." *Bird Lore* 17, no. 4 (July–August 1915): 263–273.

———. "Meditations on the Posting of Bird Laws." *Bird Lore* 5 (1903): 205–206.

———. "Song Bird Reservations." *Bird Lore* 3 (1901): 114–115.

———. "The Spread of Bird Protection." *Bird Lore* 5 (1903): 36–37.

———. *Tommy-Anne and the Three Hearts.* New York: Macmillan, 1896.

Wright, Mabel Osgood, and Elliot Coues. *Citizen Bird: Scenes from Bird-Life in Plain English for Beginners.* New York: Macmillan, 1897.

Index

Packard, Alpheus, 18
Page, Walter Hines, 191
Palmer, E. Laurence, 186, 205, 207
Parker, Clayton F., 77–78
Parker, Francis, 23, 52–54, 55, 56, 71, 79–80, 82
Parsons, Fannie G., 115
Pearson, T. Gilbert, 104–5
Peckham, Morse, 45
Penikese Island, Mass., 15, 18, 20–21
Pennsylvania, Bird Day in, 97–98, 100, 101
Peru (Neb.) Bird Lovers' Club, 102, 140 (photo)
Peru State Normal School (Neb.), 23
Pestalozzi, Johann, 22, 48–49, 51, 52
Pestalozzian theory, 25
Peterson, Roger Tory, 126
Phelps, Almira, 25–26
Phelps, William Lyon, 165
Philippon, Daniel J., 125, 126
Phillips, Helen B., 102
Phillips, John, M., 101
photography, 150, 158–64, 244n42
Physics (Comenius), 47
Pinchot, Gifford, 5, 9, 10, 96, 103, 191
Pingree, Hazen, 114
Porter, Gene Stratton, 165–68, 210, 247n78
Powell, George T., 180
"Prayer of Agassiz, The" (Whittier), 15
preservation, 9
progressivism
    education, 3, 5, 7, 12, 22–23, 24, 42–62, 64, 73, 80, 114, 153–54, 177
    goals of, 12, 202
    political strategy of, 7
    scientific inquiry and, 24, 61, 63
Public lands, 101, 148–49, 169
Putnam, Frederick Ward, 18

Quincy, Mass., schools, 52–53

racial stereotypes, 73–74, 76, 77, 78, 80, 81–83, 86, 87–88, 89, 128
Rauschenbusch, Walter, 198

recapitulation, theory of, 73–79, 81, 82, 84, 90–91, 212
Reck, Franklin M., 188
Reese, William J., 43
"Reverie of Gardens, A" (Bailey), 111
Riis, Jacob, 3, 113, 117
Roberts, Isaac P., 187
Robinson, C. H., 160
Rodgers, Daniel T., 6
Roe, Alfred S., 107
romanticism, 30–34, 38, 39, 44–49, 51, 52–53, 57, 64, 65, 69, 74, 78, 81, 90, 109, 150
Roosevelt, Grace, 47
Roosevelt, Theodore, 5, 28, 75, 78, 85, 86, 87, 113, 162–63, 191, 192
Ross, E. A., 12
Roth, Charles, 204
Rousseau, Jean-Jacques, 47–48, 49, 51, 52, 74
rural life
    education and, 175, 176, 177, 178, 180, 181, 185–86, 190, 192
    reform of, 120, 134, 170–78, 180, 182, 184–86, 191–94
    values of, 36, 43, 170
Ruskin, John, 6
Russell, Bertrand, 213–14
Russell Sage Foundation, 191

Saginaw, Mich., school gardens, 120–21
Sand County Almanac (Leopold), 207
Sargent, Frederick Leroy, 99
Schiff, Jacob, 180
Schmitt, Peter J., 13, 158
School Arts Book, 148, 151, 152, 154, 156–57
school arts movement, 153–54, 155, 156
School Garden Association of America, 121, 239n40
school gardens, 113–16, 120–22, 135–36, 144–46 (photos), 172, 197, 200
School Nature League, 119
Science magazine, 34–35, 59, 61, 96
Scientific management, 2, 9